Colonial Legacies

Colonial Legacies

The Problem of Persistence IN LATIN AMERICAN HISTORY

Edited by
JEREMY ADELMAN

Routledge
New York and London

Published in 1999 by
Routledge
29 West 35th Street
New York, New York 10001

Published in Great Britain by
Routledge
11 New Fetter Lane
London EC4P 4EE

Printed in the United States of America on acid-free paper.
Text Design by Debora Hilu

Excerpt from "La Luna" by Jorge Luis Borges (in Personal Anthology, 1983) is reprinted with permission of Grove/Atlantic, Inc.

Chapter 11 is adapted in part from *Crafting the Third World*, by Joseph L. Love, with the permission of the publishers, Stanford University Press © 1996 by the Board of Trustees of the Leland Stanford Junior University.

10 9 8 7 6 5 4 3 2 1

Library of Congress Cataloging-in-Publication Data

Colonial legacies : the problem of persistence in Latin American history / edited by Jeremy Adelman.
    p.   cm.
    Includes bibliographical references and index.
    ISBN 0-415-92152-X (cloth). — ISBN 0-415-92153-8 (pbk.)
    1. Latin America—History—To 1830.   I. Adelman, Jeremy.
F1412.C634   1999
980'.01—dc21   98-35714
                                                          CIP

History tells us that in such time past
when so many real, imaginary
and doubtful things took place,
one man conceived the unwieldy

Plan of ciphering the universe
in one book and, infinitely rash,
built his high and mighty manuscript,
shaping and declaiming the final line.

But when about to praise his luck,
he lifted up his eyes, and saw
a burnished disk upon the air; startled,
he realized he'd left out the moon.

Though contrived, this little story
might well exemplify the mischief
that involves us all who take on
the job of turning real life into words.

—Jorge Luís Borges, "La luna"

Contents

Preface

History telling in Latin America has long been about colonial formations and their legacies. Our collection of essays tackles this enduring tradition of writing Latin American history and diagnosing the seemingly endemic difficulties of democracy and the rule of law. More than other Atlantic societies, Latin America appears shackled to its past, especially to its colonial heritages. For some, this yields to postcolonial exotica; for others the past is a scourge on the present. What persists is persistence itself.

More than in any other region, the formulation of the past as persistence has shaped regional and national narratives of Latin American societies. We do not, in this volume, wish to dismiss the notion of colonial legacies in favor of other, equally totalizing views of the past. Instead, we take seriously the proposition that institutions, social and economic asymmetries, and the habitus of power can be deeply embedded in historical paths. Indeed, efforts to surmount binding legacies have often floundered and even reinforced old patterns. For good or ill, this is the history, and historiography, with which we contend.

Rather, the aim is to disentangle what it means to have a past that looms so heavily on the present—the present of the practitioner, the activist, and the historian. We offer three points. First, colonial legacies have multiple origins rooted in a triangular relationship between Europe, Africa, and the Americas. No single corner or force determined the shape of transatlantic colonialism; each continent was bound by economic, political, and cultural threads which, twined, created a complex pattern. Furthermore, neither dimension of colonialism is strictly reducible to one logic. The silver and slave trades—just to name two commodity chains of the Atlantic exchange system—enabled and motivated economic quests for rents but also presumed deep-seated cultural perceptions of race, ethnicity, and modernity. Colonialism was as multipolar as it was multifaceted.

Second, the bequests of colonialism did not go uncontested. Empire and dominion seldom obeyed their own internal laws of motion. Were it so, our stories would be flat, straightforward accounts of how architects of empire translated their interests and projects into plans and realities. Outcomes of colonialism would bear some resemblance to the intentions of its framers. In fact, the stories are not only more complex but they also testify to the agency both of colonialism's victims as well as competitors that wanted a piece of the imperial pie. So instrumental was the enterprise to economic and military hegemony that Iberian colonialism could not help but invite interlopers whose actions destabilized and redirected policy and praxis. Likewise, interstitial groups—like peasants living on the margins of the commodity nexus (described in Patch's chapter)—presented alternative projects that more often undermined dominant relationships unintentionally than they did mount full-throated oppositional movements. Then there were the cases of most outright contestation, from angry Creole merchants frustrated at peninsular mercantilism to slaves and their progeny fighting, literally, for their freedom. Either way, the constant undermining of colonial and postcolonial orders implied that the dominant orders had to adapt to circumstances over which they had much less control than is often inferred by static accounts of historical legacies. Herein lies an essential and powerful ambiguity of colonial legacies— they aggregate into legacies precisely because they appear so capable of reconstituting themselves.

Third, historians and social scientists of Latin America have taken these first two propositions seriously and have offered a rich and often combated set of master narratives for the region's past. Sometimes legacies are cultural, other times they are institutional. Sometimes the stories offer dismal laments on the impossibility of reform (as José Martí once noted, North America was born with a plow in its hand, Latin America with a sword); other times they animate a historical imagination with very explicit transcendental goals (the self-same distinctiveness of Latin America could, and did, become the rallying identity for nationalist causes, especially after 1930). These themselves have become kinds of historiographic inheritances within which Latin American historians and social scientists operate—whether they like them or not. Most commonly, "heritage" is simply reduced to dependency. This was certainly one of the dominant formulations in post-1930 accounts. Latin America, in this view, emerged as a dependent side of the Atlantic economy in the sixteenth century and has remained so. For all their merits and demerits, dependency approaches comprised but one set of tools to look at one set of legacies. Indeed, the last decade's hammering of dependency approaches—much of it warranted on empirical and logical grounds, though the rush to dismiss external conditions on Latin American development may push the critique too far—has helped highlight other types of deep-legacy arguments. More recently, some historians have folded back into even more aged narratives of cultural or even civilizational predilections rooted in the titanic struggle between the Reformation and the Counter Reformation. From a literary vantage point, Latin America is the theater for Calibanesque countermodernism—as Roberto Fernández Retamar has recently argued. Legacies are not of a piece but jostle with each other to offer competing narratives of the past. The point is: persistence—whether economic or cultural—is as heterogenous as it is prevalent in formulating the Latin American past.

This book does not advance one theory or approach—it simply explores the origins and refractions of a set of arguments about the Latin American past. Broadly speaking, what we do share is the conviction that nomothetic models or stylized archetypes of what Latin America should have been, or failed to become, put arguments about persistent structures of mind and society to specific kinds of uses, not of all which are entirely salutary. The most regrettable was the recent habit of Latin American dictators and their epigones to excuse their brutality by arguing that history did not prepare Latin Americans for the promise of modernity, and that it would take a profound praetorian rupture to tutor and reshape an irresponsible citizenry. (Some nineteenth-century liberals trotted out analogous apologies, albeit usually riddled with considerably more anxiety.) We very clearly do not wish to advance such hypotheses. Two points about persistence arguments, therefore, require clarification.

Persistence is not necessarily essence. Arguing that the past bears inordinately on the present, even in unintended ways, does not necessarily mean that Latin American societies—any society—are trapped within an identifiable essence, a rooted personality immune to the forces of time or contingency. To be sure, many of the deep-legacy arguments do advance essentialist formulations. But highlighting the genealogy of persistences does not necessarily imply transhistorical immutabilities.

Nor is persistence eternity. Inheriting legacies does not necessarily imply that the present is the captive of the past, but simply, as Marx once argued in the "Eighteenth Brumaire of Louis Napoleon," people are not the makers of the tools with which they make history. Accordingly, we want to rescue the idea that cultures, institutions, and social forces can be embedded in historical trajectories without trampling on any appreciation of the internal tensions and contradictions of the past. This is why we stress the multiple origins of the Atlantic world, the contested nature of colonial and postcolonial societies, and the manifold ways in which historical paths have been described. Furthermore, to say that the past persists is not to say that the present is bereft of choices. Persistence, as a way of telling stories about history and accounting for the present, is simply one way of narrating the past. In Latin America, there are good and bad reasons why it has become the dominant framing device for historians and social scientists. It is not necessarily wrong or misguided; it merely needs to be problematized, especially if we want the past to inform our present and to amplify visions of the future.

This book grew out of a conference held at Princeton University in the Fall of 1995 to mark the twenty-fifth anniversary of the publication of Stanley Stein and Barbara Stein's landmark book, *The Colonial Heritage of Latin America*, whose very title inspired the theme of this volume. Indeed, the conference, like so many collective ventures, had the unintended consequence of generating a discussion about heritages and legacies more generally. At Princeton, I am grateful for the support of the Department of History, the Shelby Cullom Davis Center for Historical Studies, the Council for Regional Studies, and the Program of Latin American Studies—the latter having been Stanley Stein's enduring legacy while Barbara Stein built the Iberian and Latin American collections of Princeton's Firestone Library into one of the world's finest repositories, bequeathing two institutional heritages to us all. I am also grateful to Noelina Hall and Stuart McCook for their help. Arno Mayer, John Murrin, Kathryn Burns, Barbara Corbett, Brian Owensby, Bob Levine, and Emilia Viotti da Costa were important contributors to the discussion. The authors are also to be thanked for their patience in handling my pressures and editing. Rebecca Scott and Stuart Schwartz are especially to be thanked for their encouragement. Finally, I want to express my gratitude to Karen Caplan for her editorial skills and good cheer.

one

Introduction:
The Problem of Persistence
in Latin American History

Jeremy Adelman

COLONIAL LEGACIES

For many, Latin America seems condemned to repetition. Troubled politics, boom-and-bust economics, a healthy passion for personal loyalties over impersonal identities all appear as common features of the region. Observers, journalists, and scholars trace these attributes to recent and remote pasts. This image contrasts with the United States, a country born "free" in Alexis de Tocqueville's compelling view. If the United States constantly adapted to future horizons, Latin America remained anchored to social relations, modes of behavior, and cultures of an earlier era. Where the United States made perpetual ruptures the hallmark of its history, Latin America forged its historic time lines out of deep continuities. Latin America still bears the shackles of its birth. The past is destiny.

This introductory essay explores the genealogy of this colonial legacy and some of the uses to which this particular formulation of history has been put. It examines the origins of deep-continuity arguments, the ways in which these arguments adapted to new circumstances, and then the types of legacies invoked by historians to account for Latin American development. Less concerned to test whether these representations of the past are valid (many, no doubt, are; others are better treated as myths), this essay is concerned with the idea that persistence is a powerful organizing framework for understanding particular kinds of historical processes.

Politics is never far removed from Latin American historical inquiry. If narratives of the past help make sense of experiences, then they offer clues about how to amend, transform or perpetuate these experiences. It should not surprise us to find that many of the authors offering scripts for continuity do so with programmatic intentions. A common aspect of these intentions, however, is the deep undertow of pessimism. Arguments about Latin American historical legacies—like accounts of the ethnic butchery in Bosnia or religious enmities in the Middle East—frequently serve to explain why modest, gradual, cumulative change is so difficult. The result, in political terms, is a rocking between periods of unchanging stasis and massive social upheaval. So if the past is destiny, then the prospects for a stable progressive present are seldom great. For some this helps justify voluntarist calls for revolutionary ruptures to break the grip of inertial forces; for others it is a warning against tinkering with explosive social arrangements lest they be plunged into irretrievable chaos.

This book is an effort to reexamine the idea of binding historical legacies in Latin America. The first group of authors (chapters 2 to 5) place Latin America into a transatlantic context to probe how the social features which were seen as stubborn colonial bequests came into being, especially in the triangulated relationship between Europe, Africa, and Latin America. The idea of legacy does not imply, however, unchanging stasis, as chapters 5 to 7 argue. Recent scholarship, while often agreeing that some political, social, and cultural forces resist temporal pressures, tends to show that these structures did not go uncontested. These social and political changes sometimes led to unintended consequences which deflected Latin America onto alternative courses. Other times, stories about contestation ask readers to think of continuity in more dialectical terms—as the products of interaction, even conflict, between historical actors. Finally, chapters 8 to 12 look at the way historians and writers have scripted Latin American history along the lines of deep continuities, sometimes with explicit political purposes in mind. What all the authors in this volume show is that the time lines of Latin American history cannot be reduced to simple linear accounts of cumulative change and evolution.

At first blush this is a simple proposition. Yet the implications for understanding Latin American cultures and explaining large-scale macrohistorical change can be unsettling. We are often accustomed to thinking that historical actors adapt to changing circumstances, and that if they are forbidden, then societies accumulate forces that may erupt in more abrupt change. Either way, the time lines of history may be linear, almost evolutionary, or punctuated by moments of accelerated change followed by calm.

Neither of these visions of the past is absent from Latin American historiography, especially when examining shorter-term processes or episodic events. But they take place against a backdrop of a great propensity to continuity. Semihidden structural forces inhibit social adaptability to external circumstances. For instance, rural productivity remains low for long periods of history while it is soaring in other corners of the Atlantic world (see Richard Salvucci's chapter). In other circumstances, large-scale ruptures often fold societies back into their old ways, as Kenneth Maxwell argues in his chapter. All this means that historians of Latin America often have had to balance sensibilities to change often within continuity. They cannot presume that change was natural or congenital even though modern historical inquiry often rests on the notion that stasis and failure to adapt are aberrational. Latin America, because it so often seems to resist modernization, "fails" to follow the natural course of "Western" history.

Setting up Latin American history in this way, however, itself rests on an age-old trope: colonial legacies, the social and cultural bequests of Iberian expansion into the New World, set Latin American societies on a track which would, by definition, distinguish them from English colonies. In effect, arguing that Latin America has been stuck in an inherited mould compared to other New World societies, is itself a rehearsal of old arguments. These arguments themselves are bequests of colonialism.

LEGACIES OF HISTORY

The notion of deep continuities in Latin American history was invented from the moment the region came into being as a contact between European, African, and American peoples. Once it became clear that Counter Reformation Spain possessed the financial might to wage a war against heresy in Europe, propagandists for the Reformation embarked on the mission to vilify the Iberian enterprise in the Americas (see the chapter by Stein and Stein). Especially with the spread of Bartolomé de las Casas's *Brevísima relación* (if seldom with his moral purpose), this "Black Legend" became a mythic image of the founding of Spain's New World colonies. It offered the apologists of English expansionism a set of images against which to pose a better, more benign, purpose. Spain, rather, was bent on spreading obscurantism, locking the minds of neophytes into medieval cells, and plundering Amerindian civilizations of their magnificence to thwart the Reformation's greater purpose in the Old World. The image of the brutal, pillaging conquistadors dominated the mythic landscape of Iberian expansion in the same way that the bucolic pioneer became the founding personality of Anglo-American colonies.[1]

Dichotomizing survived the centuries. Evidence that the English purpose was not as benign as its propagandists made out, and proof that the Spanish mould was hardly monolithic dented but did not dislodge the accepted contrast. Indeed, the view of backward introspective Iberian America hardened in the face of mounting evidence that the colonies were as heterogenous as they were dynamic, and that patterns of rulership were contested horizontally—within dominant elites—and vertically—from popular classes.

In the late eighteenth century, Black Legending of the Hispanic world received a new bill of health just as the fabric of the Atlantic world began to shred. Starting with the English colonies, and intensifying with the slave uprising in Saint Domingue, this process culminated in the riptide of revolution across the Spanish American world after 1810. The ways in which the colonial heritage set the terms for revolutionary and postcolonial possibilities found expression in Abbé Raynal's oracular 1770 account of New World history, the *Histoire des Indes*—a tract which enjoyed almost Talmudic status on the bookshelves of enlightened reformers across the Iberian American world.[2]

For Raynal, Spain, once again, looks bad from the start, so bad that the author felt that separating the colonies from the metropole would be easy business—though of course any "liberator" would face the arduous task of figuring out how to tutor these new subjects out of bad habits. Referring to Creoles, he argued that "from inclination, from laziness, from ignorance, from custom, and from pride, they are strictly attached to their religion, and their government, and will never conform to new laws. Their prejudices will furnish them with weapons sufficient to repel their conqueror." So, they might be militarily and formally liberated, but Creole mind-sets would retain the hallmarks of their formative experience. For Raynal, "the natural pride of the conquerors, the particular temper of the Spaniards, their ignorance of the true principles of commerce; all these, and many other causes, prevented them from giving good laws, a sound administration, and a solid basis to their American conquests, at first setting out."[3]

Histoire des Indes was a landmark referent for the generation challenging Spanish absolutism. The combination of physiocratic advice and moral condemnation of imperial domination (especially against the Saint

Domingue and Hispanic possessions—Abbé Raynal shared the propensity to see the English ventures as exceptions to the European pattern) helped nurture hopes of an alternative political configuration. If not quite espousing revolution (he did not think Creoles capable of mastering their own fate), it helped justify revolution when Creoles openly questioned Spanish and Portuguese authority.

The course of the crisis after 1810 need not be rehearsed here—and its aftermath is well known. Less well known is how, in the hands of "liberators," the very same language of colonial legacies twisted to serve a pessimistic postcolonial diagnosis. Take Simón Bolívar. As his efforts to set republics on stable liberal paths began to implode, his liberated communities slid into civil war, and the project of a confederation of Spanish American provinces splintered into localist *patrias chicas* (small homelands), Bolívar's optimism gave way to gloom. His eschatology of failure pointed to the lockjaw of Spanish America's particular colonial heritage. "It is harder, Montesquieu has written, to release a nation from servitude than to enslave a free nation. This truth," wrote Bolívar in his 1815 Jamaica Letter, "is proven by the annals of all times, which reveal that most free nations have been put under the yoke, but very few enslaved nations have recovered their liberty . . . Such a marvel is inconceivable and without precedent. There is no reasonable probability to bolster our hopes."[4] By 1830, his despair was absolute, and by then the eschatology made good cover for dictatorial constitutions in the effort to force the erstwhile colonies from their mind-sets.

Thus, when the foundational "national" tracts of American letters emerged in the 1830s and 1840s, the binding structures of colonial legacies were etched into historical templates for nation building. Nothing could better capture the difference than the gloss placed by de Tocqueville on the civic, grassroots assembly-based democracy of the former English colonies, compared to Argentina Domingo Faustino Sarmiento's bleak perspective of the vulgar and crude polities emerging under the helm of militarist caudillos. "From these characteristics," noted Sarmiento in his *Facundo*, "arises in the life of the Argentine people the reign of brute force, the supremacy of the strongest, the absolute and irresponsible authority of rulers, the administration of justice without the formalities of discussion."[5]

This was inhospitable terrain for the kind of sociability necessary for a virtuous republic. The Black Legend survived the test of time and entered, in modified, form the nineteenth-century lexicon of constitutionalism. In the minds of Latin American jurists (who were often the first to inscribe nation-building histories), North Americans could afford to vest basic rights in society; Latin Americans enjoyed no such luxury. The outcome of the revolutions, although sharing the same liberal telos, only confirmed what Raynal had predicted: Creoles were unprepared to be liberal of their own volition and aptitude.

BLACK LEGEND REDUX

The ideological and institutional pinnings of empire and their colonial legacies came to explain why New World colonies turned out so differently. By the time historians and social scientists tackled these big themes in the 1950s, especially animated by modernization theory, the Black Legend had mutated into an historical truism. In the 1950s, in the wake of European fascism and bordered by mass populism in Latin America, the prevailing "liberal consensus" sought to explain the sources of American exceptionalism. Louis Hartz and a generation of scholars in the 1950s and 1960s wanted to retrieve the approach to transatlantic continuities to account for the differences among New World societies. The English colonies, as Hartz once argued, were created free from feudal remnants. Borrowing from de Tocqueville, Hartz argued in his *The Liberal Tradition in America* that the distinguishing mark of United States society was that it was "born equal . . . instead of becoming so."[6] Bereft of a native aristocracy, free from the shackles of absolutism, peopled by possessive individualist proprietors (slaves, of course, notwithstanding), the colonies had no ancien régime, required no revolution to topple the old order, and faced no revanchist efforts to restore a defensive world of privilege. Everything converged around a whig framework. The revolution of 1776 wasn't even a real break; indeed the founders and framers did not have to dismantle the old order; they struggled instead to shimmy "a good past" into a hybrid liberal mould. In this fashion, the fragments of colonialism bequeathed the conditions under which new liberal experiments would flourish—or flounder.

This call for comparative ideological and institutional histories of "new" societies propelled Hartz to edit the landmark volume, *The Founding of New Societies*.[7] Richard Morse, the author of the Latin American essay in *The Founding of New Societies* extended this formulation into the region south of the Rio Grande.[8] Morse shared the Hartzian call for transatlantic continuities but felt compelled to accept that the ideas and institutions of empire did not implant in new territories without mediation or refraction. Indeed, from the start, the imposition of "neomedievalism of Spanish American colonial institutions" interacted with, and adapted to two other heritages: the indigenous and African presences. Out of the mingling came, as Morse argued, a "paradoxical syncretic" blend that crossed the cultural frontiers. Yet, from the point of view of the dominant political culture (Morse's chief concern), hybrid mixing only redoubled Iberian orthodoxies and scholastic fundamentalism. Specifically, Iberians sharpened their lurking propensity to dominion, forcible exploitation, and the status-quest for glory. Two legacies stand out: first, the aversion to settle the New World with small farmers, in favor of large *hacendados* (landowners) and feudal baronies; second, a municipal tradition of noble representation to preserve the hierarchies of status and potentate influence. Both the landed estate and *cabildo* (town hall) reinforced racial and ethnic hierarchies and patrimonialism in order to bolster control over subaltern populations. Accordingly, the syncretic mix (which was not all that hybrid as it turned out, even though it was the product of interethnic and interracial dialectics) inhibited the formation middle social strata—the heroic agents of change in the modernizationist plotlines. Herein, Morse located the structural conditions for Latin America's inability to make the smooth transition to modernity: the region lacked a true "bourgeois" force. Indeed, colonialism in Iberian colonies intensified (to put this in Max Weber's terms) "traditional" authority over more modern "rational-legal" forms of domination.

The consequences for postcolonial Latin America were almost predictable. When Napoleon's Iberian adventure shattered Bourbon authority, Latin America lost the anchor of traditional authority and quickly drifted into centrifugal chaos. If the mainland English colonies flourished into a dynamic capitalist and democratizing society in the wake of 1776, then Spanish republics plunged into the vortex of civil war. From this mess the *caudillo* emerged as the incarnation of a reconstituted "traditional authority." This historiographic master narrative stylized divergent time lines of postcolonial development. The United States made the transition to democratic capitalism relatively smoothly because it already hosted the preconditions for its modernity; Latin America did not, reinforcing the landed estate, local autocratic rulership, and a "vegetative decentralized non-urban economy"—variables already nestled in the fabric of Latin American colonialism.[9] Like dark mirrors for each other, the United States "succeeded" while Latin America "failed." These outcomes were practically determined at the outset.

This formulation was not restricted to Anglo-American authors. Indeed, Morse's touchstone in many ways came from the pen of

Mexico's Nobel poet laureate, Octavio Paz, whose *The Labyrinth of Solitude* built explicitly on comparative Anglo-Iberian personality types.[10] Spanish America was a land of "feudal aristocracies" descended from Iberian colonists. The break with Spain did not imply a break with its heritage since the very same leaders of independence came from the ranks of this Creole aristocracy and were thus existentially "incapable of creating a modern society." Then, when the colonies became fitful republics, hortative "liberators" became pessimistic "dictators." In a subsequent essay published in *The New Yorker*, Paz encapsulated the divergent historiographic paths as the product of conditions lurking even before conquest.[11] On the Amerindian side of the story, Latin America was home to settled dwellers, living in nucleated villages with extractive and agrarian economies propitious for tributary levies. In North America, Indians were nomadic, elusive, and difficult to induct into mercantilist political economies. At the very least, Paz brought the Indian "back in" to the picture. On the European side, England went the way of the Reformation; Spain under Charles V became the bulwark of Counter Reformation reaction. Thus when Madrid happened upon the tributary and mining wealth of Amerindians, they found the means to finance the war against infidels in Europe itself and champion the resistance against modernization. The Spanish Catholic political economy incorporated Indians into a hierarchical and centralized mission. English Protestants excluded Indians from an egalitarian, diffused political community. The Reformation, by vindicating the critique of religion, was a toehold for a broader critique of the old order and a precondition for the Enlightenment. Thus, from the start—indeed even before Europeans and Native Americans met each other—English colonies were destined to be the ideal hosts for a flourishing, unitary, and linear drive to modernity; Inquisitionist Latin America became the foil, a host for multiple, fragmented, and superimposed pasts, at once Indian and European, universal and particularist, driven yet static.

The two New World patterns presented the idealized, and idealist, conditions for divergent responses to transatlantic modernization. They reflected inescapable continuities with colonial legacies, whose differences magnified in counterposition to each other. Whatever one may think of this teleological setup, it remains the dominant explanatory framework for social change in the Americas.

Untangling Legacies

This does not mean scholars explain structural constraints on secular change in the same way. Indeed, when looking at the "colonial legacy" arguments, at least three distinctive narratives emerge, each one delineating the problematic of persistence. Continuities are explained in different ways, evoking different, sometimes complementary, sometimes contradictory time lines.

Deep Structures

Some scholars build explicitly on the type of model presented by Hartz and Paz—that elements of the Black Legend account for foundational characteristics of colonial societies, and that these features pose strict constraints on the subsequent maneuvering room of social actors.

Some have argued that the personality of founding agents created lasting patterns of domination. John J. Johnson's classic study, *The Military and Society in Latin America*, maintained that the conquest and conquistador heritage created a pattern of rulership noted for its personalism, individualism, pride, and violence—features which helped account for the sharp praetorian inflection of Latin American politics in the post-World War II years (see Michael Jiménez's chapter).[12] Militarism redoubled in the nineteenth century when the postcolonial states failed to make the transition to stable republican civilian rule. The result of the political culture was a tradition of clientelism and the weakness of impersonal loyalties to public offices in favor of the officers.

Others point to the binding constraints of colonial material structures. For Benítez Rojo, for instance, the plantation bequest left an indelible imprint on the Caribbean.[13] Indeed, where indigenous populations were wiped out and islands transformed *de haut en bas* to fit the exigencies of the Atlantic sugar economy, slavery and plantations thoroughly dominated the social formations of colonial societies. So extreme was the pattern of restructuring, that entirely new societies emerged, forged out of a shock of races and cultures—yielding to accultured and syncretized identities of Creoles. For Benítez Rojo, the plantation was like a "machine" churning society in a perpetual cauldron. If cultures and people mingled and fought to create new, hybrid identities, they could not escape the logic of their formative structure. For this reason Benítez Rojo argues that the plantation was more than a means of production: it was itself a type of society.

Deep structures of colonialism, whether forged out of conquistador cultures or the material dictates of the imperial enterprise, locked the region into a course of development from which it could not escape—a kind of large-scale historical path dependency in which the obstacles to change were insurmountable.[14] Starting in the 1960s, *dependency theory* refracted this strain of analysis into a model explaining the obstacles to change in terms of *developed* economies exploiting *underdeveloped* ones.[15] If this idea has, of late, fallen upon hard times—in some cases for good reason—it fit into a larger explanatory tendency that presented colonial legacy as a set of institutions and mind-sets resilient to change.

Reconstituted Legacies

There is a softer version of the determining power of colonial origins. Many find the deterministic flavor of deep structures difficult to swallow. Yet they remain aware that continuities pose constraints on agents' ability to break inherited moulds. In this approach, exogenous events (like international wars or technical change) or internal contestation (social upheaval or political crises) break continuous time lines.[16] For instance, in modern Latin American history, the wars for independence shattered ancien régime rulership, the Great Depression dashed the scaffolding of liberal international trade, and the emergence of manufacturing tilted the social scale away from rural to urban sectors. The examples are many—enough to compel students to treat strict continuities with caution.

But these ruptures seldom demolish old structures. Independence may have done away with absolutism, but it did not eviscerate patrimonial forms of rule. And in spite of a groundswell of genuinely liberal democratic struggle, exemplified by Artigas's movement in Uruguay, or Guerrero's in Mexico, the constitutional coalitions that emerged by the mid-nineteenth century were seldom concerned to integrate large swaths of Latin American popular sectors into the political community. In turn, the Great Depression hammered staple-led growth, but it did not diminish the importance of external markets to the health of Latin American economies—a fact which would come back to haunt policymakers in the 1950s. And manufacturing did not necessarily fully break the hold of agrarian elites over power or even mean that the majority of workers found industrial jobs. Change did not necessarily imply deep discontinuity.

This approach allows scholars to see legacies as constraints on peoples' actions—but it does not mean that people are unable to stretch or bend these constraints. In this volume, Robert Patch shows how indigenous Yucatecan material cultures survived alongside the dominant matrix of colonial extractive economies. This allowed Yucatecans to resist the forcible induction into broader trading networks later in the nineteenth century—and even then they did not do so without putting up a stout fight. Sometimes these processes deflected the course of Latin American histories onto slightly new paths; sometimes the reaction redoubled earlier patterns. They did not fully dislodge binding legacies but reconstituted them in new ways. Generally, this allows observers to tell stories about change within continuity.

Ruptures

Then there are discontinuities. Much less common, but nonetheless important to the larger sagas of Latin American histories, are the moments when the continuous time lines were irrevocably snapped. These usually appear in moments of revolution. The wars of independence, in some places, did destroy old formations. Mining wealth, for instance, emerged greatly debilitated across the hemisphere. The slaves of Saint Domingue, and the wars they fought, laid waste to Europe's single most valuable New World colony. Later, the Mexican Revolution pummeled the Porfiriato's patrician oligarchy and created wholly new alignments. The same holds true for Cuba and Nicaragua. Indeed, these episodes have become somewhat romanticized narratives of people finally able to topple the seemingly insurmountable barriers to change—perhaps most movingly rendered in C. L. R. James's story of the Haitian Revolution, *The Black Jacobins*, which borrowed a script from the French saga unleashed in 1789.[17]

What all these episodes did was puncture the previous patterns of social and political exclusion. Ruptures permanently altered the ways in which political subjects imagined their place in the new order of things, offering them new terms for discussing their membership, their rights, and their entitlements. Indeed, with time the lexicon of liberalism, the idea of equality and the autonomy of the private sphere, did refashion the political universe across Latin America, even if the moments of seismic ruptures were singular and idiographic. Few would argue that Latin Americans discuss politics or imagine their identities in the same way they did a century ago, never mind two centuries ago. This change has also had material consequences, even if Latin America remains open to the shocks of world market forces, incomes spread unequally, while ethnic, racial, and gender frontiers remain powerful barriers to realizing more democratic aspirations. Moments of large-scale upheaval, however, rupture the unalloyed continuities of colonialism, even if the outcome of these struggles do not conform to the expectations and hopes of their protagonists.

CONCLUSION

In Latin American history then, persistence is itself a historical problem. Things remain remarkably continuous but not for the same reasons and not without contestation. Moreover, features can have likenesses, but this does not mean they are the same features. Accounting for persistence does not preclude admitting change. But by problematizing persistence, untangling deep structural barriers from contingent obstacles, and distinguishing external (accidental or unanticipated) forces from internal (cumulative and strategic) pressures, historians and social scientists may come to a better reckoning of why change itself has been so difficult to realize. Moreover, admitting that Latin American histories can follow several overlapping time lines enables students to appreciate the extent to which change itself may be an unintended consequence of tugs between the pressures to conform and the will to resist.

At the same time, we must be aware of some teleological traps. The long-standing conventions of accounting for Latin American failures in terms of deep colonial legacies of premodern mind-sets (this is a favorite trope for the culture-as-destiny crowd) or dependency on world market forces (this once vibrant field has lost much of its allure—despite the very obvious vulnerabilities of Latin American societies to the caprice of exogenous forces) flattens the great diversity within the region. Moreover, the Black Legending of Latin American history inverts the causal order: it converts what needs to be problematized into fundamental causes (static cultures or entrenched power imbalances) and thus mystifies them into transhistorical truisms. Dimensions of persistence may remain, but this does not mean that the past itself should be depleted of its complexity or deprived of inquiries into the paths that were not taken, either by force or by choice. Continuities, in short, have to contend with the indeterminacies of life if they are to mean anything historically.

This volume seeks to set the problem of persistence itself on the table. Such an endeavor requires exploring the tropes and images of persistence in historiography and pluralizing the agents involved in perpetuating social structures as well as challenging them. Deliberately, this volume does not seek to offer an alternative, monolithic vision of Latin American pasts. Not all constraints are bequests of the conquest or foundational religious dichotomies. Most, indeed, are indeterminate products of struggles for power, resources, and personal quests. Nor does all change modify the sum total of social relations. The time lines of Latin American histories are manifold, not necessarily cumulative, and frequently disjointed.

Making sense of constraints on change and understanding protagonists of transformation require different, multiple sorts of narratives. For a comprehensive understanding no single approach will do. Nor is one tack necessarily better than any other—though we all have our preferences and aversions. Our hope is that identifying, questioning, and problematizing the sources of persistence will help enrich the meanings ascribed to past experiences. In this fashion we can begin to spare Latin America one of posterity's most presumptuous departure points: the stigma of "failure" to follow the path of sustained change laid out in the idealized models of other New World societies.

two

Europe and the Atlantic World

Philip D. Curtin

The usual view of Europe in the Atlantic world is bipolar, with Europe on one side and the Americas on the other. Europe is usually portrayed as the most prominent actor, and in fact Europe *was* the most prominent actor. It was Europeans who developed the maritime technology that made it possible to reach the Americas. Aside from some Inuit who seem to have made it from Greenland to Scotland, few Native American mariners reached Europe, except in European ships. But Europe was not the only actor in the relationships that came to involve four continents—the two Americas, Europe, and Africa.

European maritime prowess was the decisive factor shaping the Atlantic world, but the influences it carried were not merely from Europe outward. Especially in the early centuries, the maritime connections also involved relations between Africa and the Americas in ways that were neither intended nor predictable. Once Europe came to be equipped with the power of early industrialization, it became by far the most important of the four continents in shaping the Atlantic world, but that was not until the last decades of the eighteenth century at the earliest.

The very discovery of the Americas, so recently celebrated in the quincentennial recognitions, was more accidental than the usual view. The original maritime breakthrough did not originate with an effort to get to the Americas but with an attempt to reach down the African coast in search of gold. In 1444 the first European mariner to reach beyond the Sahara sailed back to Europe. The achievement was greater than may appear at first. It was a coastal voyage, like many other voyages Europeans made in the Mediterranean or around the coasts of northwestern Europe. The Saharan coast posed a special problem. While sailing ships could tack back and forth to make progress against a contrary wind, they could rarely make progress against both wind and current. On the Saharan coast, the wind blows from the northeast all year round creating a strong current setting toward the southwest. In the fifteenth century, however, Portuguese sailors learned that it was possible to return against wind and current if they took advantage of the fact that the winds veered inshore in daylight hours and offshore at night. By sailing in a series of long tacks to take advantage of these changes, it was possible to make progress toward the northeast.[1]

That discovery led on to another that was to be still more important. Sometime between 1444 and the 1470s, Portuguese mariners, now unknown, discovered that by sailing on a single long tack to the northwest, keeping as close as possible into the trade winds, they would arrive at the latitude of the Azores, where the winds were variable but generally westerly and fair for the Portuguese coast, and where the drift of the current carried in the same direction.

This discovery not only made it possible to sail easily to Cape Verde and back but also it was the first clear recognition that the ocean winds in the North Atlantic followed a circular pattern. From a little north of the equator to about 30 degrees north latitude, winds generally blow strongly and uniformly from the northeast, pulled in that direction by a combination of rising air over the heat equator and given an easterly twist provided by Earth's rotation. In the 40s and 50s north latitude, prevailing winds blow from the west. What the Portuguese navigators discovered, in short, was a corner of the world wind system that made long distance navigation far easier than mariners had previously recognized. This was the first step toward the science of oceanography, to be systematized by Matthew Maury in the early nineteenth century.

In the 1470s and 1480s the Portuguese exploited the first phase of this breakthrough by reaching into the South Atlantic. Before 1470 no European ship had sailed beyond Sierra Leone. By 1481 the Portuguese began building a castle at Elmina on the Gold Coast. By the end of the 1480s they had explored the equatorial coasts and those of the southern savannas and had reached the Cape of Good Hope. These voyages taught them how to use the wind system south of the equator. Along the coast of the Gulf of Guinea, the winds and currents often tend toward the east, but the Portuguese learned to escape a difficult return by dropping south across the equatorial calms to catch the southeast trades, recrossing the equator further to the west. It was these discoveries off the African coast that made possible the North Atlantic explorations of Columbus and his successors.

Further Portuguese voyages along the African coast south of the equator showed that the wind system was replicated in the South Atlantic. Vasco da Gama's voyage to India in 1498 used these findings to avoid the African coast and to use the northeast and southeast trades to reach the prevailing westerlies that would take him east into the Indian Ocean. With the help of African mariners, he then learned the rudiments of the Indian Ocean wind patterns with its seasonal reversal of the monsoon in the northern part of that ocean.

This important discovery of the uniformities of the world wind system began about 1430 and ended in 1522, when Sebastian del Cano brought Magellan's fleet back to Spain, having discovered that trade winds are uniform and tend to blow in the same direction in similar latitudes in the Pacific as well. Once this knowledge was assimilated and spread to European mariners at large, Europeans could go nearly anywhere.

AFRICA AND THE DISEASE EXCHANGE: SYPHILIS

The importance of the African factor reappears in disease aspects of the Atlantic exchange.[2] The diseases usually mentioned are syphilis, smallpox, yellow fever, and *falciparum* malaria—with measles, whooping cough, and the range of childhood diseases following. Syphilis is significant because many people believe that it originated in the Americas and came to Europe only with Columbus—that it was thus a kind of payback for the damage done in the Americas by pathogens from Europe.

An American origin of syphilis, however, is unlikely. The family of the treponemal diseases, which includes venereal syphilis (*Treponema pallidum*), consists of four distinct diseases—yaws, venereal syphilis, endemic syphilis, and pinta. The analytical problem begins with the fact that all four of these pathogens look the same under the microscope, are identical in their response to the usual serological test, and cannot be cultured to produce samples large enough for other tests. Some authorities once thought they were different manifestations of a single disease. Recent biomedical opinion, however, treats the treponemes as four closely related but distinct pathogens.

Their clinical and epidemiological manifestations are certainly distinct.[3] Venereal syphilis is transmitted by sexual intercourse, has worldwide distribution, is mainly urban not rural, and occurs most frequently in young adults. The characteristic primary lesion appears at the site of infection. Congenital transmission from mother to child is common and often results in stillbirth.

Endemic syphilis occurs among nomadic and seminomadic people in the Middle East and in northern and southern Africa, most frequently among young adults. The usual route of transmission is infected utensils, and the initial lesions occur in the mucous of the mouth or nose. It is not transmitted from mother to child.

Yaws is confined to the humid tropics throughout the world. It is common among children and adolescents, especially in tropical Africa, where a large proportion of the population was infected before the World Health Organization began its successful anti-yaws campaigns in the 1940s.

Pinta is found rarely and only among isolated rural populations in Mexico and South and Central America. The precise mode of transmission is unknown, but it seems to require several years of close personal contact with an infected person. No congenital transmission is reported.

As to the geographical range of the treponemes, yaws probably originated in Africa. It certainly moved from Africa to the Americas by way of the slave trade, and it is confined to the humid tropics, even today, on account of its mode of transmission by person-to-person contact through breaks in the skin. Pinta is still confined to the Americas, and endemic syphilis is also geographically limited to its present arid climatic conditions.

Only venereal syphilis is geographically unlimited. When and where, then, did this universal treponeme originate?[4] Pre-Columbian skeletal evidence suggests that *some* treponeme was present in the Americas before contact.[5] Today, pinta occurs in the Americas and nowhere else, but it is comparatively rare. On the face of it, syphilis appears to be a more likely candidate than pinta to be the pre-Columbian treponeme in the Americas, but no fifteenth-century account from the Caribbean describes either yaws or the violently contagious venereal syphilis that appeared in Europe in the 1490s.[6]

That form of syphilis first occurred in Naples in 1494 or 1495 and spread rapidly thereafter to become the syphilis Europe has known ever since, though the recent strain is less virulent than the one that ravaged Europe in the first half of the sixteenth century. No contemporaneous account for 1492, 1493, or 1494 describes any such disease in the Caribbean, among Columbus's crews, in the Azores or Lisbon (where the fleet landed on its return), or in other Iberian ports where the sailors might have gone. The only evidence to support the Columbian origins of syphilis in Europe is the coincidence in dates. Columbus's fleet reached

Lisbon on March 4, 1493. Syphilis first appeared in the French army at the siege of Naples, which began in January 1494. The first undoubted descriptions of the disease date from July 1495.[7] The problem is the complete lack of evidence for the transmission of this disease from one or more of the few hundred sailors and Native Americas who returned with Columbus, across more than 1,200 miles between Lisbon and Naples.[8]

Several hypotheses have tried to explain the appearance of syphilis.[9] Recently, M. D. Grmek, on one hand, and Brenda Baker and George Armelagos, on the other, have leaned toward a Columbian origin. Grmek looked extensively at the literary, while Baker and Armelagos surveyed the skeletal evidence for a sign of *any* treponeme in Europe, Asia, or Africa before the fifteenth century; they found none. For humid tropical Africa, however, no possible evidence exists—either literary or skeletal—and that is precisely where yaws would be expected and was recently so prevalent. More recently, some skeletal material with marks of treponemal infection and a pre-Colombian date has been found in the Mediterranean basin, so that the possibility of non-American origin is somewhat strengthened.[10] Still more recently, yaws has been detected in *Homo erectus*, dating from the Middle Pleistocene (or about 1.5 million years ago). This suggests that the ancient migration from Africa across the land bridge from Asia carried the treponemal pathogens found in the pre-Columbian Americas.[11]

This leaves us without hard evidence that modern syphilis existed *anywhere* before Naples in 1494. For lack of evidence to the contrary, the most probable explanation is that one of the other treponemes mutated into syphilis near that time and place. While the Columbian hypothesis appears viable though weak, another possibility is worth considering. The second half of the fifteenth century was also the beginning of an African presence in Europe. Some slave trade across the Sahara had been going on for several centuries, no doubt bringing many yaws-infected people into North Africa, though yaws cannot maintain itself in places that arid. The direct maritime slave trade from tropical Africa began in the 1440s— made possible by the new Portuguese ability to navigate along the Saharan coast. This slave trade introduced about 500 Africans each year into southern Europe during the second half of the fifteenth century—or a total of about 25,000 people during the half century before the outbreak of syphilis. The great majority of these African immigrants arrived first in Portugal, but they soon spread widely through the Mediterranean basin. If these people had been infected with yaws at levels prevalent in West Africa early in the twentieth century, then 10 to 50 percent would have been infected. This would have meant that between 2,500 to 125,000 yaws victims entered the European disease environment over that half century. If any treponeme mutated into venereal syphilis in the 1490s, yaws would have been the most probable candidate, being the most common treponeme in the Mediterranean basin at the time. This remains an inconclusive possibility, but if the appearance of syphilis was in any sense an unintended payback, it was more likely a payback for the beginning of the slave trade not for the later Atlantic exchange.

MALARIA

If Europeans may have been instrumental in bringing treponemes to Europe, they certainly carried malaria to the Americas in two different ways. *Plasmodium vivax*, the cause of debilitating ague and fever, was the species of malaria common in Europe and rare in West Africa. It appeared in the Americas shortly after maritime contact, perhaps carried by Columbus's first or second voyage.

P. falciparum is the most deadly form of malaria and the one most widely found in the tropical world today and probably originated in tropical Africa. It seems to have arrived in the Americas only in the sixteenth century, with the increase of the slave trade from Africa. European ships carried both diseases to the Americas, but *falciparum* came from Africa and *vivax* came from Europe. Though *vivax* arrived early in the Atlantic exchange, *falciparum* arrived only when the flow of slaves from Africa became significant, and it then played a major role in the depopulation of the tropical American lowlands.

On the North American mainland, *vivax* arrived with the first settlement of Jamestown, but *falciparum* became common in the American South only in the 1670s and later when slaves from Africa began to arrive in large numbers.[12]

YELLOW FEVER

Yellow fever, like *falciparum* malaria, originated in Africa and it is also transmitted by insect vector. Aside from these shared attributes, the two diseases are very different. Yellow fever is a virus, not a protozoa. Where *falciparum* malaria can lead to a quick death or to lifelong infestation, yellow fever either kills or leaves the victim with a lifelong immunity. The principal vector, *Aëdes aegypti*, is a single species that originated in

Africa but now occurs throughout the tropical world. While the case-fatality rate is very high for adults, it is comparatively low for children, who can often achieve a lifelong immunity without serious clinical symptoms. The result was an acquired immunity that looked like an inborn immunity among people who grew up where yellow fever was a frequent visitor.

The serious occurrences of yellow fever are typically urban and epidemic—urban because the vector flies only a few hundred yards, epidemic because concentrations of nonimmunes in towns or a military organization have a high rate of infection. In such groups, the morbidity could reach to more than 80 percent, with the death of more than half of the group within a few months, before the immunity of the survivors bars the further progress of the infection.

Europeans carried yellow fever to the Americas as still another by-product of the trade in slaves. Its date of arrival is uncertain. Yellow fever symptoms mimic those of many other diseases, including malaria. In children and some adults, yellow fever may show no clinical symptoms at all. The first secure reports of the disease in the 1640s are therefore probably later than its actual arrival. The epidemiology of yellow fever commonly followed one of two patterns. Where the only animal hosts were human beings, an epidemic would often leave so few nonimmunes that the resulting herd immunity would cause the disease to die out altogether. In time, as new generations of nonimmunes were born, it could be reintroduced from the outside and a new epidemic would follow.

In other circumstances, nonhuman animal hosts, primates who lived in the canopy of tropical forests, made it possible to keep the infection alive so that each new generation could be infected and thus acquire immunity in childhood. When this happened, observers at the time often came to believe that some populations like those of tropical West Africa had a racial, inherited immunity. In the Caribbean, however, some islands lacked the forest reservoir and a monkey population, so that yellow fever passed through its epidemic stage and then disappeared for a generation or more, until new victims were available to new infection from the outside. In Cuba, for example, yellow fever struck in 1649–55 and then vanished until the 1760s.

Though yellow fever mortality was great when it first arrived in the Americas, its later consequences were extremely variable, depending on the size of the community, the existence of alternate hosts, and the intensity of intercommunication. In some circumstances, the disease was devastating. In others, it could even protect the local populations from outside, human enemies, as it did with the with the spectacular death rates among invading armies, while the local militia was protected by immunity resulting from childhood infection. The notable cases of this kind included the defense of Cartagena against the British in 1740 and Saint Domingue against a French effort to reconquer it after a slave rebellion in the 1790s.[13]

SMALLPOX

Smallpox was a third disease the Europeans carried from Africa to the Americas with devastating results. *Variola major*, was present in both Europe and Africa at the time of Columbus's voyage. It had a case-fatality rate of 20 to 30 percent, and it caused the facial scarring that was the lifelong evidence of an attack. It was a virus, like yellow fever, and it too caused a lifelong immunity among the survivors. Unlike yellow fever, it has no alternate host in the forest, which made possible its ultimate extinction.

The Europeans introduced epidemic smallpox to the Americas but not until 1518, a quarter century after maritime contact. The epidemiology of smallpox suggests an explanation for this delay. Smallpox spread easily from one person to another through respiratory droplets. Actual physical contact was not necessary. In large communities with intense intercommunication, smallpox was largely a childhood disease; almost all adults were infected as children and thus acquired a lifelong immunity. In sixteenth-century Spain smallpox apparently followed this pattern. Only already immune adults went to the Caribbean in the earliest decades of contact, which meant that no carriers were available to infect the American populations. With a voyage of six weeks or more, an individual who had acquired smallpox in Europe would have run through the disease; by the time he reached America, he would either be dead or immune. In the seventeenth century smallpox was slow to spread to the English colonies for similar reasons.

In smaller communities, with less intense intercommunication, the epidemiology of smallpox was different. Whenever the population at risk was too small to sustain smallpox as an endemic childhood disease, it appeared instead in periodic epidemics. Like yellow fever in the Caribbean, a severe epidemic would kill or immunize so many people that the disease would die away—only to reappear from the outside when new births had provided enough susceptible victims. The intervals between epidemics were variable but tended to be five years or more.

This epidemiological pattern was still in effect in nineteenth-century West Africa and was highly probable for the sixteenth century as well.[14]

In the Atlantic basin of the early sixteenth century the most likely people to carry smallpox to the Americas would have been nonimmunes or infected children. The ideal carriers would be a group of nonimmunes traveling together, who could then pass the disease from one to another during the course of the voyage. A cargo of African slaves fits that specification.

People of African descent were present in the Americas from the early years of maritime contact, but the first to arrive came from Europe and shared the European pattern of acquired immunity to smallpox. In the 1510s, however, a few Africans began to come directly from Africa through an incipient and largely illegal slave trade. Late in 1518, the first smallpox broke out on Hispaniola in a camp of African slave mine workers and spread rapidly to the Indian population.[15] Contemporaneous estimates put the Indian death rates for the Antilles at nearly 50 percent in that first epidemic. A case-fatality rate at this level would be higher than recent experience, but the reports may have been exaggerated, or the death rate might have been exceptional for lack of background immunity—the *virgin soil* effect.

From the Caribbean, the epidemic spread to Mexico, and the reported carrier was again an African. In 1518–19 the Cortés expedition began the conquest of Mexico. Even though the epidemic had already begun in the Antilles, this force of Spanish soldiers carried no smallpox. In 1520, however, the governor of Cuba sent a second expedition to bring Cortés under control. That expedition included one African who had been infected in Cuba, and he set off an epidemic among the native Indians, first in the Yucatan and then in central Mexico. It was this epidemic that gave the Spanish their easy victory over the Aztec empire and killed up to half the population of what was to be New Spain.[16]

That epidemic continued and spread throughout South America by stages, merging with other introductions of smallpox from Africa to Brazil. By the 1560s smallpox had reached so much of northern South America that the disease died down, waiting for a new, nonimmune generation to be born. South America, in short, fell into the tropical African pattern of periodic epidemics.[17]

During the seventeenth and eighteenth centuries a new pattern of smallpox interaction across the South Atlantic grew out of an African pattern of drought, disease, and slave trade. The African savanna country is subject to periodic dry periods, a climatic fragility common to many parts of the world in the latitudes ten to twenty degrees north or south of the equator. On the African side, a dry period had a number of consequences. Smallpox in tropical Africa was more contagious in dry periods than in wet. Drought also encouraged epidemics by forcing scattered people toward more secure sources of water along whatever streams maintained their flow, and drought increased the flow of captives into the slave trade. People who had a hard time feeding themselves and their closest kin could release some dependents into the trade for the sake of those who remained. Thus slave exports and smallpox increased simultaneously, and the epidemic moved across the Atlantic to trigger a similar epidemic in Brazil. The African connection is not certain for the first major Brazilian pandemic of the 1560s, but it is clear for those that followed in the 1680s and 1690s, the 1740s, and in the 1780s, each of which is associated with drought in Africa and a peak in slave exports.[18]

On the disease front, then, the European maritime outburst into the Atlantic may possibly have led to the introduction of treponemal infection to Europe, and it was certainly Europeans who later spread syphilis worldwide. European shipping certainly introduced yellow fever and *falciparum* malaria into the Americas. These, the most deadly of tropical diseases, depopulated the American tropical lowlands and opened the way for their repopulation from Africa and Europe at a later time. Smallpox would no doubt have got to the Americas from Europe in due course, but the first introduction was from Africa. The major demographic and epidemiological consequences of the Atlantic exchange thus had their origins in Africa, though the exchange was made possible by European maritime prowess and mediated through the slave trade. The slave trade itself partly arose because these disease patterns, mediated by European shipping, linked the disease environments of tropical Africa with those of the tropical Americas.

THE PLANTATION COMPLEX

The complex of slave plantations and the slave trade linking Europe, Africa, and the tropical Americas is a familiar aspect of Atlantic history—possibly the most important aspect of Atlantic history from the 1550s to the 1840s. Yet we are used to the model of North American history, where the Europeans came as settlers and created a new Europe by blanket migration imposing European culture. This view of European agency is right but not until the nineteenth century. The institution of the plantation complex was unlike that of contemporaneous Europe, and its spread had something in common with the spread of disease. European maritime technology made possible a new disease environment in the tropical Americas; it also made it possible to assemble in the Americas institutions of non-European character to create the plantation complex.

I have outlined elsewhere a number of characteristics that strike me as central to the complex.[19] The first was slavery of a particular kind, different from the residual slavery in southern Europe or the serfdom of the North. Slavery in the plantation complex was for agricultural labor, and it was the dominant form of labor. The plantation societies were also demographically different from any European society. They normally had a net natural decrease in population—among slaves and masters alike. This meant that plantation populations could be maintained only with a continuous input of slaves from Africa and managers from Europe. Agricultural production was organized with a pattern of work organization and management different from any agriculture practiced in Europe at the time. The plantation complex was based on large-scale, capitalist plantations, where the planter owned the land, the capital, and the labor force and managed production through his agents on a day-by-day and hour-by-hour basis. Finally, the products were few and highly specialized, at first mainly sugar but later coffee or cotton, destined for markets an ocean away. A larger part of total production entered long-distance trade than in any other segment of the world economy at that time.

Even though it was not the European way of doing things, the complex operated under European management and under the ultimate control of European states. The wholesale export of European people and European culture belonged to a later period in Atlantic history. It was not until the 1840s that more Europeans than Africans crossed the Atlantic. The plantation complex that reached its apogee in the eighteenth century pulled together some institutions and techniques from Europe and others from elsewhere. The European directors and managers molded them into a genuinely new kind of society—not admirable, just new.

The crops themselves were one aspect of this novelty. Sugar, the most important of all, came into the Mediterranean basin from India with the rise and spread of Islam. Coffee came from Ethiopia by way of Java, indigo from India, cacao from Mexico, and rice ultimately from China, though some was grown in Europe as well.

The labor supply was even more exotic, mainly from Africa, of course, and dependent upon some crucial African institutions for its availability. One significant problem here has to be seen in the context of world history. Some societies seem to serve as recurrent sources of slaves for export, while others have been chronic importers. Western sub-Saharan Africa, like Ukraine, was a chronic exporter. Some explanations have suggested overpopulation as the reason, but tropical Africa in the centuries of the slave trade was not overpopulated in any usual sense of that term. A more likely explanation is that warfare in most of western tropical Africa was based on the convention that the entire conquered population could be enslaved. Europeans in Europe sometimes took and ransomed prisoners, but the capture and enslavement of civilians was not considered legitimate. The African convention made the capture of the enemy population a legitimate object of warfare, whereas the European objective was to defeat the enemy army in the field and to seize his territory.[20]

In tropical Africa this military objective encouraged an internal slave trade. Women and children could sometimes be reduced to servitude and kept within the victorious society, but young male adults were too dangerous to keep around. In later centuries such captives were often sold to merchants who followed the armies. A few hundred miles from the scene of capture, they might be sold into a society more capable of absorbing them, with less chance of successful escape. The prevalence of these patterns of capture and commercialization of prisoners meant that slaves were available for an export trade as well, once North Africans appeared on the desert edge or Europeans appeared on the coast.[21]

These patterns of enslavement were related in turn to other aspects of society in western tropical Africa. Control over land was rarely transferable by purchase. Low levels of population density might have contributed to this pattern, in the sense that land, being plentiful, earned no rent.[22] It is unlikely, however, that African population densities were that low. John Thornton recently suggested that slavery was prevalent because slaves were the most readily available form of revenue-producing property recognized by African law and custom. In the traditions of medieval Europe land was considered the key to productive capability, and ownership of land often included the control over a labor force to work it. In contemporaneous Africa land was owned, but it was mainly cooperative ownership by kinship groups or by the state. It was not always plentiful, but it was readily available at a low price or no price to those who could make use of it—that is, to those who owned the labor to work it.[23] In Europe, then, land ownership tended to imply easy control over labor, while in Africa ownership of labor tended to make for easy control over land.[24]

It was the intersection of European maritime technology with African social and legal ideas about rights in people that made the slave trade possible. In the longer run these two factors combined with the epidemiological conditions to make possible the enormous scale the slave trade was to achieve at its height in the eighteenth century.

In effect, and to oversimplify only slightly, the Europeans carried Africans to the tropical Americas, where their diseases wiped out the Amerindian populations. The new American disease environment that resulted was one where people with West African patterns of immunity were better able to survive than either the Native Americans or the Europeans who were the ultimate carriers of goods and people and managers of the Atlantic world.[25] The growth of the slave trade from the sixteenth to the late eighteenth centuries, however, altered West African societies in fundamental ways, just as the growth to the American plantations created a new kind of society that had never existed anywhere before on such a scale.

In addition to remaking the world of the tropical Atlantic through the Atlantic exchange, the European plantation complex was to have a long and important influence on Europe itself. It was ultimately based on European maritime technology, and the associated carrying trade led to cheaper ocean shipping as the complex itself grew and changed. In this connection it is important to remember that the sailing ship was the most important source of nonanimal, nonhuman power before the development of the steam engine.

Because the complex involved such intricate relations between planters, agents, bankers, insurers, and shippers, the transaction costs were very high at first, but with the passage of the decades, transaction costs came down paralleling the falling cost of ocean shipping. Although it is difficult to sustain the full weight of Eric Williams's thesis[26] that the plantation complex in some sense helped to cause the industrial revolution, such intensive intercontinental trade over these centuries surely helped to develop and refine business methods. The bundle of lower transaction costs, along with cheaper and safer oceanic transportation, were at least a part of the technology that paved the way for the industrial world to come.

three

Colonial Africa through the Lens of Colonial Latin America

Robert L. Tignor

Fascination with empire is unceasing. Despite having entered the post-colonial period, contemporaries continue to be intrigued by the imperial era. Biographies of the great empire builders abound. New studies reinterpret the European partition of Africa. Yet, in spite of this intense interest in empires, the comparative study of the early modern Iberian empires in the New World and the European empires in Africa can hardly be said to have received much attention. Two of the most recent overviews of imperial history (Michael Doyle, *Empires* [Ithaca, 1986]; and Paul Kennedy, *The Rise and Fall of the Great Powers* [New York, 1987]) treat the Spanish and Portuguese imperial record only briefly. Most generalists dealing with colonialism tend to skimp on colonial Latin America, seeming to accept a notion prevalent among modern historians that there is little to compare between what many regarded as the inefficient, albeit long-lived, Iberian empires of the mercantile era, with the seemingly purposeful and rationalized British and French colonies of twentieth-century industrial and financial capitalism.

By ignoring the comparative value of Iberian colonialism, contemporary scholars are being true to their sources and also echoing the opinion of the colonial practitioners of this later form of imperialism. The European proconsuls, as articulate and well-read as any comparable group of public officials, had searched for colonial guidance in antiquity, particularly in the practices of the Roman empire, and had neglected the closer and potentially more insightful experiences of the Spanish and Portuguese. Lord Cromer, perhaps the most erudite and prolific writer among the British colonial administrators, in his famous essay

Ancient and Modern Imperialism completely ignored the Spanish and the Portuguese empires of the Americas and went straight to classical Rome for his historical analogies.[1]

Two fundamental concerns animate this paper: first, whether the Atlantic economy, created in the era of mercantile capitalism, survived the abolition of slavery and the attainment of political independence in the Americas and thus was able to influence the later European empires in Africa; and, second, whether useful structural comparisons can be made between the Spanish empire of early modern times, undeniably the most self-conscious and rationalized of the colonial states of this era, and the later British and French colonies. This chapter suggests that significant benefits flow from this kind of comparative work.

THE ATLANTIC ECONOMY—AN ENDURING INTELLECTUAL LEGACY OF THE "OTHER"

The existence of an Atlantic economy, binding together early modern Europe, Africa, and the Americas, has by now gained an unassailable status in the historiography of these three continents. Few would contest the claim that a group of Caribbean historians and intellectuals made the original breakthroughs in demonstrating the linkages that bound Africa, Europe, and the Americas together. First, C. L. R. James traced the spread of the ideas of the French Enlightenment and the French revolution to the planters, free blacks, mulattoes, and slave populations of Haiti and described the resulting war of Haitian independence.[2] Eric Williams's discussion of the triangular trade highlighted the economic bonds among three continents. His work argued for the centrality of Atlantic trade to European capital formation and industrialization.[3] From these sturdy foundations, a vast army of scholars uncovered the web of connections that drew these three land masses and peoples together. Recent work has provided information on the number of Africans transported to the Americas, their locations in Africa and the Americas, the impact of this population exodus on African societies, and the varying slaveholding arrangements in the Americas.[4] A still grossly underresearched aspect of the Atlantic economy remains the influence of African practices on the Americas, in spite of the early insights of Melville Herskovits on African continuities.[5]

Given the importance so many scholars now attach to African and Latin American contacts in the early modern era of European history, one must ask whether any of the legacies of the Atlantic economy spanned the historical watershed of the European Industrial Revolution. The conventional historical wisdom is that the dissolution of mercantile capitalism and the spread of abolitionism and an ideology of free labor marked the end of the old Atlantic system and set the African and American continents on different historical courses.[6] Undeniably, the seismic changes that brought political independence to the peoples of North and South America also altered Europe's economic relationship to Africa. No longer did Europeans view Africa as a reservoir of slave labor. They now measured Africa's worth by the value of its raw materials, the so-called legitimate commerce of the nineteenth century, its import of European manufactures, and its centrality for Christian conversions.[7]

Yet one continuity can hardly be denied, overriding the impact of industrialization and abolitionism on European relations with Africa. This was the persistence of certain European images of Africa and Africans that outlasted the revolutions of the eighteenth century. However varied and even contradictory the European imagery of Africa was, certain views of the African continent and its peoples were crystallized in Europe's early modern period and proved to be obdurate from that moment onward. These perceptions owed much to the early European expansionism of the fifteenth and sixteenth centuries which not only intensified Europe's relationship with Africans but also brought the Europeans into contact with the native peoples of the Americas. Here was for Europe its first and formative encounter with peoples outside the European historical experience, notwithstanding the European experience with their own domestic "other" populations like the Irish for the English and the Moors for the Iberians.[8] So powerful and long-lived was this mental rift between Europe and "the other" that it easily spanned the great historical watershed between commercial and industrial capitalism. Indeed, Europe's hierarchy of the races, having evolved in its relationship to Asia, the Americas, and Africa, gained pseudoscientific authority with the emergence of social Darwinism in the nineteenth century.[9]

The attitudes of the peoples living in the northwestern portion of the Eurasian land mass toward the outside world hardened at a propitious moment in European history. At just the moment when Italian, Portuguese, Spanish, Dutch, English, and French explorers, merchants, conquerors, and missionaries were fanning out throughout the globe, Europe had come to view itself as a distinct cultural entity—a people

inhabiting a unified geocultural region—rather than a community organized around a singular religious identity. Renaissance scholars expostu-
lated that being European meant being descendants of Europa, or
Japheth, and hence separate from the other two historical branches of
mankind. European scholars also traced these branches of mankind to
roots in antiquity. The non-European world was now decisively set off
from Europe. Shem, or Asia, extolled as the birthplace of the prophets
and Christ, was expected to yield to the might of Japheth; Africa,
wherein resided the children of Ham who bore the stigma of that early
people of Israel, were subject to enslavement.[10] Europe, no longer a
mere region, had become an "idea."[11] This newfound European differentiation from the non-European world implied an unwillingness of the
peoples of northwestern Europe to enslave each other, even those as far
away as the Caucasus from whence earlier European slave cadres had
been drawn.[12]

At this moment in Europe's self-definition, Europeans encountered
the peoples of the New World. These "newly discovered" peoples had no
obvious Biblical antecedents (though some European commentators
quickly and ingeniously found some for the Amerindians) yet needed to
be incorporated into the European view of the other. To some scholars
the Europeans experienced little difficulty in fitting the Amerindian peoples, their environments, and their practices into already existing models.[13] But if this effort was accomplished with relative ease, it was done so
only by ransacking Europe's highly developed world of fantasy.
Assimilation of this new universe only heightened the European sense of
separateness from non-European communities.

The Europeans had long believed that lands lay to the west, inhabited,
in all likelihood, by bizarre, ugly, and indescribable forms of life. They,
thus, imposed on the indigenes of North and South America as well as the
peoples of Africa below the Sahara that phantasmagoria that existed in
their own world of belief. They inherited many of these images from the
ancient world or incorporated them from chivalric tales and folklore.
Where they expected to encounter man-eaters, women of incredible
strength, and giant animals, for this is what Herodotus and other classical
scholars had said existed at the peripheries of civilization, they did,
indeed, "discover" cannibals, amazons, and giant mammoths.[14] But there
was more at stake than projecting European fears and fantasies onto the
peoples of the Americas. While the Europeans were creating a hierarchy
of civilizations, with Europeans at the top, followed in descending order

by Asians, Amerindians, and Africans,[15] they were also debating the critical question of how the resources of the Americas were to be exploited. They struggled intellectually and pragmatically with the question of the labor systems best suited to these new lands. Whether the philosophical and theological interventions of clerics like Las Casas, Acosta, and Vitoria, opposed to the enslavement of the Amerindians, were more decisive than the sheer unwillingness of native Americans to accept the role of slavery that the New World conquerors thrust upon them is not nearly so relevant as the fact that American Indians avoided massive enslavement while Africans did not.[16] This crucial historical development was justified, if it did not actually spring from, many of these same early European images of African peoples as primitives, pagans, and violators of natural law, hence enslaveable. The images themselves persisted in Euro-African relations right through the era of abolition and into the partition and conquest of the African continent. In contrast, the Amerindian peoples, though they worked no less hard and often under as much compulsion as Africans, enjoyed a more elevated status since they were regarded as wards of the imperial state and peoples fit for Christianization.

It would be inaccurate to contend that these European views of the other did not change. Indeed, a vast array of images competed for acceptance, many of which, like those that argued for Africans and Native Americans as "noble savages" and those that portrayed these same peoples as bestial and unworthy of esteem, were contradictory. Views of the other changed as Europe's relationship, knowledge, and needs toward these continents altered. Certainly, the negative stereotypes of Africans became stronger during the Atlantic slave trade while views of Africans as noble savages and people whose souls could be redeemed enjoyed more credibility in the era of abolition. In the nineteenth century Europe clothed its attitude toward Asians, Amerindians, and Africans in scientific racism. But the continuity of the imagery, if not the vocabulary, is striking. It permitted the Europeans to move easily from enslaving Africans to "civilizing" them under colonial rule.[17]

STRUCTURAL COMPARISONS OF COLONIALISM IN LATIN AMERICA AND AFRICA

Colonial experiences can be compared in numerous ways. But structurally six categories have obvious relevance for comparing the colonial experience of Latin America with Africa. These are the motivations for empire, the imperial administrative systems, imperial economies, social and cultural consequences of colonial rule, nationalism, and neocolonialism. Although much of this essay will highlight the similarities between colonial Latin America and colonial Africa, if only for heuristic and corrective purposes, two differences distinguished the colonial experiences of the two continents and had an impact on every one of the six areas of comparison. The first was the time frame of the colonizing effort. Latin American colonial developments seem to occur almost in slow motion, stretching out over three centuries, in comparison with Africa's telescoped colonial history of less than a century. Second, no population catastrophe, comparable to that of the Americas, occurred in colonial Africa.

Imperial Motivations, Conquest, and Early Administrative Arrangements

The Iberian empires in the Americas appear at first glance radically different from the British and French colonies of Africa. To begin with, Iberian rule did not enrich the Portuguese and the Spanish as much as it did the Dutch, French, and English. The bounty of Spain and Portugal's overseas possessions was transmitted to Europe's more developed metropoles. The intensity of Spanish and Portuguese missionary zeal and the maritime achievements of the Iberians did not overcome the late medieval nature of their societies. The Iberians proved unable to take full advantage of the extraordinary economic and other opportunities that the Americas offered to them. Concomitantly, the long-term relative economic retardation of Latin America itself arose from the continent's misfortune to be subjugated to the least dynamic fragment of Europe and to serve mainly as a transmission belt for riches on their way to the rising commercial entrepots of England, France, and the Netherlands.

Most commentators on later European imperialism highlight the contrasts with this earlier mercantilist version. They point out that, in contrast to this earlier era, the most dynamic European nation states led the expansionist surge while the lesser European powers—the Belgians, Portuguese, Italians, and Spanish—fought for smaller places in the imperial sun. Yet the similarities in motivations, impact of conquest, and the nature of the colonial administrative systems are surely worth noting. If, in fact, we focus on the overarching motives that impelled the Europeans into conquest and territorial control, then we quickly catch sight of the palpable continuities between these two ages of conquest and empire formation. Historians of the *new imperialism* are likely to object to the notion that the mentality and motivation of the European colonizers and early administrators of Africa, steeped in the science and rationality of the late nineteenth century, can be seen as similar to the worldview of individuals caught up in the *Reconquista*, the Reformation, and the Spanish Inquisition as well as bullionism. Yet there are striking parallels if one only adjusts the vocabulary of the two eras.

Nineteenth-century European expansion was driven by the same inflated personal ambitions and unrealistic visions of undiscovered El Dorados that hypnotized the Iberian conquerors. It is not inaccurate to characterize late-nineteenth-century imperialism as driven by the same three crudely stated motivations that nearly all of the textbooks on Latin American history attribute to the Iberians—God, gold, and glory.[18] Just as Cortés exclaimed, "We came to serve God and King and also to get rich,"[19] so we can find similarly unvarnished statements of imperialist motivations echoing from their latter-day counterparts. No one spoke more candidly or was a more blatant aggrandizer than Cecil Rhodes. He believed in Britain's divine imperial mission and was as compulsive in the acquisition of mining contracts and mineral wealth as any El Dorado-driven conquistador.

No one would gainsay the dominant role that the early explorers and conquerors played in the Iberian expansion into the Americas. Throughout these decades of ceaseless expansion, the men on the spot outstripped their superiors in Hispaniola and Spain in extending the empire. Their desire for personal enrichment and glory and their Christianizing zeal made them formidable adversaries to their much more numerous hosts. Nor were they solely interested in the fame that flowed from conquest, for they wanted to enjoy the spoils of the New World and set themselves in positions, as *encomenderos* (patrons), to exploit, usually in brutal fashion, the labor of the Americas.

If, then, we are justified in viewing the partitioners and conquerors of Africa as latter-day conquistadors, what about the impact of these individuals on colonized and conquered populations? Did they have as deleterious an effect as Cortés, Pizarro, and their compatriots? In truth, the early exploitation of the African continent, relegated by the metropoles to men on the spot, took on the same features of uncaring self-enrichment that had characterized the rule of the conquistadors in the New World. One easily observes examples of a late-nineteenth-century conquistador mentality toward empire and native peoples.

Archinard, the French military zealot and conqueror of the western Sudan, Leopold, his majesty incorporated, Karl Peters, father of German imperialism and architect of the German empire in East Africa, and, the omnipresent Cecil Rhodes, the most visible and voracious apostle of British expansionism, conquered and ruthlessly exploited. Like their sixteenth-century analogs, these men were inspired by a vision of Europe's civilizational superiority and were certain that the forces of Christian Europe would prevail over the larger African armies whom they had to best.[20]

The conquerors of Africa also stamped their personalities and visions on the early relations between Europe and its subjugated populations; hence the first economic and administrative arrangements in colonial Africa can usefully be compared with those of Spanish America. The early decades of European colonial rule in Africa were nearly as chaotic and disruptive as the Spanish-Portuguese era in the Americas. An era of pillage and plunder followed the conquest of Africa as surely as it did in the Spanish and Portuguese Americas. The nineteenth-century European powers, much like their Spanish counterparts, delegated authority to men on the spot and then watched in horror as "the new hunters and gatherers" of Africa spoliated the continent's resources, human and nonhuman. Exploiting Africa's most accessible, albeit non-renewable, resources of wild rubber and ivory, the merchants, military men, and colonial officials lined their own pockets without concerning themselves with the effect of these policies on local peoples and environments. These grossly exploitative arrangements would have persisted had it not been for a series of wrenching African rebellions that called attention to these economic iniquities while simultaneously announcing the exhaustion of the resources and, in some cases, the exhaustion of local populations.[21]

Nor do the similarities between the early colonial eras end with rule by "men on the spot." The early colonial reforms in Africa and Latin America have much in common, in spite of differences in vocabulary. Everywhere in colonial Africa, just prior to or after World War I, metropolitan regimes and colonial administrations adopted new policies. While hardly rid of the hard edges of racism and economic exploitation, these programs, nonetheless, proclaimed Africa's primary asset to be its human capital rather than its cash crops and its precious metals. Arguing that without attending to matters of health and education Africa's raw material resources would lie idle, the new colonial rationalizers articulated a different vision of Europe's colonial relationship to the continent. This new rationalized and metropolitan-controlled colonialism employed different rubrics in the different colonial empires, but the similarities were striking. The British used ideals like the dual mandate, indirect rule, and the doctrine of native paramountcy to represent the new ideological and administrative thrust. The Germans spoke of scientific colonialism, which emerged out of the Herero and Maji-Maji rebellions and the 1906 election, partly fought over colonial issues. French Minister of Colonies Georges Sarraut referred to a *mise en valeur* to herald an effort to "civilize" Africans under their control.[22]

The rationalizations of African colonial rule stemmed directly from gross abuses in these early and unregulated colonial arrangements and from a lack of metropolitan oversight. They have an obvious analog in the Spanish royal efforts to assert authority over the conquistadors and early settlers.[23] In this case the reformists were humanitarians and theologians like Montesinos, Las Casas, Acosta, and Vitoria. These men upbraided the *encomenderos* for their abusive treatment of Native Americans and spurred the monarchy to insert itself vigorously into the debate over colonial issues. The crown used this groundswell of colonial criticisms to limit the powers of these men on the spot in favor of royal appointees. In both imperial experiences, colonial debates and revelations about widespread maladministration compelled colonial agents to assume larger social and cultural responsibilities and resulted in more rationalized colonial administrative systems.

Yet the population catastrophe still stands out as the glaring difference in the early colonial effects. The demographic destruction in the Americas has intrigued the historians of Africa, only a few of whom, however, have claimed similar results on the African continent. Whether the Amerindian population was in the neighborhood of sixty to one hundred million in 1500 or a more modest forty million and whether the spread of pandemic diseases was the primary cause of death remain hotly contested issues. Unchallenged, however, is the devastating population decline, which from nearly all accounts was no more than seven million at the end of the eighteenth century.[24] A few Africanists have argued for similar demographic results in the early European colonial contact with African populations, basing their judgment on the regions of the most intensive economic exploitation, such as the lower Congo basin in Leopold's Congo and the gold and diamond mines in southern Africa.[25] The assertion that Africa suffered population depredations on as widespread a scale as Latin America has not, however, been widely accepted. Indeed, in comparing the American and African colonial expe-

riences, perhaps no factor stands out more distinctly than the population destruction of the New World, which paved the way for the repeo-
pling of large parts of North and South America with Western
Europeans and Africans, and the inability of the later European conquerors to accomplish the same outcome in Africa. Try as the Europeans
and their Asian subordinates did during the African colonial era
nowhere did the colonists accomplish the goal of establishing an enduring, European-dominated polity.

Imperial Administration

Having partitioned and occupied Africa, the European colonial powers
set about the task of governing. When the inexpensive and effortless
solution of devolving power to those on the spot or creating chartered
companies along the lines of the defunct East India Company did not
prove viable, the metropolitan authorities undertook a more rational
fashioning of colonial power. They established ministries of colonies,
elaborate recruitment and training procedures for colonial officers, and
a roster of colonial political and technical agents from colonial governors
and district officers to agricultural and educational inspectors.

At first glance these later colonial systems appear altogether removed
from the prebendal Spanish empire in the Americas. But appearances
are once again deceiving. A comparison of the table of administration
and the training of colonial bureaucrats reveals clear similarities. Despite
the fact that the Spanish did not possess specialized colonial schools for
the training of elite colonial administrators comparable to those created
by the British and French they did recruit the frontline colonial administrators from the leading metropolitan universities.[26] In other respects
as well the imperial structures were alike. Spain had its own Ministry of
Colonies (the Council of the Indies), its governorships (the viceroys of
New Spain and Peru), its judicial structures, and even its commissions
of enquiries (*visitas*), empowered to investigate abuses in the system
and to recommend change.[27]

In the final analysis, however, the critical agents in the colonial
bureaucracy were not the Spanish viceroys or the British and French
governors; nor even the British and French provincial commissioners or
the Spanish presidents, *oidores* (judges), and *fiscales* (attorneys). They
were the district officers, the *commandants de cercle*, and the African
headman and chiefs in colonial Africa and their Spanish American
equivalents, the *corregidores* (magistrates) and local *caciques* (political

bosses). These men do, indeed, deserve their appellation as the real rulers of empire.[28] Comparing these local agents of administration proves immensely rewarding. Scholars have cited the levels of venality and education among these local officials as evidence for the palpable difference between the Spanish empire and British and French Africa. To be sure, British and French district officers were men of considerable education who were by and large incorruptible, at least once the colonial systems had been rationalized. In contrast, local Spanish administrators, owing their office to social and political influence in the metropole, undertook their colonial assignment with a view to enriching themselves and even returning to Spain as wealthy persons. Having paid a high fee to obtain their positions, they were compelled to extort wealth from local populations to achieve their goals. Indeed, the only real incentive to assume the office of *corregidor* was "because of widespread power that went with it."[29] Even the eighteenth-century Bourbon reforms, in which intendants sought to tighten control over *corregidores*, did not succeed in expunging corruption and reducing the oppressive nature of the system.

Yet, despite their specialized colonial training and their commitment to an ethos of personal integrity, made possible of course because the African colonial government compensated its officials much more realistically than did the Spanish empire, the British and French did not eradicate corruption at the local administrative level. Quite the contrary, they allowed it to take root, even admitting its necessity for colonial rule.[30]

Beneath the European political officers in imperial Spain as well as colonial Africa indigenous subordinates operated in ways that were similar, usually oppressive, and extremely venal. The Spanish, like their later European counterparts, endeavored to recruit indigenous collaborators of traditional legitimacy and to associate the authority of these traditional rulers with colonial power. Indian *caciques*, like the later African chiefs, often performed heroically in defense of their communities. Yet there can be no gainsaying the fact that in many locales, especially those of the most intensive social and economic change, *corregidores* held the *caciques* accountable for internal security and collection of taxes and swept aside those officials who balked at these demands, even those with long-standing traditional legitimacy. At the local level the Spanish created an environment where "massive corruptions prevailed."[31]

In colonial Africa the results and methods were the same. The colonial governments of Africa, pressed for funds and forced to operate at the district level on minimal resources, could not help but regard colonial chiefs as a primary extension of colonial authority. Chiefs and headmen carried out a myriad of formal administrative tasks and were also fully involved in numerous duties that lay outside their formal table of duties but were essential to the success of the colonial system. African chiefs and headmen, like Spanish *caciques*, were the day-to-day executors of colonial *dicta* (dictates). They facilitated the spread of the new colonial currencies, wage labor, missionary education, and European consumer goods. As the advance guard of colonial capitalism, they encountered opposition and employed force to overcome it.

To be successful in achieving these goals African chiefs and headmen were compelled to create, at their own expense, a cadre of supporters—a subadministration, so to speak—that existed outside the formal colonial apparatus yet was recognized by all knowledgeable observers as essential to the colonial mission. To maintain this shadow administrative corps, a coercive arm was composed of young strongmen willing to do the bidding of the chiefs and to coerce reluctant local populations into unwanted colonial obligations. In this fashion the chiefs extracted resources from the local populations as ruthlessly as the *caciques* in Spanish America had, spreading this bounty to themselves, their followers, and their family members. Local administration in colonial Africa, notwithstanding its protestations of good government and incorruptibility, was venal and operated like Spanish American administration at the grassroots level. Nor were its oppressive and violent foundations unknown to its colonial overlords.[32] Just as the oppressive nature of Spanish rule undermined the legitimacy of local Indian officials so in colonial Africa, even in areas drenched in the administrative ethos of indirect rule, local chiefs and headmen ultimately were seen for what they truly were—agents of European rule.

Imperial Economics

Much of the work on colonial Latin American economic issues has reflected the powerful imprint of dependency analysis in this field. Dependency advocates have stressed the incorporation of Latin America into a European-dominated economy as exporters of raw materials and importers of manufactures—a mode of incorporation that destined these countries, in their opinion, to political subordination and economic vulnerability. Although this dependency perspective found an immediate echo in African historical literature, by and large Africanists have doubted its applicability to Africa. Even sympathetic studies have offered correctives to the original dependency perspectives, as has also occurred in Latin American social science. The revisionists, from Latin America as well as Africa, have argued that dependency, as originally formulated, underrated local innovation and was insufficiently attentive to the economic gains that took place in colonial and neocolonial environments.

Research into the economic effects of colonialism, whether undertaken from a dependency or a modernization perspective, is nonetheless a field of obvious comparative value in which, unfortunately, to date few rigorous studies exist. Of the research areas likely to produce useful comparative findings, the recruitment and retention of labor in labor-needing colonial areas come readily to mind. In the mining zones of Mexico and Peru as well as those in southern Africa, European colonial capitalists and administrators confronted similar problems of procuring massive labor supplies.[33] In each region the locally available labor resources were grossly inadequate. Zacatecas and Potosí in Spanish America were distant from populated areas, as was Katanga province in the Belgian Congo. Additionally, the labor needs in all of these regions were felt immediately and precluded a gradual buildup of populations in these locales.

The mines of Zacatecas in northern Mexico and Potosí in Peru came into operation in the 1530s. By the beginning of the seventeenth century the imperial mining city of Potosí had already grown to the size of 60,000 residents, including some 19,000 Indian mine workers.[34] Similarly, the diamond mines at Kimberley had a massive work force while the gold mines of the Rand, where a labor force already numbered 200,000 at the turn of the twentieth century, placed the whole of southern Africa under acute labor-procuring pressures.[35] The labor recruitment techniques employed in labor-supplying areas were remarkably alike in spite of prohibitions on using unfree labor in the later empires. In both eras the state supported labor recruitment, conducting population censuses with a view to identifying the labor potential of neighboring areas and tolerating, if not encouraging, highly coercive labor-recruiting systems.[36] In Spanish America mine workers were mainly free-born Amerindians. Recruited through modified pre-Columbian corvée labor devices like the *mita* in Peru and the *repartimiento* in Mexico, these systems adapted Incan and Aztec compulsory labor forms. To date scholars have not investigated in detail the mechanisms of recruitment and their impact on local Amerindian populations in a way that would permit rigorous comparisons with the more minutely researched mining economies of colonial Africa and their labor-supplying hinterlands.[37]

The studies of mining in southern Africa have demonstrated that the levels of coercion employed by private recruiting agencies in procuring labor supplies in the early decades of mining were little short of slavery and that African mine workers suffered as grievously as their Amerindian counterparts from the same combination of arduous journeys to the work destinations and debilitating and dangerous work routines. Using the mining compound first introduced in the diamond mines at Kimberley to keep labor forces under control and to compel laborers to honor their contracts, mine owners all across southern Africa were able to hyper-exploit unskilled African laborers.[38] For the Peruvian and Mexican mining experiences we have much less data. Yet the apparently similar mechanisms of procuring, retaining, and exploiting workers as well as the high levels of mortality and morbidity of workers provide rich arenas for comparative analysis. From the perspective of workers, the fact that the colonial state in Latin America was the primary agent of labor procurement while the African colonial state permitted private labor supplying agencies to undertake this unpleasant task seems inconsequential.

The impact of these pressures on the traditional values and institutions of labor-supplying areas has been one of the most fully researched areas in African historiography and ethnography. Early ethnographic studies argued for the resilience of these communities, highlighting the numerous techniques developed to integrate stints in the mines within the framework of traditional communal life. In labor-supplying locales of Mozambique it was common for young men to work in the gold mines on the Rand prior to marrying and settling down. Work outside the community was ritualized as a rite of passage and became integrated into the family system by means of bride payments based on monies made in the wage-earning economy. Similar kinds of studies on colonial Latin American villages in labor supplying areas warrant research.[39]

Culture of Colonialism

The culture of colonialism, including such topics as education, urbanization, art and architecture, the role of women, and law and society is a voluminous field and almost without exception noncomparative. Problems even venturing comparisons arise, in the first instance, because so much of the work on education, art, architecture, and the like in colonial Latin America focuses on the immigrant European population. In contrast, most of the African scholarship deals with indigenous communities. Still there are many areas where comparative work is likely to yield significant results, the most apparent at this time being comparative religious change. Already scholars of religious change and religious resistance in Latin America and Africa are finding common ground both in the Christianization of the two continents and the use of traditional religious beliefs and syncretistic Christianity to resist externally imposed belief systems. In studying conversion and religious resistance the boundaries between African and Latin American studies have been crumbling.

The original works on the Christianization of the two continents depicted religious conversions in optimistic hues, a progressive force, bringing increased literacy, liberation from the bondage of premodern religious beliefs, and in the African case, increased literacy and awareness of Western learning. Based as they were on the archives of missionary organizations and unaware of or unable to gain access to indigenous sources, these authorities extolled the heroism of missionary efforts and underlined the obstacles to success that missionaries and their first converts had to overcome.[40] In African studies, however, even before some of these early mission-centered studies had appeared, occasional and lonely voices presented a more Afrocentric perspective. They stressed the African contributions to religious change and identified the creativity of African spiritual leaders, steeped in their own religious traditions, in blending elements of their traditional spiritual life with missionary-preached Christianity.[41]

Not long after the publication of the first studies of the spread of Christianity in Africa, Robin Horton offered a broader, more philosophical, and African-centered explanation for the spread of Christianity (and Islam as well) in the nineteenth and twentieth centuries. He attributed the appeal of world religions in Africa to the rapidity of social and economic change, population movements into cities and over long distances, and the unsatisfying nature of traditional religious beliefs and explanations that stressed local gods and were embedded in the life of small-scale societies. In his view Christianity and Islam were a good fit with traditional African cosmologies. As Africans became involved in activities of a wide geographical frame, they were prepared to embrace the notion of a high god, which had always been part of their traditional beliefs, lying behind the pantheon of small-scale gods that had dominated the religious perspectives of these local communities.[42]

Similar religious reappraisals are under way in Latin American studies where the work of Horton has been influential. Scholars have concluded that indigenous religious traditions did not disappear with the spread of Christianity but were incorporated in ways that merged traditional beliefs and practices.[43] Whether one sees these changes as a form of religious resistance or as the way in which these communities accommodated themselves to political and cultural conquest the new emphasis places local populations and local religious leaders at the center of the story and attaches much less importance to missionary exertions. This revisionist work has required searching for new sources, similar to oral accounts on the African side, and reading the traditional sources, like the missionary records, notably the notorious extirpation trials in colonial America, from a different and more sympathetic perspective.[44]

There is a final area of scholarship on religious change and religious resistance that appears to have considerable potential for the comparativist: literary criticism and deconstruction. Recent works emphasize the many misunderstandings that occurred along the dialogic frontier between Europe and the peoples of the Americas and Africa. They stress the incapacity of one community, having its own cultural assumptions and operating in a different economic and technological milieu, to communicate complicated religious messages to another group.[45] Some of the best work in the field has been done by Latin Americanists; the inspiration from these studies has flowed into Africanist work where, for instance, the Comaroffs have explored the frontier of symbols between European missionaries and the southern Tswana people in the early nineteenth century.[46]

Nationalist Protest

Much African historiography arose in conjunction with the struggle against colonialism; Latin American historiography took shape against a broader intellectual canvas of state building and economic development. Not surprisingly, the two bodies of work have had widely divergent perspectives on the nationalist struggles of indigenous peoples. Yet in recent years these different streams of thought appear to be converging and are ready to profit from the findings in the other's work.

Reflecting their earlier intellectual preoccupations, the two fields have approached resistance movements of indigenous peoples from opposite polls. Africanists have stressed the continuity and high levels of anticolonial resistance; the Latin Americanists have emphasized political quiescence. But as the two areas of scholarship have come more fully into dialogue they are finding common ground.

Scholars of African resistance movements, working in one of the richest fields of historical research, have identified overt and violent acts of resistance at all phases of the colonial experience. Indeed, some African historians argue for an unbroken chain of connection between the earliest acts of resistance, often misleadingly referred to as primary resistance, to the later anticolonial nationalist parties of the decolonization era.[47] Even in the intervening decades, when the movements of violent confrontation between African peoples and the colonial authorities were less frequent, some scholars have argued that the so-called age of improvement was a period when Africans self-consciously mastered the techniques of European strength so as to be able to repel their colonial masters.[48]

In contrast, the first two centuries of Spanish and Portuguese rule in the Americas offer many fewer movements of heroic resistance on the order of the Maji-Maji rebellion in German East Africa, the uprising in southern Rhodesia, the Satiru revolt in northern Nigeria, and the Aba women's protest movement in southeastern Nigeria. Explanations for this relative political calm are readily at hand, most notably the population catastrophe and the severity of Iberian colonial policies in the Americas. Yet recent historical work has dramatically narrowed the gap between African resistance and Latin American anticolonial protest. To begin with, early Incan resistance is now viewed for what it was—prolonged and bloody. The Incan opposition to the Spanish was not crushed until Viceroy Toledo executed Titu Cusi's successor, Tupac Amaru, in 1572.[49] A resistance effort that stretched across four decades would appear unnaturally drawn out in the telescoped context of African colonial history. Moreover, Indian confrontations with the imperial state in Peru occurred periodically—first in 1666–67—and culminated in the Tupac Amaru rebellion of the 1780s. John Rowe's comment that "the record of Inca activity in the colonial period is thus one of repeated protest against Spanish rule and the conditions associated with it" highlights the continuity of this opposition and underscores the parallels with African resistance.[50]

The understanding of African resistance has also changed in recent times in part because of disappointments about Africa's postcolonial record, and this understanding has made African protest seem more similar to the Latin American experience. It no longer seems feasible to view the evolution of anticolonial protest in Africa as an unbroken chain of nationalist assertions, culminating in political independence. For the Africanists, a Latin American historiography that demonstrates the intermingling of overt acts of resistance with periods of silence and political quiescence now has more relevance. Such a perspective opens up a more complex analysis of resistance and collaboration. In particular, Steve Stern's work on Peruvian resistance should have saliency for

Africanists. It stresses the multiple time frames of protest and invokes a historical memory drawing on "legacies from distant colonial times."[51] Employed in an Africanist setting, this perspective would undercut the naive notion of a straight-line evolution of anticolonial opposition from the earliest protests to political independence. Africanists can also profit from observing the rhythms of overt opposition to colonial authority and their giving way to periods of creative collaboration.

Although much of the luster has vanished from Africanists views of anticolonialism, certainly the groundswell of enthusiasm for African nationalism that existed in the 1950s and 1960s intensified Latin Americanist efforts to recover Amerindian perspectives from the time of conquest. The publication of *Broken Spears* in a Spanish edition in 1959 and an English translation in 1962 is the best known of these restorations. But the Peruvian intellectual, Guaman Poma, has also been presented as a culminating figure in a line of Native American commentators on their lost civilization and the violence of the Spanish intrusion.[52] Poma's writings and the symbolism of his complex woodcuts revealed a pre-Columbian world order of coherence and integrity torn asunder by the coming of the Europeans.[53]

Neocolonialism

Much of the work on colonial Latin America insists on the persistence of a colonial and dependent world in Latin America, all the way into the twentieth century. Racism and racial hierarchies, economic dependence on cash crops, the dominance of overseas capital, retarded manufacturing, extreme vulnerabilities to the vagaries of the world economy, and gaping income disparities took root in colonial Latin America and were far from being eradicated even after nearly two centuries of formal political independence. This dependency model, always intriguing to Africanist scholars, became more tempting as the early promise of African political independence in the 1960s gave way to the disillusionment of the 1980s and 1990s. Should one seek, these observers asked themselves, explanations for Africa's political instability, failed economic programs, famines, and falling income levels in the colonial heritage as many scholars have done for Latin America? Is Africa, then, destined to recapitulate the postcolonial experience of Latin America, failing to realize the goals articulated at independence?

A first wave of African pessimists—Samir Amin questioning the economic miracle in the Ivory Coast and Colin Leys pointing out the palpable problems of economic growth in Kenya—openly credited Latin America dependency studies for their insights into Africa's postcolonial condition. Challenging the conventional scholarly wisdom of the 1970s concerning Kenya's postcolonial economic success, Leys predicted that Kenya's aggrandizing bureaucratic and *comprador* business classes would be incapable of launching sustained economic development. In a similar vein, Amin predicted that the Ivory Coast would fail to lift itself from poverty through the export of cocoa just as the Gold Coast and Nigeria had. In his view the Ivorian economy was no different from the export economies of Ghana and Nigeria of the colonial era except that its cocoa development had occurred later in the twentieth century. Amin contended that once the cultivation of cocoa had reached its outermost geographical limits in the Ivory Coast as it had in Ghana and Nigeria that country, too, would experience economic stagnation. In the same way, scholars, critical of the influence of multinationals on African development goals, argued that foreign-based firms exercised inordinate influence over African governments and devised sophisticated mechanisms for transferring profits from their enterprises in the periphery to the metropole.

In spite of the obvious potential for comparative analysis in these *longue dur'ee* approaches, there may be more value in comparing the immediate events and political chronology of postcolonial Africa and Latin America. If one examines the first forty years of independence in Africa and Latin America, with a view to understanding the common problems and common solutions to the postcolonial condition, the similarities of events and underlying forces are striking. To begin with, the political boundaries of the independent Latin American and African states were those established in the imperial age. In Spanish America these boundaries had evolved over a long period of time and were more attuned to political and economic realities than the boundaries of Africa were at independence. But in both situations the postcolonial regimes were heirs (or captives, as the case may be) to their colonial legacies.[54]

Second, the drive for independence on both continents owed more to seismic changes in the world political system, initiated outside Latin America and Africa, than internal impulses. In 1808 the French invasion of Spain triggered political revolts in Spain and throughout the empire. Just as the Spanish at home refused to accept French authority and join Napoleon's continental system against the British, so the *peninsulares* and Creoles abroad dissented. In the Americas Creole patriotic sentiments prevailed so that by the 1820s, as Metternich was erecting his European concert, all of the Spanish territories in the New World, with the exception of Cuba and Puerto Rico, had seceded from Spain and were in the process of claiming their independence.[55]

In much the same fashion, African independence succeeded because of shifts in world power that witnessed the rise of the United States and the Soviet Union and the spread of decolonizing sentiments from Asia into the Middle East and Africa.[56] In the 1960s scholars found it fashionable to compare Asian and African independence movements with that first anticolonialist revolt—the American War of Independence.[57] In truth, the obvious comparison for the African continent was Spanish America. The deep ethnic and social divisions of Africa, the export-oriented nature of the economies, and the absence of powerful business communities make Latin America the more relevant analog for Africa.

A third similarity entails the political instability and strongman government that regimes on both continents experienced after independence. The political instability of the Latin American states stemmed directly from the struggle waged there for self-rule from Spain. Spanish American independence took two decades to achieve at a considerable expense in wrenching and destabilizing military conflict. Parts of Latin America knew no respite from war for up to two decades. In the Mexican struggles for independence 600,000 people, or one-tenth of the total population, may have perished.[58]

In contrast, most of Africa, except for territories of European settlement, achieved independence swiftly, constitutionally, and without bloodshed. Ghana's independence in 1957 set off a chain reaction that engulfed nearly all of Anglophone and Francophone Africa in the next half decade. A second round of more violent decolonizations took place in the southern part of the continent in the 1970s. Yet Africa's more orderly pathway to independence did not secure stable postcolonial regimes. African postcolonial polities failed to evolve organically from the African past, and the new polities were overwhelmed with ethnic jealousies, which owed much of their emotional charge to colonial divide-and-rule policies. Once the steel grid of European colonial administrations had disappeared, coups d'etat, bloody civil strife, and ethnic, religious, and regional enmities tore the artificial states into shreds. Nor did the belated efforts of the colonial regimes and African nationalist leaders to endow these states with constitutions and parliamentary government stand up well against the aggrandizing impulses of early charismatic political leaders and military plotters. The Latin

American *caudillos,* so well exemplified by Rosas in Argentina, had their counterparts in Africa's military dictators. The prebendary polities of contemporary Africa underscore the fertile ground for examining the immediate aftermath of decolonization on these two continents.[59]

four

Financing Empire:
The European Diaspora of Silver by War

Barbara Hadley Stein and Stanley J. Stein

La révolution de l'argent a été presque générale... ; n'est-ce pas cette unité du monde que l'argent américain a ainsi créee par son universelle présence, fruit d'une universelle convoitise?
> –Frank G. Spooner, *Economie mondiale et les frappes moné-taires en France* (26).

En este negocio [la plata americana] va la seguridad y firmeza de mi Monarquia.
> –Philip IV, quoted in Domínguez Ortíz, "Los caudales de Indias y la política exterior de Felipe IV," *Anuario de estudios americanos*, xiii (1956) (319 n. 16).

The Spanish credit system... depended absolutely on specie and principally on the treasure of the Indies landed at Seville for the king.
> –Geoffrey Parker, *The Army of Flanders* (152–153).

1

Tracking the diffusion of Peruvian and Mexican silver under the Spanish Hapsburgs involves pursuing strands of the fabric now perceived as the nascent Atlantic economy. The task is complicated, often elusive, and difficult to quantify. As Felipe Ruíz Martín once wrote: "How can we calculate the funds carried by couriers . . . (despite periods of restricted licensing) . . . often lost in the Pyrenees, the Alps and the Apennines to lurking bandits? Merchant-shippers and crews were also involved in similar activities . . . And even more important in such fraudulent activity was payment in certain highly desirable goods."[1]

The patterns of silver mining in colonial Mexico and Peru as well as the complementary structures of the "managed" Atlantic trade forged by Spanish colonialism are now generally understood. Some of the conduits of silver into Europe are well known: the open and covert ways by which importers in lower Andalusia covered chronic trade deficits with their European suppliers of manufactures, the exchange of silver for goods smuggled from foreign Caribbean ports, and the surreptitious transfers ship to ship off the Azores, the Canaries, and Cádiz. What remains to be assessed is silver's diaspora by warfare on the European continent in the sixteenth and seventeenth centuries as a result of Castile's commitment to Hapsburg dynastic expansionism, championship of the Counter Reformation, and its opposition to emergent states pursuing economic and political policies conflictive with those of the Holy Roman Empire. In a general sense, the development of North Atlantic Europe was a response to the stimuli of war as well as trade. In tracing the impact of American silver on Castile's relations with Europe, we may begin to understand the creative but "chaotic fluctuations" that invariably followed the irregular arrivals of silver fleets at Europe's commercial and financial centers at Sevilla, Medina del Campo, Villalon, Florence, and Genoa, Besancon, Lyon, Augsburg, Paris, Antwerp, and London.[2] Here our focus is on some internal and external ramifications of Castile's initial ad hoc financial practices that later became policy. By 1539 analysts in Castile's bureaucracy could see that "there are many unknown debts . . . which every day leads to more, and which make no sense in the books."[3] Clearly Castile's new international projection now required creating a "serviceable, long-term debt at low rates of interest."[4]

Pursuit of silver for financing war was the leitmotif of Castile's Treasury operations under the five Hapsburg reigns in Spain between 1517 and 1700. For continuing warfare was the outcome of the late medieval vision of Charles V ("caballero andante perdido en el mundo moderno" [wandering gentleman lost in the modern world]) of a universal Catholic empire centered on Europe, a vision received from his grandfather Maximilian, architect of a revitalized Holy Roman Empire dominated by Austria, and emperor from 1494 to 1519.[5] The basic incompatibility of that vision with the aspirations for sovereignty of the emergent states in France under the Valois, in England under the Tudors, and briefly in the Spain of Ferdinand and Isabel provided the underlying rationale of European conflict in the sixteenth and seventeenth centuries.

Once initial protonationalist opposition to the accession of Charles of Hapsburg was overcome by suppression of Castile's *Comunero* Rebellion in 1521 and, above all, once Peruvian and Mexican silver appeared in volume at midcentury, Spanish officials had to license large-scale export of precious metals to meet the needs of Charles's military enterprises as well as to advertise Castile's capacity to handle the growing problem of debt liquidation (*fomentando la liquidez*) when silver flows were interrupted or when demand exceeded supply.[6] Opening these floodgates enabled Spain to subsidize its European networks of Hapsburg power over the following seven decades in Italy, North Africa, Flanders, Germany, Austria, Portugal, Hungary, and the Balkans by attracting investment in the Spanish public debt by "magnates of public finances, members . . . of the *grand capitalisme*, and isolated members . . . of the *petit capitalisme.* . . ."[7] At the same time investment in fixed-interest, short- and long-term government bonds (*juros*, offering the attractive rate of 5 to 7 percent interest) by Spain's aristocrats, bureaucrats, merchants, provincial gentry, and enriched peasants as well as by convents, monasteries, cathedral chapters and hospitals furnished continuing sources of relatively secure income.[8] They added to the justifications of religion, political power, and national prestige and united supporters of Hapsburg policies in Spain and abroad. Silver built consent if not always consensus.

Never before had western Europe enjoyed the buoyant sense of access to such unparalleled financial resources promising liquidity for both private and public enterprise.[9] In 1598 perhaps as much as 4.6 million *ducados* annually were being paid to *juro*-holders from a budget of 9.7 million; in the seventeenth century the Treasury of Philip IV managed to expand the public debt to twelve times Castile's annual revenues.[10] Unloaded from incoming convoys from New Spain and South America, silver came to be perceived as a harvested exportable comparable, for example, to the wool exchanged for Flemish textiles. The perception of silver as crop, or *fruto*, combined with the Hapsburg conception of a dynastic patrimonial empire linking Central Europe, Germany, Burgundy, the Netherlands, and Spain in a kind of international division of labor transformed Castile into the financial core of the Catholic order in Europe. In this context, warfare on multiple fronts from the Mediterranean to the Baltic, from the Atlantic to Central Europe further rationalized Castile's long-term borrowing based on American silver. In Hapsburg cosmography the role of Spain and its colonial world in underwriting Hapsburg dynasticism and papal hegemony in Europe had little to do with the atrophy of Spanish development relative to that of northwestern Europe. If sacrifice there were, it was God-ordained.

2

Fiscal policy emerging under Charles V shaped the general patterns of Castilian state finance until the end of the seventeenth century. The financial needs of the Castilian protostate of the late fifteenth century had been controllable, matching an economy of erratic agricultural output, extensive sheep farming, and a low level of manufacture.[11] Raw wool exports to Flanders's workshops constituted the principal source of export earnings and imported goods: merchant intermediaries financing wool exports then constituted the majority of lenders to this state. They were what Ruíz Martín has called petty capitalist intermediaries, *regatones* and *colporteurs*.[12] Collapse of the *Comunero* Rebellion coupled to heavy outlays on Spain's campaigns against French competitors in Italy introduced what became the characteristically ad hoc, disorganized borrowing practices and the pile-up of the Castilian public debt.

With the influx of precious metals from conquest and occupation of Hispaniola, Mexico and Peru and the initial output of silver mines in central Mexico and then upper Peru, the borrowing capacity of Castile's treasury expanded. Charles's treasury officials could now bypass the limited capital resources of Spanish merchant bankers (*cambiadores publicos*) to tap those of German groups like the Welsers and Fuggers (the latter's fortune came from silver mining in central Germany), of the Flemish Schetz bankers and later those in north Italy, the Spinola, Affaitadi, and the Grillo.[13] These "cosmopolitan" bankers in turn were displaced between 1538 and 1557 mainly by Genoese who would maintain their role in Spanish Hapsburg finance until at least the third decade of the next century.[14] Unlike Castile's merchant bankers, foreigners enjoyed access to large pools of capital, understood the credit techniques of the time, could anticipate state borrowing needs, and—this was critical—could cope with a discernible, predictable pattern of assured (if often postponed) amortization.[15]

Confidence in lending to the Castilian government was grounded on faith in sustained inflows of silver on public (royal or crown) and private account, although one should not minimize revenue from Castile's domestic taxation. Prior to Charles's accession, a placer gold boom in Hispaniola ended around 1512; what brightened Spain's financial outlook for domestic and foreign merchant capitalists was the sustained returns of colonial conquests—silver mines in Peru and New Spain.[16] Between 1526 and 1555 inflows of colonial precious metals according to official registry at Sevilla jumped by a factor of 6, from 3.2 million *ducados* per decade to 18.4 million; in one short period 1536–45 to 1546–55, annual average imports climbed almost 73 percent.[17]

American mining, however, was only one of Castile's main revenue sources. In the 1540s annual borrowing of about 1 million *ducados* was also secured on grants from the Cortes and by general taxes in which rising customs receipts from colonial trade (*almojarifazgo de Indias*) figured prominently. About this time (1532–41), too, the Vatican assigned part of its Spanish income from its *subsidio* and sales of *bulas de cruzada* (papel seal of the crusades) to the Castilian Treasury.[18] With the failure to broaden the tax base to include privileged groups enjoying exemptions, the tax burden rested on a multiplicity of excise taxes paid by the mass of consumers.[19] By 1539 Treasury officials managed to liquidate most of the public debt via domestic revenues supplemented at critical junctures by initial expropriations (*secuestros*) of precious metals arriving from America on private account. In the early 1550s the pattern began to change when the Treasury scrambled for funds to finance Charles's ill-fated siege of Metz. If to this moment Castilian revenues had covered largely the "very high expenditures of imperial policy," it was now discernible that the "open loans of (foreign) bankers" were attracted by returns from the overseas colonies and would continue.[20]

The Treasury handled incoming colonial metals shipments through two mechanisms. It received the surplus of colonial treasuries (*cajas reales*) at Sevilla's Casa de Contratación. In addition, when Charles desperately needed cash, Sevilla's authorities were authorized to seize (*secuestrar*) privately owned incoming precious metals, offering in compensation interest-bearing government bonds, or *juros*, of varying maturities. A *secuestro* is reported in 1523, another financed Charles's amphibious assault on Tunis (1535) when Contratación sequestered 800,000 *ducados*, offering in return *privilegios de juros* at 3 percent annual interest (far below an open market rate of 14 percent or higher). Other forms of security consisted of *consignaciones*, or claims (*situados*), on specific revenues such as ordinary excise taxes, crusade bulls, and offices in the military orders.[21] A *secuestro* was ordered in 1551 when Charles directed agents at Milan to procure loans backed by expected precious metals receipts from America, a moment when his Treasury officials complained that "there is nothing left of all the revenues of these dominions."[22] At Sevilla, Treasury officers proceeded to commandeer all silver available including 600,000 *ducados* belonging to passengers returning from the colonies. This coincided with Augsburg bankers agreeing to further loans to Castile providing that repayment were made from what "La

Gasca brought" from Peru. By then Spain's principal creditors were Europe's great international financiers, German and Genoese.[23]

Embryonic Castilian state finance utilized another instrument to capture funds for an expansive European policy, the sale of *juros*. Like prior short-term borrowing from the peninsular merchant capitalists, *juros* were becoming a common financial technique in the 1480s. By then Isabel and Ferdinand had lowered their inherited *juro* debt by perhaps half. While subsequently they had to augment the volume of *juro* obligations, such obligations were to explode under their grandson, Charles V.[24]

Juros represented a certificate of the *privilegio* (privilege) of participation in a royal debt obligation stipulating "occasional payment of annual interest based on the return of royal revenues."[25] They were issued in various denominations according to term and source of payment, *al quitar* (until withdrawal), *de resguardo* (guaranteed), *por vida* (for life), *por herencia* (in trust), and *perpétuo* (perpetual). *Juro*-holders knew the specific revenue source of interest and ultimate redemption. Although payments were drawn from a variety of such revenues, over time, however, colonial income became the preferred source.[26] *Juros* became a fiscal expedient "propelled by the returns from the New World fount" which drew *juro* investors from the fair towns of Villalon and Medina del Campo to Sevilla's Casa de Contratación.[27]

Diffusion of *juros* developed in two phases. Until the late 1550s Castile applied *juro* income mainly to domestic purposes, limiting sales of *juros al quitar* to Castilians. But once the scale of Spanish Hapsburg entrapment in Germany and Flanders ballooned and foreign policy dictated Castile's fiscal and financial policies, another ad hoc pattern of response developed. In this second phase, the Treasury turned to corporate bodies holding pools of investible funds, to monasteries and convents, cathedral chapters, hospitals and chaplaincies (*capellanías*). The investment pool was extended from a few merchant banking houses like the Schetz (Antwerp) and Fuggers and Welsers (Augsburg) to draw upon the larger pool of Genoese capital. Genoese merchants proceeded to market their *juros* in Spain and elsewhere, encouraged by the Castilian government's readiness after 1566 to issue export licenses (*licencias de saca*) covering precious metals exports.[28] By then the assurance of colonial silver backing for *juros* which were "flooding the money market" had made them the "most coveted form of repayment."[29] This instrument of liquidity made it possible for the Spanish Hapsburgs to bypass the Cortes of Castile by the early 1550s; in five years, 1551–55, more than one-quarter of all colonial receipts over a fifty-year period (1503–60) was unloaded at Sevilla.[30]

The rising trend of silver shipments notwithstanding, the economic situation inherited by Charles's son Philip II has been painted as "realms wracked by poverty . . . and on the brink of financial collapse."[31] Already Castile's treasury officials were—and remained—masters of fiscal brinkmanship. The conjuncture of an accumulated public debt of 25 million *ducados* in 1559 (equivalent to sixteen times estimated annual revenues)[32] but offset by colonial silver imports inspired Treasury officials to attempt to convert a regulatory agency of colonial trade, the Casa de Contratación at Sevilla, into a sort of early state bank. Under this plan, Contratación was assigned working capital for investment in colonial trade in expectation that its earnings might help amortize the public debt over a ten-year period. So-called *juros de la Casa de Contratación* would compensate owners of silver subject to *secuestros* in the 1550s. This exercise in state enterprise lasted only fifteen years (1560–75), collapsing partly by bureaucratic incompetence, partly (one suspects) by the covert opposition of Sevilla's commercial corps, and partly because Treasury officials had to appropriate Contratación funds to finance the forces suppressing insurrection in Flanders (1576–84).[33]

One facet merits emphasis. Like his father, Philip II made a cardinal point of fiscal policy the payment of interest (if not always capital) on Castile's public debt despite repeated bankruptcies, unlike the French practice of debt repudiation.[34] Philip could afford to honor at least the backlog of interest due because the overseas mining colonies from which he always "awaited new returns" were a major financial prop. In 1557, for example, 70 percent of military operations against France werefinanced by American silver receipts; the next year, 85 percent of total state borrowing was guaranteed by the same source; and in 1559 Philip, like his father, fell back upon the "disreputable policy of taking bullion from New World fleets," commandeering all private sector incoming silver at Sevilla.[35] Here was tacit recognition that state income could be augmented only minimally by what was becoming standard practice—sale of "vassals, jurisdictions, titles" and most public offices, alienation of state revenues "mortgaged to secure immediate cash loans and by *juro* commitments on a scale hitherto unknown." These practices were the genesis of structures later making it impossible for the Castilian state "to persist with real measures of centralization."[36]

To be more precise: the trajectory of Castile's financial policy over the century after 1550 is foretold by indicators appearing between 1553–59. As servicing the public debt rose from 17 to 44 percent of Castile's annual revenues, colonial income (including sequestrations) as the share of such income moved from 22 to 32 percent. To finance Philip's initial field operations in 1557 and 1558, the Treasury had to seize 2.7 million *ducados* of an incoming flota; for the next campaign, another *secuestro* netted 1.4 million.[37] There is no exaggeration in asserting that American silver, especially in the form of *juros de la Casa de Contratación*, in the 1590s represented "enormous fiscal reinforcements."[38]

Second, while the volume of *juro* obligations nearly doubled, the share of the most negotiable and hence desirable type (*juro al quitar*) was 75 percent. Here was a positive correlation between public debt, rising *juros al quitar*, and the role of colonial funds in Castile's revenues.[39] So Sevilla became the main office for handling *juros*, whose volume achieved a "scale hitherto unknown" reflecting the "appetite for *juros* as the preferred investment." At the century's end, *juros*—now the foundation of Castile's long-term debt—allowed Spain's "privileged classes" to live off this income while Castile's Treasury alienated to the private sector oversight of fiscal operations which "its own ministers had proved unable to handle."[40]

3

In the half century (1598–1648) following the reign of Philip II came repeated financial crises as the domestic and colonial resources of Castile were absorbed in what Spain's political class envisioned as a winnable war when conflict with the Dutch Republic was renewed in 1621. This coincided with what became after 1631 a downward inflexion in the already unreliable official registry of incoming silver at Sevilla.[41] War with France commencing in 1635—"a decisive year"— worsened the financial situation. Five years later came what Pierre Chaunu has called "the great crisis . . . which dragged the grandeur of the Spanish Empire into its whirlwind" in the form of uprisings in Portugal and Catalonia. Henceforth the demise of Spain as the European hegemon would become clear along with its reliance upon colonial silver. Silver continued to settle perennial trade deficits with Spain's suppliers in northwestern Europe and, in particular, expenditures on military forces—wages, arms, food, and transport. A "monetary hemorrhage" flowed from Spain into its European diaspora as "the mail of Italy, Germany and Flanders demanded . . . deliveries of what was by then the nerve of war," and it was obvious that New World silver constituted the "security and buttress" of the Spanish Hapsburg *monarquía*, a bulwark of the public debt including *juro*-based debt held by financiers (*hombres de negocio*), by Spanish noblemen, merchants, bureaucrats, clergymen, and wealthy peasants.[42]

While American silver on royal account was perhaps between 10 and 20 percent of Philip IV's revenues, its significance was multiple. It provided desperately needed liquidity—*juro* issues alienated Treasury revenues—and satisfied financiers who avoided debased copper coinage.[43] When fleets arrived intact, Madrid would decree holidays in the largest cities; when one was delayed, the premium on silver soared, domestic trade slowed, and "help for armies and allies abroad became impossible." Hence "the impatience with which everyone, monarchy and subjects, hurled onto that river of silver."[44] The financial roller coaster of the Thirty Years' War was not due, we are assured, to neglect of Treasury problems by Philip IV who is reported to have developed a "perfect knowledge of that complicated accounting." As he confessed at one point, "there is nothing I lament more than having to depend on silver," preferring "that I am afforded a way to excuse it in the state in which we are found." Options included appeals to officials, clergy, and businessmen in the colonies for gifts or loans which frequently ended in renewed sequestrations of silver consigned to Sevilla merchants—*secuestros* compensated by at least 5 million *ducados* of *juros* issued between 1621 and 1640.[45]

Broadly speaking, the appetite for silver was a measure of preoccupation with defending Hapsburg hegemony in Europe and Castilian dominions in America in the course of what has been likened to the first world war.[46] It was an instance of financial policy dominated by external over domestic considerations. This long-term factor was paralleled by the usual current account deficits with European suppliers of basic imports consumed in the peninsula and (mostly) reexported to America, e.g., textiles, writing and printing papers, hardware, glass, and even hawkers' goods. In the late 1640s the deficit was exacerbated by the continued fall in wool exports, while profit margins on other traditional Spanish exports,—oils, wines, and dried fruits—dwindled.[47] Further pressure derived from Madrid's policy of putting into circulation debased copper coinage; understandably foreign creditors insisted on repayment in silver and as a result Treasury officials often fell back on the excuse for avoiding payouts, "there was no more available money from the galleons which brought it."[48]

With an understandable but also perverse logic, Madrid's fiscal policy concentrated on augmenting the flow of Peruvian and Mexican silver into the peninsula through the port of Sevilla.[49] One element of the strategy was repeated appeals for monetary gifts and loans circulated throughout the two American viceroyalties. Response came from high colonial officeholders, the wealthy merchant communities of Mexico City and Lima, large estate owners, and from well-endowed religious corporations—so much so that by 1647 the Consejo de Indias referred without hyperbole to the "muy continuos donativos que se ha pedido en las Indias."[50] In 1628 the Council of Castile took a different tack, linking expansion of colonial trade, merchants' profits, and the silver needs of the Treasury. Colonial trade held the highest priority for, were it to decline, "it would sever the threads of benefits," reducing the already small number of financiers willing to loan to the government. From this analysis flowed a recommendation which could break Sevilla's century-old colonial trade monopoly: extend the privilege of colonial trade to other Andalusian ports, "open commerce" to Cádiz, Gibraltar, and Malaga, otherwise Spain's European suppliers would surely expand their smuggling activities in order to satisfy colonial demand. This radical proposal went no further because Sevilla's oligopolists opposed it.[51]

Equally unproductive were renewed efforts to persuade Sevilla's merchants to lend to the government. When the Treasury queried why its merchants were reluctant to lend, the Sevilla merchant guild protested that Spanish merchants did not own incoming silver; they were intermediaries, merely *consignatarios* and *encomenderos*.[52] Hoping to tax the real rather than the officially registered value of the "silver waves . . . which cause such damage," Treasury officials in 1630 properly questioned the accuracy of silver imports registered at Sevilla and insisted on copies of silver registers sent from Lima to Portobelo for transshipment to Sevilla. The Council of the Indies confessed that its investigating officials proved incompetent, even flag officers of transatlantic flotas collaborated in silver smuggling, and concluded that "the issue is so ravaged that it yields little."[53] Twenty-five years later, in trying to compel silver hoarders to convert to copper, Madrid officials ordered Sevilla's notaries to disclose the contents of legal documents that recorded silver that Spanish and non-Spanish merchants alike expected to receive for goods dispatched (often through the connivance of strawmen) to the colonies. They backed down before the combined protests of both the Council of the Indies and Sevilla's merchant guild.[54]

Liquidity crises during the Thirty Years' War and creditors' hardening insistence upon reimbursement in silver obliged the Treasury to turn to Sevilla's merchants for funds or, failing satisfactory response, to further seizures. Invariably, of course, Madrid vowed to abandon the seizure policy, a promise all too soon broken; in reaction, Sevilla businessmen took defensive action by concealing assets to protect their colonial trade operations. It was at best a cat-and-mouse game in which state and society were long-term losers.

Sequestrations were scarcely novel when the Thirty Years' War began, for the Spanish Hapsburgs had firmed the pattern early in the previous century.[55] In essence, Madrid would approach Sevilla's merchant community and when funds were not forthcoming or the volume unacceptable, would appropriate private consignments of silver in exchange for government bonds. Of course, Philip IV's regime started out disavowing sequestrations but had to change course. In 1625 Sevilla's merchant community offered a 300,000 *ducado* loan for the siege of Breda and the Flanders campaign; but when one of two expected flotas failed to arrive, Madrid expropriated 40 percent of privately consigned silver already unloaded. In 1630 Madrid again requested financing for an Italian campaign; Sevilla's merchants bargained, offering 500,000 in silver and demanding *juros* of 6 percent annual interest plus jurisdiction over the naturalization of alien merchants operating at Sevilla.[56] Over the next decade both parties joined in the dance of credits requested, funds granted, *secuestros* executed—all in return for *juros* backed by prospective silver imports on government account.

By 1641 foreign bankers were insisting on reimbursement only in silver while Sevilla's merchants underregistered or, more often than not, simply omitted registering their silver. Or they refused to commit cargo to outbound flotas "if they were not assured of not being dispossessed of the money." By agreement between flota flag officers and Sevilla merchants in 1641, a flota sailed from Veracruz with silver to be registered later (*por registrar*) on reaching Sevilla.[57] When Madrid again disavowed its sequestration tactics in the late 1650s, the damage was already irreparable. State policy rooted in expediency had disorganized Sevilla's colonial trade, driving merchants into a lasting defensive mode of smuggling and fraudulent recordkeeping, now tolerable forms of corruption. In 1649 it was clear that "for some years not a single shipment . . . in coin or bullion had appeared in the registers from America." Eleven more years elapsed before efforts to insure compliance with regulations for registry of incoming American silver were formally abandoned; by way of compensation in 1660 the merchant guilds of Sevilla, Mexico City, and Lima consented to a fixed annual silver payment to Madrid. The Thirty Years' War along with previous international involvements had proven to be a "disastrous piece of business for . . . the Spanish monarchy."[58]

At the onset of Spain's participation in the Thirty Years' War to preserve the Holy Roman Empire in Europe *and* its colonies in the western

Atlantic, *juros* were still viewed as a sound placement for individual as well as religious corporate investors. To judge by an earlier, very proximate breakdown in 1577, investors preferred readily negotiable *juros al quitar* over other types, which explains the observation concerning "the extent to which the changes, interests and usury of money has spread among so many people" in Spain's early commercial capitalism.[59] For some financiers speculative *juro* profits could be high; witness the case of Genoese speculator Doria who in 1613 bought *juros* well under par, then proceeded to cash them the following year at par. *Juros* like mortgages (*censos*), another popular investment, had come to represent "high yields."[60]

The financial requirements of Philip IV's regime were responsible for large *juro* debt increases, invariably underwritten by optimism about continued receipts of American silver to compensate periodic shortfalls in domestic revenues and by bills of exchange that some creditors were authorized to present directly to overseas colonial treasuries at Mexico City and Lima, bypassing the Treasury's agents at Sevilla.[61] Madrid also adopted new techniques of *juro* sales—forced sales to bureaucrats (obliged to convert one year's salary to *juros*), assigning *juro* quotas by province and, as a last resort, accepting *juros* when *asentistas* bought tax farms.[62] The ballooning of public debt based on *juros* plus the effects of inflation may be gauged by several measures. Between 1598 and 1621 *juro* capital rose 22 percent (from 92 to 112 million *ducados*); in 1634 *juro* interest payments alone absorbed perhaps half of Castile's annual revenues while during four decades of international conflict (1621–67) *juro* interest payments grew from 5.6 to 9.1 million *ducados*.[63]

A number of factors discouraged further *juro* investment by individuals who had inherited them as well as by corporate bodies endowed by charitable assignment of *juros*. The luster of *juro* investment began to dim in the course of repeated fiscal crises and military setbacks during the Thirty Years' War. Equally dissuasive were the tactics of Castile's Treasury: halving of annual interest payments between 1629 and 1659, then total suspension of interest in 1645; in 1677 the state decreed a 50 percent reduction in the nominal value of pre-1635 *juros* and for those issued after 1635, a halving of their interest rate. By the 1670s when "the discounting on *juros* based on Royal Revenues began," investors' disillusionment was widespread.[64]

Why Castile's Treasury began after the mid-1630s to manipulate what had long been a major source of government finance remains open to conjecture. Following the series of treaties at Westphalia (1645–48) and the settlement with France in 1659, Castile's financial commitments abroad began to contract. This appears to coincide with a decline in the level of official government (but not private) receipts at Sevilla of colonial silver which remained well below the highs of 1590–1620—hardly an incentive to prospective *juro* investors. Reinforcing the Treasury's shifting *juro* policy was the sentiment that long-held *juros* (many now in the third to fourth generation of *juristas*) had been repaid in interest many times over the initial investment, and that—given widespread speculation—the ratio of fixed interest to declining market price was intolerably skewed.[65] It is no surprise that the early Spanish Bourbon regime cut outstanding *juro* principal by one-third (1703) and in 1718 by a further 33 to 50 percent. This was a curiously silent financial revolution, a sea change by consensus.[66]

4

Europe's merchant bankers along with medium- and small-scale buyers of *juros* invested their funds in the Spanish government's financial instruments because the silver that often guaranteed their investment was a major factor in Europe's expanding regional and international economy well before 1550. Economic expansion after about 1450 had raised demand for precious metals and renewed exploitation of silver mines in the Tyrol, Alsace, Saxony, Bohemia, and Silesia. Then Peru's and New Spain's mines supplied an extraordinary increase in Europe's exchange media as American silver—cheaper to produce than Europe's—was reexported from Sevilla eastward to Barcelona and thence to Florence, Genoa, and the Low Countries, and via northern Spain into southwestern France, to its Atlantic ports and then on to Holland and its Baltic correspondents.[67] Flows of American silver into northwest Europe's regional economies were essential in shifting western Europe's economic axis from north Italy and the Rhône valley westward to the Atlantic. They turned Barcelona and southwestern France (Hendaye and Bayonne) into nuclei of "metallic fraud," late-sixteenth- and early-seventeenth-century Genoa into the financial capital of the "century of silver" and they account for the variety of prized silver coins—Segovia's *ocho reales de plata*, Antwerp's *philippes*, Elizabethan England's four reales of silver, and France's *pieces de 4 réales d'Espagne*.[68] While silver transfers from the peninsula paid for Castile's wars, diplomatic maneuvering, and growing trade imbalances, they also bought grain imports during food shortages such as the severe subsistence crisis of 1583–84.[69] Many were the roads for American silver to leak from Spain; and there were other circuits by which American silver left Spain for the Middle East, India, and China.[70]

For about a century after 1550 Genoa remained a center for diffusing Spain's American silver. Genoese banking houses lending to Madrid along with those to whom they marketed *juros* had to be serviced. More important, Spain's military forces in the Low Countries in the early campaigns insisted on payment in gold (it was less bulky than the silver equivalent) and Genoa capitalized on its network of banking connections and mastery of international exchange to supply it. For example, French exchange speculators would forward gold coins to Genoa, while at Barcelona chests of silver were loaded aboard galleys for delivery to Genoa where exchange rates oscillated in tandem with those of Sevilla.[71] Genoa's *hombres de negocio* then forwarded gold for Castile's armies in Flanders; however, the Spanish government's four subsequent bankruptcies between 1646 and 1662 led Genoese banking houses to lower their exposure in Spanish finance. It is worth noting that one of twenty-six grandee titles created under Charles II was sold to the Genoese banker Domingo Grillo—incidentally an *asentista* who supplied African slaves to Spain's American colonies.[72]

The other highway for exiting silver, at least until 1635, was the Atlantic coast of France. Most silver shipments crossed the border between Irun and Hendaye and on to the commercial center at Bayonne.[73] Also, imports of Breton grains and Anjou linens were covered by silver exports and, in addition, there were the earnings of Auvergnat field hands migrating each year into northeast Spain at harvest time. The movement of American silver fueled the regional economies of Bayonne, Bordeaux, La Rochelle, Nantes, and Rennes which served as intermediaries for Dutch trade with Spain when Holland and Spain were at war. Nor should we overlook the massive Spanish subsidies (1588–1606) to the Catholic League of the Guise, estimated at 600,000 *ecus* annually—"an enormous quantity of silver coins"—the league's soldiery were paid in silver *philippes*.[74] Fortunately there are two crude measures of France's silver imports from Spain for more than a century after the first large-scale shipments were unloaded at Sevilla. Between 1551 and 1680 only in two decades (1631–40 and 1671–80) did the proportion of silver to total coinage of France's mints fall below an average of 65 percent. In the second place, at the major mints in west or Atlantic France, Bayonne, and Rennes, that proportion remained strikingly high, 84 and 98 percent respectively; together these produced almost 65 million *livres tournois*.[75]

A third and perhaps the widest artery for the diffusion of America's silver from Spain into Europe, for the monetization of Europe and advancing a market-oriented economy there, was Madrid's reliance upon its silver to finance the corps of mercenary soldiery from Spain, Germany, Italy, Burgundy, and the Netherlands recruited for its Army of Flanders.[76] As this force expanded it absorbed a growing disproportion of Castilian revenue. In four years 1572–76, alone it required fully one-quarter of Castile's revenues to maintain an average of 63,000 men in the field; the percentage surely remained or increased when Philip IV's administration was able to muster a peak force of more than 88,000 in 1640.[77] Recruits—Spanish, Lombard, Neapolitan, Burgundian, and German—marched along two main highways: one leaving Genoa and Milan (the "Spanish Road") passed through eastern France, the other traversed Tyrol and Alsace, both converging in Lorraine to reach the Spanish Netherlands. For decades the Spanish government in a vast logistical enterprise moved thousands of troops often accompanied by women and children, contracted for weapons, food, and clothing, and arranged for mules, horses and carts, wagons and lodging. Arming these contingents (principally German and Netherlander) entailed arranging *asientos* (contracts) with suppliers at Milan, Innsbruck, and Liege—in the seventeenth century all paid in silver.[78]

Financing this military enterprise were Madrid's domestic and American silver resources. Direct transfers were made through *asientos* with Genoese financiers; indirect sources of silver for paymasters at the Antwerp headquarters often relied upon silver supplied by Dutch merchant bankers which they collected from Spanish shipping "at sea, in the Azores or off Lisbon," and which represented earnings on indirect merchandise sales to importers at Sevilla for reexport to Spain's American colonies. In point of fact, in the 1640s when the Flanders army was at its peak strength, ships detached from returning fleets from America often were sent with silver directly to Antwerp for settling the *asientos*.[79] Madrid's contracts for wages, supplies, and billeting of mercenaries in the Army of Flanders ultimately put specie in the hands of European peasants who furnished food and lodging at way-stations, or *etapes*. Over decades of Madrid's sustained maintenance of a military machine in the Netherlands, contracting for a broad range of equipment, other supplies, and services supplied at designated *etapes* for distribution to passing military contingents, American silver was diffused from the peninsula into Europe through north Italy and, via the Spanish Road and the Rhine, into the Netherlands.[80]

5

The grandeur, preponderance, and hegemony of Hapsburg Spain in Europe were the outcome of the Austrian dynasty's drive to defend Roman Catholicism and the patrimonial state as linchpins of the Holy Roman Empire in Europe and, as sovereign monarchs of Spain and its American dominions, to suppress religious, economic, and political divisions undermining that vision. Many were the reasons for the ultimate recession of Hapsburg hegemony, but beyond doubt the sustained effort to suppress rebellion in the United Provinces of the north Netherlands and retain Flanders drained the resources of Castile and its overseas empire. One must recall that during the thirty years of what was a world war Madrid was also involved in eliminating Dutch outposts in Brazil and the Caribbean as well as the Dutch Republic in Europe. The collapse of Hapsburg power in western Europe, however, followed a relentless drive to mobilize its resources in America and the Iberian peninsula—in Catalonia and Portugal as well as Castile—while keeping at bay its increasingly threatening rivals, England and France.

Such massive European and overseas entanglement had decisive economic and political consequences. In the first place, Castile was obliged to seek specie by multiplying and raising excise rates and extending taxes indefinitely, commandeering incoming silver, and setting aside preferred state revenues to guarantee obligations it owed demanding *asentistas* and bondholders.[81] But of greater long-term significance was accelerated sale of aristocratic titles and certificates of *hidalguía* (nobility) and, above all, alienation of elements of national sovereignty through the sale of seigneurial jurisdictions and public offices at all government levels—"a process of atomization and autonomization."[82] As the state privatized revenues and jurisdictions especially in Castile and Leon to purchasers often paying in *juros*, the nobility and aristocracy came virtually to control Castile, while the inflation of noble entitlements expanded tax exemptions and other immunities.[83]

Sale of public office proceeded on an even broader scale in both metropole and colonies. In the last phase of the Low Country debacle under Philip IV, the sale of office assumed an "unknown spread" while under the last Spanish Hapsburg "the alienation of revenues (was) almost complete."[84] Multiple and rising excises squeezed the mass of taxpayers.[85] At the same time a large proportion of state income as well as authority was absorbed by "administrators, collectors, receivers, treasurers, notaries, bailiffs and law enforcers, all . . . venal office holders." Buyers of office and entitlement came mainly from moneyed groups, "merchants, brokers, businessmen." At Sevilla these constituted a majority of the purchasers of *hidalguías* and municipal offices.[86]

The dissipation of effective sovereignty under the later Hapsburgs can also be traced through alienation of a principal revenue source of the *monarquía*, colonial trade at Spain's most trade-centered city and headquarters of its transatlantic trading system, Sevilla. There the treasury contracted out the customs of Sevilla (*almojarifazgo mayor*) and arranged *asientos* (with non-Spaniards for most of the seventeenth century) to manage customs collection of colonial trade, the *almojarifazgo de Indias*—a major component of Castile's general revenues (*rentas generales*).[87] Given the impressive income of the *almojarifazgo de Indias*, it was a preferred security guaranteeing interest payments under the terms of *juros de resguardo*, the fallback when other designated revenues were overcommitted. In 1583 such *juro* obligations already absorbed most *almojarifazgo* income.[88]

And Madrid had to proceed further in parting with elements of its sovereignty at Sevilla. It privatized bureaucratic posts in the Casa de Contratación; it sold to the Conde-Duque de Olivares the post of *juez conservador* along with the lucrative postmastership of the colonial mails (*correo mayor*), which he in turn proceeded to market;[89] it sold *maestrajes de plata* responsible for registry and general oversight of silver shipments from colonial ports to Sevilla; it privatized to Sevilla's merchants through their *consulado* collection and allocation of the tax financing the armament of Atlantic flotas (*avería*).[90] Small wonder that the Council of Castile lamented in 1652 that "the keys to the doors are in Portuguese and foreign hands, feeding on profits" which facilitated their involvement in "everything that is prohibitted;" and by 1660, in exchange for an annual lump sum assessed among the merchants of Sevilla, Mexico City, and Lima "the entire machinery of registration, customs and averia was abolished for cargo from the Indies."[91] Further, the process of selling state authority was extended to colonial administration: viceregal posts were sold, viceroys empowered to sell entailments (*mayorazgos*) to wealthy landed estate owners, mine owners, and merchants, the lesser colonial posts of *gobernador* (governor), *corregidor*, and *alcalde* (mayor) easing the path for merchants in the colonies to enjoy "privileged authority for their contracts, and converting Royal rights into their fraud."[92] Understandably during the Thirty Years' War Philip IV had to petition repeatedly both colonial and peninsular elites for monetary "donations" and loans (preferably interest-free). A supplicant sovereign could hardly function as an absolute one.

There are conclusions to be drawn from the seventeenth-century process characterized as the "progressive dispossession of the state for private gain and the consequent rise of a new aristocracy."[93] War finance backed by the liquidity of colonial silver granted Spain the illusory luxury of pursuing "power and grandeur" in Europe for a century. Selling its authority and alienating sources of state income, the government at Madrid demonstrated a "failure of control" over public finance and an incapacity to handle the "enormous costs of an empire much more difficult to defend than that of any other state" of the time.[94] More significant, sales of provincial and municipal offices undermined the central government by a process fundamentally "incompatible with the practice of 'absolutism.'"[95] By the end of the seventeenth century Spain's fragmented Hapsburg administration served a fragmented state where vested interests formed a bloc of consensus maintaining what had become a mutually profitable equilibrium, in other words, the status quo. The diaspora of silver had unpredicted consequences, Spain's double dependence: on Europe for most of what was exported to the colonies in America; and on the colonies for the silver to pay European suppliers and state expenditures in the peninsula and Europe.

five

Hegemonies Old and New: The Ibero-Atlantic in the Long Eighteenth Century

Kenneth R. Maxwell

Looking at the Atlantic in the eighteenth century, we still lack a comprehensive view of what changed during this period, where we should set its boundaries, and how we might interpret the salient characteristics of the century. Perhaps we have been both too general and too specific, simultaneously seeking with the synthesizers to explain too much and with the more specialized monographic literature to explain too little. If we begin in the South, the situation is particularly frustrating. Because our historiography on the Ibero-American and Afro-American Atlantic is still in a state of development, not to say underdevelopment, we are often forced to establish context and frameworks out of thin air and to ask what must appear from the perspective of the more developed historiographers of the North Atlantic to be obvious, foolish, and even naive questions. We are obliged, I think, to look at the "big picture," if only to see if what happens in our sphere has any resonance elsewhere. Such, at least, is my apology for the title of this chapter. Perhaps a better way of explaining what I will attempt to do is to say that I will hold up a mirror from the South Atlantic to see if there are any reflections in the experience of the North.

I will tackle two themes. The first relates very broadly to economic chronologies within the Portuguese and Spanish Atlantic; it asks whether they allow one to speak sensibly of an Atlantic system in the eighteenth century and what the dimension and limits of such a system might be. The second theme relates more to geopolitics and questions of empire or, if you will, to imperial hegemonies and the challenges that these hegemonies faced as the century ended.

I

We are confined to some degree, as we must be in any historical speculation, not only by our own research but also by what our colleagues
have chosen to write about. History writing since the Second World War
has tended to de-emphasize the role of individuals, institutions, and
events, instead plotting the longer-term trends in economic development and delineating social and economic structures. Thus, recent
decades have seen an accumulation of more information about the first
theme—the economic aspects of the Portuguese and Spanish Atlantic
systems than about the second—the policies and politics of empire.
While the emphasis on conjunctural economic analysis and social history has been fruitful, it has unquestionably also led to the almost total
exclusion of detailed examinations of elites, institutions, and above all
intellectual life, politics, and policy. Hence, today, we tend to know more
about slaves than their masters, more about the forced Indian labor
drafts of the Andes than the attitudes of Peruvian merchants and
bureaucrats in Lima, more about Mexican silver production than the
political role of mining entrepreneurs.

Our understanding of this period is also compromised by its end, as
after independence a relatively cohesive imperial past was fragmented
into a series of sometimes spurious national histories. For the western
shores of the Atlantic, historical output thus falls into two broad categories, one of which might be called the *vertical dimension,* the other the
horizontal dimension. By the vertical dimension I mean history writing
confined by the geographical limits of what after independence became
national entities. National histories inevitably stress originality and
uniqueness rather than any common colonial background, and are
sometimes hostile to a point of view that places the new nations within an international or comparative framework, or even within a colonial
or neocolonial context. Most U.S. historians still seem locked within the
concept of the "singularity" of United States history. For Latin America
the situation is no less extreme. The horizontal dimension is, of course,
comparative.

There are two major traditional interpretive frameworks for examining
the impact of the North Atlantic democratic revolution in Latin America.
First, there are Robert Palmer's and Jacques Godechot's essentially political and institutional visions of an Atlantic-based transformation, which see
mutual influence in political theory, constitutional experimentation, and
the politics of democratic incorporation. In this view, the Enlightenment

is a positive, benign, and causative influence, essentially a progressive force.[1] A second view is more economic, partly Marxian but also capable of incorporating much of classical liberalism. This view sees a general crisis of the old colonial system, flowing from the shift from commercial to industrial capitalism and affecting the British empire in the 1770s and the Spanish and Portuguese empires in the early nineteenth century. In this view, the intellectual contribution is minimal. The revolutions in America, both North and South, in the broadest sense represent a shift from formal to informal domination, with the newly industrializing states of northwestern Europe, most especially Great Britain, replacing the decaying bureaucratic and mercantilist empires of Spain and Portugal.

Perhaps we would be better off speaking of process, in part by rethinking the history of ideas within their social and economic context. For Latin America and the Iberian powers, this involves a new look at the impact of the ideas of the Enlightenment, which for Spain under Charles III (1759–88) and Portugal during the predominance of the Marquês de Pombal (1750–77) led to major reforms in the management of colonial affairs. In both cases, reformers were motivated by a decision to fortify colonial links, retake the benefits of Atlantic commerce from northern competitors, and reestablish power and prosperity by adapting the techniques that Britain and France had used to surpass them. These measures in some instances served to preempt and in others to mitigate the impact of the North American revolution, although neither Spanish nor Portuguese America was able to avoid late-eighteenth-century European upheavals. The North American model did prove attractive, and indeed Spain was an important component of the European alliance that helped the thirteen colonies in North America escape from British rule. Many would-be Latin American nationalists, on the other hand, saw Britain, the erstwhile colonial power, as a potential ally against Spain for their own independence movements. What we see is a complex interaction between the two major strands of the Enlightenment: its absolutist form, which involved a reformulation of imperial policy along neomercantilist lines and redefined the rights of the state, and its more liberal form, which served as a guide to experimentation with new forms of governance and constitution making, defining the rights of the individual within the process of decolonization.

II

How do the Portuguese and Spanish Atlantic fit into this larger picture? The case of Portugal and Brazil is especially interesting, given the Atlantic focus of their trade, Brazil's large slave population and consequent links to Africa, and the penetration of the Luso-Atlantic system by the British-dominated commercial system of the North Atlantic. It is essential to establish the parameters of the eighteenth-century Luso-Atlantic commercial system; if it is characterized overwhelmingly by the rise of gold production in Brazil and its subsequent fall, both cycles took place within a broader framework which changed surprisingly little between the 1660s and 1807, the year of the Napoleonic invasion of Portugal. Hence, I would treat the period as a long eighteenth century whose origins date back to the 1660s.

The Dutch assault on the Portuguese overseas possessions during the mid-seventeenth century was transatlantic in scope. The Dutch were well aware that control of the sugar-producing northeast of Brazil was useless to them unless they also controlled the source of slaves in Africa. Hence, in 1641, the Dutch seized the slave supply port of Luanda in Portuguese Angola, the slave transshipment depot located on the offshore island of São Tomé, and the sugar-producing Brazilian captaincy of Pernambuco. These Dutch successes, however, were temporary. In 1648 an expeditionary force mounted by the Portuguese governor of Rio de Janeiro retook Angola, and after a long and bitter guerrilla campaign in Pernambuco, the Dutch were expelled from Recife in 1654.[2]

The Portuguese victories in Africa and Brazil were not repeated in Asia. The 1650s, in fact, saw the Portuguese presence in Asia reduced to a shadow of what it had been in the sixteenth century. The oceanic dimension of Portuguese imperial interest from the 1660s until the early nineteenth century therefore came to be preeminently focused on the South Atlantic. As early as 1644, moreover, direct trade between Bahia and the West African coast was authorized, with Bahia exporting tobacco and importing slaves. These trading and commercial links between South America and West Africa remained important well into the nineteenth century, making the Bahian merchants involved in African trade wealthy and, very early on, virtually independent of Lisbon.

On the mainland of South America, Portugal staked out claims to its frontiers in the seventeenth century. In 1670 the bishopric of Rio de Janeiro was created, its jurisdiction reaching in theory to the northern banks of the Rio de la Plata. In 1680 the Portuguese established a "new colony" (Nova Colonia do Sacramento) opposite the Spanish port city of Buenos Aires. The reaction of the Spaniards was rapid and Nova Colonia was seized within a few months. But in 1681 the Portuguese reestablished and fortified the outpost. The Portuguese presence on the Rio de la Plata caused continuous friction with Spain. Despite several treaties, the problem was never definitively resolved during the colonial period and continued to complicate the relations between the successor states after the independence of both Spanish and Portuguese America. In the far north, the Amazon frontier also remained subject to dispute, in this case by France, which had in 1676 established a strategic presence on the coast of South America in Cayenna. French interest in Brazil, in fact, did not abate throughout the eighteenth century, despite the fact that in 1712, following the War of the Spanish Succession, France formally renounced all claims to the left bank of the Amazon.

In the late seventeenth century, therefore, the focus of Portugal's imperial interest shifted decisively westward from the trading post thassalocracy of the Indian Ocean to the plantation-based colonies of the South Atlantic. The Afro-American Atlantic commercial complex which had predated the Asian empire and thrived even while overshadowed by the Asian spice trade, now came fully into its own.[3] Within the South Atlantic system itself, integrated by the triangular interdependence of Lisbon, the slaving enclaves of the western and central African coast, and the expanding colonies of European and African settlements in Portuguese America, imperial priorities were reordered to favor support of Portugal's territorial empire in Brazil. Portuguese America in the 1650s was also very different from the collection of small coastal enclaves it had been sixty years before at the time of the union of the crowns of Spain and Portugal. The development of a fleet system between Lisbon and Brazil in the immediate aftermath of Portugal's independence from Spain, the imposition of heavier customs duties to support the construction of warships at midcentury, and the newly imposed monopoly of the Brazil Company all proved advantageous to southern Brazil. The South had previously competed under serious disabilities with Bahia and Pernambuco for access to European markets, but now the sugar ships from all the Brazilian regions arrived at Lisbon together. The escort vessels left Rio de Janeiro toward the end of March and picked up the sugar ships of Bahia in April, arriving at Lisbon in early July or August.

Between the mid-1640s and 1650, sugar prices were high in Europe, but the price of Brazilian sugar soon plummeted on the Amsterdam market, falling constantly until the 1680s. The major cause was competition from the Caribbean. The Dutch, and later the British, were developing their own sugar trade, and in the case of the British beginning to develop a system of preferential tariffs to protect British markets for sugar grown in the British Caribbean. The response of the Brazilian sugar sector to this loss of markets is imperfectly understood. There are some indications of attempts by Brazilian mill owners to lower costs by vertically integrating their enterprise. The Jesuit-managed Sergipe mill in Bahia, for instance, which had relied entirely on sharecropping arrangements in the early years of the century, was directly producing 60 percent of its own cane by the 1680s. Producers also managed to transfer some of their losses to salaried employees whose wages suffered a substantial real decline over the second half of the seventeenth century.[4] The social and political consequences of the new economic situation were significant. Planters and mill owners tended to lose their dominant position in urban institutions. Merchants began to hold positions of importance in prestigious urban voluntary lay organizations in the Brazilian port cities. And in the municipal government the old planter domination was challenged by the appointment of a university-trained lawyer as presiding officer (*juiz de fora*) and the appearance (at least in Bahia in 1641) of representatives of the urban artisan population, "the people's tribune" (*juiz do povo*).[5]

At the same time, the municipal councils in Brazil were acquiring added importance in the broader imperial context. The recovery of Pernambuco from the Dutch had resulted as much from the actions of the inhabitants themselves and their allies from São Paulo and Bahia within Brazil as from the intervention by Lisbon; this fact undoubtedly encouraged this autonomy. Indeed, the Pernambucans had been prepared at one point to seek the support of the Catholic monarch of France when the aid of Portugal for their cause had seemed problematic. The municipal councils had raised money for defense. They subsequently instigated a vigorous opposition to the monopoly of the Brazil Company, and with the aid of the Inquisition (which opposed the privileges granted to New Christian bankers who had invested in the Brazil Company) they succeeded in destroying the company's monopolies in 1659. The fleet system which had been imposed at the time of the company's establishment, however, was retained and continued to operate under the administrative direction of a new Lisbon-based board of commerce (*junta do comércio*). The Brazilian municipal councils were represented in Lisbon by procurators, and the council of Bahia acquired the right of sending two representatives to the Cortes in 1653.[6]

The weakness of Portugal undoubtedly contributed to the relative autonomy of Brazilian institutions. Portugal was well aware of the need to treat Brazilians with care and respect since Portugal's power to coerce obedience was very limited. In the 1690s, despite the fact that Brazilian white sugar no longer dominated world markets, it was still of high quality and thus remained an important export (and for Lisbon reexport) item. The major positive impact of sugar's relative decline in value was to stimulate diversification and give new incentive to exploration and expansion into the vast hinterland of South America. Tobacco, for instance, became a key Brazilian export to both Portugal and Africa; the quantity of tobacco sent to Portugal doubled between 1662 and 1672. Attempts were made to introduce cloves and cinnamon from Asia and to develop a trade in cacao. The cattle frontier was also pushing inland, opening up connections between the São Francisco river valley and the São Paulo plateau. Since 1670 the crown had also used the Paulistas extensively for systematic exploration of the interior, rewarding them with titles of nobility and membership in the chivalric military orders. With Paulista aid, the last complex of fugitive slave settlements, known as Palmares, was destroyed.

The most dramatic and decisive consequence of Portuguese exploration of the interior, however, was the discovery of gold. The Portuguese had been less fortunate than Spain in the search for precious metals. For almost two hundred years after Portugal laid claim to the territory which became known as Brazil, they had to make do with more prosaic products, such as Brazilwood, sugar, hides, cacao, and tobacco. At the end of the seventeenth century, however, half-Indian frontiersmen from the small inland settlement of São Paulo struck it rich. São Paulo was a resource-poor community that made its living by capturing and selling Indian slaves and raiding the prosperous Jesuit missions in Paraguay. The Paulistas were ever on the lookout for booty. In the 1690s, after years of searching, they eventually came across rich deposits of alluvial gold in the streams along the flanks of the mountain range of Espinhaço, which runs north-south between the present-day cities of Ouro Preto and Diamantina in the state of Minas Gerais. Within a decade of the Paulistas' discovery, the first great gold rush of modern history was in full swing. More than anything else, it was gold that pushed Portuguese settlements deep into the interior of Brazil, first to Minas Gerais, later to Goias and Mato Grosso—well beyond the traditional sphere of Portuguese interest determined by the Treaty of Tordesillas. The issue of the interior frontier hence became a matter of acute concern to the courts of both Lisbon and Madrid.

As the negotiations for a treaty to establish boundaries between Portuguese and Spanish America progressed during the 1740s, it became generally accepted that clear topographical landmarks such as rivers and mountains should serve to delineate frontiers. The Portuguese had two major bargaining chips. First, they held Colonia do Sacramento on the east bank of the Plate Estuary. Second, the westernmost Portuguese mining region, in what is now Mato Grosso, was integrated administratively and economically with the northern Brazilian coast by means of a fluvial transportation and communications route running along the Guaporá, Mamoré, and Madeira rivers in the western Amazonia basin. When an agreement was finally reached, these rivers constituted the northwestern border of Portuguese lands, much to the satisfaction of authorities in Lisbon.[7]

It is within these broader geographical limits that the economic characteristics of the long-eighteenth-century Portuguese Atlantic system should be seen. First and foremost, the period was marked by the flow of specie and the preeminence of colonial, mainly Brazilian, staples. Second, the growth, decline, and revival of manufacturing industry in Portugal was inversely proportional to the rise and fall of gold production in the Brazilian interior. That is to say, Portuguese domestic manufacturing thrived prior to 1700 and again after 1777, but languished during the golden age, with major implications for the Portuguese foreign and colonial policy. Portugal also remained throughout the eighteenth century a chronic grain importer—from northern Europe at the beginning of the century and from North America, especially Virginia and the Carolinas, toward the end. This fact had a major impact on the attitudes of the new North American republic toward protonationalist republican movements in Brazil. These attitudes were ambivalent at best when Virginia's trade with Portugal was balanced against support for independence movements of uncertain origin in Portugal's vast South American territories.

The third important characteristic of the long eighteenth century was the British presence in Portugal and indirectly within its empire, protected by treaties and exercising de facto extraterritorial rights and privileges on the pattern later imposed during the nineteenth century in China. The whole period from the late 1660s through 1807 was marked by the domineering presence of influential British merchant communities established in Lisbon and Oporto. These British merchants in Portugal were organized within factories, which were in effect legally recognized commercial corporations, their privileges guaranteed by the Cromwellian treaty of 1657, and reinforced by the Methuen Treaty of

1703. Through their entrepreneurial skills and access to capital, British merchants penetrated the whole fabric of the metropolitan and colonial economy.[8] The need for external political and military support was at the core of the commercial concessions Portugal had made to the British and others in the seventeenth century. Political and military dependency, however, did not mean there was no room for maneuver in the national interest or options open to a skillful Portuguese nationalist to extract benefits from the Anglo-Portuguese relationship. In fact a central preoccupation of Portuguese economic thinkers and diplomats throughout the eighteenth century was precisely how to achieve balance in what had become an unequal relationship. Nor did all British economic thinkers see pure benefit in the series of treaties and tariff privileges that governed Anglo-Portuguese commerce. The issue in fact became, as the eighteenth century wore on, a central topic of debate among the leading lights of the new science of political economy, engaging both Adam Smith and David Ricardo.[9]

The eighteenth-century Luso-Atlantic world, finally, was caught up in the struggle between France and England, a struggle that increasingly compromised Portugal. Lisbon tried to accommodate both, but by its very Atlantic nature, and because of the central economic role of Brazil within the Luso-Atlantic commercial system, Portugal was tied inextricably to Britain. Although it always sought to remain neutral and thereby retain the prosperous entrepôt function of Lisbon for the reexport of colonial products, it was very rarely able to maintain neutrality for long. The role of Brazil in Portuguese calculations and diplomacy thus held much higher priority than did the colonial weight of North America in British calculations. The preoccupation with the development of the Portuguese Atlantic empire on the one hand, and with Portugal's diminished stature and apparent backwardness on the other, permeated the Portuguese intellectual milieu of the age.

The most dramatic reformulation of Portugal's policy toward Brazil occurred during the long period of rule by the Marquês de Pombal, between 1750 and 1777. Pombal himself took much from classic British and French mercantilist theory and practice in his policy making, but the use of the term *mercantilism* to describe Pombal's policy is not entirely appropriate. Mercantilism, when defined narrowly, describes a policy whereby trade is regulated, taxed, and subsidized by the state to promote an influx of gold and silver in order to achieve a favorable balance of trade. Pombal's policy was at once limited and more focused than this. Its objective was to use mercantilist techniques to facilitate capital accumulation by individual Portuguese merchants. This aid to Portuguese capitalists had wider objectives and consequences, as it was part and parcel of a scheme to fortify the nation's bargaining power within the Atlantic commercial system.[10]

The problem for an enlightened Iberian economic nationalist was not so much to encourage the influx of precious metals; this was rarely a problem for Iberian economic policymakers given the fact that the Iberian empires were the principal source of the world's bullion supply in this period. The dilemma was precisely the opposite; that is, policymakers needed to devise measures to retain capital within their own economic system and thus to multiply the positive and diminish the negative economic impact of being producers of precious metals. The theory and practice of mercantilism was, after all, the creation of bullion-poor northwestern Europe. The goal of this policy in the bullion-rich Iberian Peninsula was fundamentally different from that sought by mercantilism's progenitors. The Iberians aimed to retain bullion, the northwestern Europeans aimed to attract it.

Pombal's methods reflected, in fact, the peculiarities of Portugal's position within the Atlantic system, and the particular impact on Portuguese entrepreneurship of the Brazilian gold boom of 1700–60. Essentially, the all-powerful minister, Pombal, placed the power of the state decisively on one side of the conflict that had developed between Portuguese entrepreneurs as a consequence of the gold boom. With support from the state he hoped the large Portuguese merchants would in time be able to challenge the foreigners at their own game. His economic policy protected mutually beneficial trade (such as the Portuguese wine trade), but it also sought to develop a powerful national class of businessmen with the capital resources and the business skills to compete in the international and Portuguese domestic markets with their foreign, especially British, competitors. It was not an easy policy to pursue, at least overtly, because it was essential to achieve this outcome without bringing into question the political and military support that the treaties with Britain guaranteed and which was essential if Spanish ambitions were to be kept at bay.

At the same time in Brazil, in striking contrast to the Bourbon reformers in Spanish America, Pombal sought to incorporate and co-opt the Brazilian oligarchy. Portugal was, after all, a small country with a large empire. It did not possess the resources of Britain or France. It did not have the military capabilities or the economic resources to force Brazil into a subservient role. Indeed, as Pombal watched the British attempt to repress the rebellious colonists in English-speaking North America during the 1770s, he was fortified in his belief that conciliation was a more effective weapon against colonial uprising than military force.

Portugal's colonial policy under Pombal in effect served to diffuse tensions within the colonial nexus by preventing any polarization along colonial versus metropolitan lines. The intervention of the Pombaline state had almost always been sectoral and targeted; that is, it had swung state support behind one side in a series of preexisting conflicts which themselves bridged the metropolitan-colonial divide. Hence, Pombal supported the large entrepreneurs against their smaller competitors; he had aided the educational reformers within the church such as the Oratorians while destroying the Jesuits; he had crushed powerful elements among the old aristocracy while encouraging the access of businessmen to noble status. The benefits or displeasure of the Pombaline state, in other words, helped and hindered both Brazilians and Portuguese, forging a series of alliances across the Atlantic, as well as counteralliances that linked Portuguese and Brazilian interests at a variety of levels. Some of these results of policy were unintentional; but the conciliatory aspect of Pombal's policy toward powerful Brazilian interests was entirely explicit.

The fundamental problem for Portugal, however, arose from the Brazil-based Atlantic system within which Pombal had operated. In the final analysis, Brazil would inevitably become the dominant partner within the Portuguese-speaking empire. If the political constraints that had governed the whole period from the 1660s to the end of the eighteenth century also changed, that is, if for example Great Britain no longer saw it in its own interest to protect Portugal from her continental neighbors, then the British might opt for a direct relationship with the colony rather than with the mother country.[11] Since the whole basis of Portugal's prosperity had been built on the manipulation of colonial monopolies, cash-crop exports, colonial markets, and colonial gold, such a rupture would bring fundamental change and would close an epoch. Ironically it was the French seizure of Lisbon in 1807 that forced the effective political and economic emancipation of Brazil in 1808. The neutralization of those in Portugal opposed to recognition of Brazil's central economic and political role within the Luso-Brazilian Atlantic system collapsed the structure of the system and by eliminating Lisbon as the required intermediary between South America and Europe.[12]

III

In the Spanish-American Atlantic world, the eighteenth century had seen three major processes at work. First, the old monopolistic trading connection of convoys of protected ships sailing on a regular pattern between the Caribbean and the monopoly port of Seville (later Cádiz) had been superseded by a de facto diversification of trade. Some of this diversification was illegal and clandestine, but it had become a substantial contribution to overall Atlantic commerce. After 1715, in fact, the old fleet system was clearly limiting the growth of trade as economic and demographic expansion occurred throughout Spanish America. Spain eventually permitted other Spanish ports into Atlantic commerce, gradually ending the Cádiz monopoly between 1765 and 1789 and giving formal administrative recognition to the peripheral coastal regions in South America far from the traditional centers in the highland Indian-populated core areas. Thus, while Lima and Mexico City remained important (Mexico still accounted for half the population of Spanish America in this period), new bases also developed in the previous backwaters of Rio de la Plata, Caracas, and Cuba.

Second, starting at midcentury Spain had attempted to implement a series of major administrative, mercantile, and fiscal reforms aimed at the enhancement of the power of the metropole by the more efficient exploitation of its colonies' economic potential.[13] As in Portugal, there had been growing awareness in Spain that its role as a great power was severely undermined by the failure to adapt to modern conditions, which in eighteenth-century terms meant using the power of the state to increase revenues and impose a more centralized administrative system. During the first half of the eighteenth century, this preoccupation with national regeneration was in the forefront of the minds of high government officials who saw Spanish America as the means for Spain to recuperate its position in Europe. The 1743 proposal of José de Campillo, minister of finance, in which he called for a "New System of economic administration for America," encapsulated the intention to develop the empire as a market for Spanish manufactures and as a source for raw materials. Campillo wished to see a system of general inspectors (*visitas generales*), the creation of intendancies on the French model, and the introduction of "free trade" into colonial administration—by which he meant the ending of the Andalusian monopoly and the opening of Spanish American trade to all ports of Spain. He also proposed the creation of a more economically integrated society within

Spanish America by changing the way in which the Indian communities within the New World were governed. Campillo's proposals, however, were not published until 1789. It was the Bourbon monarch Carlos III (1759–88) whose reign was associated with the implementation of a series of far-reaching new governmental measures for the administration of the vast Spanish territories in the New World. The urgency of these reforms became more than ever evident after the seizure of Havana by the British in 1762 during the Seven Years' War.[14]

It is clear that each major Spanish crisis in the eighteenth century had a colonial component. Commercial competition between England and France for the Spanish contract (*asiento*) to supply African slaves to Spain's colonies in America had been a prominent issue in the War of the Spanish Succession. The crisis in 1759–62 was precipitated by English commercial expansion in India, Canada, and the Caribbean, gateway to Spain's colonies in Central America and northern South America. At the century's end came conflict between England and Napoleonic France in large measure over seapower and trade with Spain's colonies. What defined these crises was Spain's monopoly of American silver production, its inability to develop a manufacturing industry to supply its colonies, and the competition between two more developed European economies over exploiting the Spanish empire in America.

To England and France, Spanish America represented, above all, a market for manufactured goods and a source of silver essential for expanding international trade and settling the imbalance of payments. At the end of the War of the Spanish Succession, however, the forms of British and French commercial penetration in Spain diverged. Less developed commercially and industrially than the British, and linked to Spain through the Bourbon dynasty and wartime alliances, French merchants and shippers would expand inside the Spanish colonial trading system now centered on Cádiz. The Utrecht settlement confirmed the concessions yielded by Madrid over the last half of the seventeenth century to foreign resident merchants and shippers at Cádiz. Such concessions included extraterritorial rights, the exemption of firms and vessels from certain customs controls, and lower duties on imports such as French linens and other select items.[15]

There were on average over the decades between 1724–78 about sixty major French commercial houses established in Cádiz. Of the declared value of the Cádiz merchants, moreover, the French merchants accounted for 43 percent and the Spanish merchants only 18 percent. Until 1789, the French remained the largest foreign colony in Cádiz, always sensitive, like the British factory in Lisbon, to any infringement of their treaty rights.[16] French industry also absorbed appreciable quantities of Spanish primary exports—raw wool, soda ash, and raw silk—along with products from Mexico and Guatemala like cochineal and indigo dyes. As little as 10 percent of colonial cargoes consisted of Spanish goods, with the balance made up by the production of Spain's French ally. Sales to the Spanish colonies generated a counterflow of silver that fed into the private banking system centered on Paris and Lyons, which was vital for trade with India and China and for the deficit-plagued finances of the French state. Silver, in fact, continued to dominate the Spanish American traffic: between 1717 and 1778 it composed 77.6 percent of the annual value; and 75.4 percent of the value of the trade of New Spain.[17]

English merchants were less important at Cádiz, but they enjoyed other channels of trade with Spain's American colonies, especially along Spain's Caribbean coasts. Between Utrecht and the outbreak of war in 1739, the British managed the slave supply contract (*asiento*) at Havana, Veracruz, Cartagena, and Buenos Aires, where along with African slaves they introduced smuggled goods. From Jamaica the British developed an extensive smugglers' network to Havana and Santiago on the island of Cuba, to the Campeche and Belize coasts, and to New Spain's sole major Caribbean port of Veracruz. Jamaica also served as both entrepôt and naval base from which British naval forces could threaten the French sugar islands and Spanish American ports. This threat materialized in the war beginning in 1757, when English forces took Canada and occupied first Guadeloupe and later Martinique.[18]

The accession of Charles III offered an opportunity to reform traditional attitudes. For France, which saw its colonial empire in India and Canada collapse, and for Spain, unprepared alone to withstand English assaults upon its Caribbean trading zone, the new regime provided the opportunity at last to renew their dynastic alliance of mutual convenience. Yet Charles III wished to diminish the pressure from French commercial and manufacturing interests who had long enjoyed direct and indirect participation in Spain's transatlantic trading system. This basic contradiction of purposes within Franco-Spanish diplomatic and military collaboration was not dissimilar to that within the Anglo-Portuguese alliance.

Charles aggressively revived projects of economic reform outlined earlier by men like Campillo. His first actions were to terminate the seventeenth-century tariff concessions hampering the development of domestic industry, followed by the standardization of tariffs and procedures at all peninsular ports. Given the importance of colonial trade in Spain's aggregate external exchange, Madrid was, in effect, shifting much of the burden of customs revenue to colonial consumers. Charles's government also attempted to reduce the illegal foreign share in Spain's colonial exchanges, in effect, attempting to increase Spain's participation and advantage in colonial trade. And, in light of Franco-Spanish diplomatic and defense collaboration, symbolized in the family pact, Madrid expected French manufacturing interests to tolerate Spanish protectionism designed to make Spain's contribution in the joint containment of English commercial and naval power more effective.

The impact of the new governmental measures within Spanish America varied considerably from region to region. One immediate consequence was that tensions were aggravated between European Spaniards and the old Latin American white Creole oligarchies, the latter of which had for several centuries found a political niche within local administrations throughout the Americas. The Bourbon reforms, especially the intendant system, were therefore first introduced in the regions where the opposition of the old Creole oligarchies was less formidable; Cuba after 1764 and the Rio de la Plata after 1776. Only in 1784 was the system introduced in Peru, and in 1786 in Mexico.[19] In practice, Spanish neomercantilism proved limited in its impact. State intervention did not create an industrial base in textile manufactures, except in Catalonia whose cotton mills were the product of private rather than state initiatives. In the mid-1780s, colonial trade expanded, but the increase appears to have been based largely on the sustained surge in Mexican silver mining and colonial staple exports, more shipping in low-tonnage vessels, and Europe's appetite for silver and staples.[20]

Spain, Europe, and the East were still linked to American silver, and transforming a bullionist into a neomercantilist Spanish state was no easy process. The threat to the system from northwest Europe remained. The English manufacturers, in their preference for direct, if illegal, participation in Spanish colonial markets over the French method of participation via Cádiz were, in effect, pointing to one of the basic flaws in the Spanish neomercantilist project. The inability of the Spanish state to curb smuggling from English Caribbean ports or from the Dutch and French islands, demonstrated clearly what the merchants well understood. Multiple charges on goods within the formal Spanish trading system all raised the price of legal goods in Spanish America to levels that compensated for the risks of smuggling.

French textile manufacturers were also unable to provide the Spanish colonial system with merchandise whose quantity, quality, and pricing

was competitive with other European goods. To protect their deteriorating competitive position, the French defended traditional commercial
privileges in Spain's colonial trade. Yet it was precisely here that the
French manufacturers faced competition from Spain itself. The fundamental premise of mercantilism was economic competition not cooper-
ation. Thus, ironically, both French commercial agents and their Spanish
counterparts failed to observe that by the last third of the eighteenth
century both Spanish and French economic policies were being
bypassed by the rapid expansion of the international economy. English
industrial development was generating products whose price and quality would permit them to penetrate most mercantilist barriers.

The exercise of political and ultimately military power, however,
remained a vital component in the Atlantic equation, and the neomercantilist challenge by the Iberian states to British and French commercial hegemony was not without its successes. Between 1785 and 1790
the balance of trade between Portugal and Great Britain was brought
almost to an equilibrium. During the 1790s, for the first time in the
whole century, Portuguese exports to Britain showed a surplus over
British exports to Portugal. Brazilian raw cotton reexports from Portugal
to Britain, by the first decade of the nineteenth century, composed
about a quarter of Lancashire's cotton wool, mostly from Pernambuco
and Maranhão.[21] It was now the British who clamored for reciprocity, a
reversal of circumstances which would have gratified the subtle old
Marquês de Pombal had he lived long enough to see it. Between 1786
and 1788, extensive investigations were conducted in London into the
changed Anglo-Portuguese commercial relationship. Both the old
woolen and wine industries and the new cotton manufacturing interest
pressured the government and the committee of the Privy Council for
Trade. The cotton spinners and the calico and muslin manufacturers of
Manchester and Neighbourhoud were especially vocal, as were the
Borough Reeve and constable of Manchester.[22]

In 1801 Lord Hawkesbury instructed the British minister in Lisbon to
let it be known that "in the case of invasion, the British envoy was autho-
rised to recommend that the court of Portugal embark for Brazil . . . and
the [British] were ready for their part to guarantee the security of the
expedition and to combine with [the Portuguese government] the most
efficacious ways to extend and consolidate [their] dominions in South
America."[23] This was an astonishing change of policy. But its immediate
implementation was not easy; the traditional commercial organizations
and their lobbies remained powerful, not only in the form of the British

factories in Portugal but also among the new Portuguese merchant industrial bourgeoisie Pombal had created. But the British government was clear on the issue. As Robert Fitzgerald, Walpole's successor in Lisbon, wrote to Lord Hawkesbury, "the British property within these dominions forms no object of great national importance . . . especially where in the opposite balance are viewed the innumerable advantages to be derived from an open, unrestrained trade with the Brazils."[24] It took the French invasion of 1807 to neutralize the old interests in both countries and bring about the momentous transfer of a European court to South America.

IV

But if the policies of neomercantilism in both Spain and Portugal were ultimately thwarted, and if Iberian enlightened absolutism proved incapable in the long term of preventing the inexorable rise of the British commercial and naval hegemony within the Atlantic system as a whole, what of the forces of protonationalism on the other side of the ocean? Can we speak here of "an age of Democratic Revolution," as Robert Palmer proposed, or of "an Atlantic Revolution" in the sense Jacques Godechot used the term? Or are we indeed seeing a more economically based transformation from direct to indirect dominion, from the old formats to the new informal empire of trade and industrial power, an enterprise implicit in the Steins's *Colonial Heritage?*

The example of the American Revolution had been particularly important in Brazil for reasons that lay in the coincidence of its anticolonial message with the severe tension between Lisbon and major segments of the local elite in the one area in Portugal's American territories. In Minas Gerais, an embryonic independence movement had briefly made the idea of an economically independent republic on the North American model pertinent in the Brazilian interior in the period of 1788–89. Minas Gerais had the capacity to articulate as well as make effective an independent state, possessing as it did in the 1780s adequate revenues, military forces, administrative experience, and a close attention to international developments. That it failed despite all these elements is an indication of how difficult the achievement of independence would be in Ibero-America.[25]

In Spanish America, internal social, racial, and caste divisions permeated colonial society. It would prove very difficult for a clear regional focus of protonationalistic sentiment to emerge where there was no cohesive social base to support rebellion against Spain. Movements of social protest did, of course, emerge in Spanish America, and with much more violence, bloodshed, and disruption than ever occurred in Brazil where protonationalist movements, however articulate, never got further than conspiracy in the eighteenth century. The most significant of these movements of protest and rebellion were the Comunero Rebellion in New Granada (present-day Colombia) in 1781 and the Tupac Amaru Rebellion in Upper Peru (present-day Bolivia) in 1780–81. But social protest in Spanish America was limited in its ideological content; it did not make the leap from protest against bad government to an attack on the rule of Spain in America. Both movements, especially the latter, served to terrify the Creole elite and make them acutely aware of the risk of race and ethnic violence implicit in the complexity of Spanish America's social makeup.

Given the heterogeneity of Spanish America in the late eighteenth century, the uneven impact of imperial reform, the diversification of the economic system, its reorientation toward the Atlantic trading system in the new peripheral growth areas, and the limited anticolonial sentiment apparent in the rebellions of the 1780s, incipient nationalism was, when it emerged, more a characteristic of disgruntled individuals than of the masses. The latter were, on the whole, more preoccupied with immediate inequalities and exploitation than with intraimperial injustices, and they felt more the oppression of the local oligarchies than of the crown in Madrid. The rebels in both Peru and Colombia, in fact, had looked to the crown for redress of grievance. The notion of independence from Spain, of a colonial emancipation from Europe, was hence confined to a very small number of the white Creole elite and developed after the putative popular revolts of the early 1780s had been repressed. These aspirations were also of a reformist rather than a revolutionary nature, and while the institutional model of the new North American nation was often an inspiration in terms of overseas contacts and hope of assistance, it was to Britain that they looked rather than the United States.[26]

By the turn of the century, it is certainly true that works by John Adams, George Washington, and Thomas Jefferson were circulating in both Mexico and South America. Key leaders of the Spanish American independence movements, most notably Francisco de Miranda, visited the United States, as did Simón Bolívar, who admired Washington. Miranda perfectly summarized the complex reaction of whites to the events of 1776 in North America and 1789 in France: "We have before our eyes two great examples," he wrote in 1799, "the American and the French Revolutions: let us prudently imitate the first and carefully shun the second." After the revolt in French Saint Domingue in 1792 property owners throughout Spanish America and Brazil became even more cautious, especially if their property included African slaves. "I confess that as much as I desire the liberty and independence of the New World," Miranda observed, "I fear anarchy and revolution even more."[27]

The impact of the American Revolution would be confined mainly to the periphery in Spanish America. Very little effect can be discerned in the two great core regions of Spanish dominion, Peru and Mexico. In many respects, the North Americans, in terms of trade, influence, and contact, followed the sea-lanes, and their role was more significant in the Caribbean and along the coastlines where they had long been involved in the transatlantic commercial complex. Trade, more than republican ideology, would be the watchword in the United States's dealings with both Spain and Portugal. Spain in particular had substantially aided in the attainment of American independence; it was a connection that made for some caution when it came to aiding and abetting revolutionaries to the south, at least until the Napoleonic period, when for all effective purposes the United States gained direct access to Spanish American ports and Spain lost direct administrative control of its empire in America.[28]

In the case of Portugal, the impact of the American Revolution in Brazil, and most especially its republicanism, was diluted and eventually rejected by the mid-1790s. This rejection was partly due to the failure of the republican conspiracy in Minas Gerais, but it was due also to the counterinfluence of the French Revolution in the Americas, the great slave revolt in the French Antilles. The white Brazilian elite, slave owners, and those opposed to slavery alike, found by the 1790s that republicanism and democracy were concepts too dangerous for experimentation within a slave society where blacks outnumbered whites two to one. The consequence was that those who avidly and approvingly followed the events in North America before 1790 turned away from the North American model and, encouraged by the Portuguese government, embraced monarchy in the interest of preserving the status quo against racial and social upheaval. A similar interaction between the chronology of revolutions and elite attitudes took place in all the American states and former colonies where slavery was entrenched.

In mainland Spanish America, independence followed from external more than internal events: the collapse of the Bourbon monarchy in Spain itself in the face of the Napoleonic onslaught in 1808. In Portugal the French invasion brought about a denouement to the dilemmas of the metropolitan-colonial relationship with the de facto (later de jure) establishment of Rio de Janeiro as the seat of a New World monarchy. But in Spain the invasion in effect cut Spanish America loose of the old metropolis for a critical six years between 1808 and 1814, with major consequences for Spanish American unity and stability. The successor Spanish American republics often took shape within the boundaries imposed by the eighteenth-century reformers, but they all faced massive problems of social cohesion and economic and administrative dislocations. The development of broad-based anticolonial sentiment prior to 1808 was limited, and the fragmented social bases diminished the potential impact of the North American example. As in the lowland tropical areas of the Western Hemisphere, the example of Haiti reinforced the fears arising from the uprising in Upper Peru in the early 1790s. Those who saw the North American model as relevant tended after 1800 to see it as the conservative option; a solution to the colonial dilemma that preserved the basic social organization, especially the system of slavery, but brought, at the same time, political emancipation from Europe. For an effective partnership in achieving this latter goal they more often looked to Great Britain than to the United States and to trade: espousing "liberalism" in the sense of access to world commerce rather than liberalism in the sense of democratic government.

Thus, for Latin America, especially the areas where plantation economies and African slavery predominated, it is essential, if we are seeking to mark the end to the long eighteenth century, to look at the relationship between the revolutions in North America, France, and Haiti and at the vicissitudes of the eighteenth-century experience with reform and rebellion. From the perspective of the Americas, the great slave revolt of 1792 in French Saint Domingue was a second "American" revolution that seemed no less important than the first. Whereas in the 1780s would-be Latin American revolutionaries had found inspiration in George Washington; after the 1790s, they would recoil in fear before the example of Toussaint L'Ouverture.

The Haitian revolt also had a major impact on the attitudes of the governments of Spain, France, and Britain toward independence movements in the Americas. For Britain in particular, Haiti brought great caution to the encouragement of colonial rebellion if such revolts threatened to bring about instability and violence and to destroy the very wealth which had attracted British traders and merchants to the region in the first place. Here, the British soon began to see the advantages of the Luso-Brazilian solution to the dilemmas of the epoch of the Atlantic revolutions. As John Barrow summarized the issue in 1806:

Revolutions in states where each individual has some interest in their welfare are not effected without the most serious calamities. What, then, must be the consequences in a country where the number of slaves exceeds the proprietors of the soil? In promoting revolutions, I trust England will never be concerned, being fully convinced that however much South America might gain by a quiet change of masters, she will be soon thrown back into a state of barbarianism by revolutions.[29]

The recently independent North Americans were the first to see through such stratagems and their implications for Spanish America and Brazil. The American secretary of state, John Quincy Adams, writing on June 28, 1818, summed up the British attitude toward the political emancipation of South America when he wrote:

The Revolutions in South America had opened a new world to her commerce, which the restoration of Spanish colonial domination would again close against her. Her Cabinet, therefore, devised a middle term, a compromise between legitimacy and traffic. . . . She admits all the pretension of legitimacy until they come in contact with her own interests, and then she becomes the patroness of liberal principle and colonial emancipation.[30]

From the early-nineteenth-century British perspective, the reasons for this essentially conservative stance are not hard to discern. Hegemonic powers with strong commercial interests always fear radical and unpredictable change.

Only two months later the British envoy in Rio de Janeiro, Henry Chamberlain, in fact was writing secretly to Viscount Castlereagh (August 22, 1818) in terms that reflected John Quincy Adam's supposition exactly.

The political state of this part of the South American continent has become so changed by the establishment of the seat of the Portuguese Monarchy in the Brazils that a change in the system under which Spain formerly governed her colonies in the Plata is become necessary and unavoidable, even if they had remained faithful; they have, however, thrown off their allegiance, and have maintained a struggle of several years for Independence. . . . For Brazil, having ceased to be a colony and being become an independent kingdom open to the commerce of the whole world, they cannot return to their former state. However, as I regard the re-establishment of Spanish authority as impossible, it appears to me that the real interest of His Catholic Majesty would be secured by his putting an end to the contest as soon as possible, . . . such as to promise stability, revolution would cease and prosperity would be restored in these fine countries to the advantage of the whole world, and of none more than of Great Britain.[31]

John Quincy Adams and Henry Chamberlain were both right. The characteristics and options that had marked the long eighteenth-century in the Spanish and Portuguese Atlantic had been permanently transformed. Yet this had occurred at least in part because the options for two very important participants in the eighteenth-century South Atlantic world—Spain and Portugal—had been largely superseded and destroyed. For them, the long eighteenth century had ended.

six

Dependency and the Colonial Heritage in Southeastern Mesoamerica

Robert W. Patch

The dependency interpretation did not burst forth, like Pallas Athena, full grown from the minds of scholars in the late 1960s. Rather, the term *dependency* came into use at that time to refer to what previous historians and economists had called *underdevelopment* resulting from the long-term relationship between Latin America and the world capitalist economy. This analysis can be traced back in part to Paul Baran's 1957 Marxist interpretation of economic "backwardness," or to the structuralist economists of the UN's Economic Commission for Latin America (ECLA) in the late 1940s (or, as Joseph Love argues in this volume, even farther back), but insofar as the interpretation emphasized the "underdeveloping" nature of foreign investment and export promotion it is possible to discover the bare bones of the theory of capitalist underdevelopment in the works of Lenin and Trotsky.[1]

The success of the dependency interpretation during the 1960s and 1970s was due primarily to the undeniable importance that exports played in Latin American history and to the failure of that sector to lead to sustained, self-generating industrialization. The scholars of the dependency school, in my opinion, succeeded in demonstrating that the great export economies, especially sugar, coffee, and mining, while generating capital accumulation and hence profits for the plantation and mine owners, were historically based for the most part on unfree labor and eventually resulted in environmental destruction, overreliance on one product as a source of export earnings, vulnerability to the vagaries of the world economy, and the creation of a large class of impoverished workers. The dependency interpretation therefore seemed to make a lot of sense for the great export economies of northern Mexico, the Caribbean, Peru, Brazil, and modern Central America.

But is the economic and social history of Latin America nothing more than the history of its export economies? In reality, in a large part of the region only a small sector was based on exports. This was especially true in the southern highlands of colonial Mexico and Central America, which is to say, the heartland of the surviving Indian population of Mesoamerica. My own research experience in the Yucatán gradually led me to conclude that the dependency interpretation had a great flaw: it failed to take cognizance of the significance of indigenous structures of production. It is clear why. Most of Latin America's agricultural exports were located in lowland tropical or semitropical regions like the Caribbean and Brazil, where after the early period of colonization there *were* no indigenous structures of production. Rather, a landscape once occupied and used by Indians was cleared to make way for the sugar or coffee plantation, and after the failure of Indian slavery, an African, that is exogenous, work force was imported to do the hard labor. Immigrants from Europe as well as from other parts of the Caribbean or Brazil—in many cases mixed-race people—occupied the middle strata of society. The Indian contribution to the structure of production, other than as the slaves in the first century of colonialism, was eventually negligible. Not even in the production of foodstuffs did indigenous people play a role.

It does not follow, however, that what was true for the Caribbean and Brazil was true for all of Latin America. In this essay, I shall attempt to show that the history of southeastern Mesoamerica (which I shall define as the area including the Yucatán Peninsula and the colonial Kingdom of Guatemala, that is Chiapas and Central America minus Panama) demonstrates that the dependency interpretation underestimated or missed the importance of indigenous structures of production in Latin American history. At the same time, however, I shall argue that this same history manifests the deep impact of export economies—which functioned in ways unnoticed in the original dependency formulation— and the nature of the colonial heritage in one of the historically most "Indian" parts of Latin America.

In southeastern Mesoamerica Spaniards found in place already existing structures of production based overwhelmingly on agriculture. These autochthonous structures of course antedated the Spanish invasion and had nothing to do with the Europe-centered world economy and therefore had not been brought into existence to serve the needs of Europe for raw materials or primary products. At the same time, the Indian economy of most of southeastern Mesoamerica was not subsistence in nature. The region was inhabited overwhelmingly by Maya and Nahua people who regularly produced a surplus and had a high degree of social stratification. The Spanish conquest meant not the destruction of this autochthonous society, as was the case in Brazil and the Caribbean, but rather its incorporation into a world system; the people in turn were neither slaves nor peons but peasants. And even though, as we shall see, ways were found to utilize this indigenous structure of production to serve the needs of an export economy, the Mayas and Nahuas had a relationship to the world system that was similar to that of the peasantry in Europe itself: they produced the surplus that permitted the continued existence of a highly stratified society yet were not directly involved in the activities of the world system's industrial core or peripheral production of raw materials and primary products.

Of course, it might be argued that the prior existence and later survival of indigenous structures of production affects the dependency interpretation not at all. Following this line of thought, the autochthonous economy could be understood simply as the provider of the goods necessary for the operation of the export economies, and such production was always taken for granted. Only rarely, as in the case of the Caribbean sugarcane economy, did dependency include reliance on outside sources for food as well as for manufactured goods. Moreover, the presence of the indigenous structure of production in colonial Latin America might be seen as completely irrelevant, for it was a subordinate economy that in the long run was destined to diminish in scale and eventually be either "ghettoized" like that in the United States or exterminated altogether by liberal and neoliberal economic policies. The autochthonous structures, in short, were quaint but doomed anachronisms that were affected by but did not affect the course of economic history.

The point, then, is not whether or not there were structures of production outside those of the export economy but rather whether or not they were important. From the perspective of southeastern Mesoamerica, the answer must be in the affirmative. First of all, the indigenous structures of production embraced the great majority of the population, not only because of the mere survival of the Indian population but also because of the great difficulty of establishing and maintaining economies geared toward the export of raw materials and primary products to the European market. (The same, of course, was true of many other parts of Latin America).

Secondly, the autochthonous structures were so productive that they could support the existence of a Spanish society not engaged in the export economy. This in turn meant the continued arrival of European immigrants who served to maintain and expand Creole America. Of course, the quantity of such people who had Yucatán, Chiapas, or Central America as their final destination was small compared to that of Mexico City, Lima, and the Mexican and Peruvian mining camps. Nevertheless, the immigrants were numerous enough to permit the survival and expansion of European society in America. This was of vital importance, for it resulted in the survival of a Spanish upper class and thus permitted the development of one of the characteristic features of Latin America: the close correlation between race, class, and culture. This pattern holds true not only in the regions historically based on export economies but also in so-called backwater areas like southeastern Mesoamerica.

Third, the existence of Spanish and Indian economies and societies not directly involved in the export of raw materials to Europe permitted autonomous development that was independent of the demands of the so-called core regions of the world economy. This meant not just the survival of Spaniards and Creoles in America but also changes within the Indian society. Most importantly, the native population eventually developed greater resistance to imported disease and then, in the eighteenth century, began to increase in numbers at a significant rate. This demographic expansion—which in fact owed nothing to European factors, events, or demands—was one of the most important historical developments of the second half of the colonial period. It led, first, to the transformation of local structures of production. In Yucatán, Guatemala, and Nicaragua, and all over most of eighteenth-century Spanish America—apparently with the important exception of the central Andes—the increased number of people, especially Indians but also Spaniards, Creoles, and so-called *castas* (those of mixed-race ancestry), led to increasing demand for food and caused estate owners to devote more and more land to agricultural production, sometimes in substitution of stock raising. They did so in order to sell food, especially wheat and maize, in the growing urban markets.[2]

At the same time, the growing number of people in the countryside resulted in a scarcity of resources and concomitant struggles for land that pitted Indian villages against haciendas and against each other. Since there was a steadily growing surplus population, *hacendados* (ranch owners) frequently found that they could increase the demands placed on laborers, renters, and sharecroppers. The demographic change of the eighteenth century therefore in some cases resulted in the lowering of the standard of living of a large part of the population in city and country. In central Mexico, for example, famine became more frequent, and as rural conditions worsened the people were pushed closer to the subsistence level. This undoubtedly helps account for the ferocity of rural rebellion when it finally came in 1810.[3] In southeastern Mesoamerica the process was delayed somewhat by the smaller number of Spaniards, but there was nevertheless a growing struggle for resources. In the case of Yucatán this contributed to the outbreak of the Caste War after independence.[4]

Finally, what the demographic expansion of the eighteenth century did was lead to the transformation of labor systems. In the case of some parts of central Mexico a full-fledged rural proletariat emerged, and landowners no longer had to rely on peonage. In the Veracruz area and in Central America even sugarcane producers came to depend less on slavery. This was possible because of the growing number of Indians who in order to survive agreed to work either part-time or full-time on the estates.[5]

In southeastern Mesoamerica, on the other hand, the movement toward free labor was much slower or nonexistent. Nevertheless, there were important changes in labor relations. In Yucatán demographic expansion resulted in the increased importance of tenancy. People known as *luneros* received the right to use hacienda land in return for the obligation to work each Monday for the *hacendado*. Moreover, the growth of landed estates allowed the royal government to abolish the *encomienda* (labor draft) in Yucatán, because the elite thereby acquired an economic base and no longer could argue that the *encomienda* was absolutely necessary for their survival.[6]

At the same time, the crown succeeded in abolishing the *repartimiento* (labor draft) system in Yucatán, Chiapas, and Central America. This was accomplished, however, in a paradoxical way: while the labor obligations of the *repartimiento* (which in southeastern Mesoamerica meant mostly the spinning of thread, weaving of textiles, or collecting raw cotton or wax) were being eliminated, villagers were made subject to a new—or rather very old but revived—labor exaction. Each village was thereafter required to provide a certain number of workers to labor on the expanding landed estates. This system, known as the *mandamiento*, produced revenues to supplement the salaries of the governors, *alcaldes mayores* (mayors), and *corregidores* (magistrates), who were permitted to charge the landowners for each worker so provided. The government officials, whose salaries were at the same time increased, thereafter no longer needed *repartimiento* income for their survival.[7]

After centuries, therefore, in many parts of Latin America the Indian population was finally responding in a major way to market forces, and sometimes a full-fledged labor market emerged. At the same time, in southeastern Mesoamerica the *repartimiento* system came to an end, a development made possible by demographic growth and the expansion of the landed estate in response to the growing internal demand for food. And for our purposes it is important to reiterate that these great social and economic changes were caused by internal factors that in no way resulted from the demands of the world economy.

One might object, as already noted, that the production of food is simply part of the process of subsistence and hence of little consequence compared to that of the great export-oriented landed estates. Yet, as also noted, in southeastern Mesoamerica the vast majority of the population belonged either to the indigenous economy or to haciendas producing for local markets and thus was engaged in activities not directly related to the export economy. The whole structure of production had come into existence for other purposes altogether. Moreover, it allowed to a certain extent for capital accumulation by the local landowners who produced for the growing markets for food. A similar situation permitted a large number of New England and Middle Atlantic farmers and merchants to make profits by selling produce to sugar producers in the Caribbean.[8] Yet this is often interpreted as an early example of the Yankee propensity toward commercial activities that eventually resulted in capital accumulation and industrialization. Would not the same have been true in Spanish America? Surely what is important, then, is not the final use of the product or the destination of production (local or distant markets for food) but rather the ability to take advantage of commercial opportunity and make money. This the landowners in Yucatán and Guatemala did. That capital accumulation did not later result in industrialization— although efforts in this direction were certainly made in Yucatán[9]—is due not to the "subsistence" nature of their activity but to the social and economic context in which it took place. The colonial heritage, in short, could very much impede England- and New England-style development.

II

The dependency interpretation, therefore, left indigenous structures of production out of the picture and as result tended to ignore a great deal of internal, autochthonous, or autonomous development. This is especially true in southeastern Mesoamerica, where export economies as important as those of Mexican or Andean silver and Brazilian or Caribbean sugar never emerged in the colonial period. Only coffee, which became significant in Central America and Chiapas in the second half of the nineteenth century, and henequen, the "green gold" of Yucatán during the Porfiriato, would result in dependency on the same scale as the colonial export economies of northern Mexico, the central Andes, and coastal Brazil.

Nevertheless, even in the so-called peripheral Kingdom of Guatemala and the Yucatán, exports historically played a role of great importance. Production of raw materials and primary products for European markets was a major goal of the Spanish colonists, for those goods, which contemporaries called "the lifeblood of commerce," were vital to connect the region to the Spanish world around it and to bring in the hard currency that allowed local people to accumulate money. At the same time, export economies in southeastern Mesoamerica and elsewhere in America served as markets for local goods produced by the indigenous people. These "backward linkages," as I shall call them, were not mentioned in the original formulations of the dependency interpretation, yet their existence and scale of operations in fact demonstrate that the "export syndrome" had a very deep impact even in areas dominated by an indigenous structure of production. In a sense, the dependency interpretation at times was more right than even its own exponents realized.

The export economies of southeastern Mesoamerica therefore had an important history. In the Yucatán, which at the time of the conquest produced nothing desired in Europe, colonists in the middle of the sixteenth century introduced indigo (*añil*) because of the world market's great demand for dyes. But the utilization of Mayas as laborers apparently contributed to the rapid decline of the indigenous population in the indigo-producing regions of the peninsula, and as a result the Franciscans fought to have the entire industry banned. It was, and *añil* quickly became insignificant.[10]

Thereafter the Yucatán's only significant export to Europe was logwood (*palo de tinte*). But in the producing regions of western Campeche and Belize there was an acute labor shortage because of the lack of a large Indian population and the expense of importing African slaves. Production levels thus were quite low for over a century after the conquest. Then, in the late seventeenth century English and French interlopers began exploiting good stands of logwood around the Laguna de Términos and in Belize, thereby provoking the Spaniards to expel them and take more interest in those regions. Shortly thereafter Campeche became a significant producer of the dye. Control of Belize, however, was beyond Spanish power, and thus the British eventually succeeded in establishing themselves in that region of difficult access. Throughout the entire colonial period, therefore, Spanish Yucatán exported little of importance to Europe other than the logwood of western Campeche.[11]

In the sixteenth century the preeminent export economy of the kingdom of Guatemala was cacao. This was produced in several regions along the Pacific coast: in Soconusco (Chiapas), Zapotitlán or San Antonio Suchitepéquez (southwestern Guatemala), and Sonsonate (western El Salvador). Spaniards acquired the beans by exacting them from the Indians, who maintained ownership of the groves and thus their own structure of production. Once European demand for chocolate began to increase significantly in the second half of the sixteenth century, exports and profits boomed. But since production depended absolutely on the native people, and since lowland areas became especially disease-ridden, the catastrophic Indian population decline of the sixteenth century resulted in an equally catastrophic decline of exports. Production never recovered from this disaster.[12] Nevertheless, enough people survived in the coastal areas to continue the industry, which remained profitable throughout the colonial period, albeit on a smaller scale. Once the kingdom's political magistracies began to be sold (in the late seventeenth century), those of the cacao-producing regions, especially the governorship of Soconusco, had high sales prices relative to many of the others.[13]

After the decline of cacao in the late sixteenth century, Spanish colonists in the Kingdom of Guatemala tried hard to find what some scholars have referred to as a *produit moteur*, that is, a product on which to base a prosperous export economy. Many things were tried, but most—such as balsam, achiote, gums, medicinal plants, vanilla, cochineal, and even smuggling—had at best limited success or were outright failures. Only two had a future. First, there was silver, found around Tegucigalpa and other places in highland Honduras. This industry started out promisingly enough in the sixteenth century but then fell into decline because of severe shortages of labor, capital, and mercury. It therefore never came to have the importance that it had in Mexico and Peru. Nevertheless, in the eighteenth century discoveries of new deposits led to a minor boom in production that helped maintain the links between the Kingdom of Guatemala and the outside world.[14]

Second, indigo was still in great demand in Europe and thus offered some hope for the future. It began to be produced in the sixteenth century and continued to grow in significance in the seventeenth, but it was only in the eighteenth that it came into its own and became "the lifeblood of commerce" of the Kingdom of Guatemala. Most production was centered in the *alcaldía mayor* of San Salvador (central and eastern El Salvador), although small amounts were also produced in Sonsonate and Nicaragua.[15]

Unfortunately for entrepreneurs, however, indigo was exceptionally vulnerable to natural disaster in the form of locusts. In the second half of the eighteenth century plagues of this insect periodically swept Mesoamerica from San Salvador all the way to Chiapas and the Yucatán. In the latter two regions it was the maize crop that was most affected, and the result was famine. In San Salvador the locusts were especially attracted to the *xiquilite* trees that produced indigo. Production was at times severely affected, and thus the region suffered the classic booms and busts typical of most export economies. The situation was especially bad at the turn of the century. Nevertheless, indigo was still the major export of the Kingdom of Guatemala until synthetic aniline dyes made it obsolete in the middle of the nineteenth century.[16]

Entrepreneurs in the eighteenth century continued to look for a *produit moteur* upon which to base an export economy. One of the most promising of these was cotton, which was indigenous to Mesoamerica and had long been used in textile production. The major producing areas were Verapaz (north-central Guatemala), western Nicaragua, northern Chiapas, and the Pacific coast of Guatemala (the *alcaldías mayores* of Escuintla and San Antonio Suchitepéquez). The crown itself took some interest in supplies of raw cotton because of its desire to stimulate industry in Spain, and consequently in 1747 it gave manufacturers in Mataró (Catalonia) the right to trade duty-free in Guatemalan cotton for four years. The raw material was to be shipped back to the factories in the mother country, while Catalan merchants would have the right to send ten registered ships with textiles to sell in Central America. Their activities were so successful at first that they began to squeeze out important local competitors.[17] Hence, long before the *Comercio Libre* of Charles III the Catalans had their eyes on commercial opportunities in America, including those in Central America.[18] However, they immediately ran up against opposition from Guatemalan merchants, who, as we shall see, had other ideas regarding markets for textiles and the uses of locally produced cotton.

Despite the existence of export economies based on logwood in western Campeche, silver in Honduras, and indigo in San Salvador, southeastern Mesoamerica's participation in overall Spanish American exports to Europe was relatively small. As already noted, most people worked in structures of production that were oriented toward markets that were mostly local or regional rather than European. This would mean at first sight that exports, and hence the "export syndrome," were not very important. This, however, is not the case. The problem is that most of the scholars who studied the economic history of the region—myself included—reached this conclusion by focusing exclusively on exports to Europe.[19] In fact, this meant looking in the wrong direction. When the whole Spanish American economy, rather than just ties to Europe, is considered, the role of exports suddenly assumes importance. In reality, southeastern Mesoamerica, like a large number of regions, was tied into a network of consumption and production for export. It is not important that most of those ties were with America rather than with Europe.

Export economies are par excellence entities of economic specialization that function within a world system of division of labor. A simplified way of interpreting this is that of Immanuel Wallerstein, who argued that Latin America was assigned the role of producer of raw materials and primary products for the European industrial core, and that to carry out this function Europeans in America used forced labor systems; Latin America thus carried out "coerced cash-crop" production, an interpretation already predicted in the dependency interpretation.[20] But as Steve Stern has shown, this is a misleading generalization, among other reasons because it ignores the complexity of the solutions reached outside the so-called industrial core—solutions that were reached through the active participation of the laborers themselves and that were not simply examples of forced labor.[21]

The historical reality thus is not so simple, and the complexity of economic integration into the world economy is partly revealed by the example of southeastern Mesoamerica. It should be remembered that all entities of economic specialization generate not only production but also demand. The effects of a market the size of Potosí—one of the largest cities in the world by the early seventeenth century—can readily be imagined. In southeastern Mesoamerica, of course, no such metropolis existed until the twentieth century. Nevertheless, the cities and exporting centers—the former allowed to grow larger because of the existence of the latter—were significant markets that consumed a plethora of goods. And just as importantly, the cities and exporting centers beyond the Yucatán, Chiapas, and Central America were also important consumers of goods produced in southeastern Mesoamerica.

Foodstuffs are the most obvious goods needed everywhere, and thus all cities and exporting centers generated considerable demand for grains, vegetables, meat, and so forth. As Eric Van Young, Carlos Sempat Assadourian, and I, among others, have shown, cities developed important hinterlands of provisioning that often brought in goods from within a wide radius.[22] Mérida was one such marketing area in southeastern Mesoamerica, as was Santiago de los Caballeros (and later its successor, Guatemala City). The *audiencia* capital in fact received most of its grains for consumption not from the Valley of Guatemala (surrounding Santiago) but from the more distant and mountainous provinces of Atitlán (Sololá), Quezaltenango, and Huehuetenango.[23] The sheer size of urban centers like Mérida and Santiago was due in part, of course, not to their importance as producers of exports but to their position as political and commercial capitals whose merchants controlled the movement of goods in all directions. On the other hand, San Salvador was a producing region that was so specialized that it had to import practically all its cattle from Nicaragua to provide its cities and towns with meat.[24]

Nevertheless, the goods demanded in export centers and cities that were most important in effecting the economic integration of provincial, regional, imperial, and world economies were textiles. Since in their finished form they combined the agricultural labor of planting and harvesting, with the manufacturing labor of carding (in the case of woolens), spinning, dying, and weaving, they were high value items. Consequently, unlike many foodstuffs, they could be transported great distances without causing transport costs to inflate prohibitively retail prices. Moreover, they were much more durable than foodstuffs and thus not as subject to spoilage, and they could be stored in warehouses for long periods of time. Finally, they were useful. Cottons in particular had advantages over wool in that they were more comfortable in warm climates and easier to wash. As a result, even before the Industrial Revolution they were important in the so-called "Country Trade" of southern Asia, were important exports to Africa that Europeans sold but did not produce, were carried on the *Nao de Manila* (Manila ship)[25] from the Philippines to Acapulco, and were already being marketed in Great Britain and Europe. World demand, in short, was already well established. The English entrepreneurs of the Industrial Revolution, therefore, did not have to create demand for their goods; that had already been established. England's accomplishment was to manufacture them cheaper and better.

The cotton manufacture of the era before the Industrial Revolution was therefore extensive. Southeastern Mesoamerica was one of the major producing *and* exporting regions. In fact, the production and marketing

of textiles was one of the major sectors of the economy.[26] Spanish
colonists and merchants tapped the already existing indigenous structure of production primarily through the institutions of tribute, religious
taxes, and—most importantly—the *repartimiento* system. Then—and
this is what is most significant—the textiles were shipped for sale in
cities and export-producing centers. In southeastern Mesoamerica this
meant the silver-mining region of Honduras and above all else indigo-
producing San Salvador and Sonsonate (modern-day El Salvador). The
latter, in fact, were voracious consumers of cotton cloth, because most
local available land had been devoted almost exclusively to the *xiquilite*
trees. Practically everything needed for survival had to be imported.

This resulted in the economic integration of the Yucatán and the
Kingdom of Guatemala into the Spanish American and world
economies. The cotton-producing regions, especially Nicaragua, Verapaz,
northern lowland Chiapas, and eastern Yucatán, provided the indigenous
villages throughout southeastern Mesoamerica with the raw material
that was then spun and woven into cloth. The huge quantity of textile
production in the highland Maya regions (Chiapas, Quezaltenango,
Huehuetenango, Atitlán, and Verapaz itself), in the Yucatán, and to a
lesser extent in some Nahua areas (Chiquimula de la Sierra,
Acasaguastlán, and Zacapa in eastern Guatemala and in western
Nicaragua), which made the magistracies there valuable posts to the
entrepreneurial-minded officials who bought them, was in fact a backward linkage of the export economies and cities that grew larger as a
result of the export economies. The Yucatán and Chiapas, far from isolated from the world economy, served as export platforms that sent cotton thread to Puebla and textiles to Mexico City and to the northern
Mexican mining camps.[27]

The Mayas, consequently, were anything but isolated from the world
economy. They were major industrial producers and exporters. The
demand for cotton textiles generated by the cities and exporting regions
of Mexico and Central America was so great that even Asia was brought
into the network as a producer. Merchants in the Philippines took
advantage of this demand by purchasing cottons in India and China, and
then sending them across the Pacific on the Manila Ship. They even
found markets in America for raw cotton.[28]

By the middle of the eighteenth century Guatemalan entrepreneurs
were so aware of their export opportunities and the marketability of
textiles that in 1748 they formed a commercial corporation, called the
Company of Guatemala, to exploit them. They planned to eliminate

their Catalan competitors, monopolize local supplies of raw cotton, import goods from China, provide the mining camps with cloth and imported mercury, and send as many *ropas de la tierra*—American-made cotton textiles—to New Spain as the king would allow. In addition, the merchants hoped to provide the growing internal market with cloth, for, as President Joseph Vázquez Prego pointed out in 1752, local people consumed little or no European-made textiles; practically all were American-made. Within two years the Guatemalan entrepreneurs had raised 675,000 pesos from shareholders—a fortune in Central America at that time.[29]

The Company of Guatemala failed to accomplish all of its goals. Increasing production to meet all the demand proved to be difficult, and in fact by the 1770s Guatemala was actually importing light cotton textiles from China, although it continued to send American-made cloth to New Spain. The merchants who engaged in the importing business referred to it as "one of the most flourishing and important branches" of their commerce, and therefore fought successfully to prevent the crown from banning Asian imports.[30] The demand for textiles, in short, was apparently insatiable in both Mexico and Central America. It is no wonder, therefore, that Spanish and then Central American leaders took measures to protect their economy once British merchants started showing up with large quantities of cheaper and better cotton cloth in the early nineteenth century.[31]

The structures of production that carried out textile production in southeastern Mesoamerica were almost entirely indigenous. The sexual division of labor existing before the arrival of Europeans continued in the colonial period: men and boys planted, harvested, and transported the cotton; women and girls did the spinning and weaving using their traditional back-strap looms. Spaniards introduced wool and woolen production techniques, but most locally made cloth was of cotton and hence nothing new was needed. Here, then, we have the important intersection of the export economies with the previously mentioned indigenous structures of production left out of the dependency interpretation. In fact, the former required the latter, learned to use it, and adapted to it. It is of course well known that the colonial regime used to its advantage previously existing labor systems, such as the infamous *mita* of Peru (although the system of forced labor for the silver and mercury mines of the Andes was so exploitative that it provoked considerable social change and resulted in the emergence of paid-wage labor in the mines—all of which demonstrates just how little the *mita* had in common with precolonial labor systems).[32] What is less known is the ability of colonists to exploit the indigenous textile industry for all it was worth, in Peru as well as in Mesoamerica.

It is also important to note that the labor system employed in textiles production in southeastern Mesoamerica was coercive in nature. It was an important component of tribute and was the basis of the *repartimiento*, which consisted of advances of credit—usually in the form of payment of tribute in arrears but sometimes for goods forcibly sold—in return for repayment in cotton or woven cloth at a later time. The Mayas and Nahuas had no choice in the matter, and flogging was sometimes employed on those who failed to deliver and even on recalcitrant *caciques* who failed to cooperate as the Spaniards desired. Consequently, even though the industrial organization was similar to that of the European putting-out system, in the Yucatán, Chiapas, and Central America this was a putting-out system maintained by the repressive power of the state. This was made clear at the time. In 1749 President of the Audiencia Joseph de Araujo defended the *repartimiento* carried out by *corregidores, alcaldes mayores*, and governors, arguing that it was "necessary that commerce be accompanied by authority, because without sales to be paid for, not in cash but in kind, over a period of six to twelve months or in personal labor, the private merchant would not be able to sell because he lacks the authority to collect."[33] Colonialism and concomitant coercion were intrinsic parts of the system.

Nevertheless, textile production was not new. Indeed, the Mayas had paid tribute in cotton cloth and even exported it to Mexico long before the arrival of Europeans in America. Spaniards therefore merely incorporated an existing structure of production into the colonial system. However, the Mayas apparently did not believe that the colonial regime was as legitimate as their own preconquest independent states, and therefore they cooperated less and resorted to the typical "weapons of the weak" (foot dragging, dissimulation, false compliance, pilfering, feigned ignorance, slander, arson, sabotage, and so forth) to resist their colonial rulers.[34] The latter in turn, lacking the authority resulting from legitimacy, needed to resort to naked coercion to accomplish their goals, in this case the production of textiles. But in practice the best way to accomplish this was to change the Indians as little as possible. As a result, colonialism accepted the survival of the indigenous structure of production, while the Mayas thereby retained the economic basis of their survival as a culturally distinct people. Exploitation meant that the textile-producing magistracies and governorships of southeastern

Mesoamerica sold for large sums of money, but it did not end up destroying the people who did the work.

The history of the Yucatán, Chiapas, and Central America thus demonstrates that in practice the indigenous structures of production not merely provided the basis for autochthonous or autonomous development but also became part and parcel of the great export economies that tied Latin America to the world economy. Far from being a region forced into coerced cash-crop production for the industrial core of the European-dominated world economy, southeastern Mesoamerica was a major industrial producer in its own right. In fact, the Yucatán, Chiapas, and Guatemala became not *less* but rather *more* industrial as time went on. Only the Industrial Revolution, the impact of which was not felt until the nineteenth century, would reverse the process.

In turn, raw materials, primary products, and above all silver flowed out of Latin America. These, however, went not just to western Europe. The economies of China, India, Persia, and the Ottoman Empire were all greatly affected by the influx of precious metals from America, while at the same time Indians and Chinese found markets for their cotton textiles in America. The impact of Latin America's great export economies, therefore, cannot be measured simply by focusing on the producing regions.[35] Rather, those economies were engines of production that produced backward linkages stretching from the Mexican, Peruvian, and Honduran mining camps and Salvadoran indigo plantations to the Maya region and all the way across the Pacific. Dependency may not always have resulted. Nevertheless, the effects of the "export syndrome" were historically deep.

At the same time, however, the survival of the indigenous structure of production into the modern era was a colonial heritage that helped lead to underdevelopment. In 1800, of course, it was by no means clear that this would be the case, for the devastating impact of the Industrial Revolution could not have been foreseen. Instead, looking at southeastern Mesoamerica as the struggle for independence broke out, one might have concluded that the per capita income generated by incorporation into the world economy as an exporter of textiles, silver, and indigo would have provided a solid basis on which to build the postindependence economy. Certainly the leaders of the independence movements had a very optimistic view of their countries' future. But the textile industry's reliance on coerced labor and pre-Hispanic technology doomed the sector to virtual extinction in the face of foreign competition. This, in turn, led to increased political conflict, as the factors integrating the colonial Central American economy were replaced by those causing disintegration. Regions were no longer tied to each other by common interest and soon fought to defend themselves. The Central American Confederation collapsed, while the Yucatán, whose ties to Mexico had been severely weakened by the collapse of textile exports, followed a historical path that frequently led to separatism.

This process of Balkanization not only resulted in the creation of countries with internal markets too small to support modern industry but it also meant increased pauperization, as long-standing patterns of trade and production collapsed. All too often Latin America's long nineteenth-century economic depression has been attributed to the violence and destruction of the struggle for independence. Yet in practice this was frequently just as much the result of the collapse of trading relationships that had been established in the colonial era but that could not survive in the postcolonial world economic order. The results were sharply declining standards of living, which of course impeded any industrial recovery. By the time the economy had "bottomed out," Latin America was far behind western Europe and North America and has been trying to catch up ever since. In southeastern Mesoamerica the only way out seemed to be the liberal policy of exporting primary products. So were founded the banana republics (in reality producers of coffee) and the henequen plantations.

But again it should be noted that the failures of the nineteenth century could not have been predicted in 1800. By the end of the colonial era the economies of southeastern Mesoamerica had not been relegated to the position of monocultural producers of raw materials and primary products. Dependency, in short, had not followed inevitably from export promotion and incorporation into the world economy. Underdevelopment did not seem to be just around the corner. The key factor that led in that direction was the Industrial Revolution, which involved significant social change and a leap forward in technology. That leap, which surprised Englishmen as much as anyone else, left Latin America behind for good.[36] The colonial heritage in southeastern Mesoamerica—industry based on coerced labor and pre-Hispanic technology and society consisting of antagonistic classes separated by race and ethnicity—then insured that comparable social change and techological development would not take place. Earlier incorporation into the world economy as an industrial producer thus neither served as a stage to modern industry nor protected society from the new world of industrial capitalism. On the contrary, it became one of the many paths to underdevelopment that Latin America followed into the present.

seven

Agriculture and the Colonial Heritage of Latin America: Evidence from Bourbon Mexico[1]

Richard J. Salvucci

INTRODUCTION: STRUCTURES OF DEPENDENCE IN AN OPEN ECONOMY?

For the past twenty-five years, a prominent way of viewing Latin American economic history has been through the lens of dependency. As one analyst has suggested, dependency thinking is part of a family of economic models in which poverty and economic progress are explained by a single cause: the nature of exploitation inherent in a capitalist system.[2] The structures of a dependent economy must therefore be those social, political, and economic characteristics that facilitate the extraction and transfer of surplus.[3] Since the economy has an export bias, growth produces a rapid increase in the supply of exportables. Trade is thus "unequal," in the sense that the terms of trade for these exportables must deteriorate. In this vein, deep structures of unequal exchange and the resilience of anticapitalist forces are treated as obstacles to sustained development.

It would be tedious to rehearse the ways in which Bourbon Mexico, the subject of this essay, fit—or did not exactly fit—such a stylized picture. Yet even so, a few observations are in order. The Mexican economy *was* surprisingly open, much as the dependency story would have it. John Coatsworth calculated that visible trade as a share of gross domestic product was 8.1 percent in 1800 which is very respectable.[4] As late as 1830, the Spanish trade coefficient was a modest 5.6 percent. The French coefficient was no more than 7.5 percent.[5] Mexico's participation in the international economy was limited only by comparison to the United Kingdom, whose trade coefficient was an astounding 21.5 percent.

Yet Mexico's *open* economy was largely its *silver* economy. Javier Ortiz de la Tabla concluded that silver accounted for more than 70 percent of the value of exports through Veracruz from 1796 to 1820.[6] This implies that exports other than silver were only about 1.2 percent of gross domestic product (i.e., 30 percent of 4.1 percent). If in 1800, as Fernando Rosenzweig observed, the Valenciana mine of Guanajuato accounted for 25 percent of all the silver New Spain produced in the late eighteenth century, then *one mine* produced nearly 20 percent of late colonial Mexico's exports (i.e., 25 percent of 70 percent).[7] It is one thing to say that Guanajuato was closely tied to the international economy but quite another to say that "Mexico" was.

On the import side, a similar picture emerges. Imports were hardly trivial, but they were mostly consumed in the larger cities. Juan Carlos Garavaglia and Juan Carlos Grosso have given us some data on excise taxes that can be crudely interpreted as yielding the share of imports in total consumption. I have rearranged some of their data for Puebla and New Spain, which appears in Table 1.

The share of imports in consumption was about three times as large in the city of Puebla as it was in small-town Tepeaca in 1789. If urban Puebla's share is typical, then the share of imports in rural consumption in Mexico in 1796 must have been less than 30 percent. The reason is that New Spain had few large cities of which to speak. Cities of 10,000 or more accounted for no more than 7.6 percent of the population, in 1790, or perhaps as little as 5 percent.[8] By contrast the European proportion in 1800 was 10 percent, or about a third higher. In this respect Mexico was more like Europe in 1600, or even 1500.[9] Such limited urbanization is itself quite revealing, and I want to return to its implications later.

Table 1

Percent of *Alcabala* in New Spain Charged on Imports

Year	New Spain	Tepeaca	Puebla (District)	Puebla (City)
1789	13.6%	26%	37.2%	
1796	28.9%			

SOURCE: Juan Carlos Garavaglia and Juan Carlos Grosso, *Las alcabalas novo-hispanas (1776–1821)* (Mexico: Archivo General de la Nación, 1987), 48, 5053. Juan Carlos Garavaglia and Juan Carlos Grosso, *Puebla desde una perspectiva microhistórica*, 90–95.

Even imports of British cottons, which had a profound impact on Mexican production, need to be kept in perspective. In 1827 Mexico imported more than thirteen million yards of cottons or about two yards per person, about enough for what David Eltis calls a "wrapper." That's a lot of cloth, but in 1828 and 1829 the volume of imports fell to about half of what it had been in 1827. In fact, Charles Mackenzie's 1824 consular report from Veracruz agrees, adding that "the annual value of the native manufactures of wool and cotton amount to a sum nearly equal to that of all the imports from every other part of the world [i.e., mostly Great Britain]."10

Looking at the *structures of dependence* mostly in terms of tradable goods is therefore not the whole story, at least in the late colonial period. Production for domestic use (i.e., nontraded goods) must also be an important part of our story. In 1800 Mexico was a rural, agrarian country, so we should examine agriculture for other evidences of the operation of a "colonial heritage."11 Yet these criticisms should not detract from the accomplishment of some of the work of dependency writers, for hindsight makes for facile judgments. This earlier emphasis on the importance of the external sector was hardly unusual. Such concerns even prevailed in the study of the United States. Douglass North, for instance, argued that "the timing and pace of an economy's development is determined by (1) the success of its export sector, and (2) the characteristics of the export industry and the disposition of the income received from the export sector"12 (Somehow, you never think of North as a *dependentista*.)

FISCAL "OTHERS" OR DIRT POOR?

In the nineteenth century foreign observers generally thought that the wealth of Mexico was being dissipated by poor government. Here was a land that would prosper under better, presumably foreign, rulers. Diplomats from the United States were especially given to invidious comparisons. From Joel Poinsett to Waddy Thompson, these envoys took a dim view of Mexican fiscal practices. Poinsett, prior to getting himself declared persona non grata by the Mexican government, wrote that "partly from ignorance and partly from villainy the finances of the country have been suffered to fall into the greatest disorder. The system adopted [in 1828 and 1829] would have ruined *my country*."[13] Thompson commented that "The government [of Mexico] seems to have been engaged in the experiment of how much taxation the people can bear, and they [*sic*] have really achieved a miracle almost as great as that of extracting blood from a turnip."[14] Poinsett and Thompson were saying little that Mexicans had not said earlier or better. For example, at the Cortes of Cádiz in 1811, Melchor Foncerrada, who had served as a judge of the Audiencia of Mexico, complained that Spain's incessant demands for funds had sucked the viceroyalty dry: "The famous wealth of its mines could not keep up with the drainage of money, money that, like lifeblood, should be left to circulate. New Spain was rich, but it has become poor."[15] Here is a sentiment that an entire generation of historians—Richard Garner, Carlos Marichal, Claude Morin, and Stanley Stein and Barbara Stein[16]—could echo. For those of liberal bent, there are the words of Mora: "No people on earth profits less from its government than the Mexican people," he concluded, "and no other pays such excessive taxes to obtain those benefits." Hence "Mexico failed to progress, and plunged daily deeper into the abyss."[17]

Such observations are striking and all are undoubtedly true. Who could disagree? Metropolitan Spain was appropriating large and growing quantities of Mexican savings in the eighteenth century. Governments in the early nineteenth century were improvident. Commercial policy for most of the century was incoherent, not to say suicidal. Defaulting on the foreign debt had serious consequences, even if default was inevitable. As long as the British (and other) bondholders were unhappy, no one would lend Mexico much of anything. Mounting political disorder made investment very risky. Chaotic institutions and property rights that scandalized Britons, Spaniards, and Yankees persuaded potential traders to look elsewhere. Mexicans became financial and commercial "others" whose conduct literally defined what was impermissible under the evolving rules of the international capitalist game. Yet our fascination with these issues obscures a logical dilemma. Can large disorders in what was surely the smaller financial and commercial sector of the Mexican economy explain its overall failure to grow? Do big disturbances in areas of modest importance matter? In Mexico—in any agrarian economy—agriculture rather than public finance, trade, or even manufacturing, leads the way.[18] Was it, perhaps, that Mexico's agriculture lagged, and that it was "dirt poor"? Was there then a "colonial heritage" in Mexican agriculture that represented a drag on overall economic performance?

I am not the only person to raise the question. I am hardly the *first* person to raise it. Adam Smith mocked what he saw as the crudely bullionist philosophy of the Spaniards in *The Wealth of Nations*. Yet the passage I am about to cite is not by Adam Smith, but by Adolphe Thiers, who was talking explicitly about Mexico. Thiers uses bizarre statistics. He is tendentious and bombastic, sounding for all the world like Monsieur Lieuvain at the country fair in *Madame Bovary*. Yet Thiers raises a crucial question: Is a country wealthy because it has mines? In January 1864, during the debate over the French "expedition" to Mexico in support of Maximillian, Thiers, who criticized the adventure, offered the following instructive commentary.[19]

"At the end of the last century," Thiers began, "Mexico was reputed to be enormously wealthy. And why? Because Spain, through its colonies, produced 90 percent of the world's precious metal. You would think that most of it came from Mexico alone." Thiers continued, "When Humboldt was writing, around 1803, when Mexico was so prosperous, do you know what Mexico grew? No more, surely, than what they grow today? 145 million a year!"[20] "Think of that," he said, "in comparison to what French agriculture produces. People say it's 6, 7, or 8 billion a year. So, according to Monsieur Humboldt, Mexico produced crops worth 145 million when this century started." Thiers continued derisively, "But it has mines, you say! The mines could yield 120 or 130 million. Well, those mines you go on so much about, they're wealth all right, but the wrong kind." And so, "When you talk about a country being rich because it's got silver or gold, you're not being serious." Thiers concluded, "That's why Mexico, with agriculture of around 150 million and mining of 120 to 140 million—around 300 million all told—has a trade, imports and exports combined, of no more than 130 million, of which we have 20 million." The point is well taken and well worth exploring. Was Mexican agriculture poor? If so, how poor was it? Why was it poor, if it was? And what difference did agricultural impoverishment make to overall levels of development? To answer these questions, we need to have some idea of just where Mexico stood in 1800.

ROADS NOT TAKEN

We conventionally say that Mexico was relatively wealthier at the beginning of the nineteenth century than by 1850. The comparatively high level of Mexican per capita income in 1800 is the basis for the statement. John Coatsworth concluded that the ratio of Mexican to United States or British per capita income was higher around 1800 than at anytime thereafter. So Mexican underdevelopment "originated" in the nineteenth century, if only in the sense of the appearance of a now irreducible gap between productivity in Mexico and the other economies with which Coatsworth compared it.[21]

Per capita income tells something about a country's relative economic performance but not everything. International income comparisons are often misleading and high per capita income levels do not resolve matters of equity or overall well-being. A society's level of development encompasses more than per capita income. In Table 2, I present some evidence of the level of Mexican development in 1800. For comparison, I use Hollis Chenery and Moises Syrquin's extremely influential *Patterns of Development 1950–1970*. Chenery and Syrquin examined the development transition and calculated the measurable characteristics of countries at different income levels. In essence, in Table 2 I measure Mexico's performance as a developing country against Chenery and Syrquin's "typical" structural characteristics.

This comparison is extremely crude. By modern standards, the Mexican data is inevitably incomplete and some of it is surely incorrect. More importantly, Chenery and Syrquin worked with data from the twentieth century, not the nineteenth. The cost of communication and transportation were considerably higher in 1800 than in 1950 and the international economy was less integrated. Poor countries now benefit from the diffusion of modern medicine and enjoy characteristically lower mortality rates than in the past, even though they are poor. Economists have identified at least a half dozen factors that account for substantially higher levels of urbanization in the late twentieth century.[22] The world of the poor country is simply not what it was in 1800. Nicholas Crafts was able to compensate somewhat for these differences in his study of British industrialization. Unfortunately, his results are too limited to be of much use. So too are Leandro Prados's calculations for Spain.[23] I must employ the Chenery and Syrquin estimates as the best alternative available.

Table 2

Mexico: Development Indicators After Chenery-Syrquin Per Capita Income in 1970 Dollars (Shares of GDP, unless otherwise noted)

	Mexico at $118	Chenery-Syrquin at Less Than $125
Urbanization	6.3% population	12.8% population
Income Distribution Highest 20 %	36.0%	50.2%
Exports	8.1%	17.2%
Private Consumption	79.6%	77.9%
Food Consumption	79.5%	41.4%
Crude Birth Rate	51.4 per thousand	45.9 per thousand
Crude Death Rate	39.6 per thousand	20.9 per thousand

SOURCES: Chenery-Syrquin: Hollis Chenery and Moises Syrquin, *Patterns of Development, 1950–1970* (New York: Oxford University Press, 1975), 20–21, adjusted for price changes.

For Mexico, as follows. *Urbanization:* The average proportion of people living in cities of 10,000 or more, according to Pescador, "Patrones demográficos," 117, 148. *Income Distribution:* Proportion of income received by top 20 percent of families in Manuel Abad y Queipo, "Representación sobre la inmunidad del clero," in *Colección de los escritos más importantes que en diferentes épocas dirigió al gobierno* (México, 1813), 57–58. Abad y Queipo put New Spain's population at 4.5 million, which is plausible, but much less than Humboldt's 5.8 million. Humboldt's estimate is the standard one, so I employed it accordingly, but I followed Abad y Queipo's usage in setting family size at five. The groupings were suggested to me by Rosenzweig, "La economía novohispana," 31–33. *Exports:* Coatsworth, "Decline of the Mexican Economy," 50. *Private Consumption:* This is the result of dividing José María Quirós's estimate of per capita consumption by Coatsworth's estimate of per capita income, expressed in 1970 prices. For Quirós's estimate, see Charles T. O'Gorman, "Translation of the Politico-Mercantile Remarks at the foot of the Balanza de Comercio of the Port of Veracruz for

25 years from the year 1796—México," 1 March 1825, FO 203/3. *Food Consumption:* Calculated from "Para vestir a la plebe de la Ciudad de Mexico: 1790–92," BN, Sección de Libros Raros, MS 15 [1338] f/29. *Crude Birth Rate:* Sherburne F. Cook and Woodrow Borah, "Crude Birth Rates in Mexico, 1700–1965," in Essays in Population History 3 vols. (Berkeley and Los Angeles: University of California Press, 1971–79) 2: 296, birth rate data for the Mixteca Alta, 1740–1800; *Crude Death Rate:* Claude Morin, *Santa Inés Zacatelco,* 89.

Those interested in comparative data for 1850 may consult Luis González, *Todo es historia* (Mexico D.F.: Cal y Canto, 1989), 98-99. González suggests that 80 percent of the population was in agriculture and that the rate of urbanization was 10 percent. His statistics for the crude birth and death rates around 1850 are 40 and 30 per thousand, respectively.

In some ways, Mexico in 1800 fits Chenery and Syrquin's distribution of characteristics for a country with per capita income of less than $125 (1970 dollars) surprisingly well. The share of private consumption in gross domestic product is nearly identical, 79.6 percent versus 77.9 percent. The crude birth rate (51.4 per thousand) is drawn from Sherburne Cook and Woodrow Borah's careful study of the Mixteca. It is close to the Chenery and Syrquin's estimate, 45.9 per thousand. It is nearly identical to David Brading's figure (51.5 per thousand) for León, Guanajuato, and close to Claude Morin's for Zacatelco.[24] The income distribution statistic is off, but that is not surprising. Manuel Abad y Queipo, who could have only been guessing, is my source for the calculations. The share of exports in gross domestic product for Mexico is low by modern standards, but as we suggested, consistent with nineteenth-century experience.

There are some telling differences in urbanization, the share of food consumption in gross domestic product, and in the crude death rate. Mexico's urbanization was quite low by modern standards, but as we said, it was low by contemporary European norms as well. The share of food consumption in gross domestic product, 79.5 percent is a problem. It is virtually identical to the share of private consumption in domestic product. This implies that Mexicans spent all their income on food, which is impossible. After all, there was some industry, which means people bought more than food! Yet virtually every effort to estimate consumption in the late eighteenth century points in the same direction.[25] Spending on food was the major "expense" for most Mexicans. For many, it must have been the only one. This has always been true. A study carried out by the Banco de México in 1963 concluded that poor families spent 62.5 percent of their monthly income on food.[26] It is hard to see how the share could have been much lower in 1800. The crude death rate in Mexico (39.6 per thousand) is twice as high as the Chenery and Syrquin estimate (20.9 per thousand). Since it is calculated for Zacatelco, a rural parish between Puebla and Tlaxcala, the death rate is probably low. Urban death rates were much higher. For instance, the average crude death rate for Guadalajara from 1823 to 1852 was 50.02 per thousand, which is nearly the same as the crude birth rate.[27] Cities in New Spain grew by virtue of migration, not by natural increase. A reasonable estimate for the overall crude death rate in the eighteenth century is a little more than 40 per thousand.

In other words, Mexico, considered as a low-income country in 1800, appears reasonably typical in all but two or three respects: the proportion of income spent on food; the rate of mortality; and the degree of urbanization. Admittedly the indicators are very imprecise. Future research will undoubtedly modify them. Yet, at the very least, they suggest an interesting hypothesis. If the relative productivity of Mexican agriculture were atypically low, the relative price of foodstuffs would be higher. People would have spent a larger part of their income on food than we might otherwise expect. Urbanization lagged because without food surpluses, city dwellers, who grow no food, cannot survive. When food supplies were tight, subsistence crises were more likely, since shocks, like bad weather, disrupted an already fragile balance between food and people. Finally, industrialization was limited. If people spent most of their income on food, they did not have much left over to pay for wage goods like cloth and shoes. My hypothesis—and given the data we have, it can be only a hypothesis—is that low agricultural productivity accounts for the indicators we have. And even if Mexico were no more than *typical* in levels of productivity, the onus for explaining "obstacles" to Mexican development or industrialization falls mainly on agriculture, at least as a first approximation. Commercial policy, trade flows, capital markets, the public debt, and political instability have a necessary role in explaining the fundamental colonial heritage of poor economic performance in its various guises: growth, development, and distribution. But even taken together, I would be surprised to find that they explained more than a small part of what needs to be explained.

The idea that Mexican agriculture "failed" in some sense in the late eighteenth century is not new. Yet the shape of the retardation, its mechanism, or even its possibly "Malthusian" character, remain obscure.[28] What, for example, would a Malthusian model look like? A very simple one, proposed by David Weir, appears in Figure 1.[29] Weir suggests we imagine an expansion in cultivated land that shifts the production function to the right. Rising per capita income raises fertility, depresses mortality, and results in natural increase. Since classical economics postulated diminishing returns, rising population drives down the standard of living (the real wage) once more, until the equilibrium between fertility (Malthus's preventive check) and mortality (Malthus's positive check) is restored.

Testing a model even as simple as this one is hardly trivial. The demographic and economic data we currently have are not equal to the task. In Table 3, I take an informal approach and present calculations for Mexican real wages (in terms of maize) at fifty-year intervals to emphasize long-run change. Even allowing for spotty data, the results are not reassuring. For instance, the urban real wage first rises and then falls back over the century, just as Weir's model predicts. Unfortunately, a more comprehensive measure that includes rural labor does not. Moreover, since silver production *and* population were growing, to what should we attribute changes in real wages? To money wages and prices that rose as a vastly increased money stock did? To the pressure from demand of more mouths to feed? To the increase in labor supply that population growth implies? To some combination of all of these? At this level, it is impossible to tell.

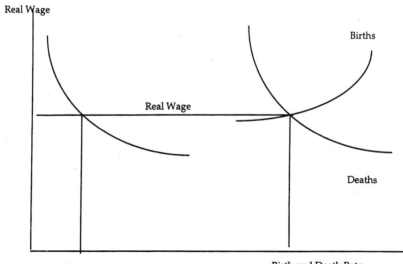

Table 3
Measures of Real Wages in New Spain, 1700–1800

Decade	Urban Wage	All Wages	Real Urban wages	Real All Wages	Maize Prices
1700/09	6.00	4.20	0.71	0.51	8.43
1750/59	5.63	2.80	1.60	0.80	3.50
1800/09	8.32	6.18	1.36	0.94	6.11

SOURCE: Richard Garner, *Economic Growth and Change in Bourbon Mexico*, appendix 2, using colonywide average annual maize prices and wage data by various categories. The real or maize equivalent wage is the ratio of the money wage to the price of maize

This is hardly the only problem. Population change is not independent of changes in food prices. Assuming that population growth will depress real wages by driving up maize prices leaves a very loose end. Rising maize prices will depress population growth, as studies in historical demography have found. What would the result on real wages then be? Population increase creates offsetting economic factors.

In Table 4, I explore this issue by using David Brading's demographic data for León, Guanajuato. I constructed a variable called *natural increase* by subtracting burials from births using Brading's five-year intervals. I then regressed this natural increase on the average price of maize, as well as on two lags of maize prices, i.e., the two preceding five-year averages. As maize prices rise, they depress natural increase and indeed would have magnified the effect of a previous increase. To make matters worse, natural increase in León did *not* drive up maize prices. It drove them down! Brading explains exactly why. There was a substantial increase in land under cultivation after 1731 in the area. That land could be worked precisely because there were more people to work it. Even though there were more mouths to feed, there was far more maize with which to feed them. Population change *alone* cannot explain changes in the price level in eighteenth-century León.[30]

Table 4
The Impact of Maize Prices on Natural Increase And Vice Versa

Dependent Variable: Natural Increase (Births-Burials)

Independent Variables:

Constant	6764.24
Maize Price Lag 0	-261.77*
Maize Price Lag 1	-310.15**
Maize Price Lag 2	174.77
Sum of lags	-397.15
Adjusted R^2	.89
DW	2.36
F Ratio	14.38
SEE	621.80

*Significant at 95%
**Significant at 90%

Dependent Variable: Maize Price

Independent Variables:

Constant	16.590
Natural Increase	-0.003*
Adjusted R^2	.65
DW	3.09
F Ratio	13.74
SEE	2.96

*Significant at 99%

SOURCE: D. A. Brading, *Haciendas and Ranchos*, 52, 54, 180–83.

Population density poses a final puzzle. In 1519 the population density of what William T. Sanders calls the "Central Mexican Symbiotic

Region"[31] was certainly no less than about 138 per km², and if one accepts the Cook and Borah estimates of precontact population, it was considerably higher. The average population density of the intendancies of Mexico and Puebla in 1803 was about 14.1 km².[32] Even granting that the intendancies were much more thinly populated than the area to which Sanders makes reference, it is difficult to understand how population pressure per se could produce a reduction in agricultural productivity by the end of the eighteenth century.[33] Something else must have been at work as well. Sanders vaguely alludes to "social and economic institutions of the seventeenth [and] eighteenth centuries which resulted in a consolidation of small, intensively cultivated holdings into large, extensively cultivated ones." Mac Chapin, in referring to contemporary difficulties in reviving the chinampa system of cultivation uses very similar language: "In pre-Hispanic times [systems of intensive agriculture such as the chinampa] thrived in the Valley of Mexico because the social, political, economic, and environmental circumstances were favorable."[34] Here I propose to turn to a stylized examination of the durable *institutions* and *circumstances—structures*, if you like—that explain various aspects of Mexican agricultural and economic performance in the eighteenth century.

MODELS OF DEVELOPMENT, STRUCTURES OF DEPENDENCY

In 1974 Jan de Vries published a pathbreaking account of rural economic development in the Netherlands, *The Dutch Rural Economy in the Golden Age, 1500–1700*.[35] While the book's title is not misleading, de Vries actually proposed an extensive framework within which to analyze the economic development of rural society in early modern Europe. His approach drew on the work of Stephen Hymer and Stephen Resnick, who proposed a model of an agrarian economy in which families produced both agricultural and nonagricultural goods.[36] Hymer and Resnick's formal model is complex and de Vries used a modified version of it. Yet the intuition guiding their reasoning is clear.

Suppose that, in the absence of trade, rural families produce two kinds of goods. One naturally enough is foodstuffs, for people must eat. The other consists of a disparate set of commodities that involve spinning and weaving, transport, processing foodstuffs, and the like—Hymer and Resnick call these "Z" activities. Homespun textiles would typify a

"Z" good, which Hymer and Resnick assume is produced by inferior means. If there is no internal trade, families must produce everything themselves. Specialization can occur only when there are opportunities for trade. Rural families will then concentrate on doing what they do best, which is growing food. What they do less efficiently—producing Z goods—they mostly stop doing. If specialization leads to predictable food surpluses, rural families will grow food and exchange them for the Z goods they formerly made. Other specialized producers, such as textile manufacturers, will take up making the Z goods. The economy grows because of increasing internal trade. Resources are allocated to their most productive uses and the labor and capital saved can be subsequently reinvested. Barriers to trade, specialization, and the reallocation of resources, whatever their nature, must be powerful obstacles to growth and development.

De Vries begins his discussion of rural development with a question. How does a self-sufficient society of peasant farmers change under the pressure of population growth and the introduction of opportunities for trade, however limited? De Vries thinks a number of responses possible, but he focuses on what he terms "the peasant model" and "the specialization model."[37] In the peasant model, increasing rural population leads peasants to divide their holdings, either because of inheritance customs, or because of the sale and purchase of lands. At the same time, population growth requires more food production and demands an intensification of land use. By intensification, deVries means an increase in the amount of labor applied to each unit of land. The result, as the typical peasant holding shrinks, is that productivity per unit of land rises while productivity per unit of labor applied falls. As the adjustment to population growth and reduced landholdings continues, the likelihood of more frequent subsistence crises increases. Peasants who cannot support themselves on their own lands will become day laborers as well.

Since an increasing number of peasants do not produce food surpluses, they must purchase grain instead. As a consequence, the price of grain rises relative to other prices, for the agricultural sector draws purchasing power away from nonagricultural activities. Moreover, the peasants can purchase few urban goods, for they have no surplus with which to trade for them. As agricultural productivity falls, peasant families will find artisan industry increasingly attractive for little is lost (and something gained) by putting family members to work in tasks such as spinning and weaving. "The result," de Vries concludes, "is a rural sector in which most peasants must respond negatively to the new trading opportunity: they strive to avoid market dependence."

Of course, some animals are more equal than others. As de Vries notices, those with capital will find ample opportunities for profit. "Moneyed men are encouraged to buy land and perhaps to organize production in order to profit from the strong demand for grain." Large landowners, who profit from increasing land and grain prices, are apt to exploit their opportunities aggressively and to seek even more land in an effort to monopolize rural production. As more peasants are forced into day labor, money wages stagnate and real wages fall. The distribution of income (and wealth) become increasingly unequal. Rising population enhances the power and wealth of an urban capitalist class even as it impoverishes rural people. Trade between the cities and the countryside does not grow much and urbanization remains limited. Peasant society remains economically undifferentiated while individual families persist is a self-sufficient production system. In this model, the rich certainly get richer, but society as a whole is poorer for their efforts. De Vries's urban "monied men" are not entrepreneurs but rent seekers.

In the specialization model, the course of economic change is different. The peasants do not divide their lands under the pressure of population increase. Indeed, they stop producing artisan goods for their own consumption and devote all their time to agriculture. Their surplus food production can be traded for the artisan goods they once produced inefficiently at home. Labor productivity in agriculture must diminish in this model as well, but there are mitigating factors. Those who remain in agriculture have more land with which to farm, which raises productivity. Moreover, those who grow food, grow food. They do not spin or weave or do things in which their productivity is lower. In other words, they benefit from specialization and from the overall reorganization of their activities.[38]

In the specialization model, the peasantry, which grows regular surpluses, gains from rising agricultural prices. Their rising income, in turn, increases the demand for nonagricultural goods. Some of these will inevitably be produced in cities, which offer considerable economies of scale. Urbanization grows and with it, employment opportunities for the surplus rural population. Expanding internal trade provides urban capitalists with a productive outlet for investment in the infrastructure needed to bring goods to market, or for investing in agriculture itself. Even so, the peasantry captures the gains from economic growth. In this model, a self-sufficient household economy grows into an economy of specialized agricultural producers whose rising income underwrites a broader process of social and economic development. The resulting distribution of income and wealth must be flatter and the potential for social conflict correspondingly reduced.

De Vries's model is by no means a "Malthusian" account of economic change. Population change is but *one* element of a larger story. Population growth does not *necessarily* trigger rural impoverishment and indeed, it may do quite the *opposite*. What matters is not just population growth but the way in which a society responds to it. The growth of the market and population change are necessary elements *of* an explanation, but they are not in themselves *sufficient* as an explanation. Institutional, cultural, political, and socioeconomic variables frame, limit, and condition the probable response.[39] If the subtext of de Vries's stylized history is to link one kind of rural commercialization to economic growth, development, and relatively egalitarian social change, it is worth asking why this change did not and could not occur in Mexico. Obviously, de Vries's specialization model does not capture many features of rural Mexico in the Bourbon age. Yet his peasant model describes *some* of the features of rural Mexico well. What were those structures, social, political, and economic, that prevented the happy outcome that de Vries's specialization model envisions?

I will focus mostly on the Bajío and adjoining portions of Jalisco, for Indian communities here were weakest and commercialization, oriented toward mining and agriculture, was most advanced. In a more general way, there are indications that the model might have broader applicability for other parts of central Mexico as well, but the evidence on which to base any such conclusion would be inevitably weaker.

A way of beginning is to discard the least relevant or persuasive elements of de Vries's analysis and to focus on the remaining essentials. Certainly his distinction between urban and rural interests did not characterize Bourbon Mexico. The extensive linkages between landholding, mining, and urban trade and commerce are well known and require no repetition here. Oddly enough, the logic of the peasant model provides an explanation for the erosion of the very distinction that de Vries proposes. If the relative price of cereals rises, rural property values, which are determined by the net present value of the income they generate, must rise as well. If the profitability of mining and commerce in Mexico fell as David Brading and John Coatsworth contend, the attractiveness of land as an investment to miners and merchants could have only increased.[40] And land values obviously rose. Brading's careful study of León in the eighteenth century concludes "all land, no matter what its quality, increased in value." Van Young's conclusion for Guadalajara is similar: "the value of land in the Guadalajara region [greatly increased] during the period between 1760 and 1820."[41] The peasant model actually provides an intuitive explanation for changing landownership in central and west-central Mexico in the eighteenth century.

De Vries's characterization of peasants as avoiding "market dependence" seems at first glance to have little to do with Mexico. His meaning is not wholly clear, for avoiding market dependence could mean shunning markets altogether. Or it could simply mean what Gavin Wright once proposed: "safety first" behavior in which families that produced cash crops for markets generally grew enough food to feed themselves if the cash crop or its market failed.[42] That contingency is not an explicit part of de Vries's model, although if markets are undependable, safety first behavior is not only rational but highly desirable. It surely explains why peasants do not specialize completely when the cash crop they grow is something other than maize, wheat, or some other foodstuff. That said, the notion of peasants avoiding markets in Bourbon Mexico sounds odd. Entire volumes detail the ways in which rural Mexicans seized virtually every commercial opportunity open to them in a catalog of Adam Smith's "propensity to truck and barter."[43]

It is easy to be impressed by the degree of rural commercialization, for most peasants bought and sold goods in markets. Yet a broad market is not necessarily a deep one. An economy with markets is not the same thing as a market economy—one in which the allocation of resources, goods, and services is determined by the free play of supply and demand. In this respect, Garavaglia and Grosso's study of rural commerce in the Puebla region comes to an interesting conclusion. For 1792 they analyzed more than 4,000 market transactions on which the *alcabala* was paid. Of these, "Indians" accounted for 57.4 percent of transactions, a proportion more or less in line with the ethnic composition of the parish of Tepeaca. Ethnic groups traded more or less in proportion to their numbers. But when Garavaglia and Grosso analyze the accounts more closely, they find that Indian and mestizo sellers typically entered the market only 1.5 times per year. Spaniards, on the other hand, did so 45 times per year. There are gross disparities in the amount of the typical transaction as well. Spanish transactions averaged 100/0(100 pesos, no reales). Mestizos averaged 6/4; Indians, 4/6. As Garavaglia and Grosso conclude, "on the one hand, more than a thousand peasants marketed a very small part of their production. On the other, a small group of merchants [were] truly employed in buying and selling goods made by others."[44] This is an important distinction. It suggests that the extent of trade and the intensity of demand for everyday goods like textiles was limited. Here is a market that seems broad but not particularly deep. Many Indians participated in rural markets, but then again, most Indians lived in the countryside. Whom else would you expect to find there?

Yet the story is obviously more complicated. Florescano eloquently describes the small surpluses produced by Indian and mestizo farmers that supplied Mexico City with maize in years of good harvests. Wheat was offered for sale by peasants as well.[45] Yet their *declining* importance in supplying foodstuffs for a growing population in the eighteenth century has been well established. Van Young argues that "the increasing share of large producers [of wheat for the Guadalajara market at the expense of small growers, including Indians] is clear during the later part of the century."[46] Florescano contrasts the prosperity of Indian sellers of maize in the Valley of Mexico from 1721 to 1778 with their declining fortunes between 1779 and 1810. Large haciendas that moved aggressively to control the supply of maize were the beneficiaries of this reversal. "During the eighteenth century," Florescano concludes, "every medium-sized and large city showed this concentration of the maize supply in the hands of the great *hacendados*."[47] Brading does not discuss the changing shares of rancheros, tenants, and *hacendados* in the cereals market of León, but his account of the redistribution of productive lands among them between 1740 and 1770 squares with the conclusions of Florescano and Van Young.[48]

The position of peasant producers in Mexico thus rested somewhere between autarchy and full commercialization. De Vries has discussed the existence of such semicommercialized peasant agriculture, which he calls "self-sufficient households with marketed surplus".[49] Such households typically "[enter] the market to gain the means to pay taxes" or land rents. The household remains self-sufficient because it supplies the Z goods it requires. Its marketed surplus is just that—the system of production and consumption from which it issues remains largely self-contained. This stratum of rural production is familiar to students of colonial history. Indian peasants in the Spanish empire faced a variety of "incentives" to market surpluses, ranging from the secular head tax or tribute to an impressive array of ecclesiastical charges, all of which required cash to be discharged.[50] For Mexico, then, a useful vision of peasant society is the "self-sufficient household with marketed surplus." Indeed, Ángeles Romero characterizes Indian agriculture in almost precisely these terms: "Indian villages planted mostly for their own consumption. Sales of maize, wheat, fruit, and other objects were a complement, rather than a central part, of their economies."[51] Once these adjustments are made, the rural development that occurs sounds much like de Vries's peasant model, at least where population densities attained were highest, such as Guanajuato which reached nearly 32 per km².[52] Indeed, you cannot read David Brading's history of León without being struck by the similarities. In the century after 1660, León experienced substantial population growth, but the rate of growth diminished after 1762 and fell to near stagnation after 1781. Between 1740 and 1770, haciendas in León underwent explosive growth fueled by "incursions of mercantile capital." Brading calculates that "the expansion of the great estate halved the supply of land open to the ranchero sector," while "the pace of natural increase within the rural population now intensified pressure on the remaining stock of land." By 1800, Brading concludes, the subdivision of rural properties among family members had led to a "continuous reduction in the size of holdings" that "yielded their owners little more than the barest necessities." As Brading puts it, "the testamentary system operated to dissipate accumulated capital." As a result, "once prosperous ranchero families [were reduced] to the condition of cottage farmers." This occurred because "the expansion of the great estate so sharply curtailed the supply of land available for purchase."[53]

Van Young describes a similar process in Guadalajara. "The evidence is overwhelming," he writes, "that during the eighteenth century Indians, particularly, had their access to land resources progressively restricted due to the conjunction of population pressure with expansion of the hacienda system." "Indians," he concludes, "withdrew from the market as sellers of . . . maize . . . and re-entered the economy . . . as sellers of . . . crafts and wage labor."[54] Van Young draws less of a contrast between the expansion of the hacienda and the erosion of small farms and village lands, perhaps because overall population density was lower (2.7 per km²) than in León.

The shift in landownership from small holdings to larger estates, or from Indian villages to haciendas in the eighteenth century had profound economic consequences. Haciendas expanded in the eighteenth century less to put additional farming and grazing land to use than to acquire labor. As more land was cultivated less intensively, agricultural productivity fell. Surely this was one reason why Manuel Abad y Queipo suggested that land uncultivated on haciendas for a generation or more should simply be thrown open to popular cultivation.[55] The apparent source of declining agricultural productivity in the late eighteenth century was less a function of population growth than it was of changes in the pattern of land tenure that produced both much larger and much smaller landholdings. Growing numbers either had too much land to use efficiently, or too little.

Unfortunately, the paucity of data on agricultural productivity in colonial Mexico makes this analysis more of a logical than a historical exercise. Yet if efficiency is defined in terms of output per unit of land, why should we assume that haciendas were as productive as small landholdings? Maize or wheat were nontradeable goods, so there was no competition from imports. Markets were small and regionalized until railroad construction drove down transportation costs in the late nineteenth century. Richard Garner concludes that "for most years [in the eighteenth century] the cost-effective distance [for shipping maize] was fewer than fifty miles."[56] In regions such as León, where the shift to cereal production by haciendas was especially marked, imperfect competition—large and increasingly concentrated producers facing limited markets—would have been the rule. Maize from León rarely if ever reached Mexico City. Even the hacienda San José Acolman, in the Texcoco district, sent no maize to nearby Mexico City.[57] In such markets, producers are then said to have "excess capacity" because they face downward-sloping demand curves. They have no incentive to expand output, for by producing more, they depress prices. Small farmers, on the other hand, cannot affect price by offering to sell more or less. No disincentive to produce exists which is why such markets are termed "competitive." Of course, an hacienda can be a competitive producer, but in the context of a national or even international market. For wheat and maize, this was not the case in the eighteenth century.[58]

Quantitative evidence for the inefficiency of the hacienda is, unfortunately, indirect at best.[59] Around León, Brading reports yields per acre of maize of 8 to 11 bushels; for wheat, the yield was 8.9 bushels. In the central valleys of the bishopric of Puebla, David Weiland finds wheat yields in the early eighteenth century of less than 12:1.[60] Around Chalco, Gibson says that maize yields were 15 to 30 bushels per acre. Seed ratios were quite high. Around León, maize yields were 90:1 and wheat, according to Humboldt, was about 35:1. For Guadalajara, Van Young gives seed ratios for maize of 100:1, with wheat at 10:1. He regards H. G. Ward's estimate for wheat in the 1820s at 25:1 as "greatly exaggerated." He may be correct. Wheat yields on San José Acolman and adjoining properties were approximately 6:1. Maize yields were 65:1, with considerable variation. Nevertheless, as Ángeles Romero observes, even though Mexican seed yields were high by European standards, yields *per unit of land* were no more than comparable, if that.[61] In other words, "sowing brought good results in New Spain because land went to waste." A significant proportion of land used by haciendas could not have been sown, given the disparity between seed ratios and yields per unit of ace. There was, in economic terms, excess capacity in land.

As it stands, the argument requires two qualifications. Imperfect competition depends not only on concentration of production and the relative level of demand. Producers must be able to exclude potential rivals and collude as they divide the market. If not, new competitors or cheaters will upset the applecart by driving down prices or trying to get a larger share of the market. In Mexico rising land prices may have constituted an important barrier to entry. For example, Brading finds a threefold increase in estate values in León in the eighteenth century, while the wages of day labor stagnated.[62] If, as he suggests, capital accumulated in mining and commerce supported the boom in estate formation, the restrictive nature of the land market becomes clearer. How many miners and merchants could actually afford to play the game? Brading supposes that "they could not have amounted to more than 3 percent of the total population."[63] Yet the context of Brading's analysis suggests he is referring to urban population, which was about 7.6 percent of New Spain's population. By implication, this is fewer than 15,000 people, a very small group indeed.

But did landowners actually collude in holding grain off the market? Here the numbers convey a different impression.[64] According to Brading, the intendancy of Guanajuato counted nearly 450 haciendas within its limits in the early 1790s. Van Young analyzes a sample of 35 "important" haciendas in Guadalajara. Gibson speaks of 160 haciendas in the Valley of Mexico by the late colonial period. Given the enormous differences between them, a precise enumeration of haciendas perhaps means little. Yet the ways in which even two or three dozen big estates colluded is simply not clear, even if Mexico's late colonial elite looked much like an extended kinship network. Florescano, in speaking of the great landowners' ability to impose a "seller's market," gives no indication of how they could manage such an inherently unstable arrangement.[65] The most promising clue comes from the research of David Weiland, whose study of agriculture in Puebla shows a marked concentration of ownership of landed properties in the hands of a small number of families. In Huejotzingo in 1793, for instance, sixteen families accounted for thirty of fifty-three hanciendas and eleven of twenty-one ranchos. In Tepeaca in 1791, twelve families owned twenty of fifty-eight haciendas and nine of forty-two ranchos. Such concentration may go some way toward explaining the sort of collusive behavior that Florescano emphasizes.[66]

Whatever the case, the productive capacity of the agricultural economy had deteriorated by the late eighteenth century, just as the peasant model predicts. The frequency of hunger and dearth increased dramatically in the second half of the century. Between 1700 and 1750, fewer than three of every ten years were attended by hunger, often occasioned by failures of the maize harvest. After 1750 nearly six of every ten years through 1800 witnessed some degree of hunger and scarcity.[67] Large changes in weather patterns were obviously responsible for some of the worsening, as Florescano's comparison of cycles in France and New Spain indicates.[68] The bad weather of the 1780s played havoc with maize stocks as far north as San Antonio de Béjar, where Frank de la Teja writes that "[t]he worst of the lean times coincided with the widespread agricultural crisis of 1785–86, although in Texas the climatic disruptions lasted until 1790." De la Teja adds, "[b]y the time the crisis was over, farmers had paid as much as twelve pesos the fanega for seed maize which was 3 or 4 times the already high prices prevailing in the 1780s.[69]

But as Jean Drèze and Amartya Sen argue, "climatic change is [not] independent of society." Moreover, "economic, social, and political factors [determine] the impact of a drought (or any other climatic change) on what people can produce and consume."[70] Exactly. Bad weather *and* the changing distribution of land were responsible for the increasing frequency of subsistence crises in the late eighteenth century. Florescano recognized this in his pioneering study nearly a quarter of a century ago. It fits precisely with the argument we have made, and with de Vries's peasant model of rural change.

COLONIAL HERITAGE AND COLONIAL INDUSTRY

The logic of de Vries's peasant model leads to a final conclusion. As a rural population that divides its land into smaller holdings grows, its members will increasingly "enter the labor market as day laborers" or form "a marginally employed 'cottar' class." Moreover, "the falling productivity of labor in agriculture as landholdings shrink makes labor in home handicrafts a relatively attractive alternative."[71] The available evidence points precisely in this direction. Both day and seasonal labor were found throughout the Bajío in estate agriculture during the eighteenth century. Tenancy on haciendas appeared as well, and may to some extent have mitigated the effects of population growth. Larger properties, including haciendas themselves, were leased. Tenants on leased haciendas were known as "subtenants" (*subarrendatarios*). Many, for instance, rented lands from haciendas around the town of Dolores, near San Miguel, although the case of Dolores was by no means unique.[72] Yet the artisan textile industry that was so widely dispersed throughout central Mexico is of even greater relevance to this discussion than day labor or tenantry.

Historians have devoted considerable attention to protoindustry in Bourbon Mexico, if only to deny its existence. One difficulty is that *obrajes* (workshops), about which we are reasonably well informed, cannot accurately be characterized as protoindustrial.[73] *Obrajes* existed to accommodate the production of woolens in an economy in which markets were thin, poorly developed, unreliable, and imperfectly integrated. Technology, transactions costs, and simple exploitation of labor explain why they existed. *Obrajes* had much in common with haciendas, for where using markets is costly, centralized production, which relies on hierarchy and internal command, makes sense, however inefficient or unproductive it might otherwise appear.

Protoindustrialization is not precisely an account of the transformation of workshops into factories, but an analysis of the economic, demographic and cultural conditions under which peasant populations will turn to artisan industry.[74] Protoindustry is not a prerequisite for industrialization. Large concentrations of household spinners and weavers may or may not lead to the rise of centralized factory production. This criticism—that protoindustrialization is neither necessary nor sufficient for industrialization—applies to Mexico.[75] Comparing the location of the artisan textile industry in the 1780s and 1790s with the distribution of factory production in the mid-nineteenth century illustrates the difficulty. There was no artisan textile industry in colonial Veracruz, but by the 1860s there was a substantial cotton industry there. Conversely, Michoacán and Oaxaca, which had relatively large artisan industries in the 1780s, were of no real significance by the 1850s.[76] How colonial industry in Puebla and Querétaro was linked to later factory production has yet to be established.

In Bourbon Mexico, protoindustry in the European sense was partly a response to diminishing returns in agriculture. For example, as population in the León district grew, and as the fragmentation of rural properties continued apace, the poor and increasingly landless families of the region turned to spinning and weaving for the balance of subsistence. Descriptions of cottage industry in and around Guanajuato, León,

Celaya, and Guadalajara in the early 1780s and 1790s describe these developments.[77] The weavers, uniformly poor, worked out of their homes, or *jacales* (shacks), on an irregular basis, and earned a few *reales* for their troubles. The phrase *por temporada*, or seasonally, often appears, as it did in a description of more than 400 looms worked by Indians and *castas* in the area around San Miguel el Grande. Near Tepeaca, the Indians "used [their looms] only half the year, because they spent the other half working in the fields." Here indeed is an industry that fit hand in glove with agriculture, and which sounds like "protoindustry."

There were variations on the theme. Where agriculture was well commercialized, the stimulus to protoindustrialization came as much from stagnating market demand as from rural population increase. In the early eighteenth century, for example, the Puebla region lost out to Guadalajara and the Bajío in supplying the interior markets of New Spain with cereals. Declining demand depressed the price of wheat, the critical regional staple. Wheat which sold for 9 pesos per carga at the beginning of the eighteenth century had fallen as low as 2.25 pesos per carga by the 1740s.[78] Falling prices mattered, because if agriculture is commercialized, the demand for labor is determined both by labor's marginal productivity and by the price of what it produces. As wheat prices fell, a unit of agricultural labor produced less revenue. Hence income and agricultural employment fell. Thus, Guy Thomson views the expansion of domestic industry in eighteenth-century Puebla as a response to agricultural stagnation.[79] As the potential income from agricultural employment fell, weaving cottons became increasingly attractive.

So the effect of low (or declining) agricultural productivity was twofold. On the one hand, low agricultural productivity depressed the demand for manufactures. On the other, it made artisan industry and the putting-out system very attractive to poor people. An odd but very plausible equilibrium emerged. Most of the cotton cloth that common people used was produced inefficiently, but then again most people could not afford to buy much cloth. What royal bureaucrats called *telares sueltos* was a dispersed, poorly capitalized, technologically backward form of industry, but by and large it met the limited needs of an impoverished people. The concentrated urban demand, which was small in any event, was satisfied by contraband, imports, and other domestic producers, such as *obrajes*. An inefficient industry was just good enough. Mexican protoindustrialization therefore offered limited potential for economic transformation, a generalization valid for most of Latin America, just as Albert Berry has observed.[80] One suspects that the role of agricultural productivity, which was generally low outside the export sector, has a major role to play in explaining what Latin Americans evocatively call this rickety (*raquítico*) pattern of industrial development.

CONCLUSIONS: TOWARD SYNTHESIS

It is easy to summarize the thrust of the argument. Agriculture was an element of Mexico's colonial heritage, and an important one. Indirect and circumstantial evidence suggests that agricultural productivity in Mexico was generally low. We emphasized two sources of low productivity: the nature of landholding, and the effects of population growth where law (or custom) of inheritance dictates equal division among survivors. The model stresses that population growth in itself does not depress rural standards of living. The response to population growth is critical and reflects institutional differences between societies. Where land is subdivided (such as New Spain), the falling marginal product of labor makes the production of Z goods (such as homespun textiles) an attractive option. Market exchange is stunted as a result. Where lands are maintained intact, specialization and exchange promote rising productivity even if population is increasing. As a result, population increase is a *necessary* element in explaining apparent changes in agricultural productivity in Bourbon Mexico, but it is by no means a *sufficient* explanation.

In significant portions of central Mexico in the later eighteenth century, a transfer of land from efficient small landholders to relatively inefficient haciendas occurred. In the Bajío, and to a lesser extent in Jalisco, the phenomenon is well documented. Since productivity and costs are inversely related, stagnating productivity growth implied higher costs and prices for commodities such as maize. The increasing frequency of subsistence crises reflected these underlying changes in productivity. The mining and commercial boom that occurred under the later Bourbons accelerated the process. Capital thus accumulated financed much of the considerable "takeover" of lands. Yet de Vries's peasant model indicates that something similar, if less intense, would have occurred anyway. Inheritance practices, mediated by law or custom, mattered a great deal. The Bourbon "reforms" may have accelerated or exacerbated the change, but they did not fundamentally alter it.

Is there much certainty that agricultural productivity was low? We need much more careful, detailed, and painstaking studies of a range of agricultural production than we currently have.[81] Our "Chenery-Syrquin" type data for the eighteenth century are suggestive and circumstantial but hardly definitive. The rising frequency of subsistence crises in the late eighteenth century certainly suggests a deterioration in the level of productivity was well underway by 1750. This sort of evidence is indirect, but it is the most abundant kind we have for Mexican agriculture. Victor Bulmer Thomas calculates that around 1913, "labor productivity in [domestic use agriculture in Mexico] was no more than one-fifth the national average."[82] And this, we must add, after a generation of radical changes in the Mexican countryside, such as the railroad, which could have only raised the productivity. If this were true in 1913, then how much more so in 1813?

As Bulmer Thomas suggests, poor agricultural performance is a drag on growth. Since export sectors typically represented a small share of GDP, they would have had to grow quite rapidly to offset poor performance in agriculture. Bulmer Thomas shows that this rarely happened. Few countries in nineteenth-century Latin America were able to grow over the long run on the basis of exports alone.[83] Yet there is also a dynamic aspect to the question. If agriculture fails to grow, and if most resources are devoted to agricultural production, then exports cannot grow if food cannot be imported. Agriculture can only release labor and capital to other activities if productivity rises, or if the price of imported foodstuffs falls. An increase in agricultural productivity offers both static and dynamic gains and is thus apt to have a disproportionate impact on the rate of growth.

While we have concentrated on two sources of productivity change in agriculture, there are others. Transportation costs were extremely important, as numerous historians have emphasized. If, as Richard Garner suggests, the typical market in New Spain had a radius of 50 miles, then we could, in view of the proportion of arable surface in modern Mexico, think that fourteen or fifteen such markets comprised the colonial economy.[84] Even if resources of homogeneous quality were uniformly distributed across these markets, a fall in transportation costs would raise productivity simply by encouraging specialization, or learning-by-doing. Yet in practice, resources varied considerably by regions, as did soil type, climate, and terrain. A reduction in transportation costs encouraged regional specialization and produced economies of scale as well. There may not have been fourteen or fifteen separate markets for artisan industry in Bourbon Mexico, but its wide dispersion indicates an inefficiently low degree of specialization. Here is why Mexican railroads had the effects they had.[85]

Institutions explain agricultural productivity as well. To speak of institutions "traditions, mores, customs, and laws" as part of a colonial heritage is singularly appropriate. In recent years, economic historians have turned increasingly to institutions as explanations for divergent economic development. The discussion has an obvious appeal to economic historians of Latin Amercia, if only because it is flexible (or vague) enough to accommodate libertarian, social democratic, neoliberal, Marxist, and other sorts of development stories. The institutions of interest to us here are laws of inheritance and types of landholding. Castilian laws were "exogenous" institutions, brought to Mexico by force of arms and inevitably modified by local need, opportunity, and circumstance. Haciendas were a more nearly "endogenous" institution that reflected the abundance of land and scarcity of labor that attendended their creation, as well as the unpredictable operation of market forces in an economy with high transactions costs. A conventional economic historian might explain the shift from intensive, irrigated Mesoamerican agriculture to extensive colonial practice in terms of factor endowments. Yet however we define our emphasis, it is clear that domestic agriculture was an aspect of the colonial heritage, not only in Mexico but more generally in Latin America as well.

eight

The Tricks of Time: Colonial Legacies and Historical Sensibilities in Latin America

Steve J. Stern

The colonial past is an unclosed chapter in Latin America. Its history seems to bequeath to its postcolonial successor an unresolved inheritance. This living inheritance, often politically charged, unsettles unilinear notions of the march of historical time. Time as a march of sequential displacement—event or pattern A is replaced by event or pattern B, B by C, and so on, in a sequence of cause and effect on a time track in which the present replaces the past and is itself replaced by the future—seems not to square well with experience and sensibilities in Latin America. Time and time again, in Latin America, phenomena apparently centuries old and "dead" somehow resurface and reassert themselves. Despite vast changes, the present seems not so much to replace the past as to super-impose itself on it, only partly altering and displacing it. Time as linear sequence and the related notion of time as progress seem questionable.

In this kind of historical and social experience, unilinear notions of time compete with other notions. This mix of sensibilities was very much a part of the milieu in Latin America in the 1950s, 1960s, and 1970s, the era of discontent marked by profound critiques of Latin America's deeply entrenched historical inheritance. Three writers of the era—makers of the "boom" that placed Latin America in the forefront of world literature—illustrate the sensibilities that undermine unilinear notions of historical time.

In his short story "The Night Face Up" ("La noche boca arriba"), Julio Cortázar plays a time trick on readers.[1] The protagonist of the story rides a motorcycle amidst the traffic of modern Mexico City, succumbs to an accident when he tries to avoid a pedestrian, and is rushed unconscious to a well-equipped modern hospital. In the hospital, he floats in and out of consciousness. When he is awake, he is reassured by the paraphernalia of medical modernity and competence; when he retreats into his dreams, he is terrified by Aztecs determined to capture and sacrifice him so that the sun will continue to rise and cast the security of light and wakefulness upon the world. At the end, we discover that the motorcycle and the accident and the hospital are the dream, that what is "real" is the terror and the imminent sacrifice of the protagonist. Mexica/Aztec times and practices still live; the modern façade of twentieth-century Mexico City is a dreamlike illusion.

In this story, time is not forward motion on a unilinear track called *History.* There are multiple levels upon which time's motion takes place. What appears to be forward motion on one track or level (the technological modernization of Mexico City) does not exclude backward motion on another track or level (travel toward the time of human sacrifice by the Mexica/Aztecs). Or perhaps one is moving in a grand circle in which there is the illusion of forward motion but the reality of returning to the place of beginnings.

Consider, as well, the way time stands still, yielding a sense of a reality outside normal historical time, in the celebrated novels of Gabriel García Márquez. There is a mix of relevance and irrelevance in the historical time markers that work their way into *One Hundred Years of Solitude (Cien años de soledad)* and *Autumn of the Patriarch (El otoño del patriarca).*[2] On the one hand, one can "date" these and other novels by reference to key historical events that find their way into them (the banana massacre of workers in Colombia, the interplay of homegrown dictators and U.S. creditors and imperialists in the Caribbean, respectively). Yet there is also a certain vagueness about time in these works, a certain irrelevance to their apparent historical anchoring. The works seem to expose their historical markers haphazardly. Indeed, they foster a sense of something quintessential or entrenched that resists or obviates specific chronological location. In the town of Macondo, the setting for *One Hundred Years of Solitude,* the rainy season might last for several years instead of several months, people might sleep a few weeks or months instead of a few hours. What difference does the length of rain or sleep make if, as the local folk are fond of saying, "Nothing happens in Macondo"? In the Caribbean of the declining patriarch, the times of Columbus and gringo imperialists blend into one another, as if the specific historical century is not all that relevant or distinctive.

In short, experienced time stands outside conventional historical time. Time stands still. Or, if it marches forward, then the march turns out to be rather irrelevant. As José Arcadio Buendía, the patriarch of Macondo, put it, "Incredible things are happening in the world. . . . [yet] we go on living like donkeys."[3]

Consider, finally, the novel that may be considered a kind of precursor or prologue of the literary "boom," Alejo Carpentier's *The Lost Steps* (*Los pasos perdidos*).[4] This quest novel is painted on a distinctively Latin American canvas. For our purposes, what is important is the way it assumes that in the Latin American context, travel across space amounts to travel across time. The protagonist, a musician who lives in the United States, experiences the vapid meaninglessness of modern life. He is alienated and passionless both in his work and in his human relationships. When he is given the task of finding primitive musical instruments in the Amazonian jungle of Venezuela, however, his life takes a new turn. His quest requires that he travel across the social landscape of a Latin American society—beginning with his landing in the capital city, moving on to a provincial city in the agrarian hinterlands, continuing on to remote trading settlements on the periphery of the jungle, and finally pushing past colonizing, exploratory settlements and establishing contact with utterly isolated, "stone age" societies deep in the jungle. He accomplishes his mission and discovers the beginnings of human musical invention.

On one level, of course, *The Lost Steps* deploys the universal symbolism one expects in great literature. Our alienated protagonist has embarked upon a search for authenticity in human relations, a return to the roots of the human psyche and its urges, unfettered by the gadgets and malaise of mid-twentieth-century life. The "lost steps" retraced by the protagonist are the "lost steps" of humankind.

On another level, however, the novel evokes the conditions of Latin American life that seem to conflate travel across physical space with travel across historical time. Caracas, the capital city, is a relatively contemporary urban setting, equipped with tall buildings, a modern business and newspaper district, a stock exchange, an infrastructure of electricity and machinery, and a great many automobiles. To be sure, it is tempered by a past that has not entirely disappeared—by colonial and fin de siècle architectural styles, by political monarchists, premodern storage habits that ruin hospital medicines, and a population of poor people who still walk everywhere. These elements of the past coexist with and entangle the present, but they do not erase the historical location of Caracas as a contemporary social setting. The provincial city, our protagonist's next major destination, is not at all "primitive," but it does seem more of a throwback to another era. People wear clothes that are out of fashion; a visitor encounters more Blacks and Indians; local people experience a sensation of remoteness, as if they are removed from "real" world places such as Paris, where culture is made; the locals read books not for entertainment but to apprehend truth; they take the celebration of patron saints seriously. This is a world with a nineteenth-century or late colonial feel, and it is here that the protagonist meets a more "traditional" peasantlike woman, for whom he develops a stronger affective sensation than he can experience in the contemporary world.

As the protagonist travels deeper and deeper into the jungle, time travel continues to the point where he meets characters who seem to have stepped out of history books. He meets, in addition to the "traditional" woman who becomes his consort, a jungle prospector ("Diamond Hunter") who fuses exploration with a lust for gems and precious metals. His party picks up a Capuchin friar committed to missionary work among pagan Indians of the jungle. He even encounters a conquistador ("Adelantado") who is rumored to have become the king of a community of runaway slaves and the lord of a secret harem of women, and who has in fact set up his own colonial city in the jungle.

As the exploratory party moves backward in time—switching from electricity to kerosene lamps to candles—the group decides to play a game in which they pretend to be conquistadors in search of the native kingdom of Manoa. The game is the truth of what they have become: a classic colonial expedition. The men now include a miner, a missionary, a conqueror, and an exiled wanderer; they are accompanied by mistresses and servants; and they finally reach "untouched" forest inhabited by Stone Age peoples who "invent" human music, pursue their own religious understandings, and have no desire to be baptized into Christianity. As the chaplain intones his primitive mass, the musician feels he has traveled back some four hundred years in time.

In Carpentier's rendition, time does not beat to the same drummer in all the varied regions of a Latin American country. This multiplicity of timescales means that in Latin America, at least, travel across regional space is travel across historical time. Different regions seem to have become "frozen" in different historical eras, so that in the society as a whole there emerges a complex coexistence and interaction among different historical eras. Even Caracas was somewhat affected by this coexistence. When political violence broke out during the hero's visit to Caracas, he observed to a lawyer that "an incredible chronological discrepancy of ideals" seemed to govern the conflict, as if it were "a kind of battle between people living in different centuries." "That's very acute," noted the lawyer. "You must remember that we are accustomed to living with Rousseau and the Inquisition, with the Immaculate Conception and *Das Kapital.*"[5]

In all three cases we have reviewed, unilinear notions of historical time coexist and compete with other notions of historical time. Cortázar's story encourages us to imagine simultaneous forward and backward motion on multiple tracks, or a grand circle of forward illusion. García Márquez's novels encourage us to imagine a time that stands still, a deep time that somehow displaces the imagined relevance of conventional historical time. Carpentier encourages us to imagine regionally distinctive rhythms of historical time that somehow bring different historical eras together within the present.[6]

In short, all three writers expose us to the "tricks of time" that render history a living, restless spirit that infects the present rather than a closed chapter or a prologue to the present. In their somewhat varied ways, all expose Latin American sensibilities about time that call attention to cycle and recurrence, continuity, and multiple motion (forward, backward, inertial) in human wanderings through history. Sensibilities such as these compete with and render superficial or illusionary the more familiar notions of change, forward motion, or progress over time.

THE COLONIAL HERITAGE
AS AN UNCLOSED CHAPTER: SIX THESES

The multiplicity that marks time sensibilities in Latin America, especially the Latin America that yielded profound yearnings for deep change in the mid- to late twentieth century, sets a context for consideration of a book which encapsulates a historiographic variant on this genre, Stanley Stein and Barbara Stein's *The Colonial Heritage of Latin America: Essays on Economic Dependence in Perspective.*[7] One of the astute dimensions of the Steins' 1970 book—one that transcends its focus on economic dependence as such—was its insistence on the living dimension of the colonial heritage, and its effort to interpret how and why this heritage proved so resilient. The Steins urged their readers to think broadly about the ways the colonial experience and its neocolonial repercussions constituted an "unclosed" rather than "closed" chapter of Latin American history, part of present-day travails and struggles rather than mere background to it.

This insistence, and the substantive historical interpretation attached to it, remain important, even if the specific focus on an economic dependence once so important in the 1960s and 1970s and that served as a conceptual foundation in *The Colonial Heritage of Latin America*—and indeed its genre—is perhaps less compelling in the 1990s. Panoramic reflection on a living colonial heritage in its international context remains important for at least three reasons. First, the problem of Latin America's unequal and neocolonial relationship with economies of the North Atlantic world remains terribly important, even in an era where the global logic of the marketplace—and internal social and economic forces within the once colonized world—have undermined an older world geography that seemed to place factories and technological advance in one part of the world, primary commodity production and occasional enclaves of technological advance in another. An updated exploration of the themes that anchored the interpretation of the Steins, in dialogue with the political and economic world of the 1990s, would illuminate much about Latin American trajectories of past, present, and future.

Second, the Steins' promotion of a panoramic interpretive vision of the colonial heritage stands as a challenging antidote to the plethora of narrower, more specialized case-study research driven by the advance of contemporary knowledge and the incentive system of modern universities. Above all in an age of monographic abundance, we need to insist on the importance of stepping back to reflect on the broad sweep of historical experience. Textbooks do not really perform this function, although a panoramic reflection can sometimes do double duty as a textbook. It is a sad but revealing comment on the state of professional historical knowledge of Latin America that the number of compelling synoptic reflections (whether in article or short book form) on the colonial experience published since 1970 is very, very small.

Third, and most important, even in a postmodern age of global immediacy—the ability to communicate images, messages, exchanges, and decisions almost instantaneously with electronics, computers, and satellites; the rush to global neoliberal policies and imitation dynamics, the pressures of transnational investment, resource flow, and competitiveness logics—even in this kind of world, the colonial and neocolonial inheritance of Latin America ends up reborn. It becomes a forgotten inheritance that bites back, shocking those whose rush to the unilinear future had led them to forget history's stubborn resilience, to interpret history as a series of "closed" chapters in a sequential march. The shock of the Chiapas uprising in 1994, in a country whose technocrats had rushed headlong toward a "new" Mexico embracing promises of transnational neoliberalism, presents a dramatic example. Chiapas reacquainted Mexicans with their past, bringing to the surface, once more, the tricks of time that complicate historical sensibilities in Latin America.

The tricks of time in Latin America render colonial history an unclosed chapter and underscore the enduring value of the Steins' interpretive essay. Yet as the content (if not the subtitle) of the Steins' 1970 book makes clear, the exploration of colonial legacies requires far more than a study of the international economic dimensions of Latin America's economic and social existence. If one agenda bequeathed us by the Steins is an updated reconsideration of Latin America's history and legacies in their international context,[8] another is an updated mapping, from a more interior point of view, of the diverse ways in which colonial legacies seem ever present, somehow reborn and "biting back," in twentieth-century conditions of Latin American life.

Let us undertake this more interior mapping by considering six "theses" (to invoke the language of an earlier era) about the colonial experience as an unclosed chapter of Latin American life.

Thesis One

In the so-called backward regions of twentieth-century Latin America, and at times even in "advanced" regions, colonial-like social and economic relations have been maintained or reinvented and put to use in modern economic contexts. In these areas, the classic colonial hybrid recurs: the profit principle that governs modern economic life has been joined not to free labor relationships but to coercive labor relations.

This thesis will not surprise students of Latin American history. Whether one thinks of the debt-and-intimidation relations that pulled tappers into the rubber boom in the Brazilian Amazon of the late nineteenth and early twentieth centuries, or the re-creation of labor drafts and roundups of alleged vagrants that channeled Indian peasant labor into Guatemalan coffee plantations through the 1940s; or the reversion of Oaxacan antimony mines, between the 1960s and mid-1980s (after the mines had been abandoned as unprofitable by a U.S. company), to a colonial-like regime of coerced Indian labor imposed by the state's local power groups; every historian has a list of ready examples.[9] Significantly, the march of Latin America into the postmodern age of electronic information and high technology does not halt the stream of examples. In

1995 the Pastoral Commission of Brazil reported that confirmed reports of forced labor had climbed to more than 25,000 in 1994. Brazilian sociologist José de Sousa Martins estimated the actual figure at about 85,000 and observed that slave labor had become part of the chain of labor relations and commodity flows within "modern" production by multinational companies. Charcoal workers subjected to a kind of de facto enslavement, for example, supplied energy consumed by modern steel plants.[10]

In June 1995 President Fernando Henrique Cardoso—himself an intellectual prominent in the exploration of dependency ideas—appointed a commission to investigate massive forced labor. In August he addressed the nation and acknowledged that, somehow, the abolition of slavery in Brazil a century earlier had not really closed the chapter of slavery in Brazilian life. The colonial and neocolonial heritage of Brazil had bitten back in Latin America's largest and most industrialized society. And it had done so in the country's southern regions, where the modernity and postmodernity of the late twentieth century were presumably most advanced.

Thesis Two

In the frontier areas of Latin America, especially the vast Amazonian basin of South America, the basic issues of conquest and first-generation native-white encounter have been confronted, often on a "first-time" basis, in the twentieth century.

Those who have read Carpentier's depiction of a party that fused classic colonial personalities—conquerors in search of riches, missionaries in search of souls, alienated seekers of a social utopia—will not be surprised at the twentieth-century history of the Amazon. The ephemeral quality of earlier direct colonization and contact experiences created a "first-time" quality to many later encounters, even for peoples and regions with extensive prior histories of contact.

To be sure, the dynamics of first-time encounter and conquest on the twentieth-century frontier were not identical with those of colonial times. In the twentieth century the magical resource might be oil rather than gold, the proselytized path to Christian salvation might be Protestant rather than Catholic, the escape to a utopia of social leadership and rule might focus on postcapitalist revolution rather than early modern kingdom making, the ideology of civilization's benefits might place a stronger emphasis on public health, a weaker emphasis on saving souls.[11] But such differences did not block the emergence of the classic colonial frontier situations: the lure and contentiousness of plunder, labor, and resources over "new" peoples and regions long governed by their own lifeways, geographies, and sovereignties; the search for pathways to religious rule and proselytizing among "pagans" whose embrace of Christianity might prove either reluctant, or differently premised, from the expectations and frameworks of colonizers; the conflictual and fragmentary meldings of different cultural and social premises into new languages of social rule, status, and right; the problems of practical sustainability and moral interpretation posed by epidemic disease and devastating mortality among populations exposed to new pathogens and cultural regimes. Time and time again, in the frontiers, the issues of first-time encounter come back to life.

Thesis Three

Although a formal racial caste system is now archaic in Latin American societies, in practice, in a number of regions and countries, the class structure interacts with the racial structure in ways that bear a strong resemblance to colonial patterns.

Of course, there are some regions within Latin America where a colonial-like racial geography seems terribly salient. In highland regions of Guatemala and Andean South America, in the northeast of Brazil and in portions of the greater Caribbean, the building of social and class privilege on a racial foundation may seem both obvious and reminiscent of colonial times. Significantly, however, colonial-like dynamics of race and class exert a presence even in less obvious cases. An unspoken coordination of racial inheritance and hierarchy, and socioeconomic possibility and hierarchy, marks even those regions where racial mixing is proudly proclaimed as a national identity that supersedes hierarchy and antagonism. In Mexico City, the capital city of a self-declared mestizo nation, the cultured elites concentrated in the southern metropolitan zones are largely white in phenotype; the laborers and street sellers in the poorer northern zones and shantytowns are largely dark in phenotype; the newcomers who stream in from the countryside and must "learn" new lifeways through domestic service or other apprenticelike relationships with patrons are, in some contexts, "Indian" or near Indian.

Perhaps most important, twentieth-century Latin America still uses a colonial device to bring class and racial geographies into rough accord—from the point of view of elites and white "respectable" folk—when social mobility, luck, or anomaly might otherwise call them into question. In colonial times, a certain plasticity marked ethno-racial labeling. One's inherited ethno-racial category turned out to depend not only on the ethno-racial labels of one's parents and ancestors but also on lineage quality, economic resources, cultural demeanor and trappings, social alliances, and personal character traits. This process allowed for selective redefinitions of racial standing that "whitened" or "darkened" individuals and families in accord with their total package of attributes and within the specific contexts of social interaction. The result, in complex societies where nonwhites might acquire significant wealth, power, or social influence, was a certain ability to move individuals or families along a racial spectrum that included intermediate racial labels and ideas of "near white," "perhaps white," and "recently white" ethno-racial location.

Such dynamics, of course, had their limits. On an elite level, they sparked a certain uneasiness among those whites or elites who considered whitened racial arrivals a threat and opened the cultural door to epithets that put apparent "whites" back into their "darkened" social place. On a subaltern level, many racially mixed plebeians and laboring folk, whose life chances did not place them near the fringes of respectable or whitened middle-sector folk, might find gradations of whiteness and darkness culturally meaningless or irrelevant.[12] And some socially mobile, wealthy, or powerful folk of Amerindian, African, or mixed-racial descent projected an ethno-racial identity explicitly contrasted with those of whites.[13] Nonetheless, selective redefinitions of "race" served to mediate the contradictions between socioeconomic privilege hierarchies and ethno-racial descent hierarchies that sometimes emerged in complex colonial societies. Such mediation somewhat restored the cultural premise of a certain parallelism of race privilege and class privilege.

In twentieth-century Latin America, the unspoken parallelism of race and class hierarchies, and the devices used to mediate contradiction and rupture of such parallelism, seem strikingly reminiscent of colonial dynamics. Despite formal discourses that have dismantled the significance of an older racial caste system, or even proclaimed racial blending a nationwide process that supersedes past divisions, the older system lives on. A certain parallelism of race and class, accompanied by flexible mediation of anomalies, still rules. The whitened society of elites and respectable folk includes a modest variety of colorations and phenotypes, a sprinkling of racially arrived folk, within its cultural premises and fictions.

Thesis Four

The honor codes and social relations of gender that shaped a ranked system of manhoods and womanhoods (and a related spectrum of gendered respectability and degradation) in colonial times have proved surprisingly durable, despite significant modifications, in postcolonial times. This durability is all the more striking because important political and economic transformations have taken place since the late nineteenth century.

Because the problem of gender in Latin American history is a relatively young research field, this thesis may not resonate as strongly as the earlier theses for many historians of Latin America. For scholars of gender, however, and readers of Latin American literature (García Márquez's *Crónica de una muerte anunciada*,[14] for example) the resonance is quite strong. The formal codes of honor that governed respectable manhood and womanhood in colonial times find striking parallels in the ethnographies and studies of more recent times.[15] At more subaltern levels of colonial society, the codes of manhood and womanhood that both engaged and contested the wider society's system of ranked manhoods and womanhoods—and that yielded conflict over gender rights within subaltern life—seem lived out, again and again, in twentieth-century contexts.[16]

In some ways, of course, emphasis on the continuity of a colonial inheritance of gendered honor, degradation, and struggle can be overdrawn. Overemphasis ignores important transformations, including the emergence of feminist and woman-centered politics and cultural sensibilities, the erosion of rural patriarchal power and elder power, and the urbanization of social and domestic life within twentieth-century Latin America. Elsewhere, I have discussed some of the ways that the gendered ghosts of the colonial past turn out to be partially illusory.[17] Yet despite the altered contexts of gendered life and struggle, the colonial ghosts reappear and turn linear sequencing of gender history into a superficial illusion. Small wonder that film depictions of female life and destiny in revolutionary Cuba moved from the linear optimism of *Lucía* to the more unresolved forward-and-backward struggles depicted in *Retrato de Teresa*.

Thesis Five

The Christian Church(es) and fragments thereof continue in many Latin American regions to exert a vital direct impact on political legitimacy. In this respect, the church and its fragments act on associations between secular (worldly) power and religious (sacred) authority built before and during the colonial period. The emergence of Liberation Theology and politicized evangelical Protestantism are in this context innovative acts within a long-playing drama, all of whose acts share a certain underlying unity.

In this arena, the colonial inheritance seems deeply powerful. It includes the profoundly important role of the colonial Catholic Church as the institutional hub around which state and colonizers built their legitimacy. It includes historically close connections between state and church authorities that sometimes merged in single authoritative persons—the familiar figure of the colonial archbishop-viceroy. It includes, as well, the remarkably widespread constructions of "folk" versions of redeployed Catholicism, service festivals, and patron saints within the constructions of subaltern community and political life. On occasion, this reworked version of Catholicism, which did not necessarily exclude "pagan" religiosity, could even legitimate popular rebellion against constituted official authority, including the official authority of the institutionalized church.

Given this history of resonance between worldly and sacred power, and its embeddedness at all levels of the cultural ladder, one would be surprised if the Catholic Church and its diverse representatives and institutional dependencies did not turn out to play vital roles during moments of political turmoil and crisis in the nineteenth and twentieth centuries. From this point of view, the political dynamics that fed the emergence of Liberation Theology and, in some regions, evangelical Protestantism constituted new versions of an old story. Disputes that surround Liberation Theology and evangelical Protestantism focused not so much on the legitimacy of a strong nexus between religion and politics as on the particular political substance or stances encouraged by "new" forms of Christian presence and mobilization in society.

Thesis Six

In popular and elite cultures in the twentieth century, memories of colonial life and struggle are sometimes woven into the fabric of contemporary life, identity, morality, and struggle. The palimpsest effect pushes to the margin historical experience as a chain of sequential cause and effect stretched along a linear time line while integrating a remembered (mentally reconstituted) colonial heritage into contemporary social and political life.

For historians of popular culture, examples abound. Zapata, when asked about the motivation for his stubborn integrity as a rebel, pointed to a box of colonial land titles, preserved and integrated into peasant understandings of right, struggle, and duty.[18] The Saramaka maroons, faced with the challenging multiethnic politics and coast-interior relations of Surinam, build their sense of moral identity on the reverential memory of "first-time," the struggle for freedom in a world of colonial sugar plantations.[19] In indigenous life, as one might expect, living colonial memory is particularly salient. The *memoristas* of southern Colombia studied by Joanne Rappaport,[20] like the elders of Guatemalan community life chronicled by Rigoberta Menchú,[21] and the Bolivian Kataristas who declare that they have been "waiting" for four hundred years to resolve pressing social issues,[22] all attest to the tricks of time within popular culture.

Significantly, the resilience of the colonial heritage as memory is not confined to Indians or subalterns. I recall a travel conversation with a respectable Bolivian in La Paz in 1983, who warned me that life in La Paz could become precarious. The Indians of the *altiplano* (high plains) might surround and besiege the city, as they had in 1781, if political order disintegrated. The sense of urgency attached to the 1781 episode made it more like an "only yesterday" reference than a "once upon a time" remark.

Similarly, in the resurgent ethnic politics that has marked much of Latin America in the 1980s and 1990s, colonial genealogies and memory have inserted themselves into the politics of land rights. To be a maroon community descended from runaway slaves ended up mattering to Brazilian law on land claims; to be an Indian from a community whose history was dispossessed ended up mattering to Colombian law on land claims. The nexus of colonial history, ethnic descent, and land claims could even lead to new ironies. In contests over land in southern Colombia, mestizo claimants argued, in a reversal of customary status assertion, that self-declared Indians and Indian communities were not really Indian at all. The colonial inheritance, as memory, had bitten back too hard.[23]

TIME'S ADDITIONAL TRICK

We have considered from an interior view the historical time sensibilities evident in Latin American literature covering long-term views of continuities and the multiple legacies ("theses") that define a living colonial heritage in the context of the 1990s. We have framed such legacies as "tricks of time" that coexist and compete with more familiar unilinear and sequential visions of time in Latin American experience.

Yet there is a pitfall to the sensibilities encouraged by the uncanny presence of the world we have not yet lost. To what extent are we to interpret the living colonial heritage as a kind of resilient inertia, a projection of times past (including the reconstitutive dynamics of times past) into the present? To what extent, on the other hand, are we to interpret the living colonial heritage not as inertial projection but as reconstitutions generated by postcolonial contexts of transformation, a reinvention of ghosts past despite ruptures that have broken linear continuity? The former orientation relies on a common sense notion of an "entrenched legacy" that carries forward into the present, somehow withstanding the forces of change, modernization, or progress. The latter orientation resonates with current intellectual sensibilities, an acute awareness of the contingent and the transitory in historical experience that exposes the constantly constructed and reinvented character of apparent legacy and tradition.

This opposition between continuity as persistence of a past that defies change and continuity as reinvention provoked and redefined by change is not necessarily a mutually exclusive antagonism. Nor does it exhaust the range of conceptual options before us as we struggle to understand the tricks of time in Latin America. But it brings to the fore a difficult intellectual dilemma. If the choices posed above are not quite as mutually exclusive as they appear at first sight, then neither are they smoothly compatible. If pressed to choose between the colonial heritage as rock formations that resist erosion for a very long period of time, or the heritage as contemporary "reinventions" of old tools and gadgets adapted to new machines and functions, then I would decide for the latter metaphor. Yet as we shall see, the choice is not entirely satisfying because it relegates an important dimension of experience to the margins.

Consider, for example, the instances mentioned above of the fusion of a profit principle with a coercive labor principle in postcolonial Latin America. The rubber boom in the Amazon, and its accompanying regime of coercive pressures on tappers, responded to the rapidly expanding world market for rubber sparked by new inventions and mass-market manufactures such as bicycles during the Second Industrial Revolution. Given this dynamic context, it goes too far to interpret the rubber regime as a rather flat projection of the extractive economy that produced cacao, nuts, spices, turtle eggs, and rubber on the eve of postcolonial times. Indeed, despite the broad resonance between the labor patterns and techniques of extraction of the late colonial Amazon and those of the early twentieth century, for the specific zones and peoples drawn into the rubber vortex, the new context of extractive commodity markets may have transformed sharply the substance of life: the specific commodities produced, the work pace of daily life, the scale and impact of debt and credit, the prevalence or fear of violence, the in-migration from other regions, and the ecological geography and sustainability of life adaptations. Similar cautions about context, transformations, and linkages to the wider economic world also apply to the examples of coffee, antimony, and charcoal mentioned above.

And yet to the historian of colonial times and to the viewer of the multifaceted pervasiveness of colonial legacies (six theses, not one thesis, embracing such varied themes as political economy, conquest encounters, race/class parallelism and mediation, gender relations and honor/degradation codes, the religion/politics nexus, and group memory), the vote for the transformational position may also seem a bit too facile. The closer one scrutinizes relationships and struggles at the more interior level, as microlevel experiences and adaptations of those directly affected, the more striking the sensation that a ghost has walked out of the past to defy our sense of historical motion. The leading extractive commodity may be rubber rather than cacao, but the dispersed geography and rhythms of collection, the economic powers and ethnic statuses concentrated in the *patrão*-merchant's seasonal credit advance to producers, the violent struggle to monopolize commodity flows along the river and tree trails in the jungle, might all suggest an eerie continuity at the concrete microlevel of human experience and interaction. Similarly, the "enslaved" charcoal worker of southern Brazil is legally free, relatively marginal to the prosperity of the wider economy of Brazil, less bound to servitude because of racial descent than the enslaved coffee and sugar workers of the early 1800s. In this and other ways the contemporary reinvention of "slavery" is indeed sharply different from its older counterpart. Yet why does the reinvention spark such scandal and outrage? Precisely because at a basic microlevel of human experience, the importance of such contrasts diminishes. What one still sees and experiences are peoples of African descent in lifetime bondage to physically exhausting labor regimes marked by heavy mortality, fear of capture, and severe violence for those who dare to escape.

Time's additional trick is the dynamic reconstitution of entrenched legacies. This last trick exposes the ways that the literary expressions of time sensibilities reviewed earlier may illuminate and mislead at the same time. If Carpentier is understood to imply that history "freezes" in some anachronistic regions, if Cortázar's story is read to imply that Aztec values persist as "national character" values passed on from generation to generation, if García Márquez is consumed as the idea that Latin America is an exotic realm outside the flows of change and movement that seem more normal elsewhere, then we remain at a superficial level of understanding. The tricks of time pose a deeper problem: reconciling an undeniable sense of continuity that seems to render historical motion irrelevant, with an understanding of the historical motion that itself generates cycles of apparent repetition or continuity while transforming their social meaning and consequences. This is the agenda I have tried to take up recently in a study of continuity and change in gender relations and experiences in Mexico between late colonial times and the late twentieth century.[24] In principle it is a problem that we may take up for all six theses presented above.

As we search for an understanding of time's additional trick, the one that poses the most intractable and difficult conundrum for historical analysis, we are steered back toward the enduring insights of appraisals of dynamic reconstitutions of entrenched colonial legacies, within a history that includes rupture and transformation. Embodied in their own literary and historiographic perspectives, Latin American scholarship and imaginations less rooted in the quest to treat the past as closed and sealed, are free to see it as open, surprising, and therefore contestible.

nine

Argentines Ponder the Burden of the Past

Tulio Halperín Donghi

Exploring the past and its legacy—frequently in the hope of finding the origins of present calamities—is an exercise that Latin American intellectuals have always found tempting. Argentine history in particular, where trends often found in other Latin American countries reach a feverish intensity reflected in a puzzling oscillation between dizzying rises and catastrophic falls, multiplies the opportunities for engaging in such self-congratulatory or anguished explorations.

In all of Spanish America the decades that followed the breakdown of the colonial order were full of disappointments. But to many Spanish American witnesses, the rise of the Rosas regime—one in which they discovered not only a hitherto unsurpassed despotism but also an unmatched disposition to inflict unspeakable barbarities on its subjects—represented a violent backlash against the brief liberal awakening of the 1820s, to such extremes that the Argentine experience appears qualitatively different from to those of its sister republics.

Much later, in the 1920s, Argentina not only had achieved a comparatively uneventful transition toward what Juan Bautista Alberdi, the ideologue of the project of national reconstruction launched after the fall of Rosas, had called the *república verdadera*, one in which the representative institutions did actually represent the popular will (expressed in free elections based on a universal male franchise) but its level of economic activity and its social profile moved it closer to western Europe than to its Latin American neighbors. To many outside observers, the difference was again qualitative: as the Mexican José Vasconcelos was to remark in 1922, while for the rest of Latin America the problem continued to be how to become a civilized country, Argentina already faced the problems of being one.[1]

A half century later, Argentina faced instead the consequences of a no less dramatic reversal of fortune. A witty economist had by then classified the countries of the world into four categories: developed countries; under-developed countries; Japan, that did everything right; and Argentina, where everything went wrong. And soon after that, during the sad years when much of Latin America witnessed the flourishing of regimes described (with variable degrees of understatement) as bureaucratic-authoritarian, Argentina suffered the experience of the terrorist state in a more extreme form than even its unfortunate neighbors of the Southern Cone.

Today, the country that finally emerged from that horrifying experience has to find its bearings in a world in constant transformation toward goals that cannot as yet be fathomed. The effort to reestablish an intelligible link with the nation's origins and its past appears more elusive than ever.

The starting point for this incessant exploration of a constantly changing object begins in 1838, when Esteban Echeverría, speaking on behalf of the first generation risen in the postrevolutionary era, defined their task as the total elimination of the colonial legacy of cultural and ideological inertia. Eight years later, in 1846, that hope had been dashed, and from his refuge in besieged Montevideo Echeverría drew in his *Ojeada retrospectiva* the portrait of a country ruled again by the forces of the past, which had found their deadly champion in Rosas.

In the meantime, Sarmiento had already offered in *Facundo* a richer and more complex view of the country's predicament and its colonial roots. To avoid opposing ideological principles (tradition and progress, despotism and liberty) that obsessed Echeverría, Sarmiento focused on conflicts between lifestyles and worldviews developed in the context of specific collective experiences. His approach allowed him to conclude that Argentina was victimized less by the deadening legacy of Counter-Reformation Spain than of Spain's inability to root its peculiar style of civilization in the vast spaces of the pampas. After locating Echeverría's abstract dilemmas in the concrete reality of two River Plate cities—Buenos Aires, open to all the winds of trade and hospitable to new ideas and new men that incessantly reached it from the outside world, and Córdoba, the landlocked capital of the Interior, an introspective city of spires and convents that turns to the past with pride and contemplates the future with foreboding—he refused to recognize in the contrast between the two cities a key to Argentina's predicament.

Córdoba and Buenos Aires represented two successive stages in the effort to ground the civilization of Europe in the deserted pampas. Sarmiento's *Recuerdos de Provincia* (1851) offers a monumental self-portrait of a man destined to reconcile these two civilizatory influences: as heir to a family tradition of service to God and king, he both continued and overcame it by putting the virtues inherited from his colonial ancestors at the service of the political and social ideas of the modern world.

This necessary reconciliation—achieved through the absorption of the older by the younger rival—would make it less difficult for the forces of civilization, so weakly implanted by Spain, to claim Argentina for themselves. Their victory would finally solve the Argentine dilemma, that—as Sarmiento had already proclaimed in the title of his 1845 book—did not oppose two ideals of civilization, but—more starkly— civilization *and* barbarism. As always in the case with Sarmiento, these terms do not denote two opposite abstract principles but rather the distillate of two parallel collective experiences: one grounded in the cities; the other in the insufficiently populated plains.

Giving enduring meaning to Sarmiento's construct is less its central polarity than an integration of vast social and historical configurations that does full justice to their contradictory complexity. Moreover, Sarmiento's passionate conviction that Latin America needed to open itself to the forces of change from the outside world was not based on any illusions about their benevolent natures but on a somber view of the world that recognized that historical progress required the ruthless annihilation of all those peoples and cultures unwilling or unable to sustain its constantly accelerating pace.

Sarmiento was thus well aware that Latin America's opening to the world was fraught with dangers ignored by his contemporaries. His rationale for change is close to that of the enlightened reformers of the previous century. Indeed, there was no viable alternative to radical change (even less so—Sarmiento would argue—after independence "had broken the glass walls" of the hothouse in which Spain had both imprisoned and sheltered its overseas possessions). Moreover, if an immense effort was not immediately launched to prepare for its challenge by improvising a new society capable of providing schools and land for all, the untrammeled opening to the outside world would place Spanish America at the mercy of enemies "who will come to take our place, to put us in the street, while doing the country the immense service of endowing it with the means to prosper, but exploiting these by and for themselves."[2]

As is frequently the case with Sarmiento, here he reached in a brief moment of illumination insights that anticipate concerns that would only become dominant much later. But stressing these insights' prophetic link with the future can obscure their more obvious connections to disappointments that followed the breakdown of the Spanish empire. The memory of the conquest frequently dominated such reflections for having led to an original sin blemishing forever Spain's New World creation.

Sarmiento fully shared this somber view of the Spanish, but he refused to waste any sympathy on the victims of an enterprise whose barbarity and illegitimacy he did not dispute. The memory of Spanish conquest offered instead a precious cautionary tale: in his native corner of Andean Argentina—he reminded the readers of *Recuerdos de Provincia*—the conquerors had found a powerful and prosperous native kingdom, that of the Huarpes. Yet, nothing had survived of this proud people or of its language beyond a few geographic names. This was the inevitable price paid by those left behind in the forward march of civilization. Now, if the heirs of the Huarpes' conquerors failed to awake in time to the imminent danger, they would share the same fate as their victims.

Sarmiento's awareness of the ruthless underside of historical progress was not a singular intuition. For instance, the Chilean writer J. V. Lastarria's *Investigaciones sobre la influencia social de la conquista y del sistema colonial de los españoles en Chile* (1843) gave Sarmiento his first opportunity to develop his dark view of historical progress. Andrés Bello, undoubtedly the towering figure among Spanish American intellectuals of the previous generation, argued for an even more negative reflection. Bello acknowledged life's advances in each individual society, but "in the relations among peoples and races savagery survives under hypocritical appearances, with all its original injustice and rapacity." Admittedly, the marauders of barbaric times have been replaced by merchants, "but these have on their counters Brenno's scales: *Vae Victis*."[3]

The second half of the century saw the birth of a more positive view of the postrevolutionary transformations and the role of the expansion of trade in fostering them. There is a specific reason why in Sarmiento this transition is especially abrupt. His *Memoria* of 1855 coincided with the end of his Chilean exile and his settlement in Buenos Aires, where he discovered that his alarm about the future had been excessive. "Buenos Aires is the people in South America that comes closest to the United States. . . . Mingling with the multitude that filled the main square to overflow on the national holiday I have not found rabble, plebs, *rotos* [impoverished]. . . . The dress is the same for all classes, or more properly speaking there are no classes. The gaucho relinquishes his poncho; the countryside is invaded by the city and this by Europe." The spectacle led to "strange conclusions that frighten *him* . . . Chile would have to prove that thirty years of peace have been useful to her. Forty thousand *rotos* in Santiago do not argue for the country's progress, and if Buenos Aires shows instead riches, cultivation, growing population and immigration, it is possible to conclude that without war and tyranny it would have fallen victim to the same stagnation as other peoples."[4]

This discovery of Argentine exceptionalism differed from the historical constructs of Bartolomé Mitre, in 1862–68 the first constitutional president of the reunified country, and the creator of modern Argentine historiography. Mitre did not find the key to exceptionalism in the tormented history of the postindependence decades but in the very origins of the Argentine historical experience. Mexico and Peru were feudal societies in which the heirs of the conquerors continued to oppress and exploit those of the conquered. In the River Plate, necessity forced settlers, faced with a sparse and indomitable Indian population, to organize the only Spanish colony sustained by its own productive labor. They were admirably prepared for the task: coming as they did from the largest cities and the most developed regions of the peninsula, they had very little in common with the illiterate and ferocious conquerors of Mexico and Peru. Initially their economic achievements were modest, and this was indeed fortunate: universal penury created an egalitarian society in which an "instinctive democracy" could flourish. During this early period few new settlers migrated to this unpromising region. This, again, was fortunate: the mestizo offspring of the early pioneers occupied the leading positions in society. From these "sinews of the colony" came "the historians of the colony, the governors who were to rule it, the citizens of the fledgling municipalities," men who brought to public life a spirit of "wild independence, that announced the type of a new people, with all its shortcomings and qualities"; thus racial equality complemented economic equality.[5]

The ensuing history validated this violently stylized narrative of Argentina's social origins, a course that unrelentingly pushed the River Plate colony forward and upward. Ignored and neglected by a petty and greedy imperial regime, the River Plate grew and expanded using the opportunities opened to its pioneers's initiative by a ruling power whose inefficiency counterbalanced its arbitrariness. When the imperial order threatened to stifle a flourishing clandestine outlet, revolution was the response, and through it the River Plate society became a nation. After ten years of revolutionary wars, a new leadership emerged from the struggle, one which better represented the masses it mobilized, thereby dislodging the initial revolutionary elites. Through this "social revolution" the "instinctive democracy" bequeathed by the humble colonial origins found its first political expression.

Mitre, however, quickly acknowledged that this was a very defective order. Mitre's own generation faced a clear task: to enshrine this democratic instinct within the institutional framework of modern liberal democracy. Mitre did not doubt the success of the enterprise. Argentina's good fortune differed from the rest of Spanish America. If liberal democracy was an exotic import whose triumph required a total repudiation of the legacy of the past, which for Andrés Bello (among many others) defined the political predicament of postrevolutionary Spanish America, the triumph of liberal democracy was the goal toward which the River Plate society had striven—albeit unknowingly—since its most remote origins. Mitre's faith in this unproblematic view of Argentina's political destiny rested on willful oversights of the political course following the fall of Rosas.

Other factors reinforced Mitre's optimism. Economic expansion, supported by the immense land resources of the pampas, that in Mitre's view underlay the creation of a democratic society and a democratic polity on the shores of the River Plate, flourished unabated and without apparent limits. It is difficult to argue with success and it helped to persuade Mitre's contemporaries of the wisdom of his view of the country's economic trajectory. To Mitre Argentina once again stood out from the rest of Spanish America. The rapid settlement of the pampas, at the price of implanting in it only the most primitive kind of pastoral economy, far from resulting in the barbarism denounced by Sarmiento, only marked the first stage in the development of civilization in the region, one in which "progressing on all fours" was natural.[6] The Argentine path of economic development appeared to Mitre as unproblematic as the nation's progress toward a democratic republic. Mitre's programmatic optimism about the Argentine present and future radically eliminated the problems that occupy us here; rather than reassessing the burden of the past, he looked back toward it in the same celebratory spirit that inspired his prophetic speculations.

While Mitre's contemporaries only occasionally objected to his belief in the country's manifest destiny of unlimited economic progress, many soon harbored reservations about the country's political course. In the economic field, neither the enthusiasts who embraced the path, nor the industrial protectionists who pleaded for careful modifications, had any reason to examine the colonial era for any clues to present problems. Since the new course emerged out of the total repudiation of colonial habits, past legacies could hardly explain present shortcomings. Moreover, even the most severe critics of these shortcomings could scarcely justify a turn to the past in search of better alternatives.

There was admittedly a pressing aspect of the country's socioeconomic development that inspired universal dissatisfaction. If not for Alberdi, for most of his contemporaries, the *república posible* was supposed to include a strong class of independent farmers who would rescue the pampas from gaucho barbarism. This did not happen. The desert plains continued to be appropriated instead by a class of large landowners rooted in the traditional Argentine elite. This disappointment evoked a vast literature that deplored the economic and social consequences of these overwhelming latifundia. Indeed, by the next century the consensus embracing radical rural transformation was as universal as it had been after the fall of Rosas; of the two books that reconstructed the consolidation of the large estate in the pampas, one was written by a rising star in the conservative party,[7] and the other by a socialist labor organizer.[8] Both shared the same dismal conclusions about existing land tenure patterns.

But there was something peculiar about this negative consensus. Ritual condemnations of the rural order acquired an increasingly fatalistic tone; rather than arguing for necessary reforms, they deplored the consequences of an irretrievably lost opportunity. Was this so because— as Sir Herbert Gibson, an Anglo-Argentine landowner and stock-raising expert, mischievously remarked in a 1914 pamphlet[9]—urban public opinion could not leave the issue alone, even though it only inspired indifference among people of the countryside? But, what very soon vanishes from this melancholy literature is the conviction, so pronounced in the aftermath of Rosas's fall, that rural transformation necessarily played a central role for the country at large. Now everybody recognized that the continuing predominance of large properties tarnished the otherwise admirable progress, yet almost everybody agreed to leave the matter there.

Regarding political developments, dissatisfaction was far more general. Here the legacy of the past also found relevance, and for decades to come its exploration was to provide dominant themes in Argentine political literature. In 1883 Sarmiento offered with his *Conflicto y armonías de las razas en América* the first significant contribution to a durable genre. Described by its author as a "*Facundo* that has reached old age," *Conflicto* is the testimony of an old man ruthlessly pushed to the margins of political life by a younger generation of leaders more interested in the spoils of victory than in loftier goals. Looking back on his career and those of his generation, Sarmiento concluded that their apparent triumphs could not hide the failure to realize social transformation and political redemption. "Our material situation"—he grudgingly admitted—"is not bad." Fields yielding golden harvests covered whole provinces, and signs of progress were everywhere. But such progress, lacking in unity and consistency, did not stifle concerns about political retrogression: Argentina was falling back to the level of Mexico, Venezuela, and other specimens in the museum of political monstrosities that was Spanish America. "The persistence of the ills that we hoped to have overcome through the introduction of the federalist constitution, and the generality and similarity of the events that take place in all of Spanish America made me suspect that the disease was more deeply rooted than the superficial features of the landscape had led us to believe."[10]

While in *Facundo* the key to the country's ills lay in the primitive lifestyle unavoidably associated with an excessively scarce population, now Sarmiento found it in the racial heritage of the Spanish conquest. In this fashion, racism finally raised its ugly head. But it was a very peculiar version of racism. As Nancy L. Stepan has stressed, Latin American spontaneous views on race better approximated Lamarckism than Darwinism; rejecting principles of nonhereditability of acquired traits is no less strong because in most cases it remains implicit. The reasons for such rejection are complex. Ambitious projects of social transformation militated against views of racial heritage as an insurmountable obstacle. Moreover, for all their scientific ambitions, in Latin America racial theories offered little more than a new vocabulary for earlier views. Comparative assessments of virtues and shortcomings of blacks and mulattoes already occupied the minds of Latin American thinkers as frequently as the exploration of the social impact of *mestizaje*. Their miscegenetic conclusions depended less on racial views than on attitudes toward social mobility. In Argentina negative views of mulattoes and admiration for the heroism displayed by black slaves in protecting their masters from Rosas's persecution (developed at length in José Mármol's lengthy excursus in his novel *Amalia* of 1851 or Sarmiento's celebration of the mulattoes's striving for personal improvement and social advancement) blurred distinctions between the racial and the social.

These views endowed racial heritages with the possibility of historical change, thereby disrupting inherited social arrangements.

Everywhere in Latin America, these influences made it difficult for fully fledged racism to flourish. Stanley Stein and Barbara Stein, in their *The Colonial Heritage of Latin America*, speak of a tendency toward racial pessimism. But in a country that looked to its future with more pride than concern, even pessimism tended to pale. This was already the case with Sarmiento. His drift to pessimistic conclusions were cut short by the discovery that French craneal capacities expanded with every century; now that Spaniards and Spanish Americans were free from the Inquisition's deadly grip, they too would follow French progress. Thus, to accompany his pessimism, Sarmiento offered a salve. Notwithstanding his generation's dashed hopes, it was still possible to keep the faith in historical progress: humankind's self-redemption, while slower than he had hoped in his youth, went even deeper than he had once imagined.

Even more revealing of this Argentine bias for hope than Sarmiento's convoluted argument, is the sudden optimistic closure of Carlos Octavio Bunge's unrelentingly pessimistic portrait of Spanish America in *Nuestra América*. We are told there how Spanish Americans owed their arrogance, indolence, and theological uniformity to their Spanish heritage and their fatalism and ferocity to their native ancestors, while Africans injected servility and malleability to the ethnic legacy. What follows is a passionate identification with this tainted section of humankind: "Perhaps from an anthropological viewpoint I am a pure European, but as far as psychology is concerned, I feel as Spanish-American as the Aztec or Guaraní *mestizo* or the mulatto. I am assimilated to them. I am one of them, and feel proud of it, in the hope than once the shortcomings sketched in this book are corrected we Spanish Americans shall be not just equal to Europeans and yanquis. The best!"[11]

What has the racial approach contributed to the idea of a legacy of the colonial past? The truth is, very little beyond a shift of emphasis from the notion of a Spanish American original sin, from the conquest as crime, to the presence of a collective blemish founded in the original shortcomings of the racial stock of the three peoples that mixed their blood in Spanish America. What counted was more their blending than the violence and oppression of their encounter. But this transfer had an important consequence: the blemish doesn't taint the Spanish American elites in the same way as the conquest-as-crime once had; if the problematic Spanish American ethnic inheritance can be studied "objectively" it is because it is nested in the object, in the Spanish American masses.

This objectification of the issue is not strictly new: it was already there in Echeverría, Sarmiento, and Alberdi. There is however a crucial difference: each one of them confronted a globally problematic society and offered his own very personal solution. Now the students and critics of Argentine society began to see themselves as members of a cultural and political elite and their writings as part of a dialogue within that elite, in whose name they offer verdicts.

This shift in emphasis toward the masses as inheritors of such a problematic legacy is even more marked in the writings inspired by another new influence, that of collective psychology, in its two versions, *Volkerpsychologie* (psychology of the people) and *psychologie des foules* (crowd psychology). The most distinguished product of the first influence is Juan Agustín García's *La ciudad indiana*. In exploring the colonial past, García discovered psychological tendencies that were already imposing "a fixed direction" to society: the cult of physical courage, contempt for the law, an exclusive concern for the acquisition of wealth, and faith in the country's future greatness.[12] This was certainly a mixed but less than calamitous heritage. Indeed, its negative repercussions appeared comparatively marginal.

The explorations inspired in the dubious insights of *psychologie des foules* also generated more pessimistic conclusions than the general drift the discipline's European masters might have delivered. In *Las multitudes argentinas*, José María Ramos Mejía turned to crowd psychology in search of a scientific explanation of the transition after 1810 from revolutionary emancipation to tyranny. If the conventional view had always recognized this descent as pathological, he certainly did not believe that this bleak period of the nation's past offered any special insights into the dark recesses of twentieth-century Argentina. A similar shift in emphasis to the masses, followed by the same moderate pessimistic conclusions, can also be found in a work that restores the conquest to its central position in the Spanish American past, Lucas Ayarragaray's *La anarquía argentina y el caudillismo*. Here, the breakdown of Imperial Spain destroyed the thin veneer hiding the survival of a power system based on the personal authority of a caudillo, descendant of the Spanish conquistador lurking under the burnished surface of an increasingly bureaucratized monarchical system. Emancipation allowed caudillismo to flourish, enabling nature to triumph over artifice. Caudillismo still survived even in the constitutional era, hidden again under the surface of an even more sophisticated institutional system but influencing and modifying it in decisive ways. Above all, its heritage survived in political parties that were little more than the following of personalistic leaders, and politics were less about issues and policies than about the personal rivalries among leaders.

Thus a national mood dominated by a more thoughtful but still vigorous optimism overwhelmed the cultural pessimism that characterized the Zeitgeist in the prewar years. Some writers went even further. While recognizing the negative aspects in the heritage of the past, both Juan B. Justo, the founder of the Socialist Party, and José Ingenieros, a central figure in Argentine intellectual life from the turn of the century until his premature death in the 1920s, did not doubt that the unstoppable advances of a new capitalist order successfully erased past legacies. And, in perhaps the most admirably balanced view of past and present developed under these ambiguous auspices, Joaquín V. González offered in his *El juicio del siglo* (1910) an essentially coincident—albeit less programmatically optimistic—assessment of the link between past and future. Unlike his fellow conservatives who denounced new social conflicts as exotic and irrelevant imports spread by the misguided apostles of the Left, González saw an Argentina integrating into a modern industrial world in which social issues provided the dominant theme for politics. Albeit with more problematic consequences than the founding fathers had imagined, Argentina was shedding its colonial heritage to enter, as they had prophesied, the orbit of the advanced North Atlantic countries.

This optimistic temper did not, however, survive the shock of the First World War and its aftermath. The breakdown of the nineteenth-century liberal capitalist civilization devastated a country that had accepted as its goal the full incorporation into that civilization. Argentina could not reach the true republic under worse auspices, and after the first disappointments with authentically elected governments, the temptation to proclaim that their failure was inevitable only mounted. The whole historical experience Mitre had so enthusiastically celebrated now collapsed. Notwithstanding the unheard-of prosperity of the 1920s, expressions of massive pessimism spread, targeting the past as much as the present and future, and not only from the conservative establishment disempowered by the political transition. Ezequiel Martínez Estrada, a man of the independent Left best known until then as a poet, took on an in-depth exploration of the Argentine past and present. In contrast to Mitre's celebrations, Martínez Estrada offered a relentlessly somber evocation of a land of mud and sterile stone, fated to host a corrupt and inhumane society, whose dwellers misguidedly tried to hide their hopeless physical and moral landscape under a false veneer of civilization. On publication, his *Radiografía de la Pampa* was greeted with enthusiasm and crowned with a state prize.

This was 1933, and the country was ready to receive its desperate message. Since 1929 the economic world order that had proved so hospitable to Argentina lay in ruins, the Invisible Hand had lost its prodigious powers, Mitre's manifest destiny had suddenly vanished, and the country had to find its way in an unfamiliar and (it was to be feared) hostile world. Not surprisingly, it was now ready to look at its past with new and disenchanted eyes.

The Depression paved the way for an alternative image of the nation's past and present by integrating in novel ways motifs which had already helped undermine the disarray of an old image it once struggled to replace. First, reticence toward the democratic republic, once celebrated by Mitre in the 1880s as "the highest rational form [of government], and the last word of human logic, that conforms to reality as well as to the ideal in matters of free government,"[13] gave way to an outright rejection of the democratic experiment, and with it of the whole experience of the *república posible*, justified in the past as a new economic and social order which would finally set the possible stage for genuine democracy.

The Depression pushed another ideological motif still marginal during the 1920s closer to the center of political discussion. The term *imperialism* had already entered the vocabulary of politics, but usually associated with expressions of solidarity with Latin American peoples directly affected by the economic dominance and the political and military interventions of the United States. It was only after the shock of 1929 that significant sectors of public opinion began to turn to theories of imperialism in their search for keys to the unexpected predicament that had struck the country.

To be sure, even before 1929 the course of the economy had inspired some preoccupation, but it usually did not go as far as pleading for a radical change in orientation, preferring a more proactive attitude than reliance on the restorative powers of the Invisible Hand. Thus Alejandro Bunge, a statistician who since the Great War had dominated economic debate, had proclaimed the end of the era in which the dynamism of the agricultural export sector fueled economic expansion. The old export sector had matured and could neither expand production nor absorb the swelling labor force. Future growth depended on the rise of manufacturing, and it was the duty of the state to facilitate this necessary transition.

But these proposals did not reject previous achievements. Indeed, for Bunge the successful completion of agricultural expansion itself necessitated and enabled industrialization. By entering this higher stage in its economic development, the country would not deviate from the route traced by the founding fathers, who in fact had always recognized in industrialization the ultimate goal for the Argentine economy.

The view of continuity with the past rather than its rupture did not completely disappear. It inspired, for instance, *Historia de la independencia económica*, published in 1949 by Eduardo B. Astesano, a former Communist who swung to Peronism. If the title echoed the recent proclamation of economic independence by Perón, suggesting that the country was undergoing a new beginning, the portrait of Carlos Pellegrini (the conservative statesman who had presided during the financial and economic restructuring after the Baring crisis of 1890) on the book's cover offered a more accurate reflection of its true spirit. Aldo Ferrer's *La economía argentina: las etapas de su desarrollo y problemas actuales* (1963) even more explicitly portrayed the period of rapid economic expansion prior to 1929 as a decisive stage in Argentina's progress toward a mature industrial economy.

These nuances clashed with much more negative views fanning out across ever larger sections of public opinion. At first glance there is nothing puzzling in the rancor with which a country suddenly cheated of a promising and prosperous future looked back at those who failed to prepare it for such an unexpected reversal of fortune. But it so happens that, after passing the first shock, the haphazard economic order that slowly emerged from the ruins of the Depression proved less inhospitable to Argentina than once feared: from 1932, when the economy touched bottom, until 1947, the country enjoyed an economic expansion as vigorous as anything it had known in the agrarian export era.

The rejection of past inheritances was less a reaction to economic adversity than to the blatantly illegitimate political regime that took charge of expanding the role of the state in the economy. In 1930 the first successful military coup of the constitutional era overthrew President Yrigoyen, elected in 1928 with the largest majority in Argentine history. The revolutionary leaders hoped that the shortcomings of his administration had forever alienated the electorate. An exploratory election in the province of Buenos Aires only brought dismay: six months after their fall from power, the Radicals garnered a larger majority than one year earlier. The military and the conservative forces, determined to remain in power at whatever cost, now faced a stark dilemma: establish a dictatorial regime akin to those coming into fashion in the Old World, or manipulate the electoral system in order to generate artificial majorities allowing them to govern against the will of those they ruled.

Only a minority of army officers and an even more minuscule faction within the political class favored the first solution. In 1932, after the provisional military government had forced the Radicals to abstain by imposing the most humiliating conditions for their electoral participation, a coalition of conservatives and dissident Radicals and Socialists elected president General Agustín Justo. The return of the Radicals to the electoral arena in 1935 forced Justo to supplement his subtle intrigues with blatant electoral fraud and open violence. Not surprisingly, his government's unpopularity only mounted.

In this context, an unforgivingly hostile public was prepared to discover the most sinister motives behind the financial and economic measures designed to counteract the Depression. While public opinion at large believed that government policies only offered better opportunities for the people in power to indulge their personal greed, left- and right-wing enemies of the administration (and those Radicals who felt the need to develop an interest in ideological issues) preferred less simple explanations.

In this pathological political setup alternative views of the Argentine past and present began to flourish. Two different versions emerged, having however, more in common than their supporters appreciated. For both the critical exploration of the past shifted its focus from the inventory of political shortcomings usually linked to the cultural or ethnic aspects of the Spanish legacy, to the link with the North Atlantic economy that in Mitre's view had sustained the enormously successful performance of post-Rosas Argentina. One feature of the new economic policies especially invited such a shift: the almost total incorporation of Argentina into the British trade and currency system, reflected in the terms of the Roca-Runciman treaty of 1933, that intended to keep the British market open to its pastoral exports. Such evidence of the enormous impact of the unequal links between Argentina's peripheral economy and its metropole also revealed the salience to Argentina of the imperial *problématique*. Both the Right and the Left opposition placed this new theme at the core of their revised views of the Argentine past and present. Remarkably, however, the Left, for which imperialism was a familiar topic, proved less able than the authoritarian Right, for which this was a new concept, to integrate it into a coherent view of the nature and roots of the Argentine predicament.

In 1934 the brothers Julio and Rodolfo Irazusta developed in *La Argentina y el imperialismo británico: Los eslabones de una cadena* the right-wing argument about imperialism. Strongly influenced by Maurras, they discovered the key to the country's political and economic misfortunes in the "oligarchy," a group defined less by its social background than its ideological inspiration. Having ruled the country since the fall of Rosas, opened it to the influence of the western nations in the vain hope of refashioning Argentina as a replica of liberal democracy and free trade, the oligarchy condemned the country to merciless plunder of its wealth and robbed Argentina of its soul by turning its back on its Hispanic and Catholic roots.

Notwithstanding its indignant rejection of the previously dominant view, the Irazusta brothers had more in common with it than it would appear: political regeneration through a return to the ideological legacy of the Spanish colony did not include any return to the closed economy of colonial times. This was no doubt unavoidable in a region which once existed as a depressed backyard and backdoor to Potosí and had later developed the most powerful national economy in Spanish America after the last Spanish viceroy of the River Plate opened its harbors to foreign trade.

In their search for a usable past the Irazustas turned instead to Rosas, who harbored a healthy skepticism about the socioeconomic and political utopias of his enemies, saw western powers's invocations of their *mission civilisatrice* as a rationalization for their hegemonic ambitions, and used what had survived of the colonial traditions to consolidate his political authority. The increasing popularity of the Irazustas's view of the past did not depend on the dubious accuracy of this monumental portrait of a hero whom Julio Irazusta was later to describe as Argentina's Cavour. What made their view even more attractive was, while sternly condemning the historical experience that had just closed in economic and political bankruptcy, they did not prescribe any drastic social or economic restructuring. What is more, they even suggested that entrusting national interests to more patriotic and knowledgeable advocates, the intimate links with the developed economies could be maintained without threatening the country's independence and prosperity. Accordingly, this view gave voice to the reactions of a public opinion chafing under the rule of a blatantly illegitimate government that boasted its roots in the post-Rosas era while recognizing—albeit grudgingly—that the economic results of the government's policies were not entirely negative.

Lending the Irazustas's views a more permanent attraction was their promotion of solutions not only less than radical but also remarkably imprecise. Thus, while they denounced the Justo government's complicity with imperialism, they emphasized the plight of the stock raisers, sacrificed by the Roca-Runciman treaty to the tender mercies of the American and British packers (and the small minority of privileged fatteners with whom they traded), the British shipping companies, and the large buyers in London's Smithfield market. Yet there was no intrinsic reason why similar arguments could not apply to other interests. Indeed, by the early 1940s another spokesman for this right-wing version of anti-imperialism, José María Rosa, used them for a proindustrialist plea in the essays he gathered in 1943 in his *Defensa y pérdida de nuestra independencia económica*.

The Leftist reply to this right-wing anti-imperialism was much less effective in shaping public opinion. While it could rely on a much larger body of doctrine than the views the Right was improvising on the matter, both the national and the world context inhibited efforts to build a new view of the Argentine past and present around the *problématique* of imperialism. For one thing, in a context where fake democracy jostled with authentic dictatorship, for the Left, the defense of political freedoms assumed the highest priority, and this prompted them to treasure the legacy of the liberal constitutionalist tradition, to which most of them looked back with a respect verging on veneration.[14]

The world context also militated against an exclusive emphasis on the notion of imperialism. Thus the Socialists—the only party in Congress steadfastedly opposing policies that had inspired the right-wing anti-imperialist protests—continued referring to British and United States imperialism but carefully distinguished their limited critique from the larger dilemma of a world inexorably careening toward a new war created by the triumph of fascism. Here a very different set of political and ideological responses was needed. From the Spanish Civil War on, the conflict between democracy and fascism dominated the socialists' concerns, prompting them to downplay anti-imperialist topics, and finally to recognize that the fascist threat was serious enough to force its enemies to rally behind the imperialist powers that were— albeit belatedly and for self-serving reasons—leading the antifascist cause.

As for the Communists, they moved in the same direction but through more brusque transitions that reflected a wholly manipulative use of anti-imperialist topics. During the Popular Front years these themes yielded the limelight to calls for a democratic, antifascist struggle which included an explicit commitment to nonrevolutionary social transformation. Imperialist themes returned with a vengeance after the Soviet-German pacts, and were totally dropped after the German invasion of the USSR, to which the Argentine Communists responded with a complete and unqualified allegiance to the Grand Alliance against Nazi Germany.[15] By 1945, a senatorial candidate in the Communist-backed coalition in Buenos Aires claimed that "today anti-imperialism is Fascism," thereby confirming that the Right had won the anti-imperialist high ground by default.

Within the Radical Party, the reception of the anti-imperialist *problématique* reflected similar trends. While it found a sympathetic echo among most currents within the deeply divided Party, only a very minor faction, the youthful FORJA, placed it at the core of its political project. FORJA's following within the party remained negligible, and within the public at large it was even smaller than the right-wing appeal. To be sure, the movement enjoyed a decisive posthumous influence after Peronism's radical social and political innovations gave FORJA's ideological message greater relevance. This message took its inspiration from APRA (the Peruvian nationalist movement led by Haya de la Torre), from which it derived two motifs that distinguished it from even moderate Marxist versions of anti-imperialism. For one, since the struggle against imperialism took precedence over the class struggle, the anti-imperialist party could not be an exclusively workers' or a peasants' and workers' party. Instead, the middle classes, thanks to their superior political culture and skills, were to play the leading role. Perhaps even more important, anti-imperialist goals did not include breaking the links with imperial metropoles but a renegotiation of those ties so that imperialism could—in Haya de la Torre's striking formula—function in peripheral economies as the first and not the last stage of capitalism. The agent charged with such renegotiation was a state refashioned as the reincarnation of the political will of the anti-imperialist party. The Second World War forced FORJA supporters to choose aligning with right-wing anti-imperialists, who in 1940 decided after long vacillations to entrust their future to an imminent German victory, or with mainstream Radicals, who, with varying degrees of enthusiasm, finally took the opposite tack.

The best-known FORJA intellectual, Raúl Scalabrini Ortiz, chose the first alternative, when in 1941 he wrote: "the simple souls say: by attacking England you play Germany's game. This is in fact true. But it is no less true that Germany is playing our game, if we know how to take advantage of it."[16] And with this alternative in mind, in 1940 he published two books that by 1972 would reach fifth editions, *Historia de los ferrocarriles argentinos* and *Política británica en el Río de la Plata*. The first book explored the finances of the British railway companies, gathering for the first time a vast mass of partially new information to bolster old accusations against these companies. The author concluded by justifying Lenin's casting of Argentina as the archetypal semicolony, which he reproduced almost verbatim in the introduction—albeit without attribution. The second book was a different matter. An exploration of alleged British interventions in Argentine politics elaborated in a decidedly paranoid style, Scalabrini Ortiz assigned to Britain the role of counterprovidence, leaving the author both horrified and awed by his discovery that this diabolical agent shared the omniscience and omnipotence of its heavenly rival.

The durable success of books displaying the iron logic of a *délire systématique* suggests that their views were so convincing that readers ignored the telling signs of their author's near paranoia. Indeed the posthumous ideological success of *forjismo* owed less to its theoretical rationale for Peronism than the fact that FORJA prophecies and Peronist policies reflected a consensus which crossed the Right, Center Left, and Left spectra, even while they refused to support to the new regime.

More thoughtful versions of the critique of the legacy of the export economy that underlay the anti-imperialist currents also forged independent lines of argument. Here the role of Raúl Prebisch is of course crucial. Having participated in the planning and implementation of the economic policies of the Justo administration—and thereby becoming the brunt of opposition attacks—and having been forced into semiexile by the military government established in 1943 and its heir the Peronist regime, Prebisch sought to build a theoretical framework to define and justify a specific role for the state in integrating national economies at the periphery of the world economic system. Prebisch offered an infinitely more valuable diagnosis than the economic rhapsodies of the right- and left-wing ideologues who rallied to Peronism. But it appeared less and less relevant in a country overwhelmed by the increasingly authoritarian turn under Peronism. Prebisch's views at best justified an early assessment of the new regime's achievements, complaining humorously that it *hace mal lo bueno y bien lo malo* (makes bad the good, and good the bad). But, once Peronism rabidly polarized Argentine society, almost everybody found this assessment excessively nuanced.

By the latter 1940s the anti-imperialism legacy translated into simpler and cruder versions, underpinning the economic policies of Peronism, massive redistribution from agriculture to manufacture, and within the latter to wages, and the most extreme industrial protectionism. By 1948 it was clear that a correction was needed, but the regime's deep social transformations made it extremely difficult. Gradually, Perón accepted its inevitability and attempted a partial opening to foreign investment. Now, this debased nationalistic and anti-imperialistic view of the Argentine past and present became the ideological girding of exhausted economic policies. The regime could scarcely afford to repudiate the very policies responsible for the unparalleled prosperity—and indeed existence—of enlarged social sectors, in spite of its oblique maneuvers.

This popularized version of the critical view of Argentine history did not look too far into the past: it emphasized the 1930s, now universally designated as the *década infame* (infamous decade), and characterized it as a period in which a corrupt political class ruled the country against its will and systematically sold it out to foreign interests. The more remote past lurked in a depressing but imprecise landscape of arbitrariness and misery for the poor.

The Peronist regime's collapse only radicalized this view of the past among the faithful, drawing it closer to its sources in the right-wing anti-imperialism of the 1930s. After long vacillations, Rosas now became an illustrious precursor to Peronism which, having lost almost its entire following among the propertied classes and the middle class, became even more closely identified with the memories and the objectives of the working class. But the same supple ideological tradition serviced President Frondizi's developmentalist project. A new version converted the *década infame* into a temporary victory of an oligarchic-imperialist alliance intent on barring Argentina's progress toward its industrial future by imposing an impossible and irredeemable return to an export economy. Perón's fall risked a return of these negative forces to influential positions, determined more than ever to impose their hopelessly anachronistic objectives. Only a national and popular front, in which the working class followed the industrial "national bourgeoisie," would thwart this sinister plan. However, this required a rejigged view of the imperialist threat. While the British still longed to restore a pastoral Argentina as part of their informal empire, investment from other core economies, if carefully selected and channeled by a state committed to the cause of economic development, could accelerate rather than bridle it.

Some former FORJA spokesmen, forced into hibernation by the ungrateful Peronist regime, now won the opportunity to preach this modified gospel to the mass readership of the progovernment press.

Scalabrini Ortíz recoiled from the task in horror when he discovered that he was expected to justify the opening of oil exploitation to foreign companies. His fellow *forjista* Arturo Jauretche eluded such awkward issues by launching a satirical attack on middle-class liberal traditions from the pre-1929 paradise. The middle classes was depicted as an irredeemably gullible booboisie. He later continued his crusade in books than won a vast following among a reading public that did not necessarily share his political *parti pris*.[17] José María Rosa launched a parallel enterprise in history, culminating in a multivolume global alternative to Argentina's *historia oficial*, accused now of having used Mitre's central intuitions to build a cynically falsified canonical version of Argentine history.[18] Thus the substitution of the old consensus on the Argentine past for a new one successfully completed the inversion of positive and negative formulations. Its success depended on the new version's adaptability to changing circumstances, a very necessary virtue in a country where these circumstances were changing with ever greater frequency.

These new views of history already rallied the support of the post-1955 Peronist resistance grounded in the labor movement (bizarrely rooted in the interwar right-wing ideologies but boasting a spontaneous view of social conflict remarkably akin to social democracy), and favored an industrializing project similar to Helio Jaguaribe's Bismarckian plan for Brazil.

Yet the secret of its success, this version's adaptability, also threatened to empty it of any precise content. Any assessment of the Argentine past that included the demonization of the *década infame* and a negative evaluation of the age of export-induced economic growth under the *república posible* could count on a place in this new consensus. The intensified political crisis inspired comparative indifference to the more specific social and economic issues of the past. Post-Perón administrations could neither destroy Peronism as a political force nor reintegrate it into the legitimate political arena without committing political suicide. Worsening political conflict developed a dynamism and a logic of its own, and eclipsed any single social actor's ability to influence new views of the Argentine past and present, all of them contained within the capacious boundaries of this new consensus.

The 1960s only aggravated an already hopelessly entangled situation. The Cuban Revolution for the first time rescued the socialist alternative from its indeterminate future, even though supporters and enemies alike always exaggerated the horizon of its possibilities. For Peronists, the situation now offered an opportunity to engage in occasional political blackmail. Some adversaries began to recognize it as a nonrevolutionary alternative to the revolutionary danger. But to many others the very fact that it was ready to use that danger as a political weapon confirmed that it was irredeemably unsound. Thus, while the revolutionary socialist alternative never won the active support of any significant section of Argentine society, its very presence linked the chronic Argentine political crisis to Latin America's much more extreme political and social agendas. In so doing, it restored relevance to the anti-imperialist motifs of Peronism, identities which, after 1955, emphasized the labor movement's roots and nonrevolutionary traditions of an uncompromisingly militant class strife.

The Right joined the Left's pressure on Peronism. Since 1963 Peronist labor leaders, persuaded of their firm foothold in the post-Peronist sociopolitical order, offered to cooperate with business to push for developmentalist goals it accused the second post-Peronist elected government of neglecting. This actively destabilized the government and contributed in 1966 to the establishment of a military regime, designed to implement this developmentalist program.

What followed did not exactly fulfill labor's expectations. While the working class suffered less than in previous botched efforts to shake off the economic legacy of Peronist policies, the labor movement failed to insinuate itself as one of the senior partners of the military in power. By 1969 the mainstream of Peronist labor cautiously crossed to the opposition. Massive riots in Córdoba hopelessly weakened the regime, crippled its economic policies and further deepened the political crisis. By 1970 no solution was possible without Peronist participation.

This was the context in which a new term made its triumphal entry into Argentine public discourse. Suddenly the word *dependencia* was on everybody's lips. Discontented stock raisers who for the first time lost their share of profits from currency devaluations and industrialists who themselves began to feel the pinch of multinational corporations's inroads and were now in danger of losing their enterprises to foreign creditors thanks to a cascade of devaluations joined the ranks of political radicalization propelled by the growing Left-Peronist underground. Indeed, a recent history of contemporary Argentina[19] covering the ten years after the luckless 1966 Argentine Revolution entitles this chapter *Dependencia o liberación*—the banner of the pro-Perón coalition which triumphed in the March 1973 general elections. Of course, in the transition from ideological construct to political slogan, the notion of dependence lost much of its precision, though one might wonder how much it had to start with.

The answer to this question may perhaps be found in a widely celebrated example of political-ideological cinema, Fernando Solanas and
Octavio Getino's *La hora de los hornos*. Their powerful mythical image
of the period from the fall of Rosas to the rise of Perón, faithfully follows the canonical view of the past first sketched by right-wing anti-
imperialists of the 1930s. Admittedly, Britain as counterprovidence has
only a modest place in the film, ceding its sinister role to the *Sociedad
Rural*: the film punctuates each successive downturn in Argentine history with the insertion of the society's logo. Its ominous bullhead and
the bloody rituals of the stockyard become in *La hora de los hornos* a
powerful symbol of the sordid and cruel realities hidden under the well-
oiled institutional machinery of the constitutional era. The directors
rediscovered a subliminal Argentine Minotaur, that Echeverría and
Sarmiento had proclaimed to have discovered in Rosas.

In the middle of a political whirlwind inexorably pushing the country toward state terrorism inaugurated in 1976, it should not surprise us
that the introduction of the notion of dependency did not add much to
the historical analyses already practiced under more homespun labels. A
perusal of the literature it inspired only confirms the conclusion already
embodied in Solanas and Getino's film. Instead, the banner of the struggle against dependency so dichotomized the contrasting positive and
negative poles at the very core of this view of history that an apocalyp-
tic resolution to the conflict seemed all but unavoidable.

We know now that the apocalypse could not in fact be avoided. What
followed was, in the most literal sense, a sobering experience. First, state
terror left the country in shock. Then, a succession of economic blows,
culminating in the 1989 hyperinflation, and the implosion of "real
socialism" in Eastern Europe abolished the national and world context
that had lent credence to the previous half century's conflicts and to the
view of the past they once inspired. The open economy that used to be
anathema to most Argentines is now an inescapable fact of life. While
few celebrate the change, it appears as pointless to object to it as to the
vagaries of the climate. Having lost old illusions about its future, sus-
pecting that little can be done to influence it, Argentina's relationship
with the past likewise changed. Passionate discussions on its true shape
give way to a remarkable indifference. While those authors who provide
richly anecdotal but unproblematic historical evocations can count their
readers in the hundreds of thousands, punitive excursions against the
great figures of the liberal pantheon, or the opinionated reconstructions
that imagined a past already dominated by the conflicts of the present,

so popular until yesterday, are part of a dying genre. Indeed, their withering amidst an almost universal indifference projects onto the past the vanishing of the social and political conflicts that only recently—albeit at a ruinous cost—lent structure and meaning to politics; thus the past becomes as shapeless—as meaningless—as the present.

This last turn marks a paradoxical arrival point of morose explorations of Argentina's past. What had sustained for so long this exercise in retrospective introspection was the increasing despair at the course of the country's current history. Now, leaving behind decades of obsessive self-absorption, one might celebrate Argentina's way of making peace with itself and its fate and conclude that it is finally ready to rejoin the world. But perhaps celebration is not what the circumstances demand: the world that welcomes Argentina into its fold is very different from the one Argentina had hoped to rejoin once free of its obsessions. So different is it indeed, that the Argentines' first lesson was the emptiness of their past and the absence of shape and meaning to their present.

ten

The Colonial Past: Conceptualizing Post-*Dependentista* Brazil

Stuart B. Schwartz

Brazilians and North Americans in the mid-twentieth century both viewed their colonial pasts from the perspective of the modern nation-state. They sought to explain contemporary national conditions by understanding their colonial origins, the nature of settlement, the fabric of society, especially its racial components, their political and religious traditions, and the economic bases of their history. North Americans, ebullient and confident in their power and their future, combed the colonial past for those elements that had promoted social stability, coherence, and consensus; for the foundations of democracy and the origins of economic success and American distinctiveness.[1] Brazilians faced with the political corruption of the old republic, social unrest, and economic dependence saw their past far more darkly and sought to explain their predicament in a history of personal irresponsibility, religious obscuranticism, sexual license, political failure, and above all in slavery and colonial exploitation. The commonalities of the two histories were obscured by their different results. In the formulation of Viana Moog's popular book, *Bandeirantes and Pioneers*, the *bandeirantes* were no match for the pioneers.[2]

Since the 1930s, for about half a century, one paradigm has dominated historical interpretations of colonial Brazil, becoming almost universally accepted by people of widely different political positions and historical methods. They viewed Brazil within the context of European expansion and the precocious development of Portuguese commercial capital (but not necessarily capitalism). Brazil was seen as a great colonial enterprise, based on African slavery and the exploitation of local resources and peoples for the exclusive benefit of its metropole, Portugal.

Within this formulation, Brazilian history prior to 1800 could be summarized simply. After the initial contact and desultory exploitation of dyewood, the introduction of sugar in the 1530s, and the creation of an export-oriented monoculture based on large-scale plantations using slave labor created a peculiar kind of agricultural export colony, distinct from the Spanish American centers of Mexico and Peru with their concentrated indigenous populations and silver mines. In many ways, this was a preview of what was to emerge later in the Caribbean. The acquisition of labor from Africa became, in fact, the essential element in the system so that over time, plantation agriculture, sugar exports, African slave imports, and a locally powerful planter aristocracy (*açucarocracia*) became so entwined that it was virtually impossible to conceive of these elements separately. This "plantation complex" determined the political organization and social relationships that characterized the colony as a whole, even in areas where the complex was attenuated or did not exist. Thus while the actors and their primary occupations changed over time, the situation of colonial dependency and social exploitation remained constant, whether the scenario was the gold washings of Minas Gerais and Cuiabá, the cattle ranges of Piauí, or the cotton *fazendas* (plantations) of the Maranhão. The stirrings for independence were abortive, late, and were ultimately forestalled by the conversion of the colony into a metropolis with the arrival of the Portuguese court in 1808. When political independence was achieved in 1822, neither monarchy nor slavery were unseated and Brazil's economic dependence, now as part of England's "informal empire," continued.

This understanding of colonial Brazil as a slave-based export economy had a long gestation period. Traces of it were already apparent in historians of the nineteenth and early twentieth centuries. But it was fully constructed, or more exactly codified, by three Brazilian intellectuals of the mid-twentieth century whose ideas have dominated subsequent historical thinking and whose shadow has fallen over most subsequent writing. Gilberto Freyre's *Casa grande e senzala* (1933) exteriorized the interior of the plantation house and made the relationships between white planters and their Indian, and especially African, slaves the key to an understanding of the dynamic of race, family, and social hierarchy in Brazil. Freyre's emphasis on patriarchal social relations contained echoes of a "feudal" interpretation of the Brazilian past, but it was able to ignore the economic implications of those relations within the context of

Portuguese commercial expansion.[3] The economic underpinning of this vision was outlined in detail in extraordinary books by Roberto Simonsen and Caio Prado Júnior, authors of widely different political persuasions who shared, nevertheless, a common vision of Brazil as a product of export monoculture. São Paulo industrialist Roberto Simonsen in his *Historia econômica do Brasil* (1937) created an image of the Brazilian economy which emphasized its commercial nature, its export orientation and dependence on world markets, and slavery as an "inescapable economic imperative." This extensive synthesis was soon followed by a book that reached similar conclusions about the colonial economy but which explained them in a distinct and far more negative framework. Caio Prado Júnior had already published *Evolução política do Brasil*, one of the first serious attempts to apply a Marxian framework to Brazilian history, in 1933, but it was with his *Formação do Brasil contemporâneo* (1942) that Prado Júnior made full use of the colonial era to identify and explain the underlying rationale of Brazil's past, or what he called in a now classic opening chapter, "the meaning of colonization (*O sentido da colonização*)."[4] In this remarkable book he placed material life and especially the plantation (*grande lavoura*) at the heart of his understanding of the colonial condition and the Portuguese commercial system as the fundamental principle of the colony's social organization. As he put it:

> that heterogeneous gathering of races that colonization brought here by chance with no other objective than to create a vast commercial enterprise so that white Europeans, black Africans, and American Indians would contribute according to the circumstances and demands of that enterprise.[5]

For Prado Júnior the colonial enterprise produced social pathology,

> incoherence and instability in [its] settlement, poverty and misery in the economy, dissolution in its customs, ineptitude and corruption in its civil and ecclesiastic leaders. What spark of vitality, what capacity for renewal lay concealed among the ruins, the truly catastrophic degradation into which the colony had fallen?[6]

Here was a reading of the colonial past that set Brazilian historiography on a dark path quite distinct from the happy trails of North American scholars.

The power of this vision of the Brazilian past gained broad historiographical acceptance, especially after it was buttressed by thorough quantitative work like Frédéric Mauro's study of the Portuguese Atlantic economy in the seventeenth century.[7] Its impact can be found in a series of subsequent books on Brazil like Celso Furtado's *Formação econômica do Brasil* (1959; English trans., 1963) and in more general books on the structure of Latin America like Andre Gunder Frank's *Capitalism and Underdevelopment in Latin America* (1967), and Stanley Stein and Barbara Stein, *The Colonial Heritage of Latin America* (1970).[8] These books of the 1960s exercised an enormous impact on a generation of scholarship and on the thinking of many Latin Americans and those concerned with the future of the hemisphere. With significant differences among them, these authors elaborated a structuralist interpretation of colonial history in which powerful and precociously centralized states, serving the economic interests of certain metropolitan groups or social fractions, created the political and juridical conditions that made colonial exploitation possible. The mercantilist Iberian states forged, in most periods, an alliance with local landowning and mining aristocracies for the extraction of colonial surplus by using archaic if not "feudal" labor arrangements (slavery, *encomienda, mita*).[9] This interpretation fit well with other globalizing visions of the former colonial worlds of Asia and Africa, and it eventually contributed to the formulation of a generalized theory of dependency. In Brazil this interpretation was sharpened and reached its most coherent expression in the definition of the "old colonial system," (*antigo sistema colonial*) outlined by Fernando Novais in a classic essay and fleshed out by a series of other studies of the eighteenth-century colonial commercial structures.[10] To put it in the language of world systems analysis, there was "increasing core-state penetration of the Luso-Atlantic economy," as Portugal's dependence on England facilitated the process of capital accumulation within the world economy.[11]

The structuralist-dependency interpretation presented great advantages. By emphasizing economic realities it bypassed the limitations imposed by political chronologies and allowed for new periodizations and conceptualizations. For example, the Steins' definition of a "neo-colonial" epoch extending from circa 1750 to the middle of the nineteenth century stressed the continuities of the colonial heritage and helped explain the difficulties of social and political transformations, thus making political independence a less central aspect of Latin American history and its failures less anomalous. Above all, the structuralist-dependency paradigm framed a "big picture" by giving coherence to a vast range of information, by explaining linkages between political, economic, and social phenomena, by emphasizing the role of the market, and by placing class relations at the core of analysis.

But the dependency approach came at a certain cost. First, it made Atlantic commerce the central (and almost the single) theme of colonial history and thus shifted focus and agency to imperial policy-makers and away from colonial actors and concerns. Whether its portrayal of "relentless capitalist advance" was simply "yet another form of Western teleology," is problematic, but clearly it centered history in Europe and left large segments of Latin American populations outside the story of the region.[12] For example, while in the eighteenth century silver made up more than 90 percent of the value of the goods shipped from Mexico to Spain, only about 10 percent of the Mexican population was associated with the mines or mining. The lives of the remaining population, while surely influenced by the colonial arrangement, could not be adequately examined or portrayed within the predominant explanation. Even within a Marxian framework, the emphasis on commerce and the market drew criticism from those who believed that the mode of production and its accompanying social relations needed to be placed at the heart of analysis and the emphasis given to the production rather than the circulation of goods.[13]

Clearly, there were other ways to conceptualize Latin America in order to integrate sectors of the population that the focus on colonial commerce and imperial politics had left out. Secondly, there were questions of historical action that did not lend themselves easily to the dependency paradigm: gender relations, sexuality, representations of identity, ritual behavior, and a myriad of other topics. An increasing concern with these issues and by the 1980s, a questioning of "dependency" as a theory with powers of prediction rather than as a specific historical explanation led to a shift in focus and interpretation.

This shift came in two stages. While the structuralist paradigm predominated in analyses of colonial Latin America in the 1970s and into the 1980s, a new generation of scholarship was shifting its focus to the dynamic of social relations, the destruction or transformation of indigenous societies, and the composition and actions of social groups within the colonies.[14] This was perhaps truer of Spanish America than of Brazil, but the tendency could be seen there as well in works on institutions like the *misericordias* (charitable brotherhoods) and *relações* (appellate courts), social groups like merchants, sugar planters, and New Christians, and above all in examinations of slavery in which slaves began to emerge not only as a form of labor but also as historical actors, struggling against the dominant power of the slave system but not always repressed and negated by it.[15] While most of these works accepted at least implicitly the *dependista* formulation of the colony, they shifted the focus away from the systemic aspects of economic and political structures and from the councils of Lisbon and the stock exchange of Amsterdam to suggest that the nature of colonial society was worked out by innumerable local decisions, actions, and compromises in Brazil.[16] Accepting the colonial relationship as a reality, the emphasis of these studies centered on Brazilian specificities, or as Bernard Bailyn put it in another context, on the "continuous relationship between the underlying conditions that set the boundaries of human existence and the everyday problems with which people struggle."[17] In doing so, a different range of questions and categories of analysis were also being constructed that called for new ways of conceiving the relationship between economy, polity, society, and culture. The "big picture" was becoming more difficult to see, its composition was sometimes pointillist, and some of the field's cohesion was lost.[18]

A second stage had begun by the late 1980s and 90s as the impact of women's history, cultural studies, ethnohistory, and French *histoire des mentalités* approaches shifted Brazilian historiography in other directions, related sometimes to the earlier round of social history approaches but now concentrating on new themes. Historians began to explore the dynamic of family relations with studies of childhood, sexuality, dowries, and gender roles; the mental landscapes of various colonial groups or individuals in studies of witchcraft, the devil, and the ideology of slavery; the nature of indigenous societies before and after contact; and on the language and representation of status and race.

It is not my intention in this overview to discuss in detail each of these historiographical developments.[19] Instead, I will briefly examine three themes around which much of the recent work on colonial Brazil has concentrated and where the new approaches have created challenges to the framework with which these problems have been traditionally viewed.

CONCEPTUALIZING THE COLONIAL STATE

One way to observe the intersection of metropolitan policies and goals and colonial interests or developments was a close examination of the operation of colonial government. The state or public power had long been seen as a negative force in Brazilian history and the remark of Alceu Amoroso Lima that "Brazil had a state before it had a people," was symbolic of that view.[20] While metanarratives of the nation-state had been created in the nineteenth century as part of a nationalist project, Brazil had a long tradition of both overt and ideological resistance to that process. After all, the classic of nineteenth-century Brazilian literature, Euclides da Cunha's Os sertões described with a certain sympathy a peasant struggle against both modernity and the state. The nation-state was perhaps less of an icon in Brazil than in other former colonial areas.

The problem of the state had been raised directly by Raymundo Faoro in 1958 in a book that was at first ignored but a decade later was rediscovered and in an expanded version quickly went through a series of editions. Faoro, in his essentially Weberian analysis, saw a fundamental conflict between a colonial state and its bureaucracy which operated for the interests of the metropolis, at first against local or colonial interests and by the nineteenth century against national interests. Writing from the perspective of the nation-state, he viewed state and society in opposition. Government and its especially its self-serving bureaucracy took on a life and character of its own, seizing the apparatus of the state to pursue its own goals. Faoro's vision was centered on the nation-state and it tended to view governmental institutions as distinct and separate from the dominant social groups of the society. But even while this theoretical position was gaining adherents, a new generation of scholarship was beginning to reveal a complex web of relationships between state and society, or more exactly between the state and certain social groups. Charles Boxer had already opened a path with a narrative trilogy that provided the outlines of colonial history.[21] Detailed monographs now followed that linked imperial politics to local events. This was done by focusing on the administration of a particular viceroy or governor as in Dauril Alden's study of the Marquis of Lavradio, on a particular institution like Schwartz's book on the High Court of Bahia which emphasized the "Brazilianization" of its judges and the web of social relations that linked royal officers to local interests, or on the government's reaction and procedure during a moment of crisis and its realization of a need for local support such as in Kenneth Maxwell's study of the Minas conspiracy of 1788.[22] These books of the late 1960s and early 1970s were in effect a recognition that the general lines of metropolitan policies were worked out in the colonial context through a series of conflicts and accommodations in which colonial realities and colonial interests played a not insignificant role. The state was not an independent variable but a field of action in which competing interests and groups struggled for advantage or control.

To a greater or lesser extent these studies sought to observe the political or social outcomes of the economic realities of the colony and they assumed a predominant role for public power. Implicitly, they were written as a contestation to a view of Brazilian history that emphasized the weakness or irrelevance of the state and looked instead to the private authority of the plantation owners (*senhores de engenho*) and cattle barons and the power of the slave owner. But deciding whom the state represented was not always easy. Here "coloniality" mattered because the state did not necessarily represent the dominant groups within the colony but rather metropolitan interests of social fractions.

The colonial state, after all, through its laws and actions created the conditions for the control of property and labor and the legal limitations on commerce through monopolies, privileges, and taxation. The goals of the absolutist Portuguese state tended to be conservative not transformative, designed not to break seigniorial authority but to maintain it and its support for the monarchy.[23] In moments of crisis or inventive leadership such as the Pombaline period (1757–76) or the flight of the Portuguese court to Brazil (1808–20), the power of the state and its bureaucratic apparatus could be both disruptive and innovative in bringing about a readjustment of social and economic forces.[24]

These studies of the colonial state as a field of social conflict and adjustment provided another dimension to the structuralist view which primarily emphasized metropolitan economic goals and imperial policies. Taking state power and law as a starting point, it was possible to examine local decisions and strategies over time as Muriel Nazzari did in her examination of São Paulo dowry practices, or as A. J. R. Russell-Wood did in his examination of municipal government. But studies which gave serious attention to the state have had few followers.[25] By the 1970s, a shift to a different kind of social history was already underway, one which emphasized local sources, local themes, and aspects of colonial life that seemed little connected to the policies and goals of the metropolis. The state was out and demography, the family, and social groups were in.

LITTLE BRAZIL, INTERIOR BRAZIL, PEASANT BRAZIL

From the early twentieth century there had been an alternative historiographical approach to the Brazilian past which, without denying the importance of slavery, the mercantilist system, the export sector, and the colonial government of the coast, shifted attention to the interior, the peasantry, and the local economy. By extension, historians turned to the motives, beliefs, and actions of common people in the colony. This was not "official" history and it was marginalized, partly by its content, and in part because its practioniers were often antiquarians, dilettantes, or local historians who worked without any general theme or conceptualization. But there were exceptions. João Capistrano de Abreu (1857–1927), bohemian, journalist, researcher, and brilliant historical essayist laid out an alternate trajectory of Brazilian history in a series of important studies that shifted emphases and focus toward the interior.[26] His intellectual heir was Sérgio Buarque de Holanda (1902–1982) whose *Raíces do Brasil* (1936) was of the same period as Freyre's *Casa grande* and who shared the modernist generation's desire to explain the Brazilian predicament by reference to Brazil's origins. But Sérgio Buarque increasingly turned toward the interior and toward the mental landscape of the past. His subsequent book *Monções* (1945) was written intentionally to stand *Casa grande* on its head and to present a dynamic "Brazil in movement," oriented toward itself rather than toward the Atlantic.[27] His subsequent *Visão do paraíso* (1959), a study of the edenic vision of Brazil in European eyes was conceived as an introduction to the study of the baroque in Luso-Brazilian thought.[28] It is perhaps the foundational work in the development of the history of mentalities approach which has become so important in contemporary Brazilian historiography.

Like most great slaveholding regimes (the Caribbean islands being major exceptions) slaves constituted about one-third of the population in colonial Brazil. Thus, a large percentage of the population, those who were neither slaves nor the economic elite, had been relatively ignored. Until the 1970s the term peasant (*camponês*) was rarely found in the historical or sociological literature on Brazil, and the large rural population of free born and freed were outside most historical analyses.[29] Unlike central Mexico or the Andean highlands, the Brazilian peasantry did not descend from conquered indigenous civilizations. They were, to use Sidney Mintz's term, a "reconstituted" peasantry, evolving at the margins and in the interstices of the slave-based export economy as *agregados, moradores, matutos* (all these being variations of tenant arrangements) and other such categories; the subjects of history and rarely its agents.[30]

They were always there however. The eighteenth-century observers, Santos Vilhena, St. Hilaire, Tollenare, and others had noted their presence and a few modern authors like Oliveira Viana (1922) had even paid them some attention, but in the main the free rural population remained forgotten until the 1980s when they began to emerge from the shadows.[31] But peasantry in colonial Brazil remained in the shadow of the mercantilist model and the overwhelming reality of slavery and of the export economy. Caio Prado Jr. himself had recognized the existence of the "plebe," but he had not been able to give it much attention in a conceptualization of the Brazilian past that emphasized slavery and the export economy.

The first challenge then was to explain the relationship of the export sector to the domestic economy. Were mining and slave-based plantation agriculture enclaves with little effect on the rest of the economy, or did they serve as poles around which a series of linkages stimulated subsidiary activities and the economy as a whole? This was a question that had been taken up as early as 1945 by Bailey Diffie but had been mostly forgotten or had been settled from the "enclave" perspective of dependency theorists.[32] The question has reemerged. Work on Minas Gerais, which showed that despite the decline of the mining economy in the nineteenth century its slave force was growing, raised a series of interesting questions not only about slave demography but also about the growth of internal markets, commercial agriculture, and the relationship of slavery to the internal economy.[33] João Fragoso and Manolo Florentino have argued in the case of Rio de Janeiro that it was not the landowners but the large-scale local merchants involved in both internal and Atlantic commerce who comprised the real social and economic elite of the colony.[34] A flurry of research especially concentrating on the economic expansion of the 1790s to 1840 has begun to argue for the rapid expansion of the subsistence sector and the growing role of the internal market in the colony.[35] Whether, in fact, it is fair to refer to an internal market or markets is a point of debate. In any case, the growth of the intercaptaincy coastal trade (*cabotagem*), the overland supply routes from Minas Gerais to Rio de Janeiro, and the stock trails from Rio Grande do Sul and Paraná to Sorocaba (São Paulo), or from Minas Gerais to Rio de Janeiro all point to the expansion of these internal markets and the importance of small- or medium-scale producers. To what extent this phenomenon was a result of the peculiar conjunctures of the period 1790 to 1840 or was structural in nature and existed long before remains to be questioned.[36]

The shift away from a concentration on the mercantilist structures of the Atlantic economy and toward the internal markets of the colony and the people associated with them, we might term the *Little Brazil approach*. It represents a new tendency within colonial Brazilian historiography, a turn away from the colonial, Atlantic, world system approach, and a concentration on local affairs and large segments of the population previously ignored. Works such as Laura de Mello's study of the poor of Minas Gerais in the eighteenth century or Elizabeth Kuznesof's careful examination of household economy in São Paulo demonstrated that a refocusing on a large segment of the population that figured little directly in the export economy was possible.[37]

By necessity this tendency has made the colonial peasantry an object of study, but here too the new paradigm could not escape the shadow of slavery. Curiously, much of the debate about peasantry has centered on the extent to which the slaves themselves sought to become peasants or opened up a "peasant breach" within the slave system, growing food for themselves and marketing the surplus, and by doing so, creating a rupture in, and a potential contestation to, the slave system. The extent to which slaves sought to do this in Brazil, what it represented to them, and how it was manipulated by slave owners has become a matter of considerable debate.[38] For Jacob Gorender, peasant production by slaves was a marginal anomaly extraneous to the operation of the slave system. For him, interpretations like Ciro Cardoso's that give household production any centrality or see in it some form of negotiation or conquest of space by the slaves are sadly misguided at best or an attempt to rehabilitate slavery at worst.[39]

But if focus needed to be shifted to the small farmer and free laborer, then there was another set of questions that needed to be addressed: How did peasants live in the midst of a slave regime; how were they marked by it? Did they reject, utilize, or ignore it? Old notions that slavery was primarily associated with the great export crop of sugar and with gold mining can now be dismissed. Studies of cattle ranching in Piauí, tobacco farming in Bahia, and small-scale cotton production in Pernambuco have all underlined the ubiquity of slavery.[40] Thousands of people in Brazil owned one or two slaves and the distribution of slave owning was very broad, including whites, *pardos*, (colored) and *libertos* (freed people). Recent work on the commonfolk (*arraia-miuda*) of non-slave owners reveals that sociologically there was little that distinguished them from those that owned slaves.[41] When opportunities presented themselves, peasants oriented production toward local or regional markets and many were not reluctant to use slaves for that purpose. Foodstuff production in Minas Gerais for the growing market of Rio de Janeiro is a case in point. Similar patterns can be seen in Bahia and Pernambuco. What kind of "subalterns" are these? The image of a slave-owning peasantry disrupts and subverts the categories of labor that are normally employed as well as sympathies of the historian. The political

implications of peasant slaveholding have not been analyzed. There is
very little in Brazilian historiography that parallels the studies of the
rural yeomanry in the United States South and their relation to the economics, politics, and social structures of the antebellum world.[42] But it is
clear that slavery was a widely diffused and "popular" institution which
was growing in the late eighteenth century and was not limited to large
landowners and commercial interests. In that diffusion lay the strength of
slavery's hold after independence.

If Brazilian peasants sometimes owned slaves, what was their access
to land? Here a digression may be useful to demonstrate that a change
in focus from the Atlantic system to the colony itself will not eliminate
the need for careful attention to the factors of production and the differential access of groups to them and may demand a rethinking of the
essential aspects of colonial life. A number of studies in the 1970s began
to reveal the anomalies of dealing with the internal development of the
colony and of a free and freed population within a slave regime.

Despite the long shadow of slavery, analyses of peasantry must also
take account of land. Yet for colonial Brazil few studies have considered
both factors of production. In the sugar zones of the Northeast there
were many cases of cane farmers (*lavradores de cana*) with substantial
slaveholdings who did not own land and of *agregados* and *moradores*
employed on plantations who owned slaves but no land. It would seem
that in the sugar-growing regions it was easier to control labor than
acquire land.

Land, in fact, may have been a scarcer factor of production than labor
in the form of slaves. In the northeast there is considerable evidence drawn
from travelers' accounts about the existence of latifundia often controlling
far more land than was actually under cultivation, and that the countryside was filled with a landless peasantry.[43] The size of holdings and the concentration of landed wealth are not necessarily related, but these observations point to an extreme concentration of landed wealth. While at present it is difficult to measure the concentration of land and slaves in Bahia
and Pernambuco, São Paulo presents an opportunity to do so. Detailed
census lists from that captaincy beginning in 1765 have stimulated a series
of studies that have made that captaincy the best-studied region of late
colonial Brazil. One of the most interesting of these studies is Alice
Canabrava's analysis of rural landholding in 1818.[44] She demonstrated that
the captaincy of São Paulo was characterized by an extreme concentration
of land, a situation, in fact, more extreme than the concentration of slaves
in Bahia.[45] She believed that as São Paulo was increasingly drawn into the

export economy after 1780, the situation worsened as the value of land began to rise. Canabrava viewed both slaves and land as essential elements of status and success. Jacob Gorender accepted Canabrava's findings about the concentration of landholding, but he argued that "the principal and decisive factor was property in slaves." Gorender substantiated his position by referring to the work of another Paulista historian, Maria Thereza Schorer Petrone, on the sugar industry of São Paulo.[46] Schorer Petrone had argued that there was no correlation between an *engenho*'s (sugar mill) production and the amount of land owned; therefore, the number of slaves must be the most important element in explaining productivity. The fact that there also seemed to be a lack of correlation between the number of slaves and production was explained by the stage of a plantation's growth, that is, estates with newly planted fields or in the process of formation produced less. The problem with this explanation is that the lack of correlation between land and production could also be ascribed to the same process. In fact, neither Schorer Petrone nor Canabrava provided hard data on slaveholding to match their information on landholding, so their observations about slaveholding and Gorender's position following Canabrava are limited by a lack of information.

Here, an article by Emilio Willems is particularly suggestive because it looked directly at the question of the distribution of wealth in slaves in ten Paulista communities at the time of independence (1822–24).[47] He found that the "ownership of slaves" was not concentrated among a few large landowners. In every community except sugar-growing Itú, owners with less than three slaves were the majority. Slaves did represent a considerable capital investment and as such were an index of status, not only because of their inherent value but also because they freed an individual from the onus of manual labor. Importantly, Willems argued that slave owning did not necessarily place an individual economically above those who owned no slaves.

> Whatever the social implication of slave ownership may have been, economically it did not set the slaveholders completely apart from those who did not use slave labor. Only among the higher echelons of the slaveholders does the expected correlation between income and slave ownership manifest itself, and then in a very general way.[48]

Furthermore, Willems demonstrated that in Itú, exactly the locale that Schorer Petrone had studied, there was no correlation between the number of slaves and production, citing many examples of estates with larger numbers of slaves producing less than those with fewer workers. There seems to be no more direct correlation of slaves to production in Willems than land to production in Schorer Petrone.

Table 1
Distribution of Wealth in Land and Slaves in Selected Communities of São Paulo 1818–23

	Slaveholding Agriculturalists Gini	Agricultiralists as Proportion of All Slaveholders	Land Among Total Population Gini
Itu	.56	23.2	.80
Piracicaba	.64	17.5	.85
Sorocaba	.55	11.5	.69
Itapetininga	.37	8.0	.92
Iguape	.64	20.7	.75
Cananeia	.45	23.9	.74
Areias	.58	33.1	.69
Bragança	.44	18.1	.67

SOURCES: Alice Piffer Canabrava, "Areparticão da terra" (1992), for calculations of land distribution; Emilio Willems, "Social Differentiation" (1970) provided the data on which the distribution of slaveholding was calculated.

Table 1 presents the results of Canabrava's calculations of the concentration of land in eight Paulista communities (Gini index) with my own calculations of the concentration of slaveholding based on Willems's data.[49] The eight communities represent various economic contexts. Itú and Piracicaba were sugar districts, Sorocaba and Tapetininga specialized in livestock, Iguape and Cananéia were coastal areas, the former more involved in export crops than the latter, Areias was a coffee district and Bragança a region of subsistence farming. In all eight communities, the ownership of land was more concentrated than the ownership of slaves. We should expect that the dominant class or groups in a society would attempt to control the most valuable resources. If slaves were indeed the most crucial factor of production, the key to success, then it would seem that those in power were not doing particularly well in controlling this resource. Perhaps it was not in their interest. Perhaps making slavery broadly accessible helped reinforce a social contract among proprietors.

It is now clear that the Little Brazil approach may demand a serious reevaluation of the dynamic of colonial life and economy and the way in which land, labor, and capital were utilized and appropriated. It is also apparent that in a society so profoundly shaped by slavery, recent importations of concepts of "subalterity" must be made with great caution since the existence of slaves created ambiguities and complexities for the status and position of other groups in the society, even those disadvantaged or marginalized.[50]

TROPICAL MENTALITIES

If the Little Brazil critics have questioned the nature of the colonial economy and by extension the colony's social organization, then a potentially even more radical attack on the traditional historiography has been a departure from the social and economic nexus altogether and a concentration on the ideas and attitudes that shaped social and gender relations in a multiracial slave society, on the representations of those relations, and on the creation of various kinds of identities within colonial society. In the last decade scholars have produced a growing literature in the history of *mentalidades* and of popular culture which has altered but not eliminated the previous emphasis on social and economic relations.[51] This trend reflects an increasing dissatisfaction with the inability of the *dependentista* paradigm to incorporate local human agency, especially of groups or individuals far from power, to deal with the ambiguities of class and color, to examine the possible effects of gender on historical processes, and above all to explore aspects of private life and thought and to relate them to popular forms of expression or resistance.[52] This trend has considerably reinvigorated colonial history and moved it in new directions—but not without some potential costs and dangers.

The new trend has emphasized popular culture, itself an ill-defined concept but to some extent it has been accompanied by an equally vigorous development in more traditional intellectual history, usually joined with literary analysis. Works such as João Adolfo Hansens's study of Gregório de Matos or Alfredo Bosi's analysis of elite colonial discourse have demonstrated the contribution that literary analysis can make to an understanding of colonial society. But much of the new work has, in fact, moved away from the relatively few colonial published texts and canonical authors toward other kinds of cultural analysis.[53] Let me cite just a few outstanding examples which have expand-

ed the horizons of colonial history in this direction. Closer to traditional approaches but far more concerned with mental landscapes has been
the work of Evaldo Cabral de Mello. In a series of elegant monographs
he has traced the rise of a regional elite's identity and self-fashioning
through genealogical deception, celebratory historiography, and the
manipulation of memory. These studies of the Pernambucan aristocracy's construction and justification of its status follows the regional historiographical tradition of one of Brazil's great colonial scholars, José
Antônio Gonçalves de Mello. But it explores not only the reality of
Pernambuco's colonial past but also the ways in which it was mobilized
and represented, and why.[54]

The interaction between European perception and Brazilian reality has
provided another important line of investigation. Laura de Mello's studies
of the demonization of the "other," the transference of the concept and
image of the Devil to Brazil, and the way in which African, Indian, and
"colonial" practice were perceived through that screen reveals the dynamic interaction of ideology and American reality, between Catholic ortho-
doxy and colonial deviance. The prosecution of witchcraft was not about
superstition but about the project of increasing the power of centralized
civil and religious authority.[55] This is the same line of analysis taken by
Luiz Mott in his biography of Rosa Egipciaca, an African woman who was
alternately a slave, prostitute, visionary, popular saint, and prisoner of the
Inquisition in eighteenth-century Minas Gerais, Rio de Janeiro, and
Lisbon.[56]

Intimate life has provided another approach. The writings of Ronaldo
Vainfas and Luiz Mott on sexuality have opened previously unexplored
areas of private life with implications for gender relations, race, and social
practice. Sex had long been a theme of Brazilian historiography (e.g.,
Freyre's *Casa grande e Senzala*) but these new approaches are far more
concerned than their predecessors with the interaction of dogma and
practice and with sex as a form of popular life difficult for authority to
control.[57] The burgeoning social history literature on women also has
become more concerned with the attitudes of and toward women. This is
reflected in the work of Alida Metcalf on the São Paulo frontier and in
Leila Algranti's study of cloistered women which pays far more attention
to the interior life of the convents and their underlying ideology than did
earlier social and economic approaches.[58] Mary del Priore's study of
women's bodies concentrates on the ascribed reproductive functions and
roles as mother and shows how female bodies and female sexuality
became a theological battleground where state projects, official ideology,

popular attitudes, and practices came into conflict. Since late antiquity, women had been seen as agents of sin and evil, but she demonstrates that in the colonial situation this struggle took on a distinctive nature.[59] Structuralist analyses could never really incorporate popular and learned discourse about the body or sexuality the way that the new cultural analysis has done.

The history of mentalities in Brazil naturally shares much with this approach in general with its concern for popular culture, suppressed voices, and with private and intimate life. It has for the most part avoided the pitfalls of overemphasizing the curious and the bizarre at the expense of the important, and although sensitive to language, it has not taken much of a linguistic turn. As innovative as this approach has been, however, its dependence on institutional sources like Inquisition records and in its formulation of social process, it has been forced to accept the structuralist understandings and appreciation of the power of the state, slavery, and economic conditions to set the parameters within which popular and elite mentalities and discourses develop. The shadow of the absolutist state and its ideological arm, the church, falls over much of the new historiography. Projects from the punishment of witches, to the control of women's bodies, to the establishment of schools are seen as manifestations of the increasing hegemony of the state. This acceptance is sometimes too easily conceded: the dominant power of the absolutist state and its ability to smooth out local practice and power has been too often overstated.[60] While trying to turn away from the public sphere, the historians of mentalities have sometimes recreated an all-powerful state. By doing so, they have obscured the ability of all kinds of people—freed persons, artisans, even slaves—to find the spaces and opportunities to influence, divert, or contain the state and other sources of power. The state has returned, not so much as an object of study as an almost residual explanation and ultimate cause of all social processes.

Finally, the development of the history of mentalities in colonial Brazil has revealed the continuing contribution of the historians of the "old colonial regime" and the *dependentista* paradigm. They developed a set of analytical tools for understanding global power and colonial exploitation and their description of the social and economic realities of the Brazilian colony still provides the best context for understanding its historical development. Linking the inner world of colonial Brazil's inhabitants to the public sphere, combining mental structures and the political economy, have become the locus of a new historiography—one that places state power and economic conditions in a central position to explain the thoughts of men and women at various social levels.[61] The relationship between the material bases of life and the ways in which people perceive and describe their world, the old structure and super-structure debate, is not easily resolved but must be confronted as historians seek to understand the dialogic relationship between class relations and economic behavior and mental structures. At a moment in Brazil's history when "privatization" has become a state program, historians are once again recognizing that the private sector, for better or worse, had always exercised a profound influence on the colony's social and political organization. Increasingly, the dichotomy of private and public spheres is disappearing in Brazilian historiography.

eleven

Furtado, Social Science, and History

Joseph L. Love

In the dialog between social science and historiography, there can be little doubt that the most important Latin American ideas and constructs to affect the writing of history in the last forty years were the related schools of structuralism and dependency.[1] In the endeavor to apply structuralist analysis to history, no writer was more important than the Brazilian economist Celso Furtado. His investigation of the relationship between development and underdevelopment—within Brazil as well as among nations—opened the way to dependency analysis, another perspective on development in which the historical process was central.

The structuralist school of thought associated with the UN Economic Commission for Latin America (ECLA, or in Spanish, CEPAL) was pioneered by the Argentinean Raúl Prebisch, who in 1949 characterized the international economy as a set of relations between an industrialized center and a periphery exporting foodstuffs and raw materials. Focusing on the problems of the periphery, Prebisch and his associates emphasized structural unemployment, owing to the inability of traditional export industries to grow and therefore to absorb excess rural population; external disequilibrium, because of higher propensities to import industrial goods than to export traditional agricultural and mineral goods; and deteriorating terms of trade—all of which a properly implemented policy of industrialization could help eliminate.[2] These ideas were first sketched out in *The Economic Development of Latin America and its Principal Problems*, ECLA's "manifesto" (Spanish ed., 1949).

Prebisch was primarily interested in cyclical phenomena, and it was Furtado, as noted, who did more than any other theorist to historicize structuralist thought.[3] In the decade beginning in 1954, Furtado and other structuralists sought to move economic history beyond a descrip-

tion of economic configurations, flows, and flux to a more analytic treatment of critical structures—both dynamic and relatively static elements
in the economic ensemble—which underlay long-term performance as
well as cyclical patterns. That is, they sought to specify those structures
which had contributed to economic development and those which had
impeded it. As a group, they sought to produce new periodizations of
economic history, with sharp demarcations between outward-looking
export phases or cycles and post-1930 inward-looking phases, focused
on the industrial economy. They tried to explain persistent inflation and
stagnation in new ways, seeking as well to trace and explain the distribution of income arising from the growth process. The impediments and
blockages to development, as well as the dynamic inequality of income
distribution, frequently had their roots in the colonial past. In Furtado's
case, his doctoral dissertation at Paris concerned Brazil's economy in the
colonial era, and his early books—sketches that would result in *A formação econômica do Brasil* (1959)—were long-term historical essays.[4] At
one time Furtado even preferred the term *colonial structure* to *periphery*.[5]

Furtado's structuralism, unlike Prebisch's, was conditioned by direct
contact with French structuralist economics. Almost twenty years
younger than Prebisch, Furtado entered the law program at the
University of Brazil in 1940 and then switched to public administration;
economics was not yet a permissible specialization. However, the young
man did have contact with the French economist Maurice Byé, a pro-
tégé of the structuralist and corporatist François Perroux. Byé had been
teaching in Rio at the time of Germany's defeat of France in June 1940
and remained in Brazil until 1942.[6] Furtado followed Byé to Paris after
the Brazilian's military service in the Italian campaign. He began the
study of economics in 1946, working under Byé, his thesis advisor, and
Perroux. At the time, Furtado, as he later wrote, was still an "autodidact"
in economics.[7] In 1948 Furtado presented a dissertation at the Faculté
de Droit in Paris on the Brazilian economy during the colonial era[8] and
was one of the first Brazilians to hold a doctorate in economics.

Furtado subsequently returned to his native land, where he was
employed by the Ministry of Finance to help produce *Conjuntura
Econômica* (*Business Cycle*), a new journal associated with the Fundação
Getúlio Vargas, to which he had contributed articles while in Europe.
Later in 1948 Furtado moved to Santiago, Chile, to join the staff of ECLA,
an agency which he would be associated with for a decade. At the UN
agency the works of John Maynard Keynes were being studied, debated,
and adapted, and Keynesian economics played a critical role in Furtado's

own early theorizing. Though Furtado had studied the Cambridge econo-mist's work in France, Keynes apparently had little influence on the Brazilian's doctoral thesis, and Furtado's major exposure to him may have come through Prebisch. The latter arrived in Santiago in February 1949—after Furtado—but had published his *Introduction to Keynes*[9] two years earlier. In any event, the influence of both Keynes and Prebisch was obvi-ous in Furtado's first essay in economics, "General Characteristics of the Brazilian Economy," written in 1949 and published the following year.[10] In this essay Furtado built on Prebisch's analysis of the business cycle in 1949 regarding the high import coefficients typical of Latin American coun-tries: he argued that income tended to concentrate in Brazil during the upswing of the cycle, owing in part to a highly elastic labor supply that held down wages. Further, he hypothesized that much of the effect of the Keynesian multiplier[11] "leaked" abroad, owing to the exporting groups's high propensity to import. Such analysis pointed again to the importance of an industrialization policy.

Prebisch's influence on Furtado may also have had a transcyclical dimension. ECLA's *Economic Survey . . . 1949*, directed by Prebisch and published in 1950, had treated in brief the economic history of Latin America as a whole from the 1880s to the mid-twentieth century, and had considered individually the four most industrialized nations—Argentina, Chile, Mexico, and Brazil (the Brazilian section being Furtado's responsi-bility). In some respects this volume was a model for the national struc-turalist histories to be published between 1959 and 1963—Furtado on Brazil, Aníbal Pinto on Chile, Aldo Ferrer on Argentina, and later, Osvaldo Sunkel and Pedro Paz on the whole region, as well as Villareal on Mexico.[12] But Prebisch's central interest was the business cycle not long-term his-torical development.

Furtado's *Economic Growth of Brazil*[13] ultimately derived from his pre-ECLA interests in defining the features of colonial Brazil. Although *The Economy of Colonial Brazil*, his dissertation at the Sorbonne, did not contain much formal economic analysis of any kind, *The Brazilian Economy* (1954) and *A Dependent Economy* (1956), a briefer work, are structuralist treatments of Brazil's economic history.[14] These early his-torical essays offer evidence that Furtado's contribution precedes Pinto's, even though their "classic" studies both appeared in 1959—Chile, *A Case of Frustrated Development*[15] and *Economic Growth of Brazil*.

The latter work covered the whole sweep of Brazilian history, and the colonial and nineteenth-century sections compare and contrast the structures of the Brazilian and U. S. economies, showing how Brazil's monoculture and latifundia impeded the high savings and investment rates characteristic of the American economy. Focusing on the distribution of income and the size of the domestic market, Furtado provided one of the first uses of modern income analysis in a historical framework and demonstrated the weak relationship between income and investment in an economy based on slavery.[16] The work throughout is written from the point of view of a development economist, emphasizing the heterogeneity of technologies and production functions (including the vast subsistence sector) in the Brazilian economy.

Turning to the problem of Brazil's economic cycles, examined in earlier studies by João Lúcio de Azevedo (writing on the Portuguese Empire), Roberto Simonsen, and John Normano,[17] Furtado saw in the weak monetization of the slave economy a kind of resilience, in that export stagnation or decline could be sustained as the free but plantation-oriented population moved toward the backlands: the subsistence economy absorbed the excess labor supply after the exhaustion of successive export booms. In a slave-based economy the response to depression is different from that of a fully capitalist economy; in the former, "entrepreneurs" have fixed costs (maintaining their slave populations) and are not in a position to contract their agricultural output. For example, when the sugar economy declined in the seventeenth century, the livestock economy became increasingly subsistence oriented, and average labor productivity, by inference, fell.[18] This economic "involution," as Furtado called it, was the opposite of development, since each historical export boom until coffee (brazilwood, sugar, gold, and—contemporaneous with coffee—rubber) led to retrogression, not to sustained growth.[19]

The apparent aberrations in Brazilian financial policy in the period since independence could be explained in part by the fact that the structure of underdeveloped economies was different from that of the industrial economies. In times of depression, the former suffered plummeting export prices, worsening terms of trade, and a reduction in capital inflow, together with rigid requirements in foreign capital servicing. In trying to adhere to the gold standard, Brazilian statesmen had failed to understand the nature of their predicament and had viewed their nation's inability to keep to the standard as the result of bad management, rather than a problem with deeper causes.[20]

Differences in the growth and diversification of the production structure of the Brazilian and U. S. economies in the first half of the nineteenth century were not accounted for by the greater degree of tariff protection in the United States, Furtado believed, but by the differences in social structure and income distribution, and therefore the size of the domestic market.[21] In fact, Furtado estimated that Brazil's continually falling exchange rate provided more protection for domestic industries than high tariffs would have.[22] But more importantly, Brazil suffered from a small domestic market, lack of modern technology, entrepreneurship, and capital, and its small capacity to import (defined as the unit prices of exports times quantities sold).[23] For Furtado, Brazil's national market dated from the last years of the nineteenth century, when a modern working class came into existence. Beginning in the late 1880s, when wage labor replaced slave labor in São Paulo's coffee fields, Brazil began to develop a significant home market. In Furtado's view, wages paid in the coffee sector provided the "nucleus of a domestic market economy," with the implication of an attendant multiplier effect.[24]

For Furtado, the big change in relative market size, however, occurred after the crisis of 1929, in which the coffee economy, which had risen to 70 percent of the value of national exports, abruptly collapsed. In Furtado's estimation, the decisive shift toward an economy based on the stimulus of domestic demand took shape in the early 1930s. The American economist Werner Baer has noted that Furtado's analysis of events in the Great Depression accounts for less than a tenth of the space in *Economic Growth of Brazil*, but it is the theme of the book which has generated by far the greatest amount of scholarly controversy.[25] Furtado's earliest treatment of the issue, the thesis in embryo, goes back to his "General Characteristics of the Brazilian Economy" in 1950.

Elaborating on that early analysis, Furtado pointed to Brazil's rapid industrial growth during the Great Depression, caused in part by the "socialization of losses" of coffee producers through exchange devaluation: this process helped maintain domestic demand by keeping up the employment level and purchasing power in the coffee sector, which in turn permitted the rise of a significant domestic demand for industrial goods when foreign products were unavailable, owing to the absence of foreign exchange. The stockpiling and destruction of coffee in the face of grossly excess supply were financed through credit expansion, which in turn exacerbated the external disequilibrium and caused new exchange depreciation and a further socialization of losses.[26]

Furtado viewed the expansionary fiscal and monetary policies related to coffee as a form of unwitting Keynesianism, because the wealth destroyed in coffee beans was considerably less than that created by maintaining employment.[27] He then noted that output of capital goods in Brazil by 1932 was 60 percent greater than in 1929. Furthermore, net investment in 1935, at constant prices, was greater than that in 1929 and the level of aggregate income of the latter year had been regained, despite the fact that the import of capital goods was only half of the 1929 figure.[28] Therefore, the economy was undergoing profound structural change.

Furtado, we may infer, was manifestly influenced by his Keynesian background, especially with regard to government intervention to sustain demand, and the significance of the domestic market in dynamizing production and income.[29] He shared the view of Prebisch and ECLA in the Economic Survey . . . 1949 that industrialization had historically occurred in periods of crisis in the larger Latin American economies. For him, as for other structuralist contemporaries, the Great Depression was a watershed in which the larger Latin American economies moved definitively to an economy in which the domestic rather than the international market was the motor of growth, and for which industrialization led the growth process. Furtado's views on Brazilian industrialization in the Depression touched off a long debate.[30]

Although the centrality of industrialization as the dynamic element in growth during the Great Depression has largely been confirmed for Brazil, Argentina, Chile, and Mexico, it now appears that the disruption in international trade during the First and Second World Wars and the Depression was less important in producing "inward-directed growth," in Prebisch's phrase, than was believed by some contemporaries to these events and by ECLA economists later.[31] In any event, econometric research in the 1990s suggests an important correlation between economic growth and participation in international trade.[32] A now widely held view is that investment in industry (capacity) grew in line with export earnings for the period 1900–1945, while output (but not capacity) tended to rise during the shocks of war and depression, when imports had to be curtailed. Capacity during the Depression could not grow appreciably in Brazil—nor in the several other industrializing Latin American nations—for lack of exchange credits to buy capital goods and inputs. Neither did it grow rapidly during the two world wars, because of the unavailability of capital goods and fuels from the belligerent powers.[33]

In addition to historicizing structuralism, Furtado explored the school's potential in another direction, as did Hans W. Singer, who in 1950 had developed a model of the international trading process similar to Prebisch's.[34] I refer to the problem now known as *internal colonialism*.[35] Furtado and Singer independently built their analysis in the

1950s around perceived unequal exchange between industrial centers and agricultural peripheries. I will focus on the Furtado version, which was published first and in a fuller form, though Singer's work was completed earlier.[36] It was in the context of analyzing internal colonialism that Furtado first began to link development and underdevelopment as components of a single historical process.

The model of the international trading process on which Singer and Furtado drew was that of ECLA (developed by Prebisch in 1949) and Singer's very similar one, independently arrived at and published a year later.[37] According to Prebisch and Singer, at the international level unequal exchange derived from differential productivities between industrial center and agricultural periphery in the world market, combined with different institutional arrangements in capital and labor markets. Technological progress in manufacturing, in any case, was shown in a rise in incomes in developed countries, while that in the production of food and raw materials in underdeveloped countries was expressed in a fall in prices relative to industrial goods. For Singer, the explanation of contrasting effects of technological progress was found in the disparate income elasticities of demand for primary and industrial goods. That is, the demand for agricultural and mineral goods rose less than proportionally to the rise in world income, and that for manufactured goods rose more.

Furtado addressed the issue of internal colonialism in the late 1950s, as he became more deeply involved in the problems of his native Northeast. This agrarian and latifundium-dominated region in 1956 had an annual per capita income of less than US $100, whereas the Center-South enjoyed a level of income more than three times higher, because of the dynamic industrial economy organized around the cities of São Paulo and Rio de Janeiro. The gap between the Northeast and the Center-South was larger than that between the per capita income of the latter region and those of Western Europe.[38] Furtado estimated the ratio between the growth rates of the lagging and leading regions was of the order of one to two for the decade after 1948.[39] Moreover, the distribution of income within the Northeast was highly skewed, making the situation even more desperate for the masses.

Like Prebisch, Furtado assumed the existence of market imperfections—particularly the administered pricing of industrial goods—and a virtually unlimited supply of labor in the backward region at the going wage in the industrial sector. But the Brazilian's model was more complex than Prebisch's international one, because it purported to measure the deterioration of terms of trade between the international price of agricultural goods sold abroad by Northeast Brazil against the domestic price of industrial goods which the region had to buy from the Center-South.

Furtado analyzed the Northeast in terms of a triangular trade between the backward region, the foreign sector, and the developed area of Brazil.[40] Brazil's Northeast had a surplus in its commercial balance abroad but a deficit in its balance of payments with its domestic trading partner, the Center-South. The state was also an essential element in the trading process: in implementing its policy of import-substitution industrialization, the central government was subsidizing industrialists and penalizing agricultural exporters. This support took the form of differential exchange rates for importers of manufacturing-related capital goods and importers who would use foreign exchange credits for other purposes.[41]

That the central government gave exporters poorer exchange rates than importers not only effected a sectoral transfer of income; the same action induced a regional transfer as well, because of the size of the export sector relative to real (national) income in the Northeast, compared to that of the Center-South. Furthermore, the government stimulated industrial development by financing private enterprise, a process which principally aided the Center-South. Finally, economies of scale and external economies in the industrial heartland of the Rio-São Paulo area made the hitherto large industrial advantages of the region, relative to the Northeast, even greater as development proceeded. Therefore central government policies designed to stimulate industrialization had a major inequalizing effect on the regional distribution of income in the country. Furtado estimated that in the period 1948–56, the Northeast transferred US $24 million annually to the Center-South, although a more accurate figure may be $15–17 million yearly.[42] Because of Brazil's protectionist tariffs and related exchange policies, the Northeast was in no position to seek alternative supplies abroad for its manufacturing needs. It offered a captive market for the Center-South, and its foreign exchange earnings gave it purchasing power in that region. But the relevant terms of trade now entered the picture: overall, prices of the South's industrial goods rose more rapidly from 1948 to 1956 (the years studied by Furtado) than the exchange rate fell, i.e., the rate at which northeastern exporters gained more *cruzeiros* per unit of foreign currency.[43]

Furtado proposed industrialization as a solution to the Northeast's economic problems.[44] He also stressed the need for agricultural development, implying the need for agrarian reform, because the cost of wage-goods, i.e., foodstuffs in the largest city of the Northeast, Recife, was rising faster than that of São Paulo. Consequently, if wage differentials were narrowing between São Paulo and Recife to meet rising costs of living in the latter, there would be little incentive for private capital to invest in the Northeast.[45] Agrarian reform has yet to occur, however, and in the years following Furtado's analysis, development strategies favoring the Center-South continued. Despite efforts of the federal government to offset regional income concentration, Baer has concluded, the overall effect of development programs continued to favor the industrial Center-South over the agrarian Northeast in the three and a half decades following Furtado's analysis.[46]

In one of his regional studies examining the interaction of industrial and agrarian regions at different levels of development, Furtado had already perceived in 1959 a relationship which he, Osvaldo Sunkel, Fernando Henrique Cardoso, and Andre Gunder Frank would develop in the mid-1960s: that a structural and perverse relationship existed between the growth of developed capitalist economies (and regions) and the growth of underdeveloped countries (and regions): "[There is] . . . a tendency for industrial economies, as a result of their form of growth, to inhibit the growth of primary economies: This same phenomenon is occurring within our country."[47] It is notable for the history of dependency analysis that Furtado's first published statement of the alleged causal relationship between development and underdevelopment appeared in the context of internal colonialism rather than at the international level.

His book *Development and Underdevelopment* (Port. ed., 1961) advanced Furtado's early efforts as an analyst of dependency. His reference to the relation of development and underdevelopment in *Operation Northeast* (1959) had been explicit, but in *Development and Underdevelopment*, a work combining analytical and historical approaches, he described how the European industrial economy by the nineteenth century had penetrated and transformed precapitalistic economies. Underdeveloped economies were "hybrid structures,"[48] and not simply *un*developed economies beginning to trace the path that Europe had already defined. Consequently, underdevelopment was a "discrete historical process through which economies that have already achieved a high level of development have not necessarily passed."[49] Economic development was "emphatically an unequal process," Furtado argued,[50] and recent historical studies by Paul Bairoch and others have confirmed this observation at the international level.[51]

In *Development and Underdevelopment*, Furtado distinguished between
autonomous development, which was supply driven, and an externally
induced development, which was demand driven. In the latter process,
the manner of industrialization—substituting domestic products for
imports—led the entrepreneur "to adopt a technology compatible with a
cost and price structure similar to that . . . in the international manufactured goods market."[52] Therefore labor-saving techniques were continually adopted, despite the need for industrial employment. Even earlier
Furtado had stressed the importance of conspicuous consumption as a
driving force in underdeveloped countries's internal dynamics.[53]

In the mid- and latter 1960s structuralist theories and policy pre-
scriptions were not only challenged by a neoclassical Right but also by
a heterodox Left, some of whose exegetes had been leading figures in
ECLA itself, notably Furtado and the Chilean Osvaldo Sunkel. This
new Left would quickly make "dependency theory" famous.[54] Although
ECLA itself had produced nothing if not a kind of dependency analysis, the new variety was set off by its more clearcut "historicizing" and
"sociologizing" tendencies in both its reformist and radical versions.[55] In
the mid-sixties Furtado elaborated the contention that development
and underdevelopment were historically linked.

In an essay published in 1964, Furtado called for a return to dialectics, and "The Dialectics of Development" was in fact the Portuguese
title of *Diagnosis of the Brazilian Crisis.* He meant by this a kind of
methodological holism, without which the individual parts of a social
entity in continual motion could not be understood. This approach
required a return to history, because the tendency to focus on equilibrium concepts in neoclassical economics denied process. Even if the
developed economies could roughly be described as being in dynamic
equilibrium, this state did not apply to the underdeveloped periphery,
where the continual introduction of labor-saving techniques resulted in
a surplus labor supply beyond that already present in the large subsistence sector.[56] In this interpretation, Furtado included a class analysis
already foreshadowed in *Development and Underdevelopment.*[57] He
argued that class struggle had historically been the engine of economic
growth in the advanced West: workers "attack" through organization to
raise their share of the national produce, and capitalists "counterattack"
by introducing labor-saving technology; in this manner, a dynamic equilibrium is approximated. Since labor is unorganized in the periphery,
above all in the rural sector he asserted, the process fails to work there.[58]

In works published between 1970 and 1978, Furtado elaborated on the contention that underdevelopment was a historical process intimately related to the development of the industrial West. Upper strata in backward regions adopted the consumption patterns of the developed West as such areas entered the international division of labor.[59] This process was the "result of the surplus generated through static comparative advantages in foreign trade. It is the highly dynamic nature of the modernized component of consumption that brings dependence into the technological realm and makes it part of the production structure."[60] Novel items of consumption require increasingly sophisticated techniques and increasing amounts of capital. But capital accumulation is associated with income concentration, so industrialization "advances simultaneously with the concentration of income."[61] Thus, in underdeveloped countries, the consumption patterns of the groups which appropriate the economic surplus and their concomitant political power—and not the elastic labor supply, as Furtado had once believed—determine the differential between the industrial wage rate and that of the subsistence sector, and keep it stable.[62]

What were the decisive influences on Furtado's development? Elsewhere I have tried to establish that Raúl Prebisch was an eclectic,[63] and the same could be said of Furtado. However, they perhaps shared only one obvious intellectual ancestor, Keynes, and Furtado's eclecticism was more clearly confined to structuralist traditions. Keynes was a structuralist in the sense that he tried to specify, analyze, and correct economic structures that impede or block the "normal," implicitly unproblematic, development and functioning of a capitalist economy. Both Furtado and Prebisch extended Keynes by showing how his analysis yielded different consequences for the Latin American economies than for the developed world. In another context I have shown that Furtado was also influenced by James Duesenberry's sociological interpretation of Keynes's consumption function (Duesenberry's *demonstration effect*) and by Ragnar Nurkse's adaptation of Duesenberry's model to explain elite consumption patterns in underdeveloped areas.[64] As indicated above, the Brazilian writer was also strongly influenced by Prebisch himself, especially with regard to the latter's center-periphery conception of the world economy, and the contrasting institutional features that characterized the two constituent elements. Furtado adapted and sophisticated the Prebisch model for the analysis of unequal growth among Brazil's regions.

Unlike Prebisch, however, Furtado had been introduced to French structuralism as a student, just as it was freeing itself from Perroux's prewar corporatism.[65] Perroux, like Prebisch, had sought to explain unequal exchange early in the postwar era. In the latter 1940s his analysis focused on different elasticities of demand for the United States and "the rest of the world," and he hypothesized a *domination effect* which denied the neoclassical assumption of pure and equal exchange.[66] Perroux also contended, consistent with his former corporatist beliefs, that state intervention was necessary to offset such monopolies. It is highly probable, therefore, that among early ECLA economists Furtado's unique contact with the French school allowed him to develop the concept *structure*, quite apart from Prebisch's own contributions.[67]

Again, in contrast with Prebisch, from the beginning of his career Furtado was a student of history, and at the center of his effort to analyze the development process was the tension between model building and seeking to understand the unique features of each society's historical development.[68] For Furtado, the weakness or absence of market forces, such as segmented labor markets and monopolies in land tenure patterns, could often be explained only through an examination of the colonial past.

At an ideological level, Furtado and Prebisch shared many traits. Both were primarily public servants, who, over the course of their careers, were intermittently associated with their national states and international organizations. Furtado was a "nonpartisan politician," in the phrase of the economist Francisco de Oliveira,[69] always striving to push forward the development process, under the direction of the state. Throughout his career, Furtado believed the state could and should be the leading force in economic development, providing the leadership that market signals, feeble or distorted by monopoly in backward economies, could not. This conviction was perhaps typical of his generation of Brazilian intellectuals,[70] and it conditioned Furtado's view of Brazilian history, most obviously in his treatment of the Great Depression. It was tempered but not abandoned as Furtado moved from his initial structuralism to dependency and as he sophisticated his understanding of the limitations of state power in the development process.[71]

In review, Celso Furtado applied structuralist theory to economic history, believing that only a historical approach which began with the colonial era, could reveal the true nature of contemporary Brazilian problems and dilemmas. Thus his motivation for studying history was ultimately instrumentalist.[72] Furtado employed income analysis to analyze such problems as plantation slavery and Brazil's early recovery from the Great Depression. Furthermore, in the process of examining unequal exchange at the intranational level in the 1950s, he arrived at the position that development and underdevelopment were linked in a single historical dynamic, an insight which opened the way to dependency analysis. In both instances, ECLA's definition of underdeveloped economies—assemblages characterized by heterogeneous technologies and therefore heterogeneous productivities—specified phenomena which Furtado believed could solely be understood by combining analytical constructs and historical analysis.

twelve

The Elision of the Middle Classes and Beyond: History, Politics, and Development Studies in Latin America's "Short Twentieth Century"[1]

Michael F. Jiménez

I

Paupered students of the past abound in big cities and small towns throughout Latin America. Young, middle-aged, and older even, they have earned degrees in history or work intermittently toward the scholarly license. They teach full time at secondary schools, hold adjunct university positions, and drive taxicabs to make ends meet. Many do research for the notables of their profession, scrounging about in newspaper collections, dusty provincial archives, and gathering interview data for which they seldom receive recognition and only meager monetary compensation. This coterie of mostly men and a handful of women are enthusiasts about the past of their own countries and others. They have corners in library reading rooms, frequent bookstores, and live in seedy walk-ups and back rooms amidst precious volumes of scholarly works, theoretical writings, and old editions. And there, of course, masterworks such as the Steins's *The Colonial Heritage of Latin America* and Tulio Halperín Donghi's *A Contemporary History of Latin America* hold pride of place. These aspiring scholars are a ubiquitous presence at public lectures and late night debates in cafes and taverns. Seldom published in prestigious periodicals, their research essays and polemical notes circulate by hand or appear in mimeographed journals of short run. Whatever talents they possess or the merit of their scholarship, hopes of studying abroad on a fellowship or acquiring a secure university position are usually denied them, as they have few connections or influence. Such difficult devotion to knowledge, dreams of stable careers, and aspiration to status lead variously to admirable commitment to a life of the mind, desperate acts of protest, or bitter regret.

Near century's end, Latin America's taxicab-historians are emblematic of the plight of the middle classes throughout the globe. In the North Atlantic, the unraveling of what Hobsbawn has called the "golden age of capitalism" has sown confusion among the middle classes which emerged there over a century ago and reached their high tide in the decades after the Second World War.[2] In the United States, a vast literature laments the collapse of the "American Dream," as public and private sector employees, professionals, and small-business owners find themselves under siege in the current era of restructuring and downsizing of state and corporations alike.[3] The economic crises of recent decades and the long-term consequences of the cold war's militarized capitalism have contributed to the government's slow yet inexorable retreat from its historic shepherding of middle-class claims and aspirations. Except for the Thatcherite enterprise in Great Britain, the Western European fraying of social democracy has, for the moment, been less jarring than in the United States.[4] Yet the scaffolding of support by and for the middle classes thrown up from the late 1940s is awobble. Recent enthusiasms for a new European Renaissance have been dimmed by internal tensions within the welfare states there and challenges posed by the presence of non-European immigrants in the region and changes in the former Soviet Union and Eastern Europe.[5]

Indeed, the "fall of communism" involved parallel crises in middle-class societies constituted under a socialist form of bureaucratic authoritarianism east of the Elbe River. Whether domestic in origin or imposed from the outside, "actually existing socialism" rapidly and dramatically transformed mostly traditional agrarian societies, raising levels of education and expectations for material security and social mobility. That this process occurred under the harshest of political regimes and did not generate living standards approaching those of the North Atlantic does not diminish the profound changes which it wrought in those societies, especially in the quarter century after the Second World War.[6] But the command economies and authoritarian political cultures, given fillip by ideology and cold war pressures, led to the coming apart of communism's variant of the middle-class dream in the last quarter of the twentieth century.[7] The cultural and political disarray, and the growing incidence of ethnic and religious conflict in the former Soviet bloc mirror the despair evident in the West. The "convergence" theorists of the 1960s and 1970s may well have been right, but theirs was a more hopeful scenario than actually came to be.

Finally, in much of the so-called "Third World" (or LDCs), the middle classes created with such rapidity in the second half of this century face similarly dismal prospects. In Latin America, the Middle East, South Asia, and Africa, these offspring of "developmentalism" have found guarantees of educational advancement, material security, and political voice severely compromised. The development strategies of the post-World War II era led ultimately to the severe debt crises of the "lost decade" of the 1980s and the subsequent neoliberal restructuring project undertaken by powerfully cosmopolitan alliances of foreign and national business and technocrats.[8] As a result, government employees, white-collar workers in the private sector, professionals, and the owners and managers of modest businesses must negotiate their way through an ever more treacherous economic landscape.[9] And, as in Eastern Europe, many of these societies are riven with intense political, ethnic, and religious rivalries which jeopardize middle-class hopes for stability and improvement. No wonder so many of them have fled to the North Atlantic in search of greater opportunities or have hunkered down at home with a sense of an impeding doom. Only on the Asian rim of the Pacific Ocean, from Japan to the "Tigers" and mainland China, each with their variant of market authoritarianism, have middle classes expanded in numbers and influence.[10] Yet there as well, sanguine assessments have recently been brought up short by both structural and political limits to the reenactment of the earlier middle-class drama which constituted such a fundamental part of the making of "modernity."

If virtually everywhere the middle classes have lost their previous compass and self-confidence and find their material, political, and cultural positions steadily undermined, neither scholars nor general observers have paid much attention to this process in global terms. Indeed, most contemporary reviews of twentieth-century history and reflections on the approach of the new millennium evade the middle-class question altogether. The problem is downplayed, of course, by those who preach the triumph of possessive individualism and market societies which supposedly herald the "end of history."[11] For others, something called "globalization" has purportedly penetrated public and private life in virtually every society.[12] For the optimistic, the result could be a hybridized, tolerant, interconnected world community or, less benignly, a corralling of natural and human resources by the all too visible hand of powerful cosmocorps and their political satraps. Finally, in the wake of the cold war, North Atlantic addictions to bipolarism have found new expression in the vision of civilizational conflicts and cultural polarization, effectively code words for race wars and assaults on dissidence and nonconformity.[13]

Yet some scholarly research, anecdote, and even the experiences of the currently downsized academy in the United States and elsewhere suggest the importance of being more attentive to the dilemmas facing middle classes around the globe. The argument here is that while they will not be eliminated altogether—leaving the world divided between tiny cliques of wealthy and powerful and an immiserated, violent mass barely distinguishable by country or clime—their fate will be a crucial importance. In effect, the sense that those increasingly fragmented groups make of these changes and their responses to the downsizing of their claims to wealth and political power will certainly have much to do with the prospects for humankind as the next millennium opens.[14]

While this essay offers a broad explanation of the unmaking of the middle classes on a global scale, it does so through a rereading of Latin American history from the Great Depression to the global restructuring of the 1980s through the story of the middle classes. These reflections will first expose how Latin American development studies, through several decades after its emergence in the post-World War II era, failed to deal in any adequate and comprehensive manner with the evolution of middle classes and their relationship to the broad contours of historical change during the course of Latin America's "short twentieth century." Then the essay will lay out the elements of a prospectus for a rereading of that era—heretofore understood in terms of the paradigm of *import substitution industrialization* (ISI), referred to here as the rise and fall of national capitalism. The intention is to demonstrate how the still powerful political and ideological legacy of developmentalist scholarship might be questioned and transcended. Just as the Steins and others during the unraveling of reform and the onset of authoritarianism a quarter century ago, scholars and activists today need to be bold in the making sense of the drama and tragedy of what appears to be a new phase of global capitalism.

II

From its inception, "development studies" neglected or at best marginalized inquiry into the nature and role of the middle classes outside of the North Atlantic basin.[15] This was certainly the case for its Latin American variant which emerged after the Second World War, reached maturity in the 1960s and 1970s, and continues to have a powerful hold on policymakers and academicians concerned with that part of the world.[16] Initially, during the decade after 1945, a handful of political scientists, sociologists, and anthropologists addressed a set of questions not dissimilar from present inquiries regarding democracy in Latin America. Their attention was drawn, as much of the work on transitions in the past two decades, to the Southern Cone. The political crises at midcentury in Argentina and Brazil provided a point of departure for most academic observers of Latin America in this period. Not surprisingly, these studies identified the middle classes in the region's most industrialized countries as providing the foundation for stable, constitutional democracies and market economies. The identification and celebration of an intrinsically democratic and reformist middle class became tantamount to enlisting these countries in the family of North Atlantic democracies against the cold war adversary.[17]

Yet some scholarship of the postwar era suggested a far more complex design of middle-class politics and, by extension, of the region's political economy and culture. Most importantly, John J. Johnson argued in his 1958 book, *Political Change in Latin America*, that claims-making by middle-class groups had the paradoxical effect of both modernizing and undermining the stability of those societies.[18] His work was empiricist, untheoretical, and suffused with a language of liberal optimism; indeed, he referred to the middle "sectors" not "classes." Nonetheless, this first major interpretation of twentieth-century Latin American history combined a structuralist narrative based on extensive documentation from the Economic Commission on Latin America (ECLA) with analysis of major political conjunctures in the decade and a half after the Second World War.[19] The Stanford historian examined the role of the middle classes in the balancing act politics of the Depression era and its aftermath and the onset of crises in the region's five most industrialized societies—Mexico, Chile, Brazil, Uruguay, and Argentina—during the mid-1950s. As one of his sympathetic reviewers, George Blanksten strongly implied, Johnson's work could serve as an antidote to the emergent reductionism of *Westernization* and *modernization* models in the social sciences in its provision of "an amazingly efficient instrument for structuring what thus far has appeared to be amorphous and sprawling indices of change."[20] Moreover, Johnson displayed enormous—and still largely unacknowledged—prescience in his prediction of the collapse of parliamentary regimes and the descent into authoritarianism.

Johnson's insights into the onset of what later observers would describe as the exhaustion of the import substitution industrialization model—referred to here as *national capitalism*—convinced few of his fellow scholars, at the time or later. To begin with, neither his fusion of structuralism and politics nor the book's modernist idealism about the middle classes in Mexico and the Southern Cone squared with a strong current of culturalist interpretation among many North American scholars in the postwar era such as Kalman Silvert.[21] In their view, the near ephemeral middle-class fragments in Latin America at midcentury did not represent a dynamic, modernizing group such as those who had purportedly transformed the North Atlantic. These Latin American middle classes, trapped in the legacy of colonialism, could only mimic those above them in highly stratified societies. Others took a less-jaundiced view of the limited modernism of the middle classes. In Silvert's wake, for example, would come corporativist interpretations proffered by Richard Morse, Claudio Véliz, and Howard Wiarda, the patrimonialism of Latin America's "generic Mediterranean" culture might prove to be the region's deliverance from the perils of progress: modernization cum traditional culture, so to speak.[22]

At the same time, Johnson's structuralist political analysis was at odds with the dominant strain in North American social science which focused on "interest groups." For functional pluralists, such as Seymour Martin Lipset and his acolytes in Latin American studies, research on the church, the military, unions, and other institutions would provide a far better guide to contemporary Latin America than Johnson's decidedly makeshift and untheorized class analysis.[23] Their purpose was to identify the vehicles by which the transition from traditional to modern societies could be achieved. More concretely, this involved determining the means by which the vast majority of poor and backward Latin Americans could be uplifted. Such scholars became the first major proponents of developmentalism, an instrument designed to help bring the so-called marginal populations of the world into the mainstream of history and on their way to what propagandists of the Alliance for Progress and others called "the good life," which was understood to be determined by a vague, universalizable model of human well-being and betterment. This line of investigation and polemics reflected, of course, the general spurning of class as a category of analysis at a moment when a substantial segment of the North American academic community abandoned "ideology," sought consensus, and partook in the campaigns against communism, at home and abroad.

With this modernization paradigm triumphant in Latin American development studies during the early and mid-1960s, the middle classes as historical subjects receded ever further into the background. This elision became more salient as analyses of coalition-building emphasizing negotiations and resource mobilizations replaced the earlier rather static portraiture of interest groups. Influenced by the "Yale School" of political science, deft observers of the Latin American scene such as Albert O. Hirschman and Charles Anderson sought to intervene in discussions of social reform in Latin America, by scholars and policymakers alike. In his now classic 1963 collection of essays, *Journeys Towards Progress: Studies in Economic Policymaking in Latin America*, Hirschman proposed that identifying structural impediments to change was less important than "trying to show how a society begins to move forward *as it is, in spite of what it is and because of what it is.*"[24] This scarcely veiled anti-Marxist and anti-structuralist manifesto effectively shut the door on a class-oriented analysis which might have been helpful in examining the social interests and their relation to the resource capabilities, potential coalitions, and prospects for adequate communication and efficient decision-making as the era of "developmentalism" came to a climax.[25]

The "radical" challenges to Latin American development studies from the mid-1960s did not result in much new light being cast on the middle classes.[26] Much of the first wave of structuralist writings calculated them out of the hopeful equation of radical reform or social revolution: highly polarized societies based on wide gaps in income, social status, and access to power. Those who did, on occasion, address the "middle-class question," such as the Argentine José Nun, defined them in negative terms, by what they had not became, namely a bourgeoisie.[27] Searching for more progressive agents of history, radical sociologists such as Rodolfo Stavenhagen also discounted the middle classes in a dualist portrait of Latin Americans captive to "internal colonialism."[28]

The *dependista* approaches which flourished through the 1970s and into the 1980s were often descriptively richer and theoretically more subtle than the early structural assessments of Latin America's underdevelopment.[29] Yet they were ultimately informed by a similar social dichotomization in which, at the end of the day, capital and the masses stood against each other. Even in so powerful a volume as Fernando Henrique Cardoso and Enzo Falleto's *Dependency and Development in Latin America*, the dense and compelling class analysis of pre-Depression Latin America largely gives way to a clunky structural functionalism of the contemporary era.[30] Consequently, in this work, as in much of the *dependista* genre, the middle classes are identified as social actors, but their sensibilities and behavior remain largely unproblematized in the interstices between labor, capital, and the state, absent of any interests, culture, politics, or ideologies of their own.

Finally, the revolutionary initiatives in social history of the 1970s and beyond hardly brought the middle classes to the forefront of scholarship or political reflection. The rich mix of *dependismo*, European and North American labor studies, and a renaissance in Marxian anthropology and sociology did make for the heady recovery of the lives of workers, peasants, artisans, and the urban poor, locating their struggles within a broad narrative of global capitalism.[31] And in doing so, it set in motion a set of research strategies and methodologies focused on power, identities, and resistance which would come into full flower in the studies of gender, race and ethnicity, and the "new social movements" of the last decade. A handful of works on "populism" written in those years, notably by Paul Drake and Steve Stein, two of John Johnson's students, brought the middle classes into relief.[32] But theirs were the exception in these empirically rich, theoretically imaginative, and politically engaged "histories from below." The dualist imprint on this radical historiography effectively repudiated any authentic role for the middle classes on their own terms given the enthusiasms of these committed scholars for the Cuban Revolution and their search for a radical alternative to the failed reformism of the 1960s. The institutional and "bureaucratic authoritarianism" approaches of the 1970s and 1980s also passed up the opportunity to develop a more wide-gauged class analysis, thereby proving inattentive as well to the role of the middle classes. The former, with Juan Linz and Albert Stepan's most effective and influential 1968 assessment of the collapse of civilian rule laid the blame for the crises of national capitalism squarely on the inefficacy and weakness of formal mechanisms for conflict resolution.[33] The latter, a curious hybrid of *dependismo* and structural-functionalism, most forcefully represented by Guillermo O'Donnell, addressed the problems of national capitalism which had preoccupied Johnson a decade and a half before and advanced a sophisticated research program to examine the relationship between the phases of industrialization, class coalitions, and the emergence of a technocratic politics.[34] But these writers, for all their analytical sophistication and insightfulness, deracinated social actors, ultimately rendering them captive to a political logic whereby the state mediated between labor and capital. Consequently, they did not put the middle classes back at or even near the center of the action in the story of the rise and fall of national capitalism where Johnson had so provocatively located them. So, yet again, the members of that social group who had become at once the progenitors and victims and terrified observers of Latin America's authoritarian turn from the mid-1960s were largely excluded from that cruel tale.

Their apparent absence characterizes many writings in the most recent incarnation of Latin American developmentalist studies. Much of the current mainstream literature builds in one way or another on the political and scholarly program enunciated by Hirschman and others in the early 1960s and which had salience in the "bureaucratic authoritarian" studies.[35] On the one hand, there has been renewed attention to the dynamics of economic decision making, whereby policymakers puzzle through the dilemmas posed by the debt crisis, the legacy of stagflation, and structural inequality. Considerable attention seems devoted to determining how the neoliberal model can be implemented by technocratic elites with a minimum of upheaval and the cushioning of its costs by creative adaptive mechanisms of the lower classes, such as the informal economy and a limited recreation of welfare programs.[36] At the same time, Latin American developmentalism has come full circle to the midcentury concerns with "democracy." Collective choice and organizational theory approaches have been brought to bear on political parties, constitutions, "liberal democratic" techniques, and institutions in order to explain the transitions from authoritarian rule in the 1980s. But as with the policy-oriented studies, these tales of "pacts," "convergences," and "consolidations" are largely absent of social content, as is, unfortunately, the now widely used notion of "civil society." In effect, there has been little scrutiny of the origins, structural positions, and cultural discourses of the various political actors who play out these scenarios of convalescent parliamentarism which have come to be known as "redemocratization." Absent a critical social narrative of neoliberalism, the fragmentations, enthusiasms, and disillusions of the middle classes thus become a matter of mere anecdote or simply, yet again, the object of their historic evasion by Latin American developmentalism.

The various poststructuralist critiques and alternatives to the mainstream social sciences have yet to discern any historical agency for the middle classes.[37] For all their analytical power and conceptual subtlety, postmodern, subaltern, and new social movement studies remain captive to a social dualism which largely essentializes the construction of elite hegemony and romanticizes those below.[38] For example, the technocratic middle classes which played such an important role in the evolution of developmentalism and its discontents in the postwar era have a shadowy presence in Arturo Escobar's trenchant and influential 1995 polemic against developmentalism.[39] And readers have yet to be summoned by testimonial literature into the complex and contradictory worlds of middle-class folk whose struggles, identity crises, and engagements and disengagements in the public realm have been much the anvil on which modern and postmodern Latin America alike were forged. In effect, even for these notably insightful writers, the middle classes have neither subject nor position.

III

In their current incarnation, mainstream social sciences and their orphaned developmentalist progeny will likely run their course in the academy and their attractiveness for policymakers and the wider public. But they will surely leave in their wake, as did the modernization school of the post-World War II era, a relentlessly narrow and impoverished historicism, theoretical incomprehension, disingenuous claims of political neutrality, and a limited capability to address the political and moral questions of power, authority, and resistance in the contemporary world. The task, therefore, for historians and others is to constitute a project similar to the one undertaken by Barbara Stein and Stanley Stein a quarter century ago. *The Colonial Heritage of Latin America* sought to identify the colonial origins of Latin America as reformist efforts in most of the region gave way to dictatorships. It bears noting that these two historians understood that region's dilemmas as part of broader global transformations, noting that the United States as well, with its legacy of slavery and unrestrained pursuit of profit, had its own heritage of colonialism. We are now challenged to discern how the strains, contradictions, and promises in this current era of cosmopolitan capitalism have arisen from the unfolding political economy, society, and culture of the region's "short twentieth century." And crucial to that process were the linkages to global processes at work in the five decades after the Great Depression which have given way, more recently, to the campaigns against welfare capitalism in the North Atlantic, the crises of "actually existing socialism" in the

Soviet Union and Eastern Europe, and the utter collapse of the post-colonial modernizing projects throughout the Third World. As a foreword to the gathering here of elements to place the middle classes back into a more historically rooted and socially dense analysis of Latin America's national capitalism, it is worth keeping in mind how the developmentalist community from the late 1940s to the 1980s construed that social group.[40] If often out of sight, the middle classes were hardly out of mind. They remained, always implicitly, the principal ideal object of historical change, a goal to be reached through hopefully orderly processes of modernization. For most adherents to developmentalism, the exemplar middle classes were literate, well-fed and housed, personally responsible, individualistic, and paradigmatically male citizens. And with voice and vote given compass by a sense of themselves as the ballast of their nations, they supposedly had corner on the respect for the rule of law and the devotion to the well-being of their fellow citizens. Finally, the rare mention in the scholarship imputed to the middle classes a certain unity and coherence, though seldom independence, as political actors. This middle-class imaginary had deep roots in the Western European and North American culture and lay at the core of a powerful historical interpretative frameworks of the postwar era. And it was given fillip by the Atlanticist crusade of the cold war years with its self-conscious identification as the bulwark of Western civilization and humanist values.

The social historian of the middle classes in Latin America's "short twentieth century" must begin by acknowledging their considerable fragmentation. The diverse social ecologies, economic structures, and political institutions of the pre-1930 era had thrown up a wide array of middling groups in town and country throughout the vast continent. In the worlds of export capitalism of the late nineteenth and early twentieth centuries, between the tiny slices of oligarchies and the mass of rural and urban poor, had arisen a complex latticework of people in the middle: the artisan cobblers of large cities to the backwoods magistrates, clerks in merchant houses to medium-sized independent farmers and even more prosperous and influential tenants on large estates and traders of all sorts, schoolteachers, junior military officers, lowly clerics, scriveners, journalists, and printers. Their uneasy position in these rapidly changing societies necessitated a constant struggle to locate themselves as persons of a certain social status, members of the *gente decente*.

Latin America's middle classes expanded in size during the five decades after the Great Depression, given widespread urbanization, industrial development, expansion of secondary and university education, and growth of the state.[41] Their presence and weight varied considerably throughout the region, as did the timing and pace of their emergence. Already strongly rooted in Mexico and the Southern Cone before 1930, they quickly expanded thereafter; in Central America, the middle classes did not burst into the foreground until the 1960s. However, over the course of the half century after the Great Depression, the material circumstances, sensibilities, and status of these groups crystallized along the lines of property holding, professional licensing and practice, and employment in governmental and corporate bureaucracies. At the same time, ethnic, racial, and gender differentiation occurred within each of these structural, occupational, and status divisions. Through their relations in middle-class households and in various professional and especially salaried positions, women left their particular imprint on this social grouping.

To a very significant degree, Latin America's middle classes during its "short twentieth century" were Leviathan's children. In effect, the dramatic and fairly consistent growth of the state apparatus most everywhere from the 1930s on, if not before, profoundly affected the making of this group. To a greater or lesser degree, this social group crystallized as governments expanded their influence and functions, often in response to the demands of elites for protection of export sectors or support for manufacturing. This quite often occurred very directly through expanded employment opportunities and benefits through the growth of traditional jobs in military service, policing, fiscal controls, and education; yet also of considerable importance were the constellation of new ministries, such as labor and economic planning and public health and public and semi-public corporations which made their appearance across the decades.[42] Through the networks and strategies of bureaucratic and political entrepreneurialism, middle-class officeholders built a universe of loyalties and expectations which in turn had a profound effect on the contours and nature of the Latin American states.[43] Middle-class property holders and professionals, as well as private sector employees, also had their lives shaped by the inexorable expansion of the state during this period. The petit bourgeoisie at times benefited from governmental planning and protectionism, and in some cases depended on the fiscal and monetary policies of national capitalism. A wide variety of professionals, from the traditional physicians, lawyers, and professors to newer groupings, such as engineers, agronomists, and economists, gained ever greater authority in these societies due to official licensing and support, even as they found themselves corralled by state power.

Finally, given the frailty of their material and status positions in their societies, the middle classes repeatedly helped transform the state into an arena of intense competition over resources, power, and authority. Much of their struggle had to do with preserving their position within the dense latticework of bureaucratic clientilism. But they also sought for the state a role to settle dangerous conflicts between elites and lower-class groups, thereby conflating the protection of their own endangered prerogatives with social peace and the national good. Time and again they imputed to governments the will and capacity to ensure economic security, political stability, and the general welfare. In doing so, the middle classes gave sinew to the modern nation-state in that part of the world, buoying economic growth and populist redistribution. In their overweening reliance on the state, however, they helped shrink and debase the prospects for a dynamic, autonomous "civil society" in most of Latin America, thereby diminishing resistance to elite demands within and outside the bureaucracies.

The preeminence of the state for Latin America's middle classes had much to do with their deep ambivalence toward the market.[44] The era of export capitalism had caused these groups to be linked inextricably into the commercial networks and consumer culture of the North Atlantic. At the same time, the boom-and-bust cycles of the several decades before 1930 had left them fainthearted enthusiasts for free trade and skeptics about the ability of markets to operate in consistent and predictable ways, thereby assuring their aspirations for material security, social mobility, and status advancement. Such concerns were heightened by the Great Depression, the unsteady position of Latin American products in world markets from the mid-1950s after a brief interlude of postwar rise in export earnings, and certainly by the conundrums of the domestic manufacturing, service, and agricultural sectors which yielded stagnation and inflation in many of the region's economies during the 1960s and 1970s. Certainly, some among the middle classes felt uneasiness about the heavy hand of the state and preferred a lighter interventionism or none at all. But the rage for planning and the broad support among a wide range of middle-class groups for governmental involvement in cushioning against the perilous economic terrain of national capitalism had greater purchase in the end. Wanting to be in the market but not of it, these groups expressed their desires for consumption of mass-produced goods even as they sought to diminish the risks and sacrifices wrought by the fulfillment of such expectations within the perilous construct of dependent development.

The powerful statist orientation of Latin America's middle classes found expression in the unfolding of the contradictory legacy of what Angel Rama called the "lettered city" during the region's "short twentieth century." Education, writing, and the humanistic arts generally had been the touchstone of middle-class material security, status, and even social power and authority. On the one hand, national capitalism witnessed various rich and interconnected literary and polemical interventions in writing and other forms of expression which were emancipatory and inclusionary in their purpose and design. From the Mexican muralists to the *dependistas*, such uses of cultural capital, expanded by the increases in secondary and university education during those years, yielded extraordinary critiques of elite power and the global economic system and laid out the contours for a nationalism which would "civilize " and make citizens of all the peoples of those societies. In doing so, they engaged with and integrated into their works and programs a wide range of ideological positions, cultural forms, and intellectual methods from the North Atlantic, from Marxism to Freudian psychology. At the same time, however, these entrepreneurs of words and ideas articulated the deep concerns of fellow middle-class members with the perils of unordered markets and dangerous classes alike. Their unrelieved panic over real and potential instability in the economic, social, and political realms sometimes found expression in a nostalgic, Hispanic anti-modernism. On the Left, a renovated, more progressive, but still paternalist notion of "civilizing" or "leading" the masses had great currency. But more commonly, theirs was the pursuit of a technical rationality which could be applied to their wildly unmanageable continent. The "civilizing" vision of lawyers, engineers, agronomists, and economists, which also involved an extended transnational dialogue, meant a strategic investment of cultural capital in the pursuit of an equilibrium of social forces which only they could purportedly keep in balance by virtue of their wisdom and disinterest.[45] Such shared convictions led to an antipolitical sensibility among the middle classes which subverted the prospects of a richly combative, intellectually diverse, and socially pluralist civil society in that part of the world.

The fissures in the middle-class imagination over the public uses of cultural capital had important analogues in their private lives as well. Building on nineteenth-century dissident traditions such as bohemianism and anarchism, the some middle-class folk under national capitalism defied the conventions of family and gender relations and sought to escape the conformities of language, sexuality, and work habits. This was especially possible in the anonymity of the great cities, more dangerously

so in provincial towns and villages. But one of the principal cultural building blocks of national capitalism lay in what Susan Besse has recently
called "modernized patriarchy" which had its crucial center among the
middle classes.[46] Part of this process unfolded in the realm of public policy and politics where a masculinist vision of the nation-state came to prevail. But there is a denser, still largely unexplored chronicle in the intimate
and family lives of the middle classes in these years which maintained a
highly repressive moral universe which kept women subordinated and
gave rebuke to dissent of any sort. The psychological and social inequalities engendered within middle-class families during these years seeped
their way into nooks and crannies throughout these societies, providing
thereby crucial underpinnings for the attractions among this group toward
the military, authoritarian rule, and antipolitics more generally.

The fragmented nature of the middle classes at work and in their
homes, in public realms and in private spaces, had further expression in
the cacophony of democratic voices raised up by this social group after
1930.[47] The complex terrain of Latin America's democratic politics in
these years and especially the "redemocratizing" aftermath have been
inadequately illuminated by the prevailing institutionalist and structuralist-functionalist approaches; these have largely thrown up models
of "open," "restricted," "frozen," and "delegative" democracy largely indif-
ferent to deep-seated, long-term debates among Latin Americans themselves over democratic ideas and practices. In a region during whose
"short twentieth century" a great deal of contention occurred on this
matter, it is possible to identify at least four, interrelated and competing
paradigms of democratic belief and action substantially articulated and
undertaken by the middle classes. These alternative projects—liberal,
social, popular, and radical—all had deep roots in the era of export capitalism. They were also in close, and sometimes fatal embrace, sharing
common languages of freedom and emancipation more broadly, competing over support from lower-class groups, helping each other at times and
not infrequently dealing each other fatal blows.

To begin with, liberal democracy had limited scope for most social
classes throughout the era of national capitalism, though it had considerable salience in the transition from authoritarianism to convalescent
parliamentarism beginning in the late 1970s. Support for parliamentary
institutions, civil liberties, and the rule of law had been major banners for
portions of the *gente decente* in the nineteenth and early twentieth centuries and had been used to combat elite rule. But by the 1880s, at least,
these potentially dissident liberal values and norms, domesticated by oli-

garchical republicanism under the influence of Benthamite and positivist thought, were seen as a crucial strategy for civilizing the peoples of the region and containing middle- and lower-class challengers. National capitalism, with its statist thrust and various populist accents, proved hostile to its legal formalism, cramped constitutionalism, and social exclusiveness. Political parties, such as the Radicals in the Southern Cone, were on the defensive as they sought to keep alive a commitment of public opinion to the rights and responsibilities of liberal democracy.[48] Its most crucial and long-lasting triumph in this period occurred through the suffragist movements, most of which, with exceptions such as the feminist wing of Peronism, adhered to its individualist notions of citizenship. However, many proponents of this otherwise exclusionary liberalism among the elites and middle classes turned rightward after 1930. Early flirtations with European fascism gave way to a technocratic vision of the social order with liberal democratic institutions drained of substance and commitments to pluralism and personal freedoms largely abandoned. Such postures informed the macabre electoral incarnations of authoritarian rule in places like Chile and Brazil, not to mention Mexico, which had substantial middle-class backing. Ironically, liberalism provided the principal armature in the battle of human rights activists, largely from the middle classes, against dictatorships from the 1960s onward.

Other middle-class democrats also sought to solidify and deepen the commitment to formal democratic institutions, including individual rights and parliamentary regimes, but did so within the framework of coalitions with working-class parties. The goal for many middle-class activists in Chile and a handful of other societies with the prospect of such alliances and strong traditions of parliamentary rule was the establishment of a welfare state. Seeking greater social equality within the framework of republican institutions and activist governments, these Latin American social democrats promoted "popular front" alliances in the 1930s and 1940s. On the eve of the cold war, middle-class activists in Socialist, Communist, and populist parties had a strong electoral presence in various countries, including the Southern Cone, Colombia, Mexico, Venezuela, Costa Rica, and Uruguay. However, the frailty of trade unionism in the postwar era, splits between workers and the middle class, and cold war divisions weakened social democracy in most places. On some level, the Christian Democratic initiatives of the 1950s and 1960s represented an effort to jump start such a political project by middle-class activists outside the traditional leftist framework, but the weak labor bases of these initiatives caused them to flounder. The authoritarian turn caused a further deterioration of these alternatives, as working-class organizations and their middle-class allies fell before severe repression. Military edicts, the reorganization of manufacturing and agriculture, and the expansion of the service sector forced social democracy into further retreat. Nonetheless, the substantial middle-class involvement and support for such workers's movements during the struggles against the dictatorships did manage to keep alive a parliamentary welfarist vision in Brazil and a handful of other countries.

The most salient political voices during national capitalism came from popular democrats, commonly referred to as populists. Midwifed by *gente decente* militants amid the nineteenth-century encounters between liberalism and the *ancien régime*, popular democracy emphasized the reduction of elite economic power, improvement of the general welfare, and, in many countries, defiance of foreign influence and even direct colonial rule, as in Cuba. Despite their touted loyalty to republican institutions, these largely middle-class popular democrats were skeptical of elite-dominated parliamentarism, repeatedly turned to arms to rectify political institutions and right the social order, and saw themselves as the most knowledgeable and morally fit to act on behalf and in the name of the "people." This nineteenth-century legacy had a profound renaissance in the era of national capitalism. In the three decades after the Great Depression, this powerful Jacobin sensibility found expression in a wide range of social and political movements, from APRA to Peronism and the reformist and revolutionary initiatives in Bolivia, Cuba, and Central America in the 1940s and 1950s. While often in close relation to social democracy, it also coincided with the vanguardist logic of the communist parties which stood as a major pillar of the Latin American Left in this period. The middle-class crusaders for popular democracy in this era tended, given the fierce struggles with recalcitrant elite groups, to reaffirm the exclusionary and authoritarian legacy of nineteenth-century oppositional politics, a process reinforced by Marxist-Leninism. With all these limits, however, they must be recognized as contributing to the remarkable evolution of national politics in the region well into the 1960s, widening the degree and scope of participation in civil society, and making social equality and public welfare major concerns for public debate and state action.[49]

Popular democracy often remained at center stage in middle-class politics during the third quarter of the twentieth century as the parliamentary regimes of national capitalism collapsed. The 1960s and 1970s witnessed a wide variety of revolutionary insurrections throughout the continent led and underwritten by middle-class activists.[50] They were initially triumphant and unusually successful over the long term only in Cuba. There middle-class rebels with popular support in 1959 overthrew a dictatorship which had lost its earlier populist edge. Fidel Castro and his middle-class associates then enacted a major structural transformation from above; they socialized capital, expanded the accumulation and distributive functions of the state, and improved the common weal to an unparalleled degree in Latin America, even while holding at bay the depredations of the Colossus of the North. Elsewhere, until the victory of the Sandinistas in Nicaragua two decades later, well-equipped national armies and strong support from the United States kept the new generation of armed Jacobins at bay. But they too undercut their own insurgencies through the inability or unwillingness to mobilize lower-class groups with whom they had, with some exceptions, few substantive links but in whose name they acted with relentless certainty. And at the end of the day, even their principal compass—the Cuban Revolution—could no longer provide clear emancipatory direction for its own people or those elsewhere in the region, at least partly because of its own militarized and vanguardist practices.

Finally, throughout most of the "short twentieth century," radical democrats in Latin America tended to be cast into the background. Previously, from the 1880s through the 1920s, middle-class militants had played major roles in a variety of local, highly combative challenges to oligarchical rule, from the uprisings of indigenous and mestizo communalists to artisanal protests and anarchosyndicalist movements. Placing a high value on individual and collective transformation (e.g., the creation of "new" men and women), social equality, and local autonomy, as well as doubtful about parliamentary representation, such claims-making had invited the harshest repression under export capitalism. As national capitalism unfolded in the wake of the Depression, these highly participative, though usually quite parochial forms of political action tended to be absorbed within the social or popular democratic projects. Anarcho-syndicalism, for example, dealt a strong blow in the 1920s by the elites, could not compete with communist initiatives which helped achieve major gains for organized labor, though at a cost of a more genuinely accountable and locally oriented political culture. In short, the successful widening of the state's welfare functions under national capitalism rendered radical democracy largely moribund through the 1950s and into the 1960s. With the onset of authoritarianism, lower- and middle-class radical democrats faced off against military rulers, national elites, and cosmopolitan bourgeoisies. Their resistance engendered a host of new institutions and organizations, usually locally and regionally based and very often under the wing of a renovated Catholic Church.[51] In the process, they spearheaded the return to parliamentary rule in many places, joining with liberal and social democrats. But in general, they sought also to keep on the agenda a wide measure of local accountability and social equality. Their radical democratic project found expression in a wide array of "new social movements" as a decayed and militarized national capitalism began to give way to a new order in the late 1970s and early 1980s. In these years, radical democrats moved beyond the compass of human rights to indigenous peoples's liberation, environmental campaigns, and struggles for women's liberation and gender equality. Their conception of democracy thus involved a wide range of arenas, from the most public of institutions to the most private of domains.

IV

The fate of the taxicab-historians and others like them—downsized managers, ill-paid school teachers, underemployed bank tellers, small-time litigators, bankrupt store owners, indebted farmers, and laid-off civil servants—in contemporary Latin America would seem to lay in forces well beyond their control. From the 1970s onward, the continent has been buffeted by what contemporary observers refer to as globalization. Increasingly cosmopolitanized elites and their foreign collaborators have forged ever more inextricable links to the so-called "new world order." Academicians and other observers have long been alarmed over the widened gaps between the rich and the poor and the prospects for social protest from below. Now, however, they have begun to identify an equally significant and historically tragic decomposition of the Latin American variant of the "middle-class dream." The institutions, sensibilities, and social pacts of statist welfarism—of democratic capitalist, socialist, or bureaucratic authoritarian varieties—which underwrote the expansion of the numbers and influence of the middle classes in the decades after the Great Depression lay in ruins. Little seems recoverable after the state terrorism of the 1960s and 1970s and the ravages of economic restructuring during the subsequent regimes of convalescent republican institutions overwhelmed by the recurrent episodes of presidentialism and other legacies of dictatorship. As in the North Atlantic, the former Soviet bloc, and much of the Third World, the middle-class prospect which crystallized in the years after World War II appears to have run its course. In its wake, nervous, angry, depressed, ill-humored, and aimless crowds of small proprietors, officeholders, and professionals flee inward or abroad, barely understanding or acknowledging their own complicity in the disaster which has befallen them and their societies.[52]

Against this emergent image of the middle classes as the most recent castoffs of the inexorable flow of history must be a recognition of their crucial role in the making of the contemporary world, for good or ill. This resonates with the insistence of the Colombian sociologist Antonio Garcia many years ago that "in the middle classes there accumulates, densifies, and projects the major conflicts and contradictions of the process of development in Latin America."[53] At the same time, the unmaking or remaking of the middle classes must not be seen outside their own historical perceptions, choices, and actions. As Arno Mayer insisted in 1975 in his discussion of the lower-middle classes in Europe, "the place and movement of class in economy, society, and polity are a function not exclusively of shared economic interest, but also of ideological configurations and political relations, notably in conjunctures of dynamic conflict."[54]

These analytical suggestions find a suggestive, and somewhat more complete articulation in a comparative study by Dietrich Rueschemeyer, Evelyn Huber Stephens, and John D. Stephens in their 1992 volume *Capitalist Development and Democracy*. This book offers a powerful reprise of Johnson's problematic more than four decades earlier about the role of the middle classes in Latin America's democratic capitalist initiatives at midcentury. The authors remain somewhat constrained by a institutionalist and structural-functionalist framework at times seeming to reduce the question to what the middle classes were not or failed to become in the context of the struggles between labor and capital. Nonetheless, they acknowledge that central to the history of Latin America's "short twentieth century" lay the "propensity and capability of the middle classes to exert strong pressures and to demand full democratization."[55] Aside from the nature of specific conjunctures, such as the Great Depression, they rightly identify important elements which helped determine the extent, depth, and pace, as well as success or failure of such efforts. Some crucial variables are external to the middle classes, such as the organizational capacity of subordinate groups, especially workers, the prospect of coalitions with military or elite factions, and the institutional frameworks within which they operated, such as clientilist or mass political parties. But these careful historical sociologists also point toward factors within the middle classes themselves. On the one hand, they identify the variability of middle-class relations with other classes at various levels of development and critically important moments. And they insist that "owing to their intermediate position in the class structure and their internal heterogeneity, the interests of the middle classes were subject to a greater variety of social interpretation and construction."

The critique in this essay of the developmentalist elision of the middle-classes and its proffering of elements for a reassessment of their relationship to the rise and fall of national capitalism coincide with what Rueschemeyer, Stephens, and Stephens refer to as the "social construction of class."[56] These pages have urged that examining the positions of middle-class groups within the state and corporate capitalism over time and at particular conjunctures remains a major task. At the same time, attention to middle-class visions of themselves, their societies, and the broader world allows for their recovery as authentic social actors. In this way, it becomes possible to discern how in diverse contexts and through multiple prisms, in both public and private spheres, market relations and politics, their beliefs and behavior gave shape to the many incarnations of national capitalism. And, finally, this has included a prospectus for seeing democratic ideas and practices less through the lens of a universalistic liberal formalism, as has been characteristic of the transition literature generally, than as a highly contested terrain by which middle classes and others struggled over the rights and responsibilities of citizenship in a multitude of realms and circumstances. Such an undertaking assures that this group will no longer be the black box which the developmentalists and their antagonists alike made them out to be.

A project of this sort would provide a welcome prospect to honor, draw inspiration, and help keep alive a long tradition of critical historical inquiry. It involves acknowledging that capitalism has unfolded on an increasingly global scale over the past half millennium, thereby being attentive to its complex conjoining of economic relations, geopolitical encounters, migrations, technological shifts, and cultural changes and interactions. But it also means being eminently clear about capitalism as a social construction, as the outcome of conflicts and accommodations between and within classes and interwoven with other power hierarchies, most notably gender and race. This reminds us in powerful ways that historical understanding is not about laws, models, and ironclad narratives but about identifying the connections between patterns of human belief and action, their contingency, and their re-creation over long periods of time and at particular moments of dramatic change. Such an approach hardly denies folly or tragedy in human affairs, but it does provide hope that, as Cornel West has written in another context, "the interplay of willful self and fateful circumstances, human volition and historical limits" can yield collective as well as individual betterment.[57]

Ultimately then, in response to the common dilemmas faced by the taxicab-historians and others of the imperiled middle classes in Latin America and throughout the globe—including now a substantial portion of the North American academy—it becomes incumbent to revisit their complex involvement in modern history. Our task, as the world they helped make becomes undone and remade at the end of the twentieth century, is to sort out their legacy, to reveal how they lived and made sense of their societies, their dreams, hopes, and fears. Stanley Stein insisted that every generation of historians must "re-examine prejudices, premises, hypotheses, implicit or explicit, in the light of unfolding reality."[58] In the end, those afforded the privilege of inquiry and reflection should be fearlessly critical and generous too in understanding those who were creators and victims alike of their historical moment and our reality.

Notes

CHAPTER ONE

1. Charles Gibson, introduction to *The Black Legend: Anti-Spanish Attitudes in the Old World and the New*, ed. Charles Gibson (New York: Alfred A. Knopf, 1971), 2–27. It did not take long for this self-conscious myth-building to mutate into the Lockean language of empire as property. Spanish greed for specie and the domain of monarchic privilege was the basis for "conquest." By contrast, the English conflated colony into "plantation" to justify dominion over new lands in the cant of rugged-individualist proprietors. This, as it turned out, became part of the language justifying a rupture of English colonies from the metropole. P. J. Marshall, "Parliament and Property Rights in the Late Eighteenth-Century British Empire," in *Early Modern Conceptions of Property*, ed. John Brewer and Susan Staves (London: Routledge, 1996), 530–544; Anthony Pagden, *Lords of all the World: Ideologies of Empire in Spain, Britain and France, c. 1500–1800* (New Haven: Yale University Press, 1995), esp. ch. 3.
2. Abbé Raynal, *A Philosophical and Political History of the Settlement and Trade of the Europeans in the East and West Indies* (Edinburgh: n.p. 1792); Arthur P. Whitaker, "The Dual Role of Latin America in the Enlightenment," in *Latin America and the Enlightenment*, 2d ed., ed. Arthur P. Whitaker (Ithaca: Great Seal Books, 1961). Also see Maxwell's chapter in this volume.
3. Raynal, *A Philosophical and Political History*, Book 8, 141.
4. Simón Bolívar, "Reply of a South American to a Gentleman of this Island," 6 September 1815, in *Selected Writings of Simón Bolívar*, ed. Harold A. Bierck (New York: Colonial Press, 1951), 114.
5. Domingo F. Sarmiento, *Life in the Argentine Republic in the Days of the Tyrants, or Civilization and Barbarism* (New York: Collier Books, 1961), 30. See also Halperín Donghi's chapter in this volume.
6. Louis Hartz, *The Liberal Tradition in America* (New York: Harper & Row, 1953), 5.
7. Louis Hartz, ed., *The Founding of New Societies: Studies in the History of the United States, Latin America, South Africa, Canada and Australia* (New York: Harcourt, Brace & World, 1964).

8. Richard Morse, "The Heritage of Latin America," in *The Founding of New Societies*, ed. Louis Hartz, 123–177.

9. Ibid., 146. For similar, if prosaic renditions on the same, see Glen Dealy, "Prolegomena on the Spanish American Political Tradition," *Hispanic American Historical Review*, XLVIII, no. 1 (February 1968); and Claudio Véliz, *The New World of the Gothic Fox: Culture and Economy in English and Spanish America* (Berkeley and Los Angeles: University of California Press, 1994).

10. Octavio Paz, *The Labyrinth of Solitude* (New York: Grove Press, 1961).

11. Octavio Paz, "Mexico and the United States" (1985), reprinted in the 1985 edition of *The Labyrinth of Solitude* (New York: Weidenfeld, 1985).

12. John J. Johnson, *The Military and Society in Latin America* (Stanford: Stanford University Press, 1964).

13. Antonio Benítez Rojo, *La isla que se repite: El Caribe y la perspectiva posmoderna* (Hanover, N.H.: Ediciones del Norte, 1989).

14. For a useful review of path-dependency arguments, see Mark J. Roe, "Chaos and Evolution in Law and Economics," *Harvard Law Review* 109, no. 3 (January 1996): 641–668.

15. Perhaps the touchstone work here was Stanley Stein and Barbara Stein's *The Colonial Heritage of Latin America: Essays on Economic Dependence in Perspective* (New York: Oxford University Press, 1970). See also Love's chapter in this volume.

16. Fernando Henrique Cardoso and Enzo Faletto, *Dependency and Development in Latin America* (Berkeley and Los Angeles: University of California Press, 1979) fits this dialectical approach, arguing that situations of dependency were not stable or permanent.

17. C. L. R. James, *The Black Jacobins: Toussaint L'Ouverture and the San Domingo Rebellion* (New York: Vintage Books, 1963).

CHAPTER TWO

1. Raymond Mauny, *Les navigations médiévales sur les côtes sahariennes antérieures à la découverte portugaises* (Lisbon: Centro de Estudos Historicos Ultramarinos, 1960 [1434]); P. E. H. Hair, "Was Columbus' First Very Long Voyage a Voyage from Guinea?" *History in Africa* 22 (1995): 223–37.

2. The sections that follow are largely a condensation of my "Disease Exchange Across the Tropical Atlantic," *History and Philosophy of the Life Sciences* 15 (1993): 329–56.

3. Peter L. Perine, "Syphilis and the Endemic Treponematoses," in *Hunter's Tropical Medicine*, 6th ed, ed. Thomas G. Strickland (Philadelphia: Saunders, 1984), 247–56.

4. See, for some recent analysis, Alfred W. Crosby, Jr., *The Columbian Exchange: Biological and Cultural Consequences of 1492* (Westport, Conn.: Greenwood, 1972), 122–64; Kenneth F. Kiple, *The Caribbean Slave: A Biological History* (Cambridge: Cambridge University Press, 1984), 191–92; R. J. C. Hoeppli, *Parasitic Disease in Africa and the Western Hemisphere: Early Documentation and Transmission by the Slave Trade* (Basel: Verlag fur Recht und Gesellschaft, 1969), 71–110.

5. Brenda Baker and George Armelagos, "The Origin and Antiquity of Syphilis: Paleopathological Diagnosis and Interpretation," *Current Anthropology* 29 (1988): 703–37; Mahmoud Y. El-Najjar, "Human Treponematosis and Tuberculosis: Evidence from the New World," *American Journal of Physical Anthropology* 51 (1979): 599–618.

6. Hoeppli, *Parasitic Disease*, 102–06.

7. Claude Quétel, *History of Syphilis* (Baltimore: Johns Hopkins University Press, 1990), 10–11.

8. Crosby, *The Columbian Exchange*, 137.

9. M. D. Grmek, *Diseases of the Ancient Greek World* (Baltimore: Johns Hopkins University Press, 1989), 133–42, esp. 140; Baker and Armelagos, "The Origin and Antiquity of Syphilis," esp. 731.

10. Maciej Henneberg, Renata Henneberg, and Joseph Colman Carter, "Health in Colonial Metaponto," *National Geographic Research & Exploration* 8 (1992): 446–59.

11. Bruce M. Rotchild, Israel Hershkovitz, and Christine Rotchild, "Origin of Yaws in the Pleistocene," *Nature* 378 (23 November 1995): 343–44.

12. S. Julian Ravenel Childs, *Malaria and the Colonization of the Carolina Low Country, 1526–1696* (Baltimore: Johns Hopkins University Press, 1940), 5-52, 109–10; Darrett B. Rutman and Anita H. Rutman, "Of Agues and Fevers: Malaria in the Early Chesapeake," *The William and Mary Quarterly* 33 (1976): 31–60.

13. John R. McNeill, "The Ecological Basis of Warfare in the Caribbean, 1700–1804," in *Adapting to Conditions: War and Society in the Eighteenth Century*, ed. Maarten Utlee (Tuscaloosa: Alabama University Press, 1986), 16–42.

14. Donald Hopkins, *Princes and Peasants: Smallpox in History* (Chicago: University of Chicago Press, 1983), 8–9; Dauril Alden and Joseph C. Miller, "Unwanted Cargoes: The Origins and Dissemination of Smallpox via the Slave Trade from Africa to Brazil, c. 1560–1830," in *The African Exchange: Toward a Biological History of Black People*, ed. Kenneth F. Kiple (Durham, NC: Duke University Press, 1988), 42–45; Frank Fenner, Donald Ainslie Henderson, Isao Arita, Zdenek Jezek, and Ivan Danilovich Ladnyi, *Smallpox and Its Eradication* (Geneva: World Health Organization, 1988), 169–208.

15. David Henige, "When Did Smallpox Reach the New World (And Why Does it Matter?)," in *Africans in Bondage*, ed. Paul E. Lovejoy (Madison:

University of Wisconsin Press, 1986), 11–26; Hopkins, *Princes and Peasants*, 204–5; Salvador Brau, *La colonización de Puerto Rico* (San Juan: Instituto de Cultura Puertoriqueña, 1969), 314–16.

16. Hopkins, *Princes and Peasants*, 204–5; Charles Gibson, *The Aztecs under Spanish Rule* (Stanford: Stanford University Press, 1964), 448–51; Torobio Motolinía, *Motolinía's History of the Indians of New Spain*, ed. Elizabeth Andros Foster (Berkeley: Cortés Society, 1950), 38; Francis J. Brooks, "Revising the Conquest of Mexico: Smallpox, Sources, and Populations," *Journal of Interdisciplinary History* 24 (1993): 1–29 has recently claimed that the serious smallpox epidemic in central Mexico in the 1520s was an illusion. His case cannot be sustained and it has been corrected Robert McCaa, "Spanish and Nahuatl Views on Smallpox and Demographic Catastrophe in Mexico," *Journal of Interdisciplinary History* 25 (1995): 397–431.

17. Alden and Miller, "Unwanted Cargoes," 42–5.

18. Ibid., 39, 55-62; Philip D. Curtin, *Economic Change in Precolonial Africa: Senegambia in the Era of the Slave Trade* (Madison: University of Wisconsin Press, 1975), 110–11; Joseph S. Miller, *Way of Death: Merchant Capitalism and the Angolan Slave Trade, 1730–1830* (Madison: University of Wisconsin Press, 1989); Joseph C. Miller, "The Significance of Drought, Disease, and Famine in the Agriculturally Marginal Zones of Western Central Africa," *Journal of African History* 23 (1982) 17–61.

19. Philip D. Curtin, *The Rise and Fall of the Plantation Complex: Essays in Atlantic History* (New York: Cambridge University Press, 1990).

20. Geoffrey Parker makes the point that this contrast between the European objective to seize territory and the frequent non-European objective to seize people was an important contrast in the military history of the West and the non-West. Geoffrey Parker, "Europe and the Wider World, 1500–1750: The Military Balance," in *Political Economy of Merchant Empires: State Power and World Trade 1350–1750*, ed. James E. Tracy (New York: Cambridge University Press, 1991), 63–65.

21. John K. Thornton, *Africa and Africans in the Making of the Atlantic World, 1400–1680* (New York: Cambridge University Press, 1992), 72–97.

22. Jack Goody, *Tradition, Technology, and the State* (London: Oxford University Press, 1971), 21–38.

23. Thornton, *Africa and Africans*, 74–79.

24. These conditions in Africa of the fifteenth and sixteenth centuries bear some resemblance to the evolution of slavery in Muscovy over those same centuries, leading in the Muscovite case to the changeover from slavery to a system of serfdom attached to the land. The major region of slave supply to the Mediterranean basin at that time was, however, south of Muscovy proper and drew to some degree on captured Muscovites.

Richard Hellie, *Slavery in Russia: 1450–1725* (Cambridge: Harvard University Press, 1982), 1-26. A long discussion of the relationship between land scarcity and labor control through slavery or other means goes back at least as far as Herman Merivale, *Lectures on Colonization and Colonies Delivered before the University of Oxford in 1839, 1840, & 1841*, 2d ed. (London: Longman, Green, Longman, and Roberts, 1861), and comes down through H. J. Nieboer, *Slavery As an Industrial System* (The Hague: Martinus Nijhoff, 1910) to a variety of recent authorities.
25. Philip D. Curtin, "Epidemiology and the Slave Trade," *Political Science Quarterly* 83 (1968): 191–216.
26. Eric Williams, *Capitalism and Slavery* (Chapel Hill: University of North Carolina Press, 1944).

CHAPTER THREE

1. Lord Cromer, *Ancient and Modern Imperialism* (London: Longmans, 1910).
2. C. L. R. James, *The Black Jacobins: Toussaint l'Ouverture and the San Domingo Revolution* (New York: Vintage Books, 1963 [1938]).
3. Eric Williams, *Capitalism and Slavery* (Chapel Hill: University of North Carolina Press, 1944).
4. Much of this work took its inspiration from Philip D. Curtin, *The Atlantic Slave Trade: A Census* (Madison: University of Wisconsin Press, 1969). The more recent studies have attempted to overcome the natural divisions between Africa and the Americas and to link the three continents together. Of this rich literature it is invidious to single out a few studies, but Stuart B. Schwartz, *Sugar Plantations in the Formation of Brazilian Society: Bahia, 1550–1835* (New York: Cambridge University Press, 1985) and Joseph C. Miller, *Way of Death: Merchant Capitalism and the Angolan Slave Trade, 1730–1830* (Madison: University of Wisconsin Press, 1988) are particularly successful in revealing the transatlantic linkages.
5. See, in particular, the essays in Manuel Moreno Fraginals, ed., *Africa in Latin America: Essays on History, Culture, and Socialization* (New York: Holmes & Meier, 1984);and Sidney Mintz and Richard Price, *An Anthropological Approach to the Afro-American Past: A Caribbean Perspective* (Philadelphia: Institute for the Study of Human Issues, 1976).
6. Much of this framework stems from R. R. Palmer's early and pioneering work on the transatlantic world of political ideas and constitutionalism. See *The Age of the Democratic Revolution: A Political History of Europe and America*, 2 vols. (Princeton: Princeton University Press, 1969–70). Since then, however, scholars have stressed the economic

and social dimensions of this transatlantic world and have been interested in the population movements that linked the three continents.

7. This has become the standard view of Euro-African relations and has entered all the textbooks on African history in the nineteenth century where the authors stress legitimate commerce and Christianization. Philip D. Curtin's *The Image of Africa: British Ideas and Action, 1780–1850* (Madison: University of Wisconsin Press, 1964) elaborates many of these themes.

8. John Elliott, "Britain and Spain in America: Colonists and Colonized," The Stenton Lecture (Reading, 1994).

9. The standard treatments of European views on Africa are Philip D. Curtin, *The Image of Africa*; William B. Cohen, *The French Encounter with Africans: White Response to Blacks, 1530–1880* (Bloomington: Indiana University Press, 1980); Margaret T. Hodgen, *Early Anthropology in the Sixteenth and Seventeenth Centuries* (Philadelphia: University of Pennsylvania Press, 1964); and Michael Adas, *Machines as the Measure of Men: Science, Technology, and Ideologies of Western Dominance* (Ithaca: Cornell University Press, 1989). Unfortunately the British and French travelers had much less to say about Africans during the early European contacts than the Spanish and Portuguese, whose accounts have been much less studied. See Cohen, *The French Encounter with Africans*; and Dorothy Hammond and Alta Jablow, *The Africa that Never Was* (New York: Twayne Publishers, 1970) where the authors write that the British comments on Africa in the sixteenth and seventeenth centuries were "a sparse literature and consist of brief accounts of trading voyages. These do not compare in sophistication with the Dutch and Portuguese writings from the same period" (19).

10. Denys Hay, *Europe: The Emergence of an Idea* (Edinburgh: Edinburgh University Press, 1968), 14.

11. Robert Bartlett, *The Making of Europe: Conquest, Colonization, and Cultural Change, 950–1350* (Princeton: Princeton University Press, 1993), 1.

12. See Charles Verlinden, *The Beginnings of Modern Colonization*, trans. Yvonne Freccero (Ithaca: Cornell University Press, 1970).

13. See John H. Elliott, "Renaissance Europe and America: A Blunted Impact?", in *The First Images of America: The Impact of the New World on the Old*, ed. Fredi Chiappelli (Berkeley and Los Angeles: University of California Press, 1976); John H. Elliott, *The Old World and The New* (Cambridge: Cambridge University Press, 1970); and Anthony Grafton, *New Worlds, Ancient Texts: The Power of Tradition and the Shock of Discovery* (Cambridge: Belknap Press of Harvard University Press, 1992).

14. Besides the aforementioned studies, the work of Valerie Flint, *The Imaginative Landscape of Christopher Columbus* (Princeton: Princeton

University Press, 1987); Peter Hulme, *Colonial Encounters: Europe and the Native Caribbean, 1492–1797* (London: Methuen, 1986); Anthony Pagden, *European Encounters with the New World: From Renaissance to Romanticism* (New Haven: Yale University Press, 1993); and Anthony Pagden, *The Fall of Natural Man: The American Indian and the Origins of Comparative Ethnology* (Cambridge: Cambridge University Press, 1982) contain a wealth of information on this subject.

15. Adas, *Machines as the Measure of Men*, 21–68.

16. On the theological and intellectual dimensions of this debate one should consult the aforementioned studies of Anthony Pagden, in addition to his *The Uncertainties of Empire: Essays in Iberian and Ibero-American Intellectual History* (Aldershot, Eng.: Variorum, 1994); Lewis Hanke, *The Spanish Struggle for Justice in the Conquest of America* (Philadelphia: University of Pennsylvania Press, 1949); and Lewis Hanke, *Aristotle and the American Indians* (Bloomington: Indiana University Press, 1959). These studies demonstrate that Spanish jurists and theologians carried out intense debates on the morality of enslaving the Native American population and that their interventions, at the least, influenced colonial policy. At the same time all of the studies on the ground in the Americas also reveal the problems that the Iberians experienced in actually enslaving Amerindians who fled or died in huge numbers. Probably the most detailed treatment of this failed effort to enslave local populations and the resort to African slave labor is Schwartz, *Sugar Plantations*. Schwartz found that in the midst of this transition to African slaves an African slave commanded a market price nearly three times that of an Indian slave (70).

17. See, especially, Curtin, *The Image of Africa*; and Adas, *Machines as the Measure of Men* for a sense of the durability of images over long periods of time.

18. For early excellent accounts of Spanish and Portuguese imperial motivations that highlight the three g's of the period one should consult J. H. Parry, *The Spanish Seaborne Empire* (New York: Alfred A. Knopf, 1966) and C. R. Boxer, *The Portuguese Sea-Borne Empire, 1415–1825* (London: Hutchinson, 1969). The general Latin American history texts refer to the theme of God, gold, and glory as the essentials of expansion. See, as an example, Benjamin Keen and Mark Wasserman, *A History of Latin America* (Boston: Houghton Mifflin Company, 1988), 74.

19. J. H. Elliott, *Imperial Spain, 1469-1719* (New York: St. Martin's Press, 1963), 53.

20. The literature on these individuals is voluminous, but one can easily begin with A. S. Kanya Forstner, *The Conquest of the Western Sudan: A Study in French Military Imperialism* (Cambridge: Cambridge University Press, 1969); Neal Ascherson, *The King Incorporated: Leopold II in the*

Age of Trusts (Garden City: Doubleday, 1964); Hans Ulrich Wehler, *Bismarck und der Imperialismus* (Frankfurt: Suhrkamp, 1984); Woodruff Smith, *The German Colonial Empire* (Chapel Hill: University of North Carolina Press, 1978); and for Cecil Rhodes, about whom there are countless treatments, the most recent work is Robert I. Rotberg, with Miles F. Shore, *The Founder: Cecil Rhodes and the Pursuit of Power* (New York: Oxford University Press, 1988).

21. I take much of this analysis and periodization of the early colonial peri-od from the work of Catherine Coquery-Vidrovitch, well summarized in her *Afrique Noire: Permanences et Ruptures* (Paris: Payot, 1985).

22. The literature on the European colonial administrations in Africa is so large as to defy presentation here in a footnote. The general study of Catherine Coquery-Vidrovitch referred to in the previous footnote develops the perspective offered here, and the two volumes of essays comparing German and French colonialism with British colonialism in Africa, edited by Wm. Roger Louis and Prosser Gifford, are also good starting points: *Britain and Germany in Africa: Imperial Rivalry and Colonial Rule* (New Haven: Yale University Press, 1967) and France and Britain in *Africa: Imperial Rivalry and Colonial Rule* (New Haven: Yale University Press, 1971).

23. C. H. Haring, *The Spanish Empire in America* (New York: Oxford University Press, 1947) is as good a place as any to begin. Toledo was to the Spanish empire what Lugard was to the British colonial possessions in Africa—the rationalizer. His administration may be viewed in Ann M. Wightman, *Indigenous Migration and Social Change: The Forasteros of Cuzco, 1570–1726* (Durham: Duke University Press, 1990) while the definitive study on Lugard remains the two volume biography of Margery Perham, *Lugard*, 2 vols. (London: Collins, 1956).

24. Here the classical studies are Woodrow Borah, *New Spain's Century of Depression* (Berkeley: University of California Press, 1951), Shelburne F. Cook and Woodrow Borah, *The Indian Population of Central Mexico, 1531–1610* (Berkeley: University of California Press, 1960), and Henry F. Dobyns, "Estimating Aboriginal American Populations," *Current Anthropology* 7 (1966): 396–416. A useful overview of the demograph-ic impact may be found in the essays by Nicholas Sanchez-Albornoz and Maria Luiza Marcilio in *The Cambridge History of Latin America*, vol. 2, ed. Leslie Bethell (Cambridge: Cambridge University Press, 1984).

25. Coquery-Vidrovitch, *Afrique noire*, 44–64.

26. Richard L. Kagan, *Students and Society in Early Modern Spain* (Baltimore: Johns Hopkins University Press, 1974), 83–84.

27. Raymond Buell, *The Native Problem in Africa* (New York: Macmillan, 1928), 2 vols. and Lord Hailey, *An African Survey: A Study of Problems arising in Africa South of the Sahara* (London: Oxford University Press,

1938) are the two works that provide a comprehensive overview of the framework and policies of colonial administration on a par with Haring, *The Spanish Empire in America*. On the personnel recruited into colonial service, the Portuguese officers are treated in Stuart Schwartz, *Sovereignty and Society in Colonial Brazil: The High Court of Bahia and its Judges, 1609–1751* (Berkeley: University of California Press, 1973); for Spain, Mario Góngora, *Studies in the Colonial History of Spanish America*, trans. Richard Southern (Cambridge: Cambridge University Press, 1975), especially ch. 3; and for Britain and France in Africa, Robert Heussler, *Yesterday's Rulers: The Making of the British Colonial Service* (Syracuse: Syracuse University Press, 1963) and William B. Cohen, *Rulers of Empire: The French Colonial Service in Africa, 1880–1960* (Stanford: Stanford University Press, 1968).

28. John Leddy Phelan, *The Kingdom of Quito in the Seventeenth Century: Bureaucratic Politics in the Spanish Empire* (Madison: University of Wisconsin Press, 1967), 126.

29. John Howland Rowe, "The Incas under Spanish Colonial Institutions," *The Hispanic American Historical Review* 37:2 (May 1957): 162.

30. The French record was mixed, but as Cohen, *Rulers of Empire*, demonstrates, after a dismal beginning, French colonial administration became as orderly and dedicated, in theory, to the attainment of "good government" in Africa as the British.

31. Phelan, *The Kingdom of Quito*, 147. It is impossible for an Africanist reading some of the standard works on colonial administration at the local level in Spanish America not to observe the parallels. See, in particular, Charles Gibson, *The Aztecs under Spanish Rule: A History of the Indians of the Valley of Mexico, 1519–1810* (Stanford: Stanford University Press, 1964); James Lockhart, *The Nahuas after the Conquest: A Social and Cultural History of the Indians of Central Mexico, Sixteenth through Eighteenth Centuries* (Stanford: Stanford University Press, 1992); Steve J. Stern, *Peru's Indian Peoples and the Challenge of Spanish Conquest: Huamanga to 1640* (Madison: University of Wisconsin Press, 1982); and Karen Spalding, *Huarochiri: An Andean Society under Inca and Spanish Rule* (Stanford: Stanford University Press, 1984).

32. Although much of the scholarly work on local administration in colonial Africa offers comparisons between British and French systems of rule—direct vs. indirect rule (See A. I. Asiwaju, *Western Yorubaland under European Rule, 1889-1945: A Comparative Analysis of French and British Colonialism* [London: Longman, 1976] and the essays by Michael Crowder and Pierre Alexandre in *West African Chiefs: Their Changing Status under Colonial Rule and Independence* ed. by Michael Crowder and Obaro Ikime [Ile-Ife, Nigeria: University of Ife Press, 1970])—there is a great deal to be gained by looking at the action of chiefs and headmen on local populations. Here Jean Suret-Canale, *Afrique noire: l'ere*

coloniale, 1900–1945 (Paris: Edicions Sociales, 1962) is excellent on French rule, J. Forbes Munro, *Colonial Rule and the Kamba: Social Change in the Kenya Highlands, 1889–1939* (Oxford: Clarendon Press, 1975); Edward Steinhart, *Conflict and Collaboration: the Kingdoms of Western Uganda, 1890–1907* (Princeton: Princeton University Press, 1977); and John Tosh, *Clan Leaders and Colonial Chiefs in Lango: The Political History of an East African Stateless Society, c. 1800–1939* (Oxford: Clarendon, 1978) deal expertly with British rule. Crawford Young's recent work on the postcolonial state, *The African Colonial State in Comparative Perspective* (New Haven: Yale University Press, 1994), with its analysis of colonial arrangements provides an effective overview of the impact of colonial rule at the local level.

33. An important effort to employ insights from labor recruiting practices in Africa is that of Enrique Tandeter, *Coercion and Market: Silver Mining in Colonial Potosi, 1692–1826*, trans. Richard Warren (Albuquerque: University of New Mexico Press, 1993). Using African studies of target and oscillating labor forces, Tandeter emphasizes "the crucial role in colonial and neocolonial economies of temporary labor migrations, recruited with varying degrees of coercion" (15). Unfortunately, Tandeter's references to the African literature do not include some of the most important works.

34. On mining in Spanish America see P. J. Bakewell, *Silver Mining and Society in Colonial Mexico: Zacatecas, 1546–1700* (Cambridge: Cambridge University Press, 1971); D. A. Brading, *Miners and Merchants in Bourbon Mexico, 1763–1810* (Cambridge: Cambridge University Press, 1971); and Jeffrey A. Cole, *The Potosi Mita, 1573–1700: Compulsory Indian Labor in the Andes* (Stanford: Stanford University Press, 1985).

35. William H. Worger, *South Africa's City of Diamonds: Mineworkers and Monopoly Capitalism in Kimberley, 1867–1895* (New Haven: Yale University Press, 1987); Robert Vicat Turrell, *Capital and Labour on the Kimberley Diamond Fields, 1871–1890* (Cambridge: Cambridge University Press, 1987); and Frederick Johnstone, *Class, Race, and Gold: A Study of Class Relations and Racial Discrimination in South Africa* (London: Routledge and K. Paul, 1976).

36. Viceroy Toledo's meticulous assessments of population densities in Peru were a prelude to the introduction of a carefully calibrated mita labor coercion system. See Tandeter, *Coercion and Market*, 25. These surveys have much in common with later colonial efforts in Africa to determine how large a labor force could be extracted from local communities for work in mining regions without destroying the structure of the local societies.

37. There are numerous studies on labor recruiting in Southern Africa. One of the most graphic is Charles van Onselen, *Chibaro: African Mine Labour in*

Southern Rhodesia, 1900–1933 (London: Pluto Press, 1981).

38. See Charles van Onselen, *Studies in the Social and Economic History of the Witwatersrand, 1886–1914* (Johannesburg: Ravan Press, 1982).

39. The work of William Taylor, particularly *Drinking, Homicide, and Rebellion in Colonial Mexico* (Stanford: Stanford University Press, 1979) moves in this direction.

40. Robert Ricard, *The Spiritual Conquest of Mexico*, trans. Lesley Byrd Simpson (Berkeley: University of California Press, 1966 [1933]), and Roland Oliver, *The Missionary Factor in East Africa* (London: Longmans, Green, 1952) represent the foundational works in this field.

41. Here, the book of B. G. M. Sundkler, *Bantu Prophets in South Africa* (London: Lutterworth Press, 1948) stands out as a breakthrough.

42. Robin Horton, "On the Rationality of Conversion," *Africa, Journal of the International African Institute* 45:3 (1975): 209–235 and 45:4 (1975): 373–399.

43. Nancy Farriss, *Maya Society under Colonial Rule: The Collective Enterprise of Survival* (Princeton: Princeton University Press, 1984). The author uses Horton's ideas in her assessment of religious change and resistance among the Maya. See especially 295–297.

44. In this rich literature I would be remiss if I did not mention the work of Inga Clendinnen, "Disciplining the Indians: Franciscan Ideology and Missionary Violence in Sixteenth Century Yucatan," *Past and Present 94* (Feb. 1982): *27–45 and The Aztecs: An Interpretation* (Cambridge: Cambridge University Press, 1991); Sabine MacCormack, "'The Heart has its Reasons': Predicaments of Missionary Christianity in Early Colonial Peru," *Hispanic American Historical Review* 65:3 (Aug. 1985): 443–466 and *Religion in the Andes: Vision and Imagination in Early Colonial Peru* (Princeton: Princeton University Press, 1991). Kenneth Mills's *Idolatry and its Enemies: Colonial Andean Religion and Extirpation, 1640–1750* (Princeton: Princeton University Press, 1997) demonstrates how the records of the extirpation trials can be used for information on pre-Columbian religious beliefs and the blending of these beliefs with Spanish Catholicism.

45. See, in particular, Louise M. Burkhart, *The Slippery Earth: Nahua-Christian Moral Dialogy in Sixteenth Century Mexico* (Tucson: University of Arizona Press, 1989).

46. On the African side one would want to consult the work of Jean and John Comaroff, *Of Revelation and Revolution: Christianity, Colonialism, and Consciousness in South Africa* (Chicago: University of Chicago Press, 1991) and *Ethnography and the Historical Imagination* (Boulder: Westview Press, 1992) as well as Thomas O. Beidelman, *Colonial Evangelism: A Socio-Historical Study of an East African Mission at the Grassroots* (Bloomington: Indiana University Press, 1982). It is not just accidental that much of the work on the African side has been done by

anthropologists, and one has to hope that historians will reenter this field, armed with some of these new theoretical insights.

47. T. O. Ranger first made that argument in "Connexions between 'Primary Resistance' movements and modern Mass Nationalism in East and Central Africa," *Journal of African History* 9:3 and 4 (1968): 437–454 and 631–642. This whiggish view of African nationalist evolution, so representative of the decade of African independence, has not held up well, however.

48. See, especially, John Iliffe, *A Modern History of Tanganyika* (Cambridge: Cambridge University Press, 1979) for an elaboration of the ideas on the age of improvement.

49. See the essays in Roleno Adorno, ed., *From Oral to Written Expression: Native Andean Chronicles of the Early Colonial Period* (Syracuse: Maxwell School of Citizenship and Public Affairs, 1982) and Pierre Duviols, *La lutte contre les religions autochtones dans le Perou colonial: l'extirpation de l'idolatrie entre 1532 et 1660* (Paris: Editions Ophrys, 1971).

50. John Howland Rowe, "The Incas under Spanish Colonial Institutions," *Hispanic American Historical Review* 37:2 (May 1957) 159.

51. Steve J. Stern, "New Approaches to the Study of Peasant Rebellion and Consciousness: Implications of the Andean Experience," in *Resistance, Rebellion, and Consciousness in the Andean Peasant World: Eighteenth to Twentieth Centuries*, ed. Steve J. Stern (Madison: University of Wisconsin Press, 1987), 12.

52. Miguel Leon-Portilla, *The Broken Spears: The Aztec Account of the Conquest of Mexico* (Boston: Beacon Press, 1992) and Rolena Adorno, ed., *From Oral to Written Expression*.

53. Rolena Adorno, *Guaman Poma: Writing and Resistance in Colonial Peru* (Austin: University of Texas Press, 1986).

54. Phelan, *The Kingdom of Quito*, 39.

55. Good overviews may be found in John Lynch, *The Spanish American Revolutions, 1808–1826* (New York: Weidenfeld and Nicolson, 1973) and Richard Graham, *Independence in Latin America* (New York: Knopf, 1972). The build-up of political tension leading to the rupture is expertly traced in Scarlett O'Phelan Godoy, *Rebellions and Revolts in Eighteenth Century Peru and Upper Peru* (Koln : Bohlau, 1985).

56. See the collected essays in the volumes on the transfer of power in Africa edited by Wm. Roger Louis and Prosser Gifford, *The Transfer of Power in Africa: Decolonization, 1940–1960* (New Haven: Yale University Press, 1982) and *Decolonization and African Independence: The Transfers of Power, 1960–1980* (New Haven: Yale University Press, 1988).

57. Louis Hartz, *The Founding of New Societies: Studies in the History of the United States, Latin America, South Africa, Canada, and Australia* (New York: Harcourt, Brace & World, 1964).

58. See Tulio Halperin-Donghi, *The Aftermath of Revolution in Latin America* (New York: Harper & Row, 1973). The estimate on the loss of life in the Mexican wars of independence comes from Lynch, *The Spanish American Revolutions*, 327.

59. It is difficult to know where to begin on the literature dealing with Africa's postcolonial polities. Jean-Francois Bayart, *The State in Africa: The Politics of the Belly* (London: Longman, 1993) offers a provocative overview. The postcolonial history of Nigeria is particularly insightful and can be accessed through Robin Luckham, *The Nigerian Military: A Sociological Analysis of Authority and Revolt, 1960–67* (Cambridge: Cambridge University Press, 1971); Larry Diamond, *Class, Ethnicity, and Democracy in Nigeria: The Failure of the First Republic* (Syracuse: Syracuse University Press, 1988); and Richard Joseph, *Democracy and Prebendal Politics in Nigeria: The Rise and Fall of the Second Republic* (Cambridge: Cambridge University Press, 1987).

CHAPTER FOUR

1. Felipe Ruíz Martín, *Lettres marchandes entre Florence et Medina del Campo* (Paris: SEVPEN, 1965), xlviii-xlix. The fine introduction to *Lettres marchandes* has been published in Spanish translation: *Pequeño capitalismo: gran capitalismo. Simón Ruíz y sus negocios en Florencia* (Barcelona: Crítica, 1990). See also his *Los destinos de la plata americana* (siglos xvi y xvii) (Madrid: Ediciones de la Universidad Autónoma de Madrid, 1990). See "La difficulté, c'est de préciser quand et comment cet argent américain s'est inflitré en Europe en provenance de la péninsule," *L'économie mondiale et les frappes monétaires en France, 1493–1680* by Frank G. Spooner (Paris: A. Colin, 1956), 19.

2. Ruíz Martín, *Lettres marchandes*, lxxxvii; Fernand Braudel, in *Cambridge Economic History of Europe*, ed. E. E. Rich, and C. H. Wilson, vol. IV (Cambridge: Cambridge University Press, 1966), 447–48; Ramon Carande, *Carlos V y sus banqueros*, 2d ed., 3 vols (Madrid: Sociedad de Estudios y Publicaciones, 1965–69), I: 247.

3. Carande, *Carlos V*, II: 101.

4. M. J. Rodríguez-Salgado, *The Changing Face of Empire: Charles V, Philip II and Habsburg Authority, 1551–1559* (Cambridge: Cambridge University Press, 1988), 24.

5. Antonio Domínguez Ortíz, *Política fiscal y cambio social en la España del siglo xvii* (Madrid: Instituto de Estudios Fiscales, 1984), 20.

6. Carande, *Carlos V*, III: 371. Geoffrey Parker estimates that Charles V in 1552 was fielding in Germany, the Netherlands, Lombardy, Sicily, Naples, and Spain perhaps 150,000 soldiers, non-Spaniards in the majority. *The Army of Flanders and the Spanish Road, 1567–1659: The*

Logistics of Spanish Victory and Defeat in the Low Countries' Wars (Cambridge: Cambridge University Press, 1972), 13. Behind the Comuneros (commmoners) Rodríguez-Salgado discerns protonationalist demands for "retrenchment, a return to sound finance, and an end to the use of Spanish money for foreign ventures." *Changing Face of Empire,* 22.

7. Ruíz Martín, *Lettres marchandes,* lxxxviii. For a masterful overview of the diaspora, see Fernand Braudel, *The Mediterranean and the Mediterranean World in the Age of Philip II,* 2 vols. (New York: Harper & Row, 1972), 462–542.

8. Álvaro Castillo Pintado, "El mercado del dinero en Castilla a finales del siglo XVI. Valor nominal y curso de los *juros* castellanos en 1594," *Annales Histoire, Economie, Société,* (hereafter AHES) III (1970): 102.

9. See "la brutalité et . . . l'ampleur de cette révolution de l'argent. Cet argent arrache a l'Amérique, mal gardé par l'Espagne—économie et politique obligent—court le vaste monde." Spooner, *Économie mondiale,* 25.

10. M. Torres López and J. M Pérez-Prendes y Muñoz de Arraco, *Los juros: Aportación documental para una historia de la deuda pública de España* (Madrid: Fabrica Nacional de Moneda y Timbre, 1967), 47.

11. Rodríguez-Salgado, *Changing Face of Empire,* 24.

12 Ruíz Martín, *Lettres marchandes,* xxxvii.

13. Ruíz Martín, "La Banca de España hasta 1782," in *El Banco de España, una história económica* (Madrid: Banco de España, 1970), 15–16. Augsburg and Nuremberg merchant houses entered after 1450 into silver- and copper-mining ventures; earnings from these enterprises helped finance Maximilian's propensity for dynastic expansionism. Richard Ehrenbourg, *Le siecle des Fugger* (Paris: SEVPEN, 1955), 184–85.

14. Speculation in Castile's public debt led Genoese merchant bankers to abandon "real and honest commerce . . . to deal only with "negoziazione e dei cambi." Braudel, *The Mediterranean,* I: 462.

15. Ruíz Martín, *Lettres marchandes,* xxix, xxxvii-xxxviii; Carande, *Carlos V,* III: 399, 469; Parker, *Army of Flanders,* 60; Spooner, *Économie mondiale,* 308-09.

16. European bankers' expectations were fueled by the rapid publication at Sevilla of Francisco de Xerez's *Verdadera relación de la conquista del Perú* (1534). Carande, *Carlos V,* III: 312.

17. Carande, *Carlos V,* I: 240 (based on Carande's conversion of Hamilton's data to *ducados*).

18. Carande, *Carlos V,* II: 34–35; I. A. A. Thompson, *War and Government in Hapsburg Spain, 1560–1620* (London: Athlone Press, 1976), 81. In four years (1551–55) ecclesiastical contributions to Castilian finance were significant, totaling 1.2 million *ducados,* virtually one year's

income to the Castilian treasury. Rodríguez-Salgado, *Changing Face of Empire*, 227. For his part, Carande views the dependence of Castile upon church financial support as another "rastro de la edad media (holdover from the Middles Ages)." Carande, *Carlos V*, II: 36.

19. Carande, *Carlos V*, I: 140.

20. Carande, *Carlos V*, III: 417. See "bullion shipments soon became the most coveted form of repayment." Rodríguez-Salgado, *Changing Face of Empire*, 63. Dependence upon foreign creditors, Braudel has proposed, ultimately led to a Spanish fiscal system "organized by the money-lenders to suit themselves." Braudel, *The Mediterranean*, II: 695.

21. At least four *secuestros* were carried out at Sevilla (1523–45) which netted the government 1.5 million *ducados*. During a longer period, 1523–1664, seventeen *secuestros* were reported. Clarence H. Haring, *Trade and Navigation between Spain and the Indies in the Time of the Hapsburgs* (Cambridge: Harvard University Press, 1928), 170; Guillermo Cespedes del Castillo, *La avería en el comercio de Indias* (Sevilla: Escuela de Estudios Hispano-Americanos, 1945), 132; Carande, *Carlos V*, III: 414 and *El crédito de Castilla en el precio de la política imperial. Discurso leído ante la Real Academia de la História* (Madrid: n.p., 1940), 30–31; Thompson, *War and Government*, 83, 85.

22. Carande, *Carlos V*, III: 319.

23. Carande, *Carlos V*, III: 313. In 1551 La Gasca returned with 1.9 million *ducados* of which the government promptly assigned 1.3 million to major creditors, the merchant banking houses of Welser, Schetz, Palavicino, Gamarry, Affaitadi, Spínola, Grillo, Dueños and others.

24. Álvaro Castillo Pintado, "Los *juros* de Castilla: apogeo y fin de un instrumento de crédito," *Hispania* 23 (1963): 52–53.

25. Carande, *El crédito de Castilla*, 15. *Juros* overnight became an "inversión segura . . . denotando . . . una predilección arraigada" Carande, *Carlos V*, II: 90. Castillo Pintado, "Los *juros*," 44–45; Pierre Vilar, *A History of Gold and Money, 1450–1920* (London: Verso, 1991), 145. *Juros* had the added advantage that interest earned required no religious approval. Castillo Pintado, "Los juros," 47.

26. The Fuggers, for instance, complied with a request in 1557 from the Castilian government to send to the Netherlands 430,000 ducados on condition of reimbursement "sur les premiers arrivages d'or et d'argent des Indes...." Ehrenbourg, *Le siecle des Fugger*, 73.

27. Rodríguez-Salgado, *Changing Face of Empire*, 61; Carande, Carlos V, II: 93; Torres López and Pérez-Prendes, *Los juros*, 27-29, 45, 66; Parker, *Army of Flanders*, 150–52. Initially *juros* were a privilegio awarded for service to the crown, later becoming an interest-bearing investment: one life or inheritable (*por vida, por herencia,* or *perpétuo*), redeemable under certain conditions (*al quitar*). *Juros de resguardo* or *caución*, a backup guarantee if specific revenues assigned proved inadequate, were

issued below par to make them more attractive to special investors. A. Castillo, "El mercado," AHES III (1970): 94. *Juros al quitar* were much sought after since they were negotiable; their price fluctuated with amount, type of guaranteed repayment, and current worth.

28. *Licencias de sacas* were purchased from Castile's Hacienda at rates varying with demand. Ruíz Martín, *Pequeño capitalismo, gran capitalismo*, 36–37. See "no Genoa merchant resident in Spain . . . but has a particular licence to transport the rials and plate . . . to a certain round sum annually." Lewes Roberts, *The Merchants' Mappe of Commerce* (1939) quoted in Haring, *Trade and Navigation*, 178 no. 1.

29. Ruíz Martín, *Lettres marchandes*, xxxviii–xxxix; Carande, *Carlos V*, I, 235; Rodríguez-Salgado, *Changing Face of Empire*, 63. By the late 1550s Castile was involved in "vast indebtedness in a financial market unfettered by national or ideological restrictions," a structure favored by the Hapsburg patrimonial concept of empire. J. Tracy, *A Financial Revolution*, 41.

30. Carande, *Carlos V*, II: 105. From 1519 to 1531 annual borrowing averaged only 500,000 *ducados*; it was already at the level of about 2 million in 1552. But between 1553 and 1555 it soared from 2.5 to 4.2 million. Carande, *Carlos V*, II: 121.

31. Rodríguez-Salgado, *Changing Face of Empire*, 347. See "Many causes . . . left Castille impoverished while fugitives came and went, the most abundant treasuries of a modern economy." Carande, *Carlos V*, I: 140.

32. Rodríguez-Salgado, *Changing Face of Empire*, 343 table 12.

33. Ruíz Martín, "La Banca," in *El Banco de España*, 19–21; and *Lettres marchandes*, xxx–xxxi; Ildefonso Pulido Bueno, *El Real Giro de España, primer proyecto de banco nacional* (Huelva: n.p., 1994), 14. The failure of this essay in state enterprise Ruíz Martín blames on officers of Contratación who "only had the vocation of bureaucrats and administrators." Ruíz Martín, "La Banca," 21.

34. José Antonio Maraval, *Estado moderno y mentalidad social* (siglos XV a XVII), 2 vols. (Madrid: Revista de Occidente, 1972), II: 294. *The bankruptcies of Philip II and successors* (five between 1557 and 1647) have been likened to converting short- into long-term debt, a consolidated debt and "une forme nouvelle de *juros*." Ehrenbourg, *Le siecle des Fugger*, 331.

35. Rodríguez-Salgado, *Changing Face of Empire*, 224–25 table 10, 248–49 table 11–2, 344; Thompson, *War and Government*, 41. With reason Philip II viewed the American colonies as the "most bountiful source" Carande, *Carlos V*, III: 380, 396.

36. Rodríguez-Salgado, *Changing Face of Empire*, 344; Thompson, *War and Government*, 275. Disbursements by Philip II's Hacienda (treasury) were made from "whatever funds happened to be available whether from general funds, colonial receipts, or local sources. Thompason, *War and Government*, 71, 80.

37. Rodríguez-Salgado, *Changing Face of Empire*, 224–25 table10.
38. Torres López and Pérez-Prendes, *Los juros*, 32 table 1; Thompson, *War and Government*, 71–72.
39. Torres López and Pérez-Prendes, *Los juros*, 32 table 1, 33. In 1609 colonial income (3 million *ducados*, much understated) constituted 20 percent of total revenues (15.6 million). Castile's aggregate revenues were more than double those of France (7.7 million) although its populaton was half that of France. Based on data in Michel Morineau, in P .Léon and J. Jacquart (eds.), *Histoire économique et sociale du monde*, vol. 2, *Les hésitations de la croissance*, 1580–1730 (Paris: A. Colin, 1978), 151–53.
40. Carande, *Carlos V*, III; 468; Thompson, *War and Government*, 71, 87–88, 100; Torres López and Pérez-Prendes, *Los juros*, 31; Ruíz Martín, *Pequeño capitalismo*, 152 n. 10 and his *Las finanzas de la monarquía hispánica en tiempos de Felipe IV 1621–1665* (Madrid: Real Academia de Historia, 1990), 171. In 1597 sale of the office of general overseer of Castile's foreign monetary transfers was a "measure of . . . alienation of state authority." Thompson, *War and Government*, 88.
41. Michel Morineau, *Incroyables gazettes et fabuleux meteaux. Les retours des trésors américains d'apres les gazettes hollandaises (xvie–xviiie siecles)* (Paris: Maison des Sciences de L'Homme, 1985), 78.
42. Ruíz Martín, *Lettres marchandes*, xlviii; Domínguez Ortíz, "Los caudales," *Anuario de Estudio Americanos*, XIII (1956), 330, 319 n. 6.
43. In 1663 Philip IV's Hacienda converted its outstanding debts to *juros*, which by 1667 amounted to 9 million *ducados*. J. Lynch, *Spain under the Hapsburgs*, 2 vols. (New York: Oxford University Press, 1969), II: 274.
44. Domínguez Ortiz, "Los caudales," 335–36, 339.
45. Ibid., 360; Castillo Pintado, "Los juros," 60–61.
46. Geoffrey Parker, *Spain and the Netherlands: Ten Studies* (London: Collins, 1979), 189.
47. Domínguez Ortíz, "Guerra económica," *Hispania* XXIII (1963), 97.
48. Domínguez Ortíz, "Los caudales," 360.
49. See "the steady flow of silver from the rents of Mexico and Upper Peru became essential to the maintenance of a bankrupt government." Haring, *Trade and Navigation*, 51.
50. Domínguez Ortíz, "Los caudales," 315, 317 n.12.
51. Domínguez Ortíz, "Guerra económica," 92-93.
52. Domínguez Ortíz, "Los caudales," 342.
53. Domínguez Ortíz, "Guerra económica," 97, and "Los caudales," 328 and n. 34.
54. Domínguez Ortíz, "Los caudales," 371.
55. For example, to continue the siege of Metz, Charles approved the sequestration at Sevilla of incoming silver on private account to satisfy creditors "in order to continue relying on them." Carande, *Carlos V*, III: 401.

56. Domínguez Ortíz, "Los caudales," 339–40, 345. Without the American funds, Domínguez Ortíz has noted, tongue-in-cheek, Velázquez might not have had the occasion to paint "Las Lanzas" (339).
57. Domínguez Ortíz, "Los caudales," 361–62.
58. Haring, *Trade and Navigation*, 65, 214; Domínguez Ortíz, "Los caudales," 328.
59. Torres López y Pérez-Prendes, *Los juros*, 42.
60. Ibid., 46; Domínguez Ortíz, *Política fiscal*, 36. The large portfolio of foreign-held *juros* induced the early *arbitrista* Sancho de Moncada (1619) to record with bitterness that "Foreigners have in Spain (as they say) over one million in *juros*, without infinite censos, the entire Crusade, a great number of privileges, entitlements, benefits and pensions." Sancho de Moncada in *Restauración política de España*, ed. Jean Vilar (Madrid: Instituto de Estudios Fiscales, Ministerio de Hacienda, 1974), 102.
61. Ruíz Martín, *Las finanzas*, 121–23. See "The Spanish credit system . . . depended absolutely on specie and principally on the treasure of the Indies loaded at Sevilla for the King." Parker, *The Army of Flanders*, 152–53.
62. Torres López and Pérez-Prendes, *Los juros*, 47.
63. Ibid., 47, 51; Castillo Pintado, "Los juros," 60.
64. Castillo Pintado, "Los juros," 29–30, 47–51, 58–59, 65–70; Domínguez Ortíz, *Política fiscal*, 66, 75–76, 90–92 and "Los caudales," 349; Torres López and Pérez-Prendes, *Los juros*, 71; Manuel Garzón Pareja, *La hacienda de Carlos II* (Madrid: Instituto de Estudios Fiscales, Ministerio de Hacienda, 1980), 335–36; Henry Kamen, "España en la Europa de Luis XIV," in *Historia de España* (Menéndez Pidal), ed. José María Jover Zamora (Madrid: Espasa-Calpe, 1993), XXVIII: 277.
65. Torres López and Pérez-Prendes, *Los juros*, 78, 81.
66. Ibid., 52; Castillo Pintado, "Los juros," 52–55, 68–69.
67. Ruíz Martín, *Los destinos de la plata*, 32; Nicolas Broens, *Monarquía y capital mercantil: Felipe IV y las redes comerciales portugesas (1627–1635)* (Madrid: Ediciones de la Universidad Autónoma de Madrid, 1989), 34.
68. Robert Gascon, "La France du mouvement: les commerces et les villes," in *Histoire économique et sociale de France*, ed. Fernand Braudel et. al. (Paris: Presses Universitaires de France, 1970) I: 2, 280.
69. Spooner, *Économie mondiale*, 24–25, 136–37 and planches iii and iv; Ruíz Martín, *Pequeño capitalismo*, 97–99, 152–53.
70. K. N. Chaudhuri, *Trade and Civilization in the Indian Ocean* (Cambridge: Cambridge University Press, 1985), 218; A. Hazan, "En Inde . . . tresors americains, monnaie d'argent et prix dans l'Empire mogul," *AESC* (1969): 835–39; F. Wakeman, "Voyages," American Historical Review 98 (1993): 15; S. Panuk, "Money in the Ottoman Empire, 1326–1914," in *An Economic and Social History of the Ottoman Empire, 1300–1914*, ed. H. Inalcik (New York: Cambridge University Press, 1994), 965.

71. Parker, *Army of Flanders*, 60; Spooner, *Économie mondiale*, 144–45, 308–09.

72. Domínguez Ortíz, *Política fiscal*, 55, 127.

73. Broens, *Monarquía y capital mercantil*, 34. He notes two main routes via the western Pyrenees: Jaca to Puerto Sompart and on to Oloron Sainte-Marie, the other from Pamplona to Biarritz and Bayonne.

74. Spooner, *Économie mondiale*, 137–38, 163–64, 175, 277, 315.

75. Ibid., 356–62, 407–11, 532–34 graphic 32. Based on French consular reporting and related materials collected by Albert Girard, Ruíz Martín's table of receipts of precious metals and their reexport, 1665–98, puts France by far the principal destination of legal precious metals exports (13 percent) followed by the United Provinces (4.8 percent). Ruíz Martín, *Los destinos de la plata*, 42.

76. As early as 1578 Castilians perceived that suppressing revolt in the Netherlands "consumed the money and substance which has come from the Indies." Over the century after 1556 about 55 percent of Castile's outlay on warfare in the Netherlands came from public (that is, royal) income from colonial treasuries. Parker, *Spain and the Netherlands*, 186–88.

77. Parker, *Army of Flanders*, 137, 272, appendix A. In 1640 when the Spanish contingent was also at a peak, it represented only about 20 percent of all Spanish-subsidized forces.

78. Parker, *Army of Flanders*, 48, 51. Financing troop movements on the Spanish Road transferred Castilian funds to Milan where "the arms industry and the manufacture of quality textiles responded . . . to the demands of the market." B. Yun Casalilla, "Spain and the Seventeenth Century Crisis in Europe." in *The Castilian Crisis of the Seventeenth Century: New Perspectives on the Economic and Social History of Seventeenth Century Spain*, ed. I. A. A. Thompson and B. Yun Casalilla, (New York: Cambridge University Press, 1994), 315.

79. V. Magalhães Godinho, *L'économie de l'empire portugais aux xv et xvi siecles* (Paris: SEVPEN, 1969), 472–95; Parker, *Army of Flanders*, 155.

80. Parker, *Army of Flanders*, 50, 88–90, 92, 94.

81. In 1687, for example, at least half of state revenues were assigned to service the public debt. H. Kamen, *Spain in the Later Seventeenth Century* (London: Longman, 1980), 367, 369.

82. J. E. Gelabert, "Urbanisation and deurbanisation in Castile, 1500–1800," in *The Castilian Crisis*, 204; Thompson, *War and Government*, 42.

83. Carande, *Carlos V*, III, 396; Domínguez Ortíz, *Política fiscal*, 49, and "Los caudales," 335; Renate Pieper, *La real hacienda bajo Ferdinand VI y Carlos III: repercusiones económicas y sociales* (Madrid: Instituto de Estudios Fiscales, 1992), 104; Thompson, *War and Government*, 65.

84. Domínguez Ortíz, *Política fiscal*, 64, and "Los caudales," 322.

85. It is plausible that Castilians under the later Hapsburgs were taxed

"more heavily than any other people in Europe." Parker, *Spain and the Netherlands*, 188.

86. I. A. A. Thompson, *Crown and Cortes: Government, Institutions and Representation in Early-Modern Castile* (Brookfield, Vt.: Variorum, 1993), ch. v, 91, and *War and Government*, 63. Yun has seen in the propensity for purchasing government office and entitlement a "retreat of business capital from the investments which could have set in motion the qualitative developments which were beginning to take place in northern Europe." Yun, "Spain and the Seventeenth Century Crisis," 315.

87. See "it is not outrageous to say that the state monopoly over trade is mortgaged to the merchants themselves." E. Vila Vilar, "Las ferias de Portobelo," *Anuario de Estudios Americanos*, 39 (1982): 311.

88. Torres López and Pérez-Prendes, *Los juros*, 37–38.

89. In addition, Olivares earned in one year alone 254,000 *ducados*, e.g., as Councillor of the Indies and official in the Casa de Contratación, and by sales of cargo shipped to America—the equivalent of 56 percent of his estimated income of that year. *Semanario erudito de Valladares* III (1787): 59.

90. Domínguez Ortíz, "Los caudales," 323–24.

91. Domínguez Ortíz, "Guerra económica," 102–3; Haring, *Trade and Navigation*, 65.

92. Domínguez Ortíz, "Los caudales," 324. As a result, in 1762 the office (alienated) of treasurer in the Mexico City mint "did not give accounts to anyone, treating the Casa's business as a private affair." Fausto de Elhuyar, *Indagaciones sobre la amonedación en la Nueva España* (Madrid: Imprenta de la Calle de la Greda, 1818), 7, 35.

93. Braudel, *The Mediterranean*, II: 688.

94. Yun, "Spain and the Seventeenth Century Crisis," 311.

95. Thompson, *Crown and Cortes*, ch. v, 90, 96. Elsewhere Thompson has noted that office-holding as an honor constrained "the possibilities of discipline and reform" of the state apparatus. *War and Government*, 58.

CHAPTER FIVE

1. R. Palmer, *The Age of Democratic Revolutions*, 2 vols. (Princeton: Princeton University Press, 1959, 1964); Jacques Godechot, *Les revolutions, 1770–1799* (Paris: Presses universitaires de France, 1965) and *L'europe et l'Amerique a l'époque napolienne, 1800–1819* (Paris: Presses universitaires de France, 1967); and more recently, Peggy K. Liss, *Atlantic Empires: The Network of Trade and Revolution, 1713–1826* (Baltimore: Johns Hopkins University Press, 1983).

2. C. R. Boxer, *Salvador de Sá and the Struggle for Brazil and Angola*,

1602–1680 (London: Athlone Press, 1952) and *The Dutch in Brazil 1624–1654* (Oxford: Clarendon Press, 1957); also the fundamental works of Evaldo Cabral de Mello, *Olinda Restaurada: Guerra e Açucar no nordeste 1630–1654* (São Paulo: Editora Forense-Universitaria, 1975), and *Rubro Veio* (Rio de Janeiro: Editora Nova Fronteira, 1986).

3. Kenneth Maxwell, "Portugal, Europe and the Origins of the Atlantic Commercial System, 1415–1520," *Portuguese Studies* 8 (1992): 3–16.

4. Stuart B. Schwartz, *Sugar Plantations and the Formation of Brazilian Society: Bahia, 1550–1835* (Cambridge: Cambridge University Press, 1985), and *Slaves, Peasants, and Rebels: Reconsidering Brazilian Slavery* (Urbana: University of Illinois Press, 1992).

5. A. J. R. Russell Wood, *Fidalgos and Philanthropists: The Santa Casa da Misericórdia of Bahia, 1550–1755* (Berkeley and Los Angeles: University of California Press, 1968).

6. Carl Hansen, *Economy and Society in Baroque Portugal* (Minneapolis: University of Minnesota Press, 1981); also the classic works by C. R. Boxer, *The Portuguese Seaborne Empire, 1415–1825* (London: Hutchinson, 1969), and *The Golden Age of Brazil, 1695–1750* (Berkeley and Los Angeles: University of California Press, 1962).

7. David Davidson, "How the Brazilian West Was Won," in *Colonial Roots of Modern Brazil*, ed. D. Alden (Berkeley and Los Angeles: University of California Press, 1973); J. R. Amaral Lapa, *Economia Colonial* (São Paulo: Editora Perspectiva, 1973). Also Sérgio Buarque de Holanda, *Moncões* (Rio de Janeiro: Casa do estudante do Brasil, 1945), and João Capistrano de Abreu, *Chapters of Brazil's Colonial History*, trans. Arthur Brakel (New York: Oxford University Press, 1997).

8. Kenneth R. Maxwell, *Conflicts and Conspiracies: Brazil and Portugal, 1750–1808* (Cambridge: Cambridge University Press, 1973).

9. H. E. S. Fisher, *The Portugal Trade: A Study of Anglo-Portuguese Commerce, 1700–1770* (London: Methuen, 1971). Also, Virgilio Noya Pinto, *Ouro Brasileiro e o comércio Anglo-portugués* (São Paulo: Companhia Editora Nacional, 1979).

10. Kenneth R. Maxwell, *Pombal, Paradox of the Enlightenment* (Cambridge: Cambridge University Press, 1995); and Francisco José C. Falcón, *A época Pombalina: política, económica e monarquia ilustrada* (São Paulo: Editora Atica, 1982).

11. There had, of course, been clandestine direct trade between British merchants and Brazil, especially involving the slave trade. The rolled tobacco of Bahia, most of it from the Cachoeira and Mantiba regions, was the basic commodity of exchange on the African coast, as necessary to other European slavers as to the Portuguese. José da Silva Lisboa to Domingos Vandelli, Bahia, 19 October 1781, *Anais da Biblioteca Nacional*, Rio de Janeiro (ABNRJ), XXXII (1920), 505; J. H. Rodrigues, *Brazil and Africa* (Berkeley and Los Angeles: University of California

Press, 1965); and Pierre Verger, *Flux et reflux de la traite des nègres entre le golfe de Bènin et Bahi de todos os santos du dix-septième siècle* (Paris: La Haye, Mouton, 1968). Some fifty vessels a year, corvettes and smaller vessels, left Bahia for Africa, four-fifths of them for the Guiné Coast and the remainder for Angola. Luís dos Santos Vilhena, *Recopilação de noticias soteropolitanas e brasilicas*, 3 vols. (Bahia: Imprensa official do estado, 1922–35 [1802]). European goods and gold dust came back to Bahia with the cargoes of slaves. This clandestine commerce had outraged the secretary of state for overseas dominions, Melo e Castro, as had the degree of control that the merchants of Bahia exercised over the African commerce to the exclusion of metropolitan merchants. "Instrucção para o marquês de Valença, no qual informa a respeito da referida devassa," Bahia, 4 February 1783, ibid., 529. The contraband manufactures, however, did underprice those imported from the metropolis and restricted the market for metropolitan goods. José da Silva Lisboa to Domingos Vandelli, Bahia, 19 October 1781, ibid., 505. The profitable subsidiary trade which accompanied the slave and tobacco commerce contributed to the favorable balance Bahia enjoyed with the metropolis. Most of the capital obtained was sunk into the purchase of more slaves. Martinho de Melo e Castro held that the working of the Bahian-African trade was the same as "according to the English, French and Dutch a free trade by the ports of Africa between those nations and the Portuguese dominion in Brazil without the intervention of the merchants of the metropolis." "Instrucção para o marquês de Valença," Martinho de Melo e Castro, Queluz, 10 September 1779, *ABNRJ* XXXII (1910), 444. See also Joseph Miller, *The Way of Death: Merchant Capitalism and the Angolan Slave Trade, 1730–1830* (Madison: University of Wisconsin Press, 1988).

12. José de Andrade Arruda, *O Brasil no comércio colonial* (São Paulo: Editora Atica, 1980); Jorge Miguel Viana Pedreira, *Estrutura Industrial e Mercado Colonial, Portugal e Brasil 1780–1830* (Lisbon: DIFEL, 1994); Valentim Alexandre, *Os Sentidos do Império: Questão Nacional e Questão Colonial na Crise do Antigo Regime Português* (Porto: Ediçoes Afrontamento, 1993).

13. I am drawing here on the work of Stanley Stein and Barbara Stein in "Concept and Realities of Spanish Economic Growth, 1759–1789," *Historia Ibérica* I (1973): 103–119. Also see Carlos C. Noel, "Charles III of Spain" in *Enlightened Absolutism*, ed. H. Scott (Basingstoke, Eng.: Macmillan, 1990), 119–43.

14. John Fisher, *Commercial Relations Between Spain and Spanish America in the Era of Free Trade, 1778–1796* (Liverpool: Centre for Latin-American Studies, University of Liverpool, 1985); and António Garcia-Baquero González, *Cádiz y el Atlántico, 1717–1778*, 2 vols. (Seville: Escuela de Estudios Hispano-Americanos, C.S.I.C., 1976).

15. Lutgardo Garcia Fuentes, *El comércio español con America, 1650–1700* (Seville: Escuela de Estudios Hispano-Americanos, Consejo Superior de Investigaciones Cientificas, 1980); Miguel Artola, "América en el pensamiento español del siglo XVII," *Revista de Indias* XXIX (1969); and N. M. Sutherland, "The Origins of the 30 Years War and the Structure of European Politics," *English Historical Review* CVII (July 1992): 586–625.

16. Carlos D. Malamud, "España, Francia y el comércio directo con el espacio peruano, 1695–1730, Cádiz y Saint Marlo," in *La economia española al final del antiguo regime: comércio y colonias*, vol. III (Madrid: Alianza, 1982). Also Albert Girard, *Le commerce français à Seville et Cadix au temps de Habsbourgs: contribution à commerce étranges en Espagna aux XVIe et XVIIe siècles* (Paris: E. de Boccard; Bordeaux, Feret & fils, 1932).

17. D. A. Brading, "Bourbon Spain and its American Empire," in *Cambridge History of Latin America*, vol. I, ed. Leslie Bethel (Cambridge: Cambridge University Press, 1984), 389–439.

18. Dorothy Goebel, "British Trade to the Spanish Colonies, 1796–1823," *American Historical Review* XLIII (1938): 288–320.

19. Allan Kuethe and Douglas Inglis, "Absolutism and Enlightened Reform: Charles III and the Establishment of the Alcabala," *Past and Present* CIX (1985): 118–143; and Jacques Barbier, "Indies Revenues and Naval Spending: The Cost of Colonialism for the Spanish Bourbons, 1763–1805," *Jarhbüch für Geschichte von Staat, Wirtschaft und Gessellschaft Latinamerikas* XXI (1984).

20. Jacques Barbier, "Peninsula Finance and Colonial Trade: The Dilemma of Charles IV's Spain" *Journal of Latin American Studies* XII (1980): 21–37; John Fisher, "The Imperial Response to 'Free Trade': Spanish Imports from Spanish America, 1778–1796," *Journal of Latin American Studies* XVII (1985): 35–78; and A. García-Baquero González, "Comércio colonial y producción industrial en Cataluña a fines del siglo XVIII," *Actas del I Coloquio de história económica de España* (Barcelona: n.p., 1975), 268–294.

21. Michael M. Edwards, *The Growth of the British Cotton Trade, 1780–1815* (Manchester, Eng.: Manchester University Press, 1967); Arthur Redford, *Manchester Merchants and Foreign Trade, 1794–1858* (Manchester, Eng.: Manchester University Press, 1934); and Robert Walpole to Lord Granville, Lisbon, 12 October 1791, Public Records Office, Foreign Office, 6/14.

22. "Minute of Propositions Impeding the Treaty with Portugal," September 1786, Chatham Papers, PRO 30/8/342 (2) f. 59; Office of the Committee of Privy Council for Trade, 25 June 1787, PRO, BT 3/1. 102; [W. Fawkener] to [Borough Reeve] and [constable of Manchester], Office of Privy Council for Trade, 23 August 1788, PRO, BT, 3/1, 290.

23. D. José de Almeida de Melo e Castro to Dom João, 1 September 1801,

Arquivo Instituto Histórico e Geográfico Brasileiro, Rio de Janeiro, Lata 58, doc. 17.

24. Robert Fitzgerald to Lord Hawkesbury, Lisbon, 21 October. 1803, PRO, FO, 63/42.

25. Maxwell, *Conflicts and Conspiracies*, esp. 115–40.

26. John Leddy Phelan, *The People and the King: The Comunero Revolution in Colombia*, 1781 (Madison: University of Wisconsin Press, 1978); in particular, Steve J. Stern, "The Age of Andean Insurrection 1742–1782: A Reappraisal," in *Resistance, Rebellion and Consciousness in the Andean Peasant World*, ed. Steve J. Stern (Madison: University of Wisconsin Press, 1988), 34–93; and Lester D. Langley, *The Americas in the Age of Revolution 1750–1850* (New Haven: Yale University Press, 1996).

27. Liss, *Atlantic Empires*.

28. John Lynch, *The Spanish American Revolutions, 1808–1826* (New York: Weidenfeld and Nicolson, 1973); *The North American Role in the Spanish Imperial Economy, 1760–1819*, ed. Jacques Barbier and Allan Kuethe (Manchester, Eng.: Manchester University Press, 1984); also *The Economies of Mexico and Peru During the Late Colonial Period, 1700–1810*, ed. Nils Jacobson and Hans-Jürgen Puhle (Berlin: Colloqium Verlag, 1986).

29. John Barrow, *A Voyage to Cochinchina in the Years 1792 and 1793* (London: printed for T. Cadell and W. Davies, 1806), 133–34; Also see John Lynch, "British Policies and Spanish America," *Journal of Latin American Studies* I (1969): 1–30; Saint Dominigue had been producing about 40 percent of the world's sugar and more than half of the world's coffee, according to David Geggus, when the 1791 slave revolt occurred. The government of William Pitt and Henry Dundas sent some 15,000 soldiers to their deaths in Saint Dominigue and spent some 10 million pounds sterling trying to conquer it. Geggus call this "among the greatest disasters in British Imperial History." D. Geggus, "The British Government and the Saint Dominique Slave Revolt 1791–1793," *English Historical Review* XCVI (1981): 285–305; also, Antonio Annino, Luis Castro Leiva, and François-Xavier Guerra, eds., *De los imperios a las naciones: Iberoaméroca* (Zaragoza: IberCaja, 1994).

30. *Diplomatic Correspondence of the United States Concerning the Independence of the Latin American Nations*, 3 vols., ed. William R. Manning (New York: Oxford University Press, 1925), I: 72.

31. "Britain and the Independence of Latin America, 1812–1830," in *Selected Documents from the Foreign Office Archives*, 2 vols., ed. Sir. Charles Webster (New York: Oxford University Press, 1938), I: 190–3.

CHAPTER SIX

1. Paul A. Baran, *The Political Economy of Growth* (New York: Marzani & Munsell, 1957); Joseph L. Love, "Raúl Prebisch and the Origins of the Doctrine of Unequal Exchange," *Latin American Research Review* XV, no. 3 (1980): 45–72; See also Love's contribution in this volume. For the intellectual background of the emergence of dependency analysis in the 1960s, see Tulio Halperín Donghi, "'Dependency Theory' and Latin American Historiography," *Latin American Research Review* XVII, (1982): 115–30 and Robert A. Packenham, "Plus ça change . . .: The English Edition of Cardoso and Faletto's *Dependency and Development in Latin America*," in ibid., 131–51. James Cockcroft first drew attention to Lenin and Trotsky as precursors of the dependency interpretation: see James D. Cockcroft, *Precursores intelectuales de la Revolución mexicana* (México: Siglo XXI, 1971) (the Spanish translation of his book *Intellectual Precursors of the Mexican Revolution, 1900–1913* [Austin: University of Texas Press, 1968]), 1.
2. David A. Brading *Haciendas and Ranchos in the Mexican Bajío. León, 1700–1860* (New York: Cambridge University Press, 1978); Claude Morin, *Michoacán en la Nueva España del siglo XVIII. Crecimiento y desigualdad en una economía colonial* (Mexico: Fondo de Cultura Económica, 1979); Eric Van Young, *Hacienda and Market in Eighteenth-Century Mexico: The Rural Economy of the Guadalajara Region, 1675–1820* (Berkeley and Los Angeles: University of California Press, 1981); John C. Super, *La Vida en Querétaro durante la colonia, 1531–1810* (Mexico City: Fondo de Cultura Económica, 1983); Cheryl English Martin, *Rural Society in Colonial Morelos* (Albuquerque: University of New Mexico Press, 1985); Rodolfo Pastor, *Campesinos y reformas: La mixteca, 1700–1856* (Mexico: Centro de Estudios Historicos, El Colegio de Mexico, 1987); Robert W. Patch, *Maya and Spaniard in the Yucatán, 1648–1812* (Stanford: Stanford University Press, 1993), 138–54.
3. Enrique Florescano, *Precios del maíz y crisis agrícolas en México (1708–1810)* (Mexico City: El Colegio de México, 1969), 140–79; John R. Tutino, *From Insurrection to Revolution in Mexico: Social Bases of Agrarian Violence, 1750–1940* (Princeton: Princeton University Press, 1986), 61–90.
4. Robert W. Patch, "Decolonization, the Agrarian Problem, and the Origins of the Caste War, 1812–1847," in *Land, Labor, and Capital in Modern Yucatán: Essays in Regional History and Political Economy*, ed. Gilbert Joseph and Jeffrey Brannon (Tuscaloosa: University of Alabama Press, 1991), 51–82.
5. Tutino, *From Insurrection to Revolution, 61–90*; Patrick J. Carroll, *Blacks in Colonial Veracruz: Race, Ethnicity, and Regional Development* (Austin:

University of Texas Press, 1991).

6. Patch, *Maya and Spaniard*, 159–68.

7. Ibid., for Yucatán. I am currently engaged in research regarding the abolition of the *repartimiento* in the Kingdom of Guatemala.

8. Bernard Bailyn, *The New England Merchants in the Seventeenth Century* (Cambridge: Harvard University Press, 1955); John J. McCusker and Russell R. Menard, *The Economy of British America, 1607–1789* (Chapel Hill: University of North Carolina Press, 1985); Thomas M. Doerflinger, *A Rigorous Spirit of Enterprise: Merchants and Economic Development in Revolutionary Philadelphia* (Chapel Hill: University of North Carolina Press, 1986); Jacques A. Barbier and Allan J. Kuethe, eds., *The North American Role in the Spanish Imperial Economy, 1760–1819*, (Manchester, Eng.: University of Manchester Press, 1984).

9. Howard F. Cline, "The 'Aurora Yucateca'" and the Spirit of Enterprise in the Yucatán, 1821–1847," *Hispanic American Historical Review* 27, no. 1 (1947): 30–60.

10. Patch, *Maya and Spaniard*, 34–35.

11. Alicia del Carmen Contreras Sánchez, *Capital comercial y colorantes en la Nueva España. Segunda mitad del siglo XVIII* (Zamora: El Colegio de Michoacán, 1996).

12. Murdo J. MacLeod, *Spanish Central America: A Socioeconomic History, 1520–1720* (Berkeley and Los Angeles: University of California Press, 1973), 68–95, 145–48, 204–52.

13. Robert W. Patch, "Imperial Politics and Local Economy in Colonial Central America, 1670–1770," *Past and Present* 143 (May 1994): 77–107.

14. There is no good study of the Honduran silver mining economy at any time in its history. For some discussion, see MacLeod, *Spanish Central America*, 148–51, 253–63; Miles Wortman, *Government and Society in Central America, 1680–1840* (New York: Columbia University Press, 1982), 96–99, 113–16.

15. MacLeod, Spanish Central America, 176–203; David Browning, *El Salvador: Landscape and Society* (Oxford: Clarendon Press, 1971), 66–77.

16. Patch, *Maya and Spaniard*, 141, 218–19; Wortman, *Government and Society*, 127, 166, 185; Ralph L. Woodward, *Class Privilege and Economic Development: The Consulado de Comercio de Guatemala, 1793–1871* (Chapel Hill: University of North Carolina Press, 1966), 43–45, 48–51.

17. Archivo General de Indias, Seville (hereafter A.G.I.), Guatemala 640, Instancia de partes, Orden-en-Consejo, 2 December 1747; A.G.I. 642, Carta de la Compañía de Goathemala al Presidente, 30 January 1756; ibid., Carta del Presidente (Arcos y Moreno) al Srio. de Indias (Arriaga), 31 January 1756.

18. Carlos Martínez Shaw, *Cataluña en la carrera de Indias 1680–1756*

(Barcelona: Editorial Crítica, 1981), 114–19 passim, 133, 136, 162, 183–186, 191–98 passim.

19. In addition to MacLeod and my dissertation ("A Colonial Regime: Maya and Spaniard in the Yucatán," Princeton, 1979), see Robert Wasserstrom, *Class and Society in Central Chiapas* (Berkeley and Los Angeles: University of California Press, 1983), and Nancy M. Farriss, *Maya Society Under Colonial Rule: The Collective Enterprise of Survival* (Princeton: Princeton University Press, 1984), all of which conclude that either the Yucatán, Chiapas, or Central America is relatively isolated from the world economy because of few exports to Europe.

20. Immanuel Wallerstein, *The Modern World-System: Capitalist Agriculture and the Origins of the European World-Economy in the Sixteenth Century* (New York: Academic Press, 1974), 68.

21. Steve J. Stern, "Feudalism, Capitalism, and the World-System in the Perspective of Latin America and the Caribbean," *American Historical Review* 93, No. 4 (1988): 829-72.

22. Van Young, *Hacienda and Market*; Carlos Sempat Assadourian, *El sistema de la economía colonial: Mercado interno, regiones y espacio económico* (Mexico: Editorial Nueva Imagen, 1983); Patch, *Maya and Spaniard*.

23. A.G.I. Escribanía 359A, Residencia del Presidente Tomás de Rivera y Santa Cruz, 1747, Cuadernos 1-4.

24. Troy S. Floyd, "The Guatemalan Merchants, the Government, and the *Provincianos*, 1750-1800," *Hispanic Amereican Historical Review* 41, no. 1 (1961): 90-110.

25. This is usually mistranslated as Manila galleon. In fact, a galleon is specific kind of ship, while the term nao, which is used in the original Spanish sources, is more generic and covers all the varieties of ships, including the galeón, that made the run between Manila and Acapulco.

26. Patch, *Maya and Spaniard*, 30-32, 81-93, 154-68; Patch, "Imperial Politics and Local Economy," 101-07.

27. See previous note; in addition, for exports from Chiapas to Mexico, see A.G.I., Escribanía 356C, Residencia de Martín Joseph de Bustamante, Alcalde Mayor de Chiapa, 1730; A.G.I., Escribanía 360B, Pieza 50, Testimonio de las Diligencias remitidas por Don Antonio de Zuazua y Muxica Alcalde Mayor de Chiapa, 1744.

28. Emma Helen Blair and James Alexander Robertson, eds., *The Philippine Islands, 1493-1898*, 55 vols. (Cleveland: A.H. Clark, 1903-7), XXVII:199-200, XLV:36-37, 83-84; Pierre Chaunu, *Les Philippines et le Pacifique des Ibériques*, 2 vols. (Paris: SEVPEN, 1960–66), I, 180–89.

29. A.G.I. Guatemala 642, Instancia de la Compañía de Goathemala al Rey, 26 November 1750; A.G.I., Guatemala 525, Carta del Presidente al Srio. de Hacienda (el Marqués de Ensenada), 30 March 1752.

30. A.G.I. 555, Carta de la Diputación de Comercio al Rey, 1 October 1772; ibid., Testimonio del expediente instruido a instancia de los

Diputados del Comercio de esta Ciudad, sobre el modo, terminos, y cirunstancias, 1772, fols. 43-52; A.G.I. Guatemala 423, Real Cédula al Presidente de Guatemala, 18 September 1773.

31. A.G.I., Guatemala 690, Carta del Jefe político e Intendente de Nicaragua al Srio. de Hacienda, 13 December 1820; Consulado de Guatemala, *Memoria sobre el estado actual del comercio de Guatemala: obstáculos que impiden su progreso y medios de removerlos* (Guatemala: Beteta, 1823); Woodward, *Class Privilege and Economic Development*, 41–43.

32. This conclusion I have reached by reading Peter J. Bakewell, *Miners of the Red Mountain: Indian Labor in Potosí, 1545–1650* (Albuquerque: University of New Mexico Press, 1984); and Ann M. Wightman, *Indigenous Migration and Social Change: The Forasteros of Cuzco, 1570–1720* (Durham, NC: Duke University Press, 1990).

33. A.G.I., Lima 1119, Informe de la Contaduría, y Respuestas Fiscales correspondientes al Expediente de Intendencias, Informe de los Señores Contadores Generales de 30 de diciembre de 1800, paragraphs 344–46.

34. James C. Scott, *Weapons of the Weak: Everyday Forms of Peasant Resistance* (New Haven: Yale University Press, 1985), 29; see also Robert M. Hill II, *Colonial Cakchiquels: Highland Maya Adaption to Colonial Rule, 1600–1700* (Fort Worth: Harcourt Brace Jovanovich, 1992), 121–37; Patch, *Maya and Spaniard*, 45–56, 91–92.

35. See O. H. K. Spate, *The Pacific Since Magellan*, vol. 1, *The Spanish Lake* (London: Croom Helm, 1979), 200–28 for a superb discussion of the trade between Asia and Spanish America.

36. For a good, brief essay on the importance of technology in causing Latin American dependency in the nineteenth century, see James H. Street, "The Platt-Stein Controversy over Dependency: Another View," *Latin American Research Review* XVI, no. 3 (1981): 173–179.

CHAPTER SEVEN

Archival Abbreviations

AGNM, Archivo General de la Nación, Mexico City
BN, Biblioteca Nacional, Mexico City
FO, Foreign Office Correspondence, Public Record Office (Kew), Richmond, Surrey, UK

1. I am grateful to Kathryn Burns, Jay Kinsbruner, Rob Patch, Bill Taylor and Jan de Vries for their exceptionally helpful comments.

2. J. L. Anderson, *Explaining Long-Term Economic Change* (Cambridge: Cambridge University Press, 1995), 55.

3. I base this discussion on Stanley and Barbara Stein, *The Colonial Heritage of Latin America. Essays on Economic Dependence in Perspective* (New York: Oxford University Press, 1970), 32, 39, 95, 128.

4. John Coatsworth, "The Decline of the Mexican Economy," in *América Latina en la época de Simón Bolívar. La formación de las economías nacionales y los intereses económicos europeos, 1800–1850*, ed. Reinhard Liehr (Berlin: Colloquium Verlag, 1989), 50.

5. Albert Carreras, coordinator, *Estadísticas históricas de España. Siglos XIX–XX* ([Madrid]: Fundación Banco Exterior, [1984]), 331.

6. Javier Ortiz de la Tabla, *Comercio exterior de Veracruz, 1778–1821: Crisis de dependencia* (Sevilla: Escuela de Estudios Hispanoamericanos, 1978), 261.

7. Fernando Rosenzweig, "La economía novohispana al comenzar el siglo XIX," in Fernando Rosenzweig Hernández, *El desarrollo económico de México, 1800–1910* (Zinacantepec, Mexico: El Colegio Mexiquense, 1989), 53.

8. My calculation from Juan Javier Pescador, "Patrones demográficos urbanos en la Nueva España, 1700–1820," in *El poblamiento de México. Una visión histórico demográfica*, coord. Ana Arenzana, 4 vols. (México: Secretaría de Gobernación, 1993), 2: 117, 148.

9. Jan de Vries, "Problems in the Measurement, Description, and Analysis of Historical Urbanization," in *Urbanization in History. A Process of Dynamic Interactions*, ed. Ad van der Woude, Akira Hayami, and Jan de Vries (Oxford, UK: Clarendon Press, 1990), 45.

10. For Mexican imports, see *Parliamentary Papers*, 1836: XLVI. Also see Charles Mackenzie to George Canning, Jalapa, 24 July 1824, FO 50/7. For Eltis's measure, see David Eltis and Lawrence C. Jennings, "Trade Between Western Africa and the Atlantic World in the Pre–Colonial Era," *The American Historical Review* 93:4 (1988): 953.

11. Victor Bulmer Thomas puts it this way: "Latin America inherited a non-export economy after independence that may have suffered from extremely low levels of productivity and high levels of inefficiency but which was far larger than the export sector." Precisely. See The Economic History of Latin America Since Independence (Cambridge: Cambridge University Press, 1994), 39.

12. Douglass C. North, *The Economic Growth of the United States, 1790–1860* (New York: W. W. Norton, 1966), 1.

13. J. R. Poinsett to Francis Baring, Mexico, 3 April 1829, Baring Bros. Archive, HC 4.5.6.

14. Waddy Thompson, *Recollections of Mexico* (New York: n.p. 1846), 191.

15. *Diario de sesiones de las Cortes generales y extraordinarias que dieron principio el 24 de septiembre de 1810 y terminaron el 20 de septiembre de 1813*, 9 vols. (Madrid: n.p. 1870), 2:846. Foncerrada's exact concluding words: "La Nueva España de rica ha pasado a menesterosa."

16. Richard Garner, *Economic Growth and Change in Bourbon Mexico* (Gainesville: University Press of Florida, 1993), 215–245; Carlos Marichal and Matilde Souto Mantecón, "Silver and Situados: New Spain and the Financing of the Spanish Empire in the Caribbean in the Eighteenth Century," *Hispanic American Historical Review* 74, no. 4 (1994): 587–613; Stanley J. Stein, "<Un raudal de oro y plata que corría sin cesar de España a Francia>: Política mercantil española y el comercio con Francia en la época de Carlos III," in *Actas del Congreso Internacional sobre "Carlos III y la Ilustración,"* 3 vols (Madrid: Ministerio de Cultura, 1989), 2:219–80.

17. José María Luis Mora, *Revista política de las diversas administraciones que ha tenido la república hasta 1837* (Mexico: Miguel Angel Porrúa, 1986 [1837]), 184.

18. For a more elegant formulation of these points, see John W. Mellor, ed., *Agriculture on the Road to Industrialization* (Baltimore: Johns Hopkins University Press, 1995), esp. 1–22.

19. *Annales du sénat et du corps législatif* (Paris: Moniteur Universal, 1865), 292–93. I have extracted this from a much longer speech.

20. Thiers knew his Humboldt. Whether he understood his Humboldt is another matter. Humboldt was really talking about gross domestic product not just agricultural output. In this context, the mistake is not important, because it stengthens Thiers's case. See Richard J. and Linda K. Salvucci, "Las consecuencias económicas de la independencia mexicana," in *La independencia americana: consecuencias económicas*, ed. Leandro Prados de la Escosura and Samuel Amaral (Madrid: Alianza Universidad, 1993), 33.

21. John H. Coatsworth, "Obstacles to Economic Growth in Nineteenth-Century Mexico," *American Historical Review* 83, no. 1 (1978): 82.

22. Cristina García López and Antonio Spilimbergo, "Urbanization, Urban Giants and Shocks," *Development Policy* (June 1995), 6–7.

23. N.F.R. Crafts, *British Economic Growth During the Industrial Revolution* (Oxford: Clarendon Press, 1985), 49–69. Also see Leandro Prados de la Escosura, *De imperio a nación. Crecimiento y atraso económico en España (1780–1930)* (Madrid, Alianza Editorial: 1988).

24. D. A. Brading, *Haciendas and Ranchos in the Mexican Bajío: León 1700–1860* (Cambridge: Cambridge University Press, 1978), 53; and Claude Morin, *Santa Inés Zacatelco (1648–1812). Contribución a la demografía histórica del México Colonial* (Mexico: Instituto Nacional de Antropología e Historia, 1973), 89.

25. For example, Gabriel Haslip-Viera, "The Underclass," in *Cities and Society in Colonial Latin America*, ed. Louisa Schell Hoberman and Susan Migden Socolow (Albuquerque: University of New Mexico Press, 1986), 285–312.

26. Sergio Reyes Osorio et al., *Estructura agraria y desarrollo agrícola en México: Estudio sobre las relaciones entre la tenencia y uso de la tierra y*

desarrollo agrícola de México (Mexico: Fondo de Cultura Económica, 1974), 408.

27. My calculation of an unweighted mean from Lilia Oliver, "La mortalidad en Guadalajara, 1800–1850," in *La mortalidad en México: Niveles, tendencias y determinantes*, ed. Mario Bronfman and José Gómez de León (Mexico: El Colegio de México, 1988), 176.

28. For example, see Eric Van Young, "The Age of Paradox: Mexican Agriculture at the End of the Colonial Period, 1750–1810," in *The Economies of Mexico and Peru During the Late Colonial Period, 1760–1810*, ed. Nils Jacobsen and Hans-Jürgen Puhle (Berlin: Colloquium Verlag: 1986), 71–74.

29. David R. Weir, "Malthus's Theory of Population," in *The New Palgrave Dictionary of Economics*, ed. John Eatwell, Murray Milgate, and Peter Newman, 4 vols. (London: Macmillan Press Ltd., 1987), 3: 290–293.

30. Brading, *Haciendas and Ranchos*, 79–80.

31. The basin of Mexico and adjacent areas in southern Hidalgo, southwestern Tlaxcala, the western third of Puebla and the state of Morelos.

32. William T. Sanders, "The Population of the Central Mexican Symbiotic Region, the Basin of Mexico, and the Teotihuacán Valley in the Sixteenth Century," in *The Native Population of the Americas in 1492*, ed. William M. Denevan (Madison: The University of Wisconsin Press, 1976), 130–131. The figure is the average of Sanders's range. For 1803, see Lourdes Márquez Morfín, "La evolución cuantitativa de la población novohispana: siglos xvi, xvii y xviii," in *El poblamiento de México*, 2:49. I took the boundaries of the intendancies as given by Guillermina González de Lemoine et al., Atlas de Historia de México (Mexico: Universidad Nacional Autónoma de México, 1990), 23.

33. Ángeles Romero makes the same point in her essay, "La agricultura en la época colonial," in *La agricultura en tierras mexicanas desde sus orígenes hasta nuestros días*, coord. Teresa Rojas (Mexico: Editorial Grijalbo, 1991), 214–15.

34. William T. Sanders, "Central Mexican Symbiotic Region," p. 120; Mac Chapin, "The Seduction of Models. Chinampa Agriculture in Mexico," *Grassroots Development*, 12:1 (1988): 16.

35. Jan de Vries, *The Dutch Rural Economy in the Golden Age* (New Haven: Yale University Press, 1974).

36. Stephen Hymer and Stephen Resnick, "A Model of an Agrarian Economy with Nonagricultural Activities," *American Economic Review* 59 (1969): 493–506. In private correspondence (4 March 1996), de Vries indicated that he also drew on Sol Tax, *Penny Capitalism* (Washington, D.C., 1953) in formulating his version of the Hymer-Resnick model. He then concludes that "the application of this model to a society like Mexico is not really so surprising," which is, as we will see, what I subsequently attempt.

37. For this discussion, see de Vries, *The Dutch Rural Economy*, 4–10. In the interests of brevity, I have compressed de Vries's discussion considerably and urge readers to consult the original for a more nuanced account. De Vries does not consider the possibility of internal migration. Where land is a free good, or nearly so, peasants can avoid the choice de Vries poses by moving on. Diminishing marginal returns do not set in because the supply of land is perfectly elastic. This was apparently the case on the Meseta Central of Costa Rica in the late eighteenth century, where population increase in the face of free land produced migration. Peasant families continued to produce Z goods because the internal market, at most 65,000 people, was so small. See Iván Molina Juárez, *Costa Rica (1800–1850): El legado colonial y la génesis del capitalismo* (San Jose: Editorial de la Universidad de Costa Rica, 1991), 106–8.

38. De Vries does not dwell much on the distinction, but the peasants who farm in the specialization model have more land and thus higher productivity than those who farm in the peasant model. If the marginal product of artisan activity is the same in both models, peasants will devote more effort to farming in the specialization model than in the peasant model. Their total product, i.e., income, will be higher as a result. Even if peasants in both models faced the same prices for nonagricultural goods, the peasants in the specialization model could purchase more of them. For de Vries, people are better off because they trade. As I see it, the model says that people trade because they are better off—not quite the same thing.

39. The key text, of course, is T. H. Aston and C. H. E. Philpin, *The Brenner Debate: Agrarian Class Structure and Economic Development in Pre-Industrial Europe* (New York: Cambridge University Press, 1987). A very interesting criticism of the entire notion of a Malthusian model appears in Peter H. Lindert, "English Population, Wages, and Prices: 1541–1913," in *Population and Economy: Population and History from the Traditional to the Modern World*, ed. Robert I. Rotberg and Theodore K. Rabb (Cambridge: Cambridge University Press, 1986), 49–74.

40. D. A. Brading, *Miners and Merchants in Bourbon Mexico, 1763–1810* (Cambridge: Cambridge University Press, 1970), 114–16; John Coatsworth, "The Mexican Mining Industry in the Eighteenth Century," in *The Economies of Mexico and Peru*, 35.

41. Brading, *Haciendas and Ranchos*, 84; Eric Van Young, *Hacienda and Market in Eighteenth-Century Mexico: The Rural Economy of the Guadalajara Region, 1675–1820* (Berkeley and Los Angeles: University of California Press, 1981), 176.

42. Gavin Wright, *The Political Economy of the Cotton South: Households, Markets, and Wealth in the Nineteenth Century* (New York: W. W. Norton, 1978). De Vries now (correspondence with the author, 4 March 1996) observes that "there is no need to argue that peasants

intend to avoid markets, only that they are not capable of orienting themselves more than superficially on the market because of the limitations of their capital and their productivity."

43. For one, see Arij Ouweneel and Cristina Torales Pacheco, *Empresarios, indios y estado: perfil de la economia mexicana (Siglo XVIII)* (Amsterdam: CEDLA,1988).

44. Juan Carlos Garavaglia and Juan Carlos Grosso, *Puebla desde una perspectiva microhistórica*, (Mexico: Editorial Claves Latinoamericanas, 1994), 106.

45. Enrique Florescano, *Precios del maíz y crisis agrícolas en México (1708–1810)* (Mexico: El Colegio de México, 1969), 91–93.

46. Van Young, *Hacienda and Market*, 65.

47. Florescano, *Precios del maíz*, 187–89.

48. Brading, *Haciendas and Ranchos*, 172.

49. See Jan de Vries, "Peasant Demand Patterns and Economic Development: Friesland, 1550–1750," in *European Peasants and Their Markets. Essays in Agrarian Economic History*, ed. William N. Parker and Eric L. Jones (Princeton: Princeton University Press, 1975), 206–7.

50. An instructive example of the way these charges worked appears in Karen Spalding's *Huarochirí: An Andean Society Under Inca and Spanish Rule* (Stanford: Stanford University Press, 1984), 184–92, 199.

51. Angeles Romero, "La agricultura," 194.

52. Lourdes Márquez Morfín, "La evolución cuantitativa de la población novohispana: siglos xvi, xvii y xviii," in *El poblamiento de México*, 2: 49.

53. Brading, *Haciendas and Ranchos*, 40–41, 154, 155, 158, 172.

54. Van Young, *Hacienda and Market*, 273–274. Also see José María Muriá, *Breve historia de Jalisco* (Guadalajara: Universidad de Guadalajara, 1988), 154; and see Brian R. Hamnett, *Roots of Insurgency: Mexican Regions, 1750–1824* (Cambridge: Cambridge University Press, 1986), 93.

55. Hunt, who recently retired from teaching at Boston University, was a colleague of the Steins in the early 1970s. "The Economics of Haciendas and Plantations in Latin America" appeared as Discussion Paper no. 29 of the Research Program in Economic Development of the Woodrow Wilson School of Princeton University in 1972. The historical part of it is dated, of course, but the model Hunt proposed remains relevant. Hunt argues that, if the opportunity cost of land is low, the hacienda will recruit workers by "paying" them in access to land (*minifundios*). He does not agree that the inefficiency of the hacienda stems from imperfect competition. For Abad y Queipo, see D. A. Brading, *Church and State in Bourbon Mexico: The Diocese of Michoacán, 1749–1810* (Cambridge: Cambridge University Press 1994), 232.

56. Richard L. Garner (with Spiro E. Stefanou) *Economic Growth and Change in Bourbon Mexico* (Gainesville: University of Florida Press, 1993), 182.

57. María Eugenia Romero I. and Erendira Villamar, "San José Acolman y

anexos: 1788–1798," *Siete ensayos sobre la hacienda mexicana,* coord. Enrique Semo, 163. This hacienda did send wheat to Mexico City.

58. Compare with Bulmer Thomas, *The Economic History of Latin America,* who sees no connection between land tenure and agricultural productivity. By the late nineteenth century, when both national and international transportation costs had fallen significantly, perhaps so.

59. This paragraph is based on the following sources: Brading, *Haciendas and Ranchos,* 66–67; Gibson, *The Aztecs,* 328; Van Young, *Hacienda and Market,* 221; and Romero, "La agricultura colonial," 214.

60. David J. Weiland, III, "The Economics of Agriculture: Markets, Production and Finances in the Bishopric of Puebla, 1532–1809" (Ph.D. diss., University of Cambridge, 1995), p. 81.

61. See David Brading, "Population and Agriculture in Colonial Mexico," *Journal of Latin American Studies,* 13:2 (1981), 407.

62. Brading, *Haciendas and Ranchos,* pp. 82, 196.

63. Brading, *Miners and Merchants,* p. 230.

64. Ibid. Van Young, *Hacienda and Market,* 119; Charles Gibson, *The Aztecs under Spanish Rule* (Stanford: Stanford University Press 1964), 289.

65. Florescano, "Hacienda in New Spain," 173.

66. Weiland, "Economics of Agriculture," 187.

67. Calculated from "Cronología de las sequías y hambres en la Nueva España" in Lourdes Márquez Morfín, "La evolución cuantitativa de la población novohispana: siglos xvi, xvii y xviii," in *El poblamiento de México,* 2: 60–62.

68. For some comparative evidence for Great Britain as well, see R. B. Outhwaite, *Dearth, Public Policy and Social Disturbance in England, 1550–1800* (Cambridge: Cambridge University Press 1991), 12.

69. Jesús F. de la Teja, San Antonio de Béxar. *A Community on New Spain's Northern Frontier* (Albuquerque: University of New Mexico Press, 1995), 93–94. De la Teja points out that maize prices in San Antonio fell moderately over the eighteenth century. What transpired in the late 1780s was clearly an aberration of major dimensions.

70. Jean Drèze and Amartya Sen, *Hunger and Public Action* (Oxford: Clarendon Press, 1989), 47.

71. De Vries, *The Dutch Rural Economy,* 5–6.

72. See, for instance, "Cuaderno general de ygualas pertenecientes a el pueblo de Dolores y su partido para el año de 85," San Miguel el Grande, (copy) 28 April 1785, Collected documents on San Miguel el Grande, Maddux Library, Trinity University. Also see Heriberto Moreno García, *Haciendas de tierra y agua en la antigua ciénaga de Chapala* (Zamora, Mexico: El Colegio de Michoacán, 1989), 222.

73. The key statement is Guy P.C. Thomson, "Continuity and Change in Mexican Manufacturing, 1800–1870," in *Between Development and Underdevelopment. The Precocious Attempts at Industrialization of the*

Periphery, 1800–1870, ed. Jean Batou (Geneva: Librairie Droz, 1991), 262–64.

74. It is futile to try to summarize the literature on protoindustrialization. A concise introduction to some of the implications of the debate is Pat Hudson, "Proto-industrialisation: the case of the West Riding Wool Textile Industry in the 18th and early 19th centuries," *History Workshop Journal,* 12 (1981), 34–61, reprinted in R. A. Church and E. A. Wrigley, *The Industrial Revolutions* (11 vols., Oxford: Basil Blackwell, Ltd., 1994), 8: 84–111.

75. D. C. Coleman, "Proto-industrialization: a concept too many," *Economic History Review,* 36: 3 (1983): 435–48.

76. Compare the industry maps (1781, 1783) in Salvucci, *Textiles and Capitalism,* 22–23 with the one (1854, 1864) appearing in Enrique Florescano, coordinator, *Atlas histórico de México* 2d ed. (Mexico: Siglo XXI Editores, 1984), 110–11. Thomson makes an identical observation in "Mexican Manufacturing," 279–80.

77. The reports documenting rural industry are found in AGNM, alcabalas, vols. 37 and 521.

78. Guy P. C. Thomson, *Puebla de los Ángeles. Industry and Society in a Mexican City, 1700–1850* (Boulder, CO: Westview Press, 1989), 21.

79. Guy Thomson, "The Cotton Textile Industry in Puebla During the Eighteenth and Early Nineteenth Centuries," in *The Economies of Mexico and Peru,* Nils Jacobsen and Hans-Jürgen Pühle, 173-76.

80. Albert Berry, "The Limited Role of Rural Small-Scale Manufacturing for Late-Comers: Some Hypotheses on the Colombian Experience," *Journal of Latin American Studies,* 19, no. 2 (1987): 279-94. Also see Takashi Hikino and Alice H. Amsden, "Staying Behind, Stumbling Back, Sneaking Up, Soaring Ahead: Late Industrialization in Historical Perspective," in *Convergence of Productivity: Cross-national Studies and Historical Evidence,* ed. William J. Baumol et al. (New York: Oxford University Press, 1994), 285–315.

81. An exemplary series of studies is Bruce M. S. Campbell and Mark Overton, eds., *Land, Labour and Livestock: Historical Studies in European Agricultural Productivity* (Manchester, Eng.: Manchester University Press, 1991). See particularly the paper by Patrick K. O'Brien and Gianni Toniolo, "The Poverty of Italy and the Backwardness of Its Agriculture Before 1914," 385–409. Ángeles Romero has put the situation in Mexican studies well: "Within the field of colonial historiography the lack of studies devoted to agriculture per se is obvious." See her introductory comments in Teresa Rojas Rabiela, coord., *Agricultura indígena: pasado y presente* (Mexico: CIESAS, 1990), 30.

82. Bulmer Thomas, *Economic History of Latin America,* 123.

83. Ibid., 46–82.

84. This is just a crude thought experiment. Modern Mexico has an area of

about 2,000,000 km2, of which 15% is generally considered arable. A circular market of the size Garner proposes is about 20,000 km2. Taking 15% of 2,000,000 and dividing by 20,000 yields fifteen such markets. Coatsworth, "Obstacles to Economic Growth," 91, does the experiment a little differently.

85. See, for example, Stephen Haber, "Assessing the Obstacles to Industrialization: The Mexican Economy, 1830-1940," *Journal of Latin American Studies*, 24, no. 1 (1992): 1–32; Simon Miller, "Mexican Junkers and Capitalist Haciendas, 1810–1910: The Arable Estate and the Transition to Capitalism Between the Insurgency and the Revolution," *Journal of Latin American Studies* 22, no. 2 (1990): 229–63; Coatsworth, "Obstacles to Economic Growth," 91-2, is a classic statement of the idea.

CHAPTER EIGHT

1. A typescript of Cortázar's "La noche boca arriba" is in the Carlos Fuentes Papers, Manuscripts Division, Rare Books and Special Collections, Princeton University Libraries. It was published in several collections of Cortázar's short stories, including *Final del juego* (Mexico: Los Presentes, 1956), *El perseguidor y otros cuentos* (Buenos Aires: Centro Editor de América Latina, 1967), and *Siete cuentos* (Manchester, Eng.: Manchester University Press, 1994). An English translation by Paul Blackburn ("The Night Face Up") is in *End of the Game and Other Stories* (New York: Pantheon, 1963), later reprinted with the title *Blow Up and Other Stories*.

2. Gabriel García Márquez, *Cien años de soledad* (Buenos Aires: Editorial Sud-americana, 1967); translated by Gregory Rabassa as *One Hundred Years of Solitude* (New York: Harper, 1970); *El otoño del patriarca* (Barcelona: Plaza & Janes, 1975); translated by Gregory Rabassa as *Autumn of the Patriarch* (New York: Harper & Row, 1976). The Princeton Libraries also own a fine edition of *One Hundred Years of Solitude* (New York: Limited Editions Club, 1982), illustrated by Rafael Ferrer and printed by the Stinehour Press of Lunenburg, Vermont; it is in the Graphic Arts Collection, Visual Materials Division, Rare Books and Special Collections.

3. García Márquez, *Cien años de soledad*, 15.

4. Alejo Carpentier, *Los pasos perdidos* (Mexico: Edición y Distribución Ibero Americana de Publicaciones, 1953); translated by Harriet de Onís as *The Lost Steps* (New York: Alfred A. Knopf, 1956).

5. Carpentier, *The Lost Steps*, 53.

6. Lest one think that such sensibilities about time have disappeared, consider a more recent expression, such as Antonio Benítez Rojo's *La isla*

que se repite: El Caribe y la perspectiva posmoderna (Hanover, N.H.: Ediciones del Norte, 1989), translated by James Maraniss as *The Repeating Island: The Caribbean and the Postmodern Perspective* (Durham, NC: Duke University Press, 1992).

7. Stanley J. Stein and Barbara Hadley Stein, *The Colonial Heritage of Latin America: Essays on Economic Dependence in Perspective* (New York: Oxford University Press, 1970).

8. I have taken up this agenda as part of a debate with Immanuel Wallerstein on world-system themes: see "Feudalism, Capitalism, and the World-System in the Perspective of Latin America and the Caribbean," *American Historical Review* 93, no. 4 (October 1988): 829–72, with the debate between the author and Wallerstein in ibid., 873–97.

9. The third item on the list above is the most obscure, an example from my own personal list: see the Mexican newspaper *Uno más uno*, 10 March 1985, 2.

10. "New Slaves Scandal," *New York Times*, 10 August 1995, A1, A5. For another example of the chain of diverse technologies and labor forms that feed into production by multinational firms, see Lourdes Benería and Martha Roldán, *The Crossroads of Class and Gender: Industrial Homework, Subcontracting, and Household Dynamics in Mexico City* (Chicago: University of Chicago Press, 1987).

11. For examples, see Gerard Colby, with Charlotte Dennett, *Thy Will Be Done: The Conquest of the Amazon: Nelson Rockefeller and Evangelism in the Age of Oil* (New York: Harper Collins, 1995); Michael F. Brown and Eduardo Fernandez, *War of Shadows: The Struggle for Utopia in the Peruvian Amazon* (Berkeley and Los Angeles: University of California Press, 1991). See also Marcos Cueto, ed., *Missionaries of Science: The Rockefeller Foundation and Latin America* (Bloomington: Indiana University Press, 1994).

12. See R. Douglas Cope, *The Limits of Racial Domination: Plebeian Society in Colonial Mexico City, 1660–1720* (Madison: University of Wisconsin Press, 1994); but for a case where whiteness mattered to plebeians, see Sarah Chambers, "The Many Shades of the White City: Urban Culture and Society in Arequipa, Peru, 1780–1854" (Ph.D. diss., University of Wisconsin at Madison, 1992).

13. The late colonial insurrections and political restlessness provide important examples of this. See Steve J. Stern, ed., *Resistance, Rebellion, and Consciousness in the Andean Peasant World, 18th to 20th Centuries* (Madison: University of Wisconsin Press, 1987), Parts I and II; Charles Walker, ed., *Entre la retórica y la insurgencia: Las ideas y los movimientos sociales en los Andes, siglo xviii* (Cuzco: Centro Bartolomé de Las Casas, 1996); C. L. R. James, *The Black Jacobins: Toussaint L'Ouverture and the San Domingo Revolution* (New York: Vintage Books, 1963 [1935]); Stuart B. Schwartz, *Sugar Plantations in the Formation of Brazilian*

Society: Bahía, 1550–1835 (New York: Cambridge University Press, 1985), ch. 17.

14. Gabriel García Márquez, *Crónica de una muerte anunciada* (Bogota: Oveja Negra, 1981); translated by Gregory Rabassa as *Chronicle of a Death Foretold* (New York: Alfred A. Knopf, 1988). A typescript of this novella is among the Mauricio Wacquez Papers, Manuscripts Division, Rare Books and Special Collections, Princeton University Libraries.

15. See Steve J. Stern, *The Secret History of Gender: Women, Men, and Power in Late Colonial Mexico* (Chapel Hill: University of North Carolina Press, 1995), ch. 14. For a striking example from early revolutionary Cuba, see Geoffrey E. Fox, "Honor, Shame, and Women's Liberation in Cuba: Views of Working Class Emigré Men," in Ann M. Pescatello, ed., *Female and Male in Latin America: Essays* (Pittsburgh: University of Pittsburgh Press, 1973).

16. Stern, *Secret History of Gender*, ch. 14.

17. Stern, Ibid.; see also Heather Fowler-Salamini and Mary Kay Vaughan, eds., *Women of the Mexican Countryside, 1850–1990* (Tucson: University of Arizona Press, 1994).

18. The classic studies of Zapata are Jesús Sotelo Inclán, *Raíz y razón de Zapata* (Mexico: Editorial Etnos, 1943); and John Womack, Jr., *Zapata and the Mexican Revolution* (New York: Vintage Books, 1968). For a more recent assessment, see Samuel Brunk, *Emiliano Zapata: Revolution and Betrayal in Mexico* (Albuquerque: University of New Mexico Press, 1995).

19. See Richard Price, *First-Time: The Historical Vision of an Afro-American People* (Baltimore: Johns Hopkins University Press, 1983), and *Alabi's World* (Baltimore: Johns Hopkins University Press, 1990).

20. Joanne Rappaport, *Cumbe Reborn: An Andean Ethnography of History* (Chicago: University of Chicago Press, 1994). See also her *The Politics of Memory: Native Historical Interpretation in the Colombian Andes* (Cambridge and New York: Cambridge University Press, 1990).

21. *Me llamo Rigoberta Menchú*, ed. Elizabeth Burgos-Debray (Havana, Cuba: Ediciones Casa de las Américas, 1983), translated by Ann Wright as *I, Rigoberta Menchú*, edited and introduced by Elizabeth Burgos-Debray (London: Verso, 1984). See also Menchú's *El clamor de la tierra: Luchas campesinas en la historia reciente de Guatemala* (Donostia, Guipúzcoa, Spain: Tercera Prensa, 1993).

22. Xavier Albó, "From MNRistas to Kataristas to Katari," in Stern, ed., *Resistance, Rebellion, and Consciousness*, 405. See also Brooke Larson, *Colonialism and Agrarian Transformation in Bolivia: Cochabamba, 1550–1900* (Princeton: Princeton University Press, 1988), esp. ch. 9.

23. Rappaport, *Cumbe Reborn*.

23. Stern, *Secret History of Gender*, ch. 14.

CHAPTER NINE

1. José Vasconcelos, *La raza cósmica*, in his *Obras Completas de José Vasconcelos* (Mexico City: Libreros Mexicanos Unidos, 1958), 1066.
2. Domingo Faustino Sarmiento, "Influencia de la instrucción primaria en la industria y en el desarrollo general de la prosperidad nacional, Memoria presentada al Consejo Universitario de Chile sobre estas cuestiones," in his *Obras Completas*, vol. 22 (Buenos Aires: Luz del Día, 1951).
3. Andrés Bello, *Obras Completas*, vol. 19 (Caracas: Ministerio de Educación, 1951), 165.
4. Sarmiento, Letter to Mariano de Sarratea, Buenos Aires, 29 May 1855, in *Obras Completas*, vol. XXIV.
5. Bartolomé Mitre, *Historia de Belgrano y de la Independencia Argentina*, 5th ed. (Buenos Aires: Biblioteca de "La Nación," 1902), I:8 (this section was first included in the second edition of 1868).
6. Bartolomé Mitre, "Discurso de Chivilcoy, pronunciado el 25 de octubre de 1868," in Bartolomé Mitre, *Arengas* (Buenos Aires: Casavalle, 1889), 275 (the quote from p. 281).
7. Miguel Angel Cárcano, *Evolución histórica del régimen de la tierra pública, 1816–1910* (Buenos Aires: Peuser, 1917).
8. Jacinto Oddone, *La burguesía terrateniente argentina; Capital Federal, Buenos Aires, territorios nacionales*, 2d ed. (Buenos Aires: La Vanguardia, 1936).
9. Herbert Gibson, *The Land We Live On* (Buenos Aires: n.p., 1914).
10. Sarmiento, "Carta-prólogo a *Conflicto y armonías de las razas en América*: A Mrs. Horace Mann," in Sarmiento, *Obras Completas*, vol. 37.
11. Carlos Octavio Bunge, *Nuestra América*, 4th ed. (Buenos Aires: Moen, 1911), XXIII–XXIV.
12. Juan Agustín García, *La ciudad indiana*, 2d ed. (Buenos Aires: Estrada, 1909 [1900]), 365.
13. Bartolomé Mitre, *Historia de San Martín y de la emancipación sudamericana* (Buenos Aires: Anaconda, 1950), 53.
14. This incongruous element in the *forma mentis* (the form of a lie) of the Argentine left is admirably reflected in the 1936 letter to the minister of public education in which Aníbal Ponce, by then the most eminent Communist intellectual, protested his dismissal from his teaching positions. In it he proclaimed his pride in the roots "in the liberal traditions of *his* native land" that he owed to his "ancestors, education and culture," and in his being victimized by the same "reactionary classes" that

once engineered the dismissal of Sarmiento. At this point he couldn't find words that would do full justice to his indignation, and concluded with an admiration mark: "Sarmiento, Mr. Minister!" to him, with this misdeed the reactionaries had crossed the line between politically outrageous behavior and outright sacrilege. See "Carta abierta al ministro Jorge de la Torre," in Oscar Terán, ed., *Aníbal Ponce: el marxismo sin nación?* (Mexico City: Ediciones Pasado y Presente, 1983), 234.

15. These shifts were reflected in the publications of the two party specialists on the subject. Ernesto Giudici published in 1938 *Hitler conquista América*, (Buenos Aires: Acento, 1938), and in 1940 *Imperialismo inglés y liberación nacional* (Buenos Aires: Problemas, 1940); Luis V. Sommi published, also in 1940, *El monopolio inglés del transporte en la Argentina* (Buenos Aires: Problemas, 1940), and in 1945 *Los capitales alemanes en la Argentina. Historia de su expansión* (Buenos Aires: Claridad, 1945); in 1949 he would add to these an equally timely exposé of *Los capitales yanquis en la Argentina* (Buenos Aires: Monteagudo, 1949).

16. "La política de cambios, salarios y crédito instrumenta el coloniaje argentino," in Raúl Scalabrini Ortiz, *Yrigoyen y Perón* (Buenos Aires: Plus Ultra, 1972), 43–70 (the quote from 47).

17. Arturo Jauretche, *El medio pelo en la sociedad argentina: apuntes para una sociología nacional*, 1st ed. (Buenos Aires: Peña Lillo, 1966), 10th ed. (Buenos Aires: Peña Lillo, 1970); *Manual de zonceras argentinas* (Buenos Aires: Peña Lillo, 1968).

18. José María Rosa, *Historia argentina*, vol. 1 (Buenos Aires: Granda, 1964); vol. 17 (1993).

19. Luis Alberto Romero, *Breve historia contemporánea de Argentina* (Buenos Aires: Fondo de Cultura Económica, 1994).

CHAPTER TEN

1. Joyce Appleby, "A Different Kind of Independence: The Postwar Restructuring of the Historical Study of Early America," *The William and Mary Quarterly* 50, no. 2 (April 1993), 245–267. This consensus view of the American past changed considerably in the 1960s as Appleby points out. See also, Jack P. Greene, "Interpretive Frameworks: The Quest for Intellectual Order in Early American History," *The William and Mary Quarterly* 48, no. 4 (1991): 515–30.

2. Viana Moog, *Bandeirantes and Pioneers* (New York: Brazilier, 1964).

3. A discussion of the "feudal" versus "capitalist" interpretation within Brazilian historiography is provided by Jacob Gorender, O *escravismo colonial* (São Paulo: Attica, 1978), 15–22.

4. Maximiliano Martim Vicente, "O sentido do colonialismo," in *História e ideal: Ensaios sobre Caio Prado Júnior*, ed. Maria Angela D'Incao (São

Paulo, n.p., 1989), 87–95.

5. I have used the translation by Suzette Macedo from Caio Prado Jr., *Colonial Background of Modern Brazil* (Berkeley and Los Angeles: University of California Press, 1967). The original edition is Caio Prado Júnior, *Formação do Brasil contemporâneo: Colônia* (São Paulo: Livraria Martins, 1942).

6. Ibid., 355; see also *The Colonial Background of Modern Brazil*, 414. Compare Caio Prado Júnior's statement to the similar one of Stanley Stein and Barbara Stein. "The pre-eminent social legacy of colonialism was the degradation of the labor force, Indian and negro, everywhere in Latin America." *The Colonial Heritage of Latin America* (New York: Oxford University Press, 1970), 117.

7. Frédéric Mauro, *Portugal et l'Atlantique* (Paris: SEVPEN, 1960).

8. I mention here only a few of the key books in this tradition which continues today. An earlier study in this tradition was Sergio Bagú, *La economia de la sociedad colonial* (Buenos Aires: El Ateneo, 1949). For more recent studies see for example, Marcello Carmagnani, *L'America latina dal' 500 a oggi: Nascita, espansione e crisi di un sistema feudale* (Milan: Feltrinelli, 1975); Ruggerio Romano, *Consideraciones: Siete Estudios de Historia* (Lima: Instituto Italiano de Cultura, 1992); Heraclio Bonilla, ed., *El sistema colonial en América Española* (Barcelona: Crítica, 1991).

9. I have left aside here the influence of this paradigm on the development of Immanuel Wallerstein's *The Modern World System* (New York: Academic Press, 1974) and the subsequent debates and critiques on that formulation which are admirably covered in Steve J. Stern, "Feudalism, Capitalism, and the World System in the Perspective of Latin America and the Caribbean," *American Historical Review* 93, no. 4 (October 1988): 829–2. Stern's essay appears reprinted with other important theoretical discussions in *Confronting Historical Paradigms. Peasants, Labor, and the Capitalist World System in Africa and Latin America*, ed. Frederick Cooper, Allen F. Isaacman, et al. (Madison: University of Wisconsin Press, 1993), 23–83.

10. Fernando A. Novais, *Portugal e Brasil na crise do Antigo sistema colonial, 1777–1808* (São Paulo: Hucitec, 1979). See also Richard Graham, *Brazil and the World System* (Austin: University of Texas Press, 1991) which includes a translation of Novais's central chapter as well as an excellent introduction by the editor. For other studies in the same tradition, see, Francisco Falcon, *A época pombalina* (São Paulo: Atica, 1982); José Ribeiro Júnior, *Colonização e monopólio no nordeste brasileiro* (São Paulo: Hucitec, 1976); Virgilio Noya Pinto, *O ouro brasileiro e o comércio anglo-português* (São Paulo: Companhia Editora Nacional, 1979). A general overview and analysis is provided in José Roberto Amaral Lapa, *O Antigo sistema colonial* (São Paulo: Brasiliense, 1982).

11. Carl A. Hanson, "The European 'Renovation' and the Luso-Atlantic Economy, 1560–1715," *Review*, 4, no. 4 (spring 1983): 475–530.
12. This is a paraphrase of Ranajit Guha's formulation. See Frederick Cooper, "Conflict and Connection: Rethinking Colonial African History," *American Historical Review* 99, no. 5 (December 1994): 1516–45.
13. The general debate is nicely summarized by Stern, "Feudalism, Capitalism, and the World System," 23–84. The Brazilian debates are discussed in José Roberto do Amaral Lapa, *O antigo sistema colonial* (São Paulo: Brasiliense, 1982). Important contributions to the debate from Ciro Cardoso and Antônio Barros de Castro appear in José Roberto do Amaral Lapa, ed., *Modos de produção e realidade brasileira* (Petrópolis: Vozes, 1980).
14. This development is discussed with many examples in William B. Taylor, "Between Global Process and Local Knowledge: An Inquiry into Early Latin American Social History, 1500–1900," in *Reliving the Past*, ed. Oliver Zunz (Chapel Hill: University of North Carolina Press, 1985), 115–189.
15. For example, A. J. R. Russell-Wood, *Fidalgos and Philanthropists: A Santa Casa da Misericórdia da Bahia, 1550–1755* (Berkeley and Los Angeles: University of California Press, 1968); David Grant Smith, "The Mercantile Class of Portugal and Brazil in the Seventeenth Century: A Socio-Economic Study of the Merchants of Lisbon and Bahia, 1620–1690." (Ph.D. diss., University of Texas, 1975); Anita Novinsky, *Cristãos novos na Bahia* (São Paulo: Perspectiva, 1972); Katia de Queirós Mattoso, "Os escravos na Bahia no alvorecer do século xix (Estudo de um grupo social)," *Revista de História* 97 (1974): 109–35.
16. I think my own *Sugar Plantations in the Formation of Brazilian Society: Bahia, 1550–1835* (Cambridge: Cambridge University Press, 1985) falls into this category.
17. Bernard Bailyn, "The Challenge of Modern Historiography," *American Historical Review* 87, no. 1 (February 1982): 1–24.
18. See Kenneth R. Maxwell, "The Atlantic in the Eighteenth Century: A Southern Perspective on the Need to Return to the 'Big Picture,'" *Transactions of the Royal Historical Society*, 6th series, III (London: n.p., 1993): 209–36. The lament for lost cohesion is also to be seen in colonial North American history. See Jack P. Greene, "Interpretive Frameworks: The Quest for Intellectual Order in Early American History," *The William and Mary Quarterly* 48, no. 4 (October 1991): 515–30.
19. I have presented an overview of some recent scholarship in "Somebodies and Nobodies in the Body Politic: Mentalities and Social Structures in Colonial Brazil," *Latin American Research Review* 31, no. 1 (1996): 113–34. Readers should also be aware of the healthy growth of

works dealing with the Indigenous peoples of Brazil in the colonial era. Notable are Hèléne Clastres, *The Land without Evil: Tupí-Guaraní Prophetism*, trans. Jacqueline Grenez Brovender (Urbana: University of Illinois Press, 1995); Nádia Farage, *As muralhas dos sertões: os povos indígenas no rio Branco e a colonização* (Rio de Janeiro: Paz e Terra, 1991); John Manuel Monteiro, *Negros da terra: Indios e bandeirantes nas origens de São Paulo* (São Paulo: Companhia das Letras, 1994); and the collective volume edited by Manuela Carneiro da Cunha, *História dos Indios do Brasil* (São Paulo: Companhia das Letras, 1992).

20. Cited by Arno Wehling and Mariz José C. de Wehling, *Formação do Brasil Colonial* (Rio de Janeiro: Nova Fronteira, 1994), 299.

21. Charles R. Boxer, *Salvador de Sá and the Struggle for Brazil and Angola: 1602–1686* (London: Athlone, 1952); *The Dutch in Brazil, 1624–1654* (Oxford: Clarendon Press, 1957); *The Golden Age of Brazil, 1695–1750* (Berkeley and Los Angeles: University of California Press, 1962).

22. Dauril Alden, *Royal Government in Colonial Brazil* (Berkeley and Los Angeles: University of California Press, 1968); Stuart B. Schwartz, *Sovereignty and Society in Colonial Brazil* (Berkeley and Los Angeles: University of California Press, 1973); Kenneth R. Maxwell, *Conflicts and Conspiracies* (Cambridge: Cambridge University Press, 1973). See also Heloisa Liberalli Belloto, *Autoridade e conflito no Brasil colonial: o governo do morgado de Mateus em São Paulo* (1765–1775) (São Paulo: Conselho Estadual de Artes e Ciências, 1979).

23. I have discussed this more fully in *Sugar Plantations*, 258–63. The institutional framework of the colonial state which was a matter of considerable interest in the 1930s and 1940s still needs attention. An important example of the uses of a broad imperial perspective is António Vasconcelos de Saldanha, *As capitanias: O regime senhorial na expansão ultramarina portuguesa* (Funchal: Centro de Estudos de História do Atlantico, 1992).

24. See for example, Valentim Alexandre, *Os sentidos do império. Questão nacional e questão colonial na crise do Antigo Regime Português* (Lisbon: Arontamento, 1992).

25. Muriel Nazzari, *The Disappearance of the Dowry* (Stanford: Stanford University Press, 1991); A.J.R. Russell-Wood, "Local Government in Portuguese America. A Study in Cultural Divergence," *Comparative Studies in Society and History* 16 (1974): 187–231.

26. João Capistrano de Abreu, *Chapters of Brazil's Colonial History*, ed. Fernando Novais and Stuart B. Schwartz (New York: Oxford University Press, 1997); José Honório Rodrigues, "Capistrano de Abreu e a historiografia brasileira," *Revista do Instituto Histórico e Geográfico Brasileiro* 221 (1953): 120–38; translated as "Capistrano de Abreu and Brazilian Historiography," in E. Bradford Burns, ed., *Perspectives on Brazilian Historiography* (New York: Columbia University Press, 1967), 156–80.

27. Richard Graham, "An Interview with Sérgio Buarque de Holanda, *HAHR* 62, no. 1 (February 1982): 3–17. See also the various apprecia- tions of his work in *Revista do Brasil* 3, no. 6 (1987), "Numero especial dedicado a Sérgio Buarque de Holanda." Sérgio Buarque de Holanda, *Caminhos e fronteiras* (Rio de Janeiro: José Olympio, 1957), deals with the opening of the interior and the techniques of rural life. It shares much in common with João Capistrano de Abreu, *Caminhos antigos e povoamento do Brasil*, 2d ed. (Rio de Janeiro: Briguiet, 1960).

28. Sérgio Buarque de Holanda, *Visão do paraíso: Os motivos edenicos no descobrimento e colonização do Brasil* (Rio de Janeiro: José Olympio, 1959).

29. An early exception was Herbert Klein, "Nineteenth-Century Brazil," in David Cohen and Jack P. Greene, *Neither Slave nor Free* (Baltimore: Johns Hopkins University Press, 1973), 309–34.

30. A discussion of the development of peasant studies in Brazil is found in Ciro Flamarion S. Cardoso, *Escravo o camponês? O protocampesinato negro nas Américas* (São Paulo: Brasiliense, 1987). He notes important early works on the topic were Maria Yedda Linhares and Francisco Carlos Teixeira da Silva, *História da agricultura brasileira* (São Paulo: Brasiliense, 1981); and Stuart B. Schwartz, "Elite politics and the Growth of a peasantry in late colonial Brazil," in *From Colony to Nation*, ed. A. J. R. Russell-Wood (Baltimore: Johns Hopkins University Press, 1975), 133–55; "Perspectives of Brazilian Peasantry: A Review Essay," *Peasant Studies* 5, no. 4 (1976): 11–19.

31. Oliveira Viana, *As populações meridionais do Brasil* (1922) 4th ed., 2 vols. (Rio de Janeiro: Companhia Editora Nacional, 1938).

32. Bailey W. Diffie, *Latin American Civilization: Colonial Period* (New York: Octagon Books, 1967).

33. Amilcar Martins Filho and Roberto B. Martins, "Slavery in a Non-Export Economy: Minas Gerais Revisited," *HAHR* 63, no. 3 (1983): 537–68. Roberto B. Martins, "Growing in Silence: The Slave Economy of Nineteenth-Century Minas Gerais, Brazil," (Ph.D. thesis, Vanderbilt University, 1980); Robert W. Slenes, "Os múltiplos de porcos e dia- mantes: A Economia escravista de Minas Gerais no século xix," *Cadernos (Campinas)* 17 (1985). See the summary of this literature in Clotilde Andrade Paiva and Douglas Libby, "The Middle Path: Alternative Patterns of Slave Demographics in Nineteenth-Century Minas Gerais," *El poblamiento de las Americas*, 3 vols. (Vera Cruz: n.p., 1992), I: 185–232.

34. João Luís Ribeiro Fragoso, *Homens de grossa aventura: acumulação e hier- arquia na praça mercantil do Rio de Janeiro* (1790–1830) (Rio de Janeiro: Arquivo Nacional, 1992); João Fragoso and Manolo Florentino, *O arcaísmo como projeto. mercado Atlântico, sociedade agrária e elite mer- cantil no Rio de Janeiro, c. 1790–1840* (Rio de Janeiro: Diadorim Editora, 1993).

35. One of the first scholars to point out the growing interest in the internal market and the theoretical implications of its existence was José Roberto de Amaral Lapa, "O mercado interno colonial," in *O antigo sistema colonial* (São Paulo: Brasiliense, 1982), 38–65.

36. The pioneering work of Mafalda Zamella, "O abstiecimento da capitania das Minas Gerais século xviii" (Ph.D. diss., University of São Paulo, 1951) remained overlooked for many years. Significantly, it was republished only in 1992. The current interest was sparked by Alcir Lenharo, *As tropas da moderação* (São Paulo: Simbolo, 1979).

37. Laura de Mello e Souza, *Os desclassificados do ouro; A pobreza mineira no século xviii* (Rio de Janeiro: Gral, 1983); Elizabeth Kuznesof, *Household Economy and Urban Development: São Paulo 1765 to 1836* (Boulder: Westview Press, 1986).

38. Jacob Gorender, *O escravismo colonial*, 3d ed. (São Paulo: Atica, 1980); *A escravidão reabilitada* (São Paulo: Atica, 1990); Ciro Flamarion S. Cardoso, *Agricultura, escravidão, e capitalismo* (Petrópolis: Vozes, 1979). I have discussed some of these issues in Stuart B. Schwartz, *Slaves, Peasants, and Rebels: Reconsidering Brazilian Slavery* (Urbana: University of Illinois Press, 1992).

39. A good review of the debate is presented with new data in B. J. Barickman, "A Bit of Land which They Call *roça*: Slave Provision Grounds in the Bahian Recôncavo, 1780–1860," *HAHR* 74, no. 4 (1994): 649–87.

40. Luiz R. B. Mott, *Piauí colonial* (Teresina: Projeto Petrônio Portella, 1985); Schwartz, *Slaves, Peasants, and Rebels*, 95–102; Guillermo Palacios, "Campesinato e escravidão no Brasil," (Ph.D. diss., Princeton University, 1994).

41. Iraci del Nero da Costa, *Arraia-miúda: Um estudo sobre os não-proprietários de escravos no Brasil* (São Paulo: MGSP Editores, 1992).

42. See as a recent example of that literature, Stephanie McCurry, *Masters of Small Worlds: Yeoman Housholds, Gender relations and the Political Culture of the Antebellum South Carolina Low Country* (New York: Oxford University Press, 1995). See also Stephen Hahn, *The Roots of Southern Populism: Yeoman farmers and the Transformation of the Georgia Upcountry, 1850–1890* (New York: Oxford University Press, 1983).

43. The classic source on Pernambuco is Louis-François Tollenare, *Notes dominicales. Prises pendant un voyage en Portugal et au Bresil*, 3 vols., ed. Leon Bourdon (Paris: Presses universitaires de France, 1971),44. Alice Canabrava, "A repartição das terras na Capitania de São Paulo, 1818," *Estudos Económicos* 2, no. 6 (1972): 77–129.

45. Canabrava's study produced Gini coefficients varying by locale from .69 to .90 and for the captaincy as a whole .82. See Stuart B. Schwartz, "Patterns of Slaveholding in the Americas: New Evidence from Brazil," *American Historical Review* 87, no. 1 (February 1987): 55–86.

46. Jacob Gorender, *O escravismo colonial* (São Paulo: Atica, 1978), 292–99; Maria Thereza Schorer Petrone, *A lavoura canavieira em São Paulo: Expansão e declínio (1765–1851)* (São Paulo: Difel, 1968).
47. Emilio Willems, "Social Differentiation in Colonial Brazil," *Comparative Studies in Society and History* 12, no. 1 (1970): 31–49.
48. Ibid., 44.
49. The indices for slaveholding are elevated by the fact that Willems excluded tradesmen, artisans, and other non-agricultural slave owners. Since these people were most likely small holders, the effect of their exclusion is to raise the coefficient of concentration.
50. Fernando Coronil, "Listening to the Subaltern: The Poetics of Neocolonial States," *Poetics Today* 15 (1994).
51. Much of the new work is represented in Fernando Novais and Laura de Mello e Souza, eds., *Historia da vida privada no Brasil*, 2 vols. (São Paulo: Companhia das Letras, 1997).
52. See for example, Maria Beatriz Nizza da Silva, *Vida privada e quotidiano no Brasil* (Lisbon: Estampa, 1993); and Fernando A. Novais, ed., *Historia da vida privadano Brasil* (São Paulo: Companhia das Letras, 1997).
53. João Adolfo Hansen, *A sátira e o engenho: Gregório de Matos e a Bahia do século xvii* (São Paulo: Companhia das Letras, 1989); Alredo Bosi, *Dialética da colonização* (São Paulo: Companhia das Letras, 1992).
54. Evaldo Cabral de Mello, *Olinda restaurada, Guerra e açúcar no nordeste, 1630–54* (Rio de Janeiro: Forense Universitária, 1975); *O nome e o sangue: Uma fraude genealógica no Pernmabuco colonial* (São Paulo: Companhia das Letras, 1989); *A fronda dos mazombos* (São Paulo: Companhia das Letras, 1996). The contributions of Gonçalves de Mello are exemplified by *Tempo dos flamengos: Influência da ocupação holandesa na vida e na cultura do norte do Brasil*, 3d ed. (Recife: Massangana, 1987); *Gente da nação. Cristãos novos e judeus em Pernambuco, 1542–1645* (Recife: Massangana, 1989).
55. Laura de Mello e Souza, *O diabo na terra da santa Cruz* (São Paulo: Companhia das Letras, 1986); *Inferno atlântico: demonologia e colonização séculos xvi–xviii* (São Paulo: Companhia das Letras, 1993).
56. Luiz Mott, *Rosa Egipcíaca. Uma santa africana no Brasil* (Rio de Janeiro: Editora Bertrand, 1993).
57. Luiz Mott, *O sexo prohibido: Virgens, gays e escravos nas garras da Inquisição* (Campinas: Papirus, 1988); *Escravidão, homosexualidade, e demonologia* (São Paulo: Icone, 1988); Ronaldo Vainfas, *Trópico dos pecados. Moral, sexualidade e Inquisição no Brasil* (Rio de Janeiro: Campus, 1989).
58. Alida Metcalf, *Family and Frontier in Colonial Brazil* (Berkeley and Los Angeles: University of California Press, 1992); Leila Mezan Algranti, *Honradas e devotas: Mulheres da Colonia* (Rio de Janeiro: Jose Olympio, 1993). See Susan Soeiro, "A Baroque Nunnery: The Economic and Social Role of a Colonial Convent: Santa Clara do Desterro, Bahia, 1677–1800,"

(Ph.D. diss., New York University, 1974).

59. Mary del Priore, *Ao sul do corpo: Condição feminina,maternidades e mentalidades no Brasil colônia* (Rio de Janeiro: José Olympio, 1993); Jean Delumeau, *Le peur en Occident* (Paris, 1978), 398–449.

60. Giovanni Levi, *Inheriting Power: The Story of an Exorcist* trans., Lynda G. Cochrane (Chicago: University of Chicago Press, 1988), 175. In the case of France a similar argument is made by Robert Muchembled, *Popular Culture and Elite Culture in France, 1400–1750* trans., Lydia Cochrane (Baton Rouge: Louisiana State University Press, 1985), 312–20.

61. Michel Vovelle has directly addressed the possible relationship between materialist approaches and the history of mentalities. See "Ideologies and Mentalities—a Necessary Clarification," *Ideologies and Mentalities* (Chicago: University of Chicago Press, 1990), 1–13.

CHAPTER ELEVEN

1. For an early appreciation and critique, see Stanley J. Stein and Shane J. Hunt, "Principal Currents in the Economic Historiography of Latin America," *Journal of Economic History* 31 (March 1971): 222–53.

2. The school thus rejected the doctrine of comparative advantage, first advanced by David Ricardo in 1817, and later elaborated and extended by J. S. Mill, Alfred Marshall, Bertil Ohlin and Eli Hecksher, and Paul Samuelson. Ricardo had demonstrated that, given two countries and two goods, it was to the advantage of both countries to specialize in the production of one good and trade for the other, even if one country produced *both* goods more efficiently (i.e., at lower cost) than the other.

3. Furtado sees this effort as one of his major contributions to structuralism. Furtado to author, Paris, 22 December 1982.

4. Furtado, "L'économie coloniale brésilienne (XVIe et XVIIe siècles): Eléments d'histoire économique appliqués" (Ph.D. diss., Faculté de Droit, Université de Paris, 1948); *A economia brasileira (Contribução á análise do seu desenvolvimento)* (Rio de Janeiro: A Noite, 1954); *Uma economia dependente* (Rio de Janeiro: Ministério de Educação e Cultura, 1956).

5. Celso Furtado, "Características gerais da economia brasileira," *Revista Brasileira de Economia*, 4, no. 1 (March 1950): 11.

6. Celso Furtado, *A fantasia organizada* (Rio de Janeiro: Paz e Terra, 1985), 18, 27.

7. Ibid., 15.

8. Furtado, "Économie."

9. Raúl Prebisch, *Introducción a Keynes* (Mexico City: Fondo de Cultura Económica, 1947).

10. Furtado, "Características gerais da economia brasileira," 1–37.

11. A construct to measure the effect of a given change in investment on

income over successive periods.

12. Celso Furtado, *Formação econômica do Brasil* (Rio de Janeiro: Fundo de Cultura, 1959); Aníbal Pinto Santa Cruz, *Chile, un caso de desarrollo frustrado* (Santiago: Ed. del Pacífico, 1959); Aldo Ferrer, *La economía argentina: Las etapas de su desarrollo y problemas actuales* (Mexico City: Fondo de Cultura Económica, 1963). Translated by Marjorie Urquidi as *The Argentine Economy* (Berkeley and Los Angeles: University of California Press, 1967); Osvaldo Sunkel and Pedro Paz, *El subdesarrollo latinoamericano y la teoría del desarrollo* (Madrid: Siglo Veintiuno de España, 1970). Subsequently a more specialized structuralist work appeared on Mexico: René Villareal *El desequilibrio externo en la industrialización de México (1929–75): Un enfoque estructuralista* (Mexico City: Fondo de Cultura Económica, 1976). Villareal argues, however, that structuralism accounts more adequately for Mexico's external disequilibrium in the period 1939–58 than in 1959–70.

13. Furtado, *Formação econômica do Brasil* (1959), published in English as *The Economic Growth of Brazil* (Berkeley and Los Angeles: University of California Press, 1963). The English title is slightly misleading, since formação indicates qualitative aspects of development as well as quantitative growth.

14. Furtado, "Économie"; *A economia brasileira; Uma economia dependente.*

15. Pinto, *Chile.*

16. Werner Baer, "Furtado Revisted," *Luso-Brazilian Review* 2:1 (Summer 1974): 115.

17. João Lúcio de Azevedo, *Epocas de Portugal econômico: Esboços de história,* 2d ed. (Lisboa: Livraria Clássica, 1947 [1929]); Roberto Simonsen, *História econômica do Brasil (1500/1820)* (São Paulo: Editora Nacional, 1937); and J[ohn] F. Normano, *Brazil: A Study of Economic Types* (Chapel Hill: University of North Carolina Press, 1935).

18. Furtado, *Economic Growth,* 69–71; Ricardo Bielschowsky, "Brazilian Economic Thought in the Ideological Cycle of Developmentalism" (Ph.D. diss., Leicester University, 1985), 243.

19. On "involution" see Furtado, *Economic Growth,* 71.

20. Furtado, *Economic Growth,* 174–77.

21. See Adam Smith's celebrated observation that the extent of the division of labor depends on the size of the market.

22. Furtado, *Economic Growth,* 107–8.

23. Bielschowsky, "Brazilian Economic Thought," 241.

24. Furtado, Economic Growth, 167.

25. Baer, "Furtado Revisted," 119.

26. Furtado, *Economic Growth,* 205–6.

27. Ibid., 211.

28. Ibid., 218–19.

29. Bielschowsky, "Brazilian Economic Thought," 191.

30. For a summary of Furtado's arguments and the subsequent debate in Brazil, see Wilson Suzigan, *Indústria brasileira: Origem e Desenvolvimento* (São Paulo: Brasiliense, 1986), 21–73, ch. 7.

31. For case studies of Latin American countries, including Brazil, see essays in Rosemary Thorp, ed., *Latin America in the 1930s: The Role of the Periphery in World Crisis* (London: Macmillan, 1984). For the best overview of the Depression across Latin America, see Victor Bulmer Thomas, *The Economic History of Latin America since Independence* (Cambridge: Cambridge University Press, 1994), ch. 7. Bulmer Thomas concurs with previous revisionists and finds that import-substitution industrialization was significantly dependent on export recovery, except in Argentina (222–24).

32. On the positive association of trade and growth, see Ross Levine and David Renelt, "A Sensitivity Analysis of Cross-Country Growth Regressions," *American Economic Review* 82, no. 4 (September 1992): 942–63, examining data for 119 countries; and Hadi Salehi Esfahani, "Exports, Imports and Economic Growth in Semi-Industrialized Countries," *Journal of Development Economics* 35 (1991): 93–116, considering data for thirty-one semi-industrialized countries. Esfahani emphasizes that the correlation between export and GDP performance has mainly to do with exports foreign exchange earnings; they mitigate import "shortages," which restrict the growth of output in these countries.

33. During World War II, Brazil's growth was perhaps less hampered because of the existence of a small capital goods sector.

34. Hans W. Singer, "The Distribution of Gains Between Investing and Borrowing Countries," *American Economic Review: Papers and Proceedings*, 40, no. 2 (1950): 473–85.

35. By my definition, internal colonialism is a process of unequal exchange, occurring within a given state, characteristic of industrial or industrializing economies, capitalist or socialist. As the economy becomes more differentiated with regard to region, factors and income flow from one or more geographically definable area to another, based primarily on price mechanisms, and secondarily (or not at all) on fiscal transfers; the state may nonetheless play a decisive role in setting price ratios, and differential regional effects of foreign trade are relevant. At the minimum, the process involves a structural relationship between leading and lagging regions (or city and hinterland) of a territorial state, based on monopolized or oligopolized markets, in which growth is progressively "inequalizing" between populations of these constituent geographic elements, rather than "equalizing." Internal colonialism is distinct from colonialism per se, in which an alien state enforces monopsony in labor markets, or even prescribes wage levels and labor drafts, such as the *repartimiento* of the Spanish American empire or the corvée of French colonial Africa. The definition by itself does not, of course, establish that

the phenomenon exists.

36. See Hans W. Singer, "Trade and Fiscal Problems of the Brazilian Northeast," in *International Development: Growth and Change* (New York: McGraw-Hill, 1964). For Furtado's work, see Conselho de Desenvolvimento: Grupo de Trabalho para o Desenvolvimento do Nordeste, *Uma política de desenvolvimento econômico para o Nordeste* (Rio de Janeiro: Conselho de Desenvolvimento, 1959). That Furtado was the principal author of this statement is indicated in Furtado, *A operação nordeste* (Rio de Janeiro: ISEB, 1959), 35.

37. Singer, "Distribution of Gains."

38. Conselho de Desenvolvimento, 7, 14.

39. Ibid., 7.

40. Ibid., 22.

41. A related policy, the *confisco cambial*, also adversely affected the Northeast: the government "confiscated" a share of the earnings of traditional exporters (sugar and cocoa planters in the Northeast, coffee and cotton growers in the South) by maintaining an overvalued exchange rate—in effect, collecting a tax. This was a way of getting around the federal constitution, which prohibited the central government from levying any tax on exports. Furtado, *Operação*, 49.

42. For the estimation procedures, see Joseph L. Love, *Crafting the Third World: Theorizing Underdevelopment in Rumania and Brazil* (Stanford: Stanford U. Press, 1996), 280.

43. Conselho de Desenvolvimento, 27–28.

44. Ibid., 49.

45. Ibid., 59; Furtado, *Operação*, 37. In 1957, Furtado noted, the absolute cost of food in Recife was a quarter more than that of São Paulo, and much of the food was imported from the South (Conselho de Desenvolvimento, 60).

46. Baer, *The Brazilian Economy*, 4th ed. (New York: Praeger, 1995), ch. 12.

47. See Furtado, *Operação*, 13.

48. Furtado, *Desenvolvimento*, 180.

49. Furtado, "Elements of a Theory of Underdevelopment," in *Development and Underdevelopment* (Berkeley Calif.: University of California Press, 1964 [Port. org. 1958]), 129.

50. Furtado, *Desenvolvimento*, 122.

51. E.g., Bairoch estimates that per capita incomes in the presently developed world and the Third World in 1750 were roughly equal. By 1970 that of the Third World was only one-seventh that of the First World. Paul Bairoch, "The Main Trends in National Economic Disparities since the Industrial Revolution," in *Disparities in Development since the Industrial Revolution*, ed. Bairoch and Maurice Lévy-Leboyer (New York: St. Martin's Press, 1981), 7.

52. Furtado, *Desenvolvimento*, 192; "External Disequilibrium" (1964), 142

(quotation); Baer, "Furtado on Development: A Review Essay," *Journal of Developing Areas* (1969): 272.

53. Furtado, "Capital Formation and Economic Development." *International Economic Papers* 4 (1954 [Port. orig., 1952]), 132–33; and Furtado, "External Disequilibrium" (1958), 406.

54. I accept Fernando Henrique Cardoso's objection to the term *dependency theory* because the perspective was a partial one and not a theory in the sense of a theory of capitalist development. I therefore use the term *dependency analysis.* Cardoso, "Teoria da dependência ou análises concretas de situações de dependência." CEBRAP, *Estudos* 1 (1971): 32.

55. The essential elements of dependency analysis are a characterization of modern capitalism as a center-periphery relationship between the developed, industrial West and the underdeveloped, technologically backward Third World; the adoption of a system-wide historical approach, and the consequent rejection of Boekean dualism and Parsonian modernization theory; the hypothesis of unequal exchange, as well as asymmetrical power relations between center and periphery; and the assertion of the relative or absolute nonviability of a capitalist path to development, based on the leadership of the national bourgeoisies of the Latin American nations. E.g., see Thomas Angotti, "The Political Implications of Dependency Theory," in *Dependency and Marxism: Toward a Resolution of the Debate*, ed. Ronald H. Chilcote (Boulder: Westview, 1982), 126–27.

56. Furtado, *Diagnosis of the Brazilian Crisis* (Berkeley and Los Angeles: University of California Press, 1965 [Port. orig., 1964]), 3, 6, 13, 20.

57. See Furtado, *Desenvolvimento*, ch. 4.

58. Ibid., 48-51, 61-62. See 32, for the specific term counterattack; it occurs again in *Subdesenvolvimento e estagnação na América Latina* (Rio de Janeiro: Civilização Brasileira, 1966), 7.

59. For Furtado's first statement of this position, see *Underdevelopment and Dependence: The Fundamental Connections* (Cambridge: Cambridge University Center of Latin American Studies, November 1973 [offset]).

60. See Furtado's retrospective, "Underdevelopment: To Conform or Reform," in *Pioneers in Development*, 2d series, ed. Gerald M. Meier (New York: Oxford University Press [for the World Bank] 1987), 210-11. He believed that technological dependence, resulting from elite consumption patterns, was ultimately an aspect of cultural dependence. Furtado, *Os ares do mundo* (Rio de Janeiro: Paz e Terra, 1991), 35.

61. Furtado, "Underdevelopment" (1987), 211.

62. Furtado, *Underdevelopment* (1973), 5-6. The evolution of Furtado's thought on these matters was similar to Prebisch's between *Towards a Dynamic Development Policy for Latin America* (New York: United Nations, 1963) and *Capitalismo periférico: crisis y transformación* (Mexico City: Fondo de Cultura Económica, 1981). On Prebisch's changing views, see Joseph L. Love, "Economic Ideas and Ideologies in

Latin America since 1930," in *Cambridge History of Latin America*, vol. 6, part 1, ed. Leslie Bethell (Cambridge: Cambridge University Press, 1994), 455-57.

63. Joseph L. Love, "Las fuentes del estructuralismo latinoamericano," *Desarrollo Económico* 36, 141 (May 1996): 391-402.

64. Love, *Crafting*, 159.

65. See Perroux's apologetic defense of corporatism in "The Domination Effect and Modern Economic Theory," *Social Research* 17, no. 2 (June 1950): 198.

66. Perroux, "Esquisse d'une théorie de l'économie dominante," *Économie Appliquée* 2, no. 3 (April-September, 1948): 243-300.

67. E.g., see note 5 above. Furtado may also have been influenced by Ernst Wagemann, whose structuralist treatment of international business cycles Furtado had known in Brazil while working for Conjuntura Econômica in 1948. He met Wagemann the following year in Chile. Furtado, *Fantasia*, 47, 99-100.

68. Furtado, *Desenvolvimento*, 13, 15, 22.

69. Francisco de Oliveira, "Introdução" in Celso Furtado, *Economia* ed. by F. de Oliveira (São Paulo: Atica, 1983), 14.

70. This tendency is clearest in the orientation of the Instituto Superior de Estudos Brasileiros, a Brazilian think tank of which Furtado was a member.

71. E.g., see Celso Furtado, *Accumulation and Development: The Logic of Industrial Civilization*, trans. Suzette Macedo (Oxford: Martin Robertson, 1983 [Port. orig., 1978]).

72. As were the studies by Aníbal Pinto of Chile and Aldo Ferrer of Argentina.

CHAPTER TWELVE

1. These reflections originated in a review of the work of John J. Johnson and the responses of the academic community to his 1958 study of the middle classes for a panel at the December 1989 LASA meeting in Miami, Florida, organized by the Labor Studies Group under John French. "In the Middle of the Mess: Rereading John J. Johnson's *Political Change in Latin America* Thirty Years Later," served as the basis for "The Unmaking of the Middle Classes and the Challenge to Development Studies," a commentary for a workshop on the Development Initiatives Planning Meeting of the Social Science Research Council in November 1993. Arguments about the contours of middle-class politics and culture have fermented over several years of teaching graduates and undergraduates at Princeton University and the University of Pittsburgh. I am deeply grateful to students and colleagues in both institutions who have

helped me puzzle through these difficult questions: Jeremy Adelman, Miguel Centeno, and Stanley Stein at Princeton; and Bill Chase, Sandra Halperin, Madeline Hurd, and Marcus Rediker at Pittsburgh. Marc Chernick has been always an invaluable source of knowledge and inspiration as this project has advanced. Eric Herschberg proffered an invitation to the SSRC which led to a broadening of the scope of the original work. Professor Brian Owensby of the University of Virginia, a stalwart and bold explorer of these shadowy regions, has forced me to rethink many questions and set a high standard for scholarship with his own work on the Brazilian middle classes in the twentieth century. Not least, I am indebted to Michael Merrill, a patient, enthusiastic, and always iconoclastic interlocutor in matters of mind and heart.

2. Eric Hobsbawm, *The Age of Extremes. A History of the World, 1914-1991* (New York: Pantheon Books, 1994), part II.

3. See, for example, Katherine S. Newman, *Falling from Grace: The Experience of Downward Mobility in the American Middle Class* (New York: Free Press, 1988); Barbara Ehrenreich, *Fear of Falling: The Inner Life of the Middle Class* (New York: Pantheon Books, 1989); Kevin Phillips, *Boiling Point: Republicans, Democrats and the Decline of Middle-Class Prosperity* (New York: Random House, 1993); and Stanley B. Greenberg, *Middle-Class Dreams: The Politics and Power of the New American Majority* (New York: Times Books, 1995).

4. On the British experience, see Mike Savage, et al., *Property, Bureaucracy, and Culture: Middle-Class Formation in Contemporary Britain* (London: Routledge, 1992).

5. Pekka Sulkunen, *The European New Middle Class: Individuality and Tribalism in Mass Society* (Brookfield, Mass.: Aldershot Press, 1992); and Yasemen N. Soysal, *Limits of Citizenship: Migrants and Postnational Membership in Europe* (Chicago: University of Chicago Press, 1994).

6. Alex Inkeles, *Social Change in Soviet Russia* (Cambridge: Harvard University Press, 1968); and James Millar, *Politics, Work, and Daily Life in the USSR: A Survey of Former Soviet Citizens* (New York: Cambridge University Press, 1987).

7. Moshe Lewin, *The Gorbachev Phenomenon: A Historical Interpretation* (Berkeley and Los Angeles: University of California Press, 1988); and Miguel Angel Centeno and Tania Rands, "The World They Have Lost: An Assessment of Change in Eastern Europe," *Social Research* 63, no. 2 (summer 1996): 369-402.

8. In the case of Latin America, the contours and consequences of this restructuring is well documented in Nora Lustig, ed., *Coping with Austerity: Poverty and Inequality in Latin America* (Washington: Brookings Institution, 1995).

9. A. Minujn, "Squeezed: The Middle Class in Latin America," *Environment and Urbanization* 7, no. 2 (October 1995): 153-165. There

is a considerable literature of sociological concern and cultural lament about the decline of the middle classes in various Latin American countries. Mexican writers have been especially prolific on this question, as seen in Gabriel Carreaga, *Mitos y fantasias de la clase media en Mexico* (Mexico: Editorial J. Moritz, 1974); Francisco López Cámara, *Apogeo y extinción de la clase media mexicana* (Cuernavaca: UNAM, 1990); and Rami Schwartz and Salomón Bazbaz Lapidus, *El ocaso de la clase media* (Mexico: Grupo Editorial Planeta, 1994).

10. Michael Hsiao Hsin-Huang, ed., *Discovery of the Middle Classes in East Asia* (Taipei: Institute of Ethnology, 1993).

11. Francis Fukuyama, *The End of History and the Last Man* (New York: Free Press, 1992).

12. Roland Robertson, *Globalization: Social Theory and Global Culture* (Newbury Park, Cal: Sage, 1992).

13. A compelling exemplar of this literature is Samuel P. Huntington, *The Clash of Civilizations and the Remaking of the World Order* (New York: Simon & Schuster, 1996).

14. For a trenchant and highly suggestive account of the current transformations throughout the globe which focuses on the restructuring of the networks within which middle classes operated in the last half century, see Manuel Castells, *The Information Age: Economy, Society and Culture* 3 vols. (New York: Oxford University Press, 1997-98).

15. Much of the following section is drawn from Michael F. Jiménez, "In the Middle of the Mess: Rereading John J. Johnson's *Political Change in Latin America* Thirty Years Later" (paper presented at the LASA IV International Congress, Miami, Florida, December 1989).

16. A comprehensive and provocative study of the origins and emergence of Latin American Studies is Mark T. Berger, *Under Northern Eyes: Latin American Studies and U.S. Hegemony in the Americas, 1898-1990* (Bloomington: University of Indiana Press, 1995).

17. Exemplary in this regard was a collection of essays by historians, political scientists, and sociologists gathered by W. W. Pierson, "Pathology of Democracy in Latin America," *American Political Science Review* 41, no. 1 (March 1950): 100-49.

18. John J. Johnson, *Political Change in Latin America: The Emergence of the Middle Sectors* (Stanford: Stanford University Press, 1958).

19. A key to Johnson's culling of primary and secondary sources is his long research note and bibliographical essay, "Middle Groups in National Politics in Latin America," *Hispanic American Historical Review* 37 (1957): 313-29. Among other sources, he drew from a six volume study sponsored by the Pan American Union, Oficina de Ciencias Sociales, *Materiales para el estudio de la clase media en América Latina* (Washington, D.C.: Pan American Union, 1950-51). For a good overview of the origins and nature of ECLA's influence on the study of Latin

America, see Jorge Balan, "Social Sciences in the Periphery: Perspectives on the Latin American Case," in *Social Sciences and Public Policy in the Developing World*, ed. Laurence D. Stifel, Ralph K. Davidson, and James S. Coleman (Lexington, Mass.: Lexington Books, 1982), 211-47.

20. George I. Blanksten, "In Quest of the Middle Sectors," review in *World Politics* 11, no. 2 (January 1960): 323-27.

21. Johnson's harshest critic along these lines, political scientist Kalman Silvert, in *Annals* (May 1959): 193-94, had done early research on Guatemala which left him disinclined to accept Johnson's view of the middle classes in Mexico and the Southern Cone. Silvert's cultural dualism found full expression in works such as *The Conflict Society: Reaction and Revolution in Latin America* (New York: American Universities Field Staff, 1966). For a similar approach see John Gillin's remarks on the middle classes in "Some Signposts for Policy," in *Social Change in Latin America Today*, ed. Richard N. Adams (New York: Vintage Books, 1960).

22. Richard Morse, "The Heritage of Latin America," in *The Founding of New Societies*, ed. Louis Hartz (New York: Harcourt, Brace, and World, 1965); Claudio Veliz, *The Centralist Tradition in Latin America* (Princeton: Princeton University Press, 1980); and Howard Wiarda's collected essays in *Corporativism and National Development in Latin America* (Boulder: Westview Press, 1982). John Mander's *The Unrevolutionary Society: The Power of Latin American Conservatism in a Changing World* (New York: Alfred A. Knopf, 1969) illustrates the popularization of this view (notably see pages 258-62). The persistence of this view can be seen in Lawrence E. Harrison, *Underdevelopment as a State of Mind* (Lanham, Md.: University Press of America, 1985).

23. Seymour Martin Lipset and Aldo Solari, eds., *Elites in Latin America* (New York: Oxford University Press, 1967) proposed an "inclusive notion of the social elite . . . has to a considerable degree formed an alternative perspective to class analysis" (vii). For an indication of the predominance of institutional analyses in the 1960s, see the edited volume by Roberto Esquenazi-Mayo and Michael C. Meyer, *Latin American Scholarship Since World War II* (Lincoln: University of Nebraska Press, 1971). David M. Ricci, *The Tragedy of Political Science, Politics, Scholarship, and Democracy* (New Haven: Yale University Press, 1984), ch. 4, examines the elitist and managerial sensibility at the heart of American social sciences in those years.

24. Albert O. Hirschman, *Journeys Toward Progress: Studies of Economic Policymaking in Latin America* (New York: Twentieth Century Fund, 1963), 6. Charles W. Anderson, *Politics and Economic Change in Latin America. The Governing of Restless Nations* (Princeton: Princeton University Press, 1967). For the intellectual foundations of this project, see Robert A. Dahl and Charles E. Lindbloom, *Politics, Economics, and*

Welfare (New York: Harper, 1953). For a closer look at this connection, see Albert O. Hirschman and Charles E. Lindbloom, "Economic Development, Research and Policymaking, " in Hirschman, *A Bias for Hope* (New Haven: Yale University Press, 1971), 63-84.

25. For a trenchant review of the state of political science writing in the 1970s which had been so influenced by these structuralist-functionalist approaches, see Arturo Valenzuela, "Political Science and the Study of Latin America," in *Changing Perspectives in Latin American Studies: Insights from Six Disciplines*, ed. Christopher Mitchell (Stanford: Stanford University Press, 1988), 63-86.

26. For an example of the radical critique of developmentalism and Latin American Studies, see Suzanne J. Bodenhemier, *The Ideology of Developmentalism: The American Paradigm-Surrogate for Latin American Studies* (Beverly Hills, Cal.: Sage, 1971). The middle classes were targeted in James Petras, "The Middle Class in Latin America," in *Politics and Social Structure in Latin America* (New York: n.p., 1970), 37-53.

27. José Nun, *Latin America: The Hegemonic Crisis and the Military Coup* (Berkeley and Los Angeles: Monthly Review Press, Institute of International Studies, 1969).

28. Rodolfo Stavenhagen, "Seven Fallacies About Latin America," in *Latin America: Reform or Revolution?*, ed. Petras and Zeitlin (Greenwich, Conn.: Fawcett, 1968), 13-31.

29. For a review of dependismo and its principal writings, see J. Samuel Valenzuela and Arturo Valenzuela, "Modernization and Dependency: Alternative Perspectives in the Study of Latin American Underdevelopment," in *From Dependency to Development. Strategies to Overcome Underdevelopment and Inequality*, ed. Heraldo Muñoz (Boulder: Westview Press, 1982), 15-42.

30. Fernando Henrique Cardoso and Enzo Falleto, *Dependencia y Desarrollo en América Latina* (Buenos Aires: Siglo XXI, 1971). The English version is *Dependency and Development in Latin America*, trans. by Marjorie Mattingly Urquidí (Berkeley and Los Angeles: University of California Press, 1976).

31. The historical literature unleashed by the dependista framework is reviewed by Tulio Halperín Donghi, "The State of Latin American History," in *Changing Perspectives in Latin American Studies*, ed. Mitchell, 13-62.

32. Paul W. Drake, *Socialism and Populism in Chile, 1932-1952* (Urbana: University of Illinois Press, 1978) and Steve Stein, *Populism in Peru: The Emergence of the Masses and the Politics of Social Control* (Madison: University of Wisconsin Press, 1980).

33. Juan Linz and Alfred Stepan, eds., *The Breakdown of Democratic Regimes: Latin America* (Baltimore: Johns Hopkins University Press, 1978).

34. Guillermo O'Donnell, *Modernization and Bureaucratic-Authoritarianism: Studies in South American Politics* (Berkeley and Los Angeles: University of California Press, 1973), and a volume of essays edited by David Collier, ed., *The New Authoritarianism in Latin America* (Princeton: Princeton University Press, 1979).

35. This vast and still rapidly growing literature includes Guillermo O'Donnell, Phillippe C. Schmitter, and Laurence Whitehead, eds., *Transitions from Authoritarian Rule: Latin America* (Baltimore: Johns Hopkins University Press, 1986); James Malloy and Mitchell Seligson, eds., *Authoritarians and Democrats: Regime Transition in Latin America* (Pittsburgh: University of Pittsburgh Press, 1987); John Higley and Richard Gunther, eds., *Elites and Democratic Consolidations in Latin America and Southern Europe* (New York: Cambridge University Press, 1992); and Scott Mainwaring, Guillermo O'Donnell, and J. Samuel Valenzuela, eds., *Issues in Democratic Consolidation* (Notre Dame, Ind.: University of Notre Dame Press, 1992). For a broad review of the literature, see Doh Chull Shin, "On the Third Wave of Democratization: A Synthesis and Evaluation of Recent Theory and Research," *World Politics* 47 (October 1994): 135-70.

36. See, for example, Carol Graham, *Safety Nets, Politics, and the Poor: Transitions to Market Economies* (Washington, D.C.: Brookings Institution, 1994).

37. Illustrations of this approach can be seen in William Rowe and Vivian Schelling, *Memory and Modernity: Popular Culture in Latin America* (London: Verso, 1991); Sonia Alvarez and Arturo Escobar, eds., *The Making of Social Movements in Latin America: Identity, Strategy, and Democracy* (Boulder: Westview, 1992); and John Beverley, et al., *The Postmodern Debate in Latin America* (Durham, NC: Duke University Press, 1993).

38. A fine collection of essays from this perspective edited by George Yúdice, Jean Franco, and Juan Flores, *On Edge: The Crisis of Latin American Culture* (Minneapolis: University of Minnesota Press, 1992) reflect much of this literature's elision of the middle classes with their emphasis on peasants, workers, women, and social movements. One contribution in this volume, Kathleen Newman, "Cultural Redemocratization: Argentina, 1978–1989" (161–86) does make a notable feint in this direction.

39. Arturo Escobar, *Encountering Development: The Making and Unmaking of the Third World* (Princeton: Princeton University Press, 1995). For a thoughtful critique of this volume, see David Lehmann, "An Opportunity Lost: Escobar's Deconstruction of Development," *Journal of Development Studies* 33, no. 4 (April 1997): 568–78.

40. A model for this sort of inquiry is Dror Wahrman's *Imagining the Middle Class: The Political Representation of Class in Britain, c. 1780–1840* (Cambridge: Cambridge University Press, 1995). A good starting point

would be Leonard Binder, "The Natural History of Development," *Comparative Studies in Society and History* 28, no. 1 (January 1986): 3–33, which proposes to unmask modernization theory, within which the "middle-class paradigm" was so deeply embedded, as "essentially an academic, and pseudoscientific, transfer of the dominant and ideologically significant paradigm employed in research on the American political system" (3). Seymour Drescher points us toward the long-standing influence of this paradigm in American historical and political thought from the early nineteenth-century in his *Dilemmas of Democracy: Tocqueville and Modernization* (Pittsburgh: University of Pittsburgh Press, 1968).

41. The following preliminary sociological portrait of the middle classes in the twentieth century is drawn partly from Ralph Beals, "Social Stratification in Latin America," in *Contemporary Cultures and Societies in Latin America*, ed. Dwight B. Heath and Richard N. Adams (New York: Random House, 1965); Helen I. Saffa, "The Changing Class Composition of the Female Labor Force in Latin America," *Latin American Perspectives* 4, no. 4 (1977): 126–36; and Alejandro Portes, "Latin American Class Structures: Their Composition and Change during the last decade," *Latin American Research Review* 20, no. 3 (1985): 7–39. Additional materials which helped focus this assessment include C. Wright Mills, *White-Collar: The American Middle Classes* (New York: Oxford University Press, 1953); Nicolas Abercrombie and John Urry, *Capital, Labour, and the Middle Classes* (London: G. Allen and Unwin, 1983); Val Burris, "The Discovery of the New Middle Class," *Theory and Society* 15 (1988): 334–43; and Michael Mann, *The Sources of Social Power.* Volume II. *The Rise of Classes and Nation-States, 1760–1914* (Cambridge: Cambridge University Press, 1993), Chapter 16.

42. Recent work on the building of these kinds of institutions within which the middle classes became embedded include Colin W. Lewis, "Social Insurance: Ideology and Policy in the Argentine, c. 1920–1960," in *Welfare, Poverty, and Development in Latin America*, ed. Christopher Abel and Colin Lewis (Basingstoke, Eng.: MacMillan/St. Anthony's College, 1993), 175–200; in that same volume, see also Henry Finch, "Utopia in Uruguay Redefined: Social Welfare Policy after 1940," 221–57.

43. Larissa Lomnitz and Ana Melnick, *Chile's Middle Class: A Struggle for Survival in the Face of Neoliberalism*, trans. Jeanne Grant (Boulder: Westview, 1991) reveals the intricacies of these exchanges and networks among government employees which the authors describe as being rapidly dismantled under the Pinochet regime.

44. This crucial and heretofore unexplored arena is to be illuminated in the powerful new study by Brian Owensby, *Intimate Ironies: Modernity and the Middle Class in Brazil, c. 1850–1950* (Stanford: Stanford University Press, forthcoming).

45. Several insightful essays point toward the emergence and consolidation

of middle-class technocrats in these years and their influence on public policy. See John Markoff and Veróniza Montecinos, "The Ubiquituous Rise of Economists," *Journal of Public Policy* 13, no. 1 (1993): 37–68; Patricio Silva, "State, Public Technocracy, and Politics in Chile, 1927–1941: *Bulletin of Latin American Research* 13, no. 3 (1994): 281-97; E. A. Vasconcellos, "The Making of the Middle-Class City: Transportation Policy in Sao Paulo," *Environment and Planning* 29, no. 2 (February 1997); and Michael Ervin, "Agronomists, Revolution, and Reconstruction: The Making of Post-Insurrectionary Mexico," in *Mexico y movimiento: Concierto Mexicano 1910-1940. Reprecusión e interpretaciones*, ed. Dick Papousek (Groningen, the Netherlands: University of Groningen, 1997), 42-72.

46. Susan K. Besse, *Restructuring Patriarchy: The Modernization of Gender Inequality in Brazil, 1924-1940* (Chapel Hill: University of North Carolina Press, 1996).

47. The following discussion is drawn from "Savage Capitalism and Democratic Politics in the Americas," a presentation originally given at "Cuba and the Post Cold War World," a conference sponsored by the MacArthur Foundation, Columbia University, and the Centro de Estudios de América in Havana, Cuba, in July 1992 and reworked for a lecture at Swathmore College on 13 April 1993. These comments are further informed by John Keane, ed., *Civil Society and the State* (London: Verso, 1988); Robert Dahl, *Democracy and Its Critics* (New Haven: Yale University Press, 1989); Sidney Tarrow, *Power in Social Movement: Collective Action and Politics* (New York: Cambridge University Press, 1994); and John Markoff, *Waves of Democracy: Social Movements and Political Change* (Thousand Oaks, Cal.: Pine Forge Press, 1996).

48. The history of liberal democracy in Latin America and its middle-class progenitors is yet to be written, but a pioneering contribution is Jaime García Covarrubias, *El Partido Radical y la clase media en Chile: La relación de intereses entre 1888–1938* (Santiago, Chile: Editorial Andrés Bello, 1990).

49. Aside from the Drake and Stein works on populism cited above, indisputably the richest portrait of the deeply contradictory nature of populist initiatives is Herbert Braun's *The Assasination of Gaitán: Public Life and Urban Violence in Colombia* (Madison: University of Wisconsin Press, 1986).

50. The insurrections of the 1960s and 1970s have yet to have their historian. Despite their flaws, interesting descriptions and insights can be culled from Richard Gott, *Guerrillas in Latin America* (New York: Anchor, 1968); Jorge G. Castañeda, *Utopia Unarmed: The Latin American Left after the Cold War* (New York: Simon & Schuster, 1993), ch. 1–4; and Timothy Wickham-Crowley, *Guerrillas and Revolution in Latin America* (Princeton: Princeton University Press, 1992). One of the few solid historical works on a guerrilla movement of that era is Richard Gillespie,

Soldiers of Perón: Argentina's Montoneros (New York: Oxford University Press, 1982). Unfortunately, the current wave of biographies on leftist guerrilla leaders, such as Jon Lee Anderson's *Che Guevera: A Revolutionary Life* (New York: Random House, 1997) do little to illuminate the social terrain within which this new wave of armed Jacobinism made its appearance. A recent study which attempts to link social formations with insurgencies, in the Colombian case, is Marc W. Chernick and Michael F. Jiménez, "Popular Liberalism, Radical Democracy, and Marxism: Leftist Politics in Contemporary Colombia, 1974–1991," in *The Latin American Left: From the Fall of Allende to Perestroika*, ed. Barry Carr and Steve Ellner (Boulder: Westview, 1993), 61–82.

51. For a more thorough review of this process, see Michael F. Jiménez, "Citizens of the Kingdom: Towards a Social History of Radical Christianity in Latin America," *International Labor and Working Class History* 34 (fall 1988): 3–22.

52. For a portrait of intellectuals, largely from the middle classes, in this conjuncture, see the powerful critique by Morris Morley and James Petras, "The Retreat of the Intellectuals," in *Latin America in the Time of Cholera: Electoral Politics, Market Economies, and Permanent Crisis* (London: Routledge, 1992), 145–177.

53. Antonio Garcia, "Las clases medias en América Latina: Hacia una teoria de ambiguedad social," *Cuadernos Americanos* 60, no. 5 (September-October 1968): 126.

54. Arno Mayer, "The Lower Middle Class as Historical Problem," *Journal of Modern History* 47, no. 3 (September 1975): 425.

55. Dietrich Rueschemeyer, Evelyn Huber Stephens, and John D. Stephens, *Capitalist Development and Democracy* (Chicago: University of Chicago Press, 1992), 198.

56. A volume of edited essays by George Reid Andrews and Herrick Chapmen, *The Social Construction of Democracy, 1870–1990* (New York: New York University Press, 1995) takes up the Rueschemeyer, Stephens, and Stephens's challenge in an exemplary way, providing valuable insights into middle-class politics and culture across a wide variety of cases in the Atlantic world and Asia. In their introduction, the editors rightly insist on the "ambiguities and ambivalences" of the middle classes in the political realm which "set the stage for possible alliances and conflicts across classes. Which of those possibilities become real depends, not on abstract laws of historical causation, but rather on the specific conditions in effect in given historical settings" (19).

57. Cornel West, *The Evasion of Philosophy: A Genealogy of Pragmatism* (Madison: University of Wisconsin Press, 1989), 159.

58. Stanley J. Stein, "Latin American Historiography: Status and Research Opportunities," in Charles Wagley, *Social Science Research in Latin America* (New York: Columbia University Press, 1964), 114.

Notes on Contributors

Jeremy Adelman teaches Latin American history and is the Director of the Program in Latin American Studies at Princeton University. The author of several books, most recently *Republic of Capital: Buenos Aires and Legal Transformation of the Atlantic World* (forthcoming), he is currently working on a study of Latin America after the Second World War.

Philip D. Curtin is Herbert Baxter Adams Professor of History at the Johns Hopkins University. Author of many books, his recent works include *The Rise and Fall of the Plantation Complex* (2d ed., 1998) and *Disease and Empire: The Health of European Troops in the Conquest of Africa* (1998).

Tulio Halperín Donghi is Professor Emeritus at the University of California, Berkeley. He has written many books, including *La larga agonía de la Argentina peronista* (1994), and *Ensayos de historiografía* (1996), and is currently at work on a volume of Argentine political literature, entitled *De la República verdadera a la República imposible (1910-1944)*.

Michael F. Jiménez teaches Latin American and Atlantic Hiatory at the University of Pittsburgh. He is the author of a forthcoming book, *Struggles on an Interior Shore: Power, Authority, and Resistance in the Colombian Andes.*

Joseph L. Love, Professor of History and Director of the Center for Latin American Studies at the University of Illinois, is the author of three books, most recently *Crafting the Third World: Theorizing*

Underdevelopment in Rumania and Brazil (1995). He is currently writing a history of the Latin American structuralist school of economics.

Kenneth R. Maxwell is the Nelson and David Rockefeller Chair in Interamerican Studies at the Council on Foreign Relations in New York where he is the Director of the Latin American Program and book review editor at *Foreign Affairs* magazine for the Western Hemisphere. Author of several books, his most recent publications include *Pombal, Paradox of the Enlightenment* (1995), *The Making of Portuguese Democracy* (1995), and *The New Spain: From Isolation to Influence* (1994).

Robert W. Patch is Associate Professor of History at the University of California, Riverside. He is the author of numerous articles and *Maya and Spaniard in Yucatán, 1648–1812* (1993), and is currently writing a book on Mayan revolt and revolution in the eighteenth century.

Richard J. Salvucci teaches economics and history at Trinity University. He is the author of *Textiles and Capitalism in Mexico*, as well as numerous essays, articles, and reviews. He is writing a history of international trade and finance in nineteenth-century Mexico.

Stuart B. Schwartz is the George Burton Adams Professor of History at Yale University. His most recent book is *Slaves, Peasants and Rebels: Reconsidering Brazilian Slavery* (1992) and he is a contributor to the *Historia da expanção portuguesa no mundo* (1998). He is presently engaged in research on two books, one on the rebellion of Portugal and the crisis of the Iberian Atlantic world in the seventeenth century; and the second on doubt in the Hispanic World.

Barbara Hadley Stein was the Latin American and Iberian Bibliographer of Princeton's Firestone Library. Stanley J. Stein was the founder of the Program in Latin American Studies, also at Princeton, where he is currently Professor Emeritus. They are the coauthors of *The Colonial Heritage of Latin America* (1970) and *America, Spain and Europe, 1500–1750* (forthcoming).

Steve J. Stern is Professor of History at the University of Wisconsin in Madison. His most recent books are *The Secret History of Gender: Women, Men, and Power in Late Colonial Mexico* (1995) and *Shining and Other Paths: War and Society in Peru, 1980–1995* (1998). His current research focuses on memory struggles in the remaking of Chile since the 1973 fall of Salvador Allende.

Robert L. Tignor is the Rosengarten Professor of Modern and Contemporary History at Princeton University. Having written several studies of modern African history, Tignor recently published *Capitalism and Nationalism at the End of Empire: Egypt, Nigeria and Kenya in the Decolonization Era* (1998). He is currently working on a project on the influence of the Nobel laureate economist, W. Arthur Lewis, on African economic development.

Index